AF594079

International Political Economy Series

General Editor: Timothy M. Shaw, Professor and Director, Institute of International Relations, The University of the West Indies, Trinidad & Tobago

Titles include:

Leslie Elliott Armijo *(editor)*
FINANCIAL GLOBALIZATION AND DEMOCRACY IN EMERGING MARKETS

Robert Boardman
THE POLITICAL ECONOMY OF NATURE
Environmental Debates and the Social Sciences

Jörn Brömmelhörster and Wolf-Christian Paes *(editors)*
THE MILITARY AS AN ECONOMIC ACTOR
Soldiers in Business

Gerard Clarke and Michael Jennings *(editor)*
DEVELOPMENT, CIVIL SOCIETY AND FAITH-BASED ORGANIZATIONS
Bridging the Sacred and the Secular

Gordon Crawford
FOREIGN AID AND POLITICAL REFORM
A Comparative Analysis of Democracy Assistance and Political Conditionality

Matt Davies
INTERNATIONAL POLITICAL ECONOMY AND MASS COMMUNICATION IN CHILE
National Intellectuals and Transnational Hegemony

Martin Doornbos
INSTITUTIONALIZING DEVELOPMENT POLICIES AND RESOURCE STRATEGIES IN EASTERN AFRICA AND INDIA
Developing Winners and Losers

Fred P. Gale
THE TROPICAL TIMBER TRADE REGIME

Meric S. Gertler and David A. Wolfe
INNOVATION AND SOCIAL LEARNING
Institutional Adaptation in an Era of Technological Change

Anne Marie Goetz and Rob Jenkins
REINVENTING ACCOUNTABILITY
Making Democracy Work for the Poor

Andrea Goldstein
MULTINATIONAL COMPANIES FROM EMERGING ECONOMIES
Composition, Conceptualization and Direction in the Global Economy

Mary Ann Haley
FREEDOM AND FINANCE
Democratization and Institutional Investors in Developing Countries

Keith M. Henderson and O. P. Dwivedi *(editors)*
BUREAUCRACY AND THE ALTERNATIVES IN WORLD PERSPECTIVES

Jomo K.S. and Shyamala Nagaraj *(editors)*
GLOBALIZATION VERSUS DEVELOPMENT

Angela W. Little
LABOURING TO LEARN
Towards a Political Economy of Plantations, People and Education in Sri Lanka

John Loxley *(editor)*
INTERDEPENDENCE, DISEQUILIBRIUM AND GROWTH
Reflections on the Political Economy of North–South Relations at the Turn of the Century

Peter Utting and José Carlos Marques *(editors)*
CORPORATE SOCIAL RESPONSIBILITY AND REGULATORY GOVERNANCE
Towards Inclusive Development?

Don D. Marshall
CARIBBEAN POLITICAL ECONOMY AT THE CROSSROADS
NAFTA and Regional Developmentalism

Susan M. McMillan
FOREIGN DIRECT INVESTMENT IN THREE REGIONS OF THE SOUTH AT THE END OF THE TWENTIETH CENTURY

S. Javed Maswood
THE SOUTH IN INTERNATIONAL ECONOMIC REGIMES
Whose Globalization?

John Minns
THE POLITICS OF DEVELOPMENTALISM
The Midas States of Mexico, South Korea and Taiwan

Philip Nel
THE POLITICS OF ECONOMIC INEQUALITY IN DEVELOPING COUNTRIES

Pia Riggirozzi
ADVANCING GOVERNANCE IN THE SOUTH
What Are the Roles for International Financial Institutions in Developing States?

Lars Rudebeck, Olle Törnquist and Virgilio Rojas *(editors)*
DEMOCRATIZATION IN THE THIRD WORLD
Concrete Cases in Comparative and Theoretical Perspective

Eunice N. Sahle
WORLD ORDERS, DEVELOPMENT AND TRANSFORMATION

Benu Schneider *(editor)*
THE ROAD TO INTERNATIONAL FINANCIAL STABILITY
Are Key Financial Standards the Answer?

Howard Stein *(editor)*
ASIAN INDUSTRIALIZATION AND AFRICA
Studies in Policy Alternatives to Structural Adjustment

William Vlcek
OFFSHORE FINANCE AND SMALL STATES
Sovereignty, Size and Money

International Political Economy Series
Series Standing Order ISBN 978–0–333–71708–0 hardcover
Series Standing Order ISBN 978–0–333–71110–1 paperback
(*outside North America only*)

You can receive future titles in this series as they are published by placing a standing order. Please contact your bookseller or, in case of difficulty, write to us at the address below with your name and address, the title of the series and one of the ISBNs quoted above.

Customer Services Department, Macmillan Distribution Ltd, Houndmills, Basingstoke, Hampshire RG21 6XS, England

---

Business, Politics and Public Policy

Implications for Inclusive Development

Edited by

José Carlos Marques

Peter Utting

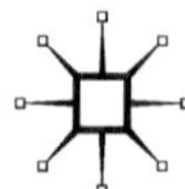

First published 2010 by
PALGRAVE MACMILLAN

Palgrave Macmillan in the UK is an imprint of Macmillan Publishers Limited, registered in England, company number 785998, of Houndmills, Basingstoke, Hampshire RG21 6XS.

Palgrave Macmillan in the US is a division of St Martin's Press LLC, 175 Fifth Avenue, New York, NY 10010.

Palgrave Macmillan is the global academic imprint of the above companies and has companies and representatives throughout the world.

Palgrave® and Macmillan® are registered trademarks in the United States, the United Kingdom, Europe and other countries.

ISBN 978–0–230–57645–2 hardback

This book is printed on paper suitable for recycling and made from fully managed and sustained forest sources. Logging, pulping and manufacturing processes are expected to conform to the environmental regulations of the country of origin.

A catalogue record for this book is available from the British Library.

Library of Congress Cataloging-in-Publication Data

Business, politics, and public policy : implications for inclusive development / edited by José Carlos Marques, Peter Utting.
p. cm. — (International political economy series)
Summary: "This is the second volume of two books on the changing nature of state-business relations. This volume focuses on the need to shift attention from what business is doing in relation to CSR and to what private regulation is doing in relation to social policy"—Provided by publisher.
Includes bibliographical references and index.
ISBN 978–0–230–57645–2
1. Social responsibility of business. 2. Policy sciences. I. Marques, José Carlos, 1972– II. Utting, Peter.
HD60.B885 2010
322'.3—dc22 2010002704

10 9 8 7 6 5 4 3 2 1
19 18 17 16 15 14 13 12 11 10

Printed and bound in Great Britain by
CPI Antony Rowe, Chippenham and Eastbourne

Contents

Tables and Figures vii

Preface x

Notes on the Contributors xii

Abbreviations and Acronyms xv

Introduction: Understanding Business Power and Public Policy in a Development Context 1
José Carlos Marques and Peter Utting

1 Organized Business and Social Policy in Comparative Perspective 30
José Carlos Marques

2 Business Power, Social Policy Preferences and Development 63
Kevin Farnsworth

3 Liberalization, Business–State Relations and Labour Policy in India 90
Kanta Murali

4 Business Participation in Free Trade Negotiations in Chile: Impacts on Environmental and Labour Regulation 110
Benedicte Bull

5 Business, Politics and Free Trade Negotiations in Nicaragua: Who Were the Winners and Losers? 134
Gloria Carrión

6 Corporate Lobbying and Corporate Social Responsibility: Aligning Contradictory Agendas 160
Bart Slob and Francis Weyzig

7 Corporate Rents and the Capture of the Peruvian State 184
Francisco Durand

8 The Ascent of Business Associations in Russia: From Capture to Partnership? 208
David W. O'Brien

9 Lobbying to Reduce the 'Brazil Cost': The Political Strategies of Brazilian Entrepreneurs 242
Wagner Pralon Mancuso

10 Government–Industry Partnership in South Africa: Social Bias in the Automotive Industry 271
Martin Kaggwa

11 New Standards and Partnerships in Latin America: Implications for Small Producers and State Policy 292
Paola Perez-Aleman

Index 312

Tables and Figures

Tables

2.1 Investment regimes and social policies 75
4.1 Trade agreements signed by Chile 116
6.1 Combined framework for analysis of channels of influence 168
6.2 Different types of regulation schemes 172
7.1 Modes of state capture in Peru, 1990–2006 187
8.1 Examples of market-supporting and market-complementing actions 211
8.2 CEO participation in business associations by regime type, 1999 (per cent) 214
8.3 Firm representation in business associations, by size and select countries (per cent) 214
8.4 Russian firms engaging government, 2002 and 2005 216
8.5 Preferred route to affect government laws, 1999 217
8.6 The relative importance of ABAs in attaining important government contacts 222
8.7 The relative importance of ABAs in attaining important contacts 223
8.8 Government and ABAs interaction (1) 223
8.9 Government and ABAs interaction (2) 224
8.10 Government and ABAs interaction (3) 224
8.11 Government and ABAs interaction (4) 225
8.12 Contribution of the ABAs to regional/policy development objectives 225
8.13 Likelihood of policy engagement and preferred pathway to affect change 226
9.1 Criteria utilized to classify decisions as successes or failures of industry 252
9.2 Impact of cases of success on the 'Brazil cost' 253
9.3 Impact of cases of failure on the 'Brazil cost' 254

9.4 Decisions classified as successes or failures of industry 255

9.5 Result of the decision, by type of decision 255

9.6 Result of the decision by impact on the status quo 256

9.7 Origin of bills by result of the decision and impact on the status quo 258

9.8 Result of the decision, by component of the decision 260

9.9 Result of the decision, by impact of the decision on the status quo, controlled by component of the decision 261

9.10 Successes: Origin of the bills, by impact of the decision on the status quo, controlled by component 262

9.11 Failures: Origin of bills, by impact of the decision on the status quo, controlled by component 264

10.1 Inflation and vehicle price indexes in South Africa 283

Figures

7.1 Tax Merger Law, legal stability agreements, and mergers and acquisitions, 1990–2001 198

8.1 Pathway choice to affect change in policy arenas 227

10.1 South Africa's OEM investment and employment, 1995–2005 279

10.2 South Africa's automotive production, export and total-industry employment growth indices 280

The **United Nations Research Institute for Social Development** (UNRISD) is an autonomous agency that carries out multidisciplinary research on the social dimensions of contemporary development issues. Through its research, events and publications, UNRISD provides government agencies, intergovernmental organizations, non-governmental organizations, scholars and others with a better understanding of how development policies and processes affect different social groups. It works to stimulate dialogue and contributes to policy debates both within and outside the UN system. Current research programmes include: Social Policy and Development; Democracy, Governance and Well-Being; Markets, Business and Regulation; Civil Society and Social Movements; Identities, Conflict and Cohesion; and Gender and Development.

UNRISD
Palais des Nations
1211 Geneva 10
Switzerland
info@unrisd.org
www.unrisd.org

Preface

A positive outcome of the financial crisis that shook the world in 2008 was the fact that it exposed the weaknesses of a particular model of capitalism that perpetuates unsustainable growth and inequality. Capitalism is characterized by competing interests, and winners and losers. What lay behind the crisis, and the problems that ensued, was intimately related to the power of business elites and the dominance of capital. In an article published in May 2009, Simon Johnson, the former chief economist at the International Monetary Fund (IMF), cogently laid out a type of analysis hitherto associated with 'radical' political economy and alter-globalization activists. He noted that financial crises the world over may have different proximate causes but they tend to have one common trait, namely the so-called capture of states by elite business interests.

The thorough analysis of business–state relations is therefore essential if problems of crisis, inequality and unsustainable development are to be addressed. Yet all too often, such relations remain opaque, under-researched and poorly understood, or explanations are locked in ideological corners. The notion of capture is itself problematic, as it conjures up images of crude mechanisms of control and influence. In the context of developing countries, which is the focus of this book, the stereotypical image is that of bribery and 'crony capitalism'. In the context of the United States, attention is usually focused on campaign financing and professional lobbying. Yet in practice, business actors have at their disposal a broad variety of means by which to access and impact the policy process. Such means relate to the very different dimensions of business power that exist, which have been conceptualized in terms of structural, instrumental and discursive power. Another stereotype suggests that when business interests do gain access and influence, the effects must be negative from the perspective of social development and equity. Here again, a more nuanced perspective is required – one that recognizes the possibility of diverse effects, depending on the nature of the firms involved and the institutional, political, economic and cultural contexts in which they operate.

This book examines the nature of business power, the dynamics of state–business relations and their implications for inclusive development. It considers these sets of issues in both less developed and emerging market economies, as well as at the global level. Particular attention is focused on public policies more immediately associated with inclusive development, namely social, labour market, environmental and fiscal policies, as well as small producer or enterprise development. Contributions also identify a variety of institutional and political arrangements that can tame business influence or ensure that such influence facilitates rather than undermines policies conducive to inclusive development.

The analysis explores in some depth the structural and instrumental dimensions of business power noted above. Aspects that relate to discursive power are given more attention in a companion volume, *Corporate Social Responsibility and Regulatory Governance: Towards Inclusive Development?* (Utting and Marques, 2010). In the companion volume we examine, inter alia, the effectiveness of CSR both in relation to inclusive development and as a means of legitimizing contemporary forms of corporate capitalism and securing the dominant position of global corporations and business elites.

Contributions to the present volume are based on papers that were originally prepared for a conference on Business, Social Policy and Corporate Political Influence in Developing Countries organized by the United Nations Research Institute for Social Development (UNRISD) in Geneva in November 2007. On behalf of UNRISD, we would like to thank the United Kingdom Department for International Development (DFID) for having provided financial support for the above conference, and the World Wide Fund for Nature (WWF–UK) for having supported the research related to the chapter on state–business relations in India. As is the case with all UNRISD research, this work would not have been possible without the core funding provided by the governments of Denmark, Finland, Mexico, Norway, South Africa, Sweden, Switzerland and the United Kingdom. We are grateful to Yusuf Bangura, Franscisco Durand, Terence Gomez, Kevin Farnsworth and Paola Perez-Aleman for having provided useful comments and criticisms on parts of the manuscript. Particular thanks are extended to Rebecca Buchholz for both comments and editorial assistance, as well as to Anita Tombez and Katrien De Moor for copyediting the manuscript.

José Carlos Marques and Peter Utting,
Montreal and Geneva, 4 September 2009

Notes on the Contributors

Benedicte Bull is Associate Professor at the Centre for Development and the Environment (SUM), University of Oslo, and Director of the Norwegian Latin America Research Network (NorLARNet). Her publications include *Development Issues in Global Governance: Public–Private Partnerships and Market Multilateralism* (co-authored with Desmond McNeill, Palgrave, 2007); and *Aid, Power and Privatization: The Politics of Telecommunication Reform in Central America* (Edward Elgar, 2005).

Gloria Carrión is Programme Officer at the International Centre for Trade and Sustainable Development (ICTSD) in Geneva. She specializes in research on trade and development, and her latest publication is *Trade, Regionalism, and the Politics of Policy Making in Nicaragua* (UNRISD, 2009).

Francisco Durand is Professor of Political Science at the University of Texas, San Antonio, and Associate Professor at the Catholic University of Peru. He has published several books and numerous articles on business and government in Peru and Latin America. His publications include *Business and Politics in Peru: The State of the National Bourgeoisie* (Westview Press, 1994); *Organized Business, Economic Change, and Democracy in Latin America* (co-edited with Eduardo Silva, North-South Center Press at the University of Miami, 1998); and *El Perú Fracturado: Formalidad, Informalidad y Economía Delictiva* (Fondo Editorial del Congreso del Perú, 2008).

Kevin Farnsworth is Lecturer in Social Policy at the University of Sheffield. He has written extensively on business and social policy, most recently, 'Business and Global Social Policy Formation', in N. Yeates (ed.), *Understanding Global Social Policy* (Policy Press, 2008). His book *Corporate Power and Social Policy in a Global Economy* was published by Policy Press in 2004.

Martin Kaggwa is a Senior Lecturer at Tshwane University of Technology, South Africa. His latest publication is 'South Africa Government's Support of the Automotive Industry: Prospects of the Productive Asset Allowance' (co-authored with Anastassios Pouris and Jasper L. Steyn, *Development Southern Africa*, December 2007).

Wagner Pralon Mancuso is Professor of Political Science and Public Policy Management, University of São Paulo. He has published several articles on entrepreneurial lobbying in Brazil and the book *O Lobby da Indústria no Congresso Nacional: Empresariado e Política no Brasil Contemporâneo*

(Industrial Lobbying in the National Congress: Entrepreneurs and Politics in Contemporary Brazil) was published by EDUSP/HUMANITAS/FAPESP in 2007.

José Carlos Marques is former Research Analyst in the Markets, Business and Regulation Programme at the United Nations Research Institute for Social Development (UNRISD). He holds an MSc in Development Management from the London School of Economics and Political Science, and is currently pursuing a PhD in Strategy and Organization at McGill University, Montreal. His latest publication is *Corporate Social Responsibility and Regulatory Governance: Towards Inclusive Development?* (co-edited with Peter Utting, Palgrave Macmillan, 2010).

Kanta Murali is a PhD candidate in Politics at Princeton University. Her dissertation focuses on the nature of state–business relations in India in the era of economic liberalization.

David O'Brien is Senior Programme Officer at the International Development Research Centre, Ottawa. His contribution to this collection draws on his PhD dissertation research, which was published as *Das Social Kapital: Institutions and Entrepreneurial Networks in Russia's Exit from Socialism* (2006, available at http://library.wur.nl/wda/dissertations/dis4018.pdf).

Paola Perez-Aleman is Associate Professor of Strategy and Organization at the Desautels Faculty of Management at McGill University, Montreal. Titles of her recent publications include 'Cluster Formation, Institutions and Learning: The Emergence of Clusters and Development in Chile' (*Industrial and Corporate Change*, 2005); and 'Building Value at the Top and the Bottom of the Global Supply Chain: MNC–NGO Partnerships' (*California Management Review*, 2008).

Bart Slob is Senior Researcher at the Centre for Research on Multinational Corporations, Amsterdam. His research focuses on codes of conduct and international soft- and hard-law frameworks for corporate social responsibility. His publications include *Verification Instrument for the Inclusion of Social Criteria in Public Procurement* (co-authored with J. Oldenziel and T. Steinweg, SOMO, 2007); *The ISO Working Group on Social Responsibility: Developing the Future ISO SR 26000 Standard* (co-authored with G. Oonk, SOMO, 2007); and *Sustainable Procurement in the European Union: Proposals and Recommendations to the European Commission and the European Parliament* (co-authored with J. Oldenziel and T. Steinweg, European Coalition for Corporate Justice, 2007).

Peter Utting is Deputy Director of the United Nations Research Institute for Social Development (UNRISD), where he also coordinates the Markets, Business and Regulation Programme. His publications include *Corporate Social Responsibility and Regulatory Governance: Towards Inclusive Development?*

(co-edited with José Carlos Marques, Palgrave Macmillan, 2010); *Corporate Accountability and Sustainable Development* (co-edited with Jennifer Clapp, Oxford University Press, 2008); *Reclaiming Development Agendas: Knowledge, Power and International Policy Making* (Palgrave Macmillan, 2006); and *The Greening of Business in Developing Countries: Rhetoric, Reality and Prospects* (Zed Books, 2002).

Francis Weyzig contributed to this book as Researcher at the Centre for Research on Multinational Corporations, Amsterdam. Currently he is Policy Advisor at De Nederlandsche Bank (DNB, the central bank of the Netherlands). His research interests include corporate social responsibility, foreign direct investment, economic development and corporate taxation. His publications include: 'Political and Economic Arguments for Corporate Social Responsibility: Analysis and a Proposition Regarding the CSR Agenda' (*Journal of Business Ethics*, 2009); and 'Corporate Social Responsibility in Mexico: How Changes in the Behaviour of Multinational Enterprises Contribute to Economic Development' (*Accountancy Business and the Public Interest*, 2007).

Abbreviations and Acronyms

AAC	Anglo American Corporation
ABAs	alumni business associations
AFL–CIO	American Federation of Labor and Congress of Industrial Organizations
AGOA	African Growth and Opportunity Act
ALADI	Latin American Integration Association
AmCham	American Chamber of Commerce
ANC	African National Congress
ANITEC	Asociación Nicaragüense de la Industria Textil y Confección (*Nicaraguan Apparel and Textile Manufacturers' Association*)
APA	Asociación de Productores Avícolas de Chile
APROCER	Asociación Gremial de Productores de Cerdos de Chile
ASEXMA	Asociación de Exportadores de Manufacturas y Servicios
ASSOCHAM	The Associated Chambers of Commerce and Industry of India
BAC	Banco de América Central (*Central American Bank*)
BANCENTRO	Banco de Crédito Centroamericano (*Central American Credit Bank*)
BANPRO	Banco de la Producción
BBBEE	Broad-Based Black Economic Empowerment
BCRP	Banco Central de Reserva del Perú (*Central Reserve Bank of Peru*)
BDF	Banco de Finanzas
BEE	Black Economic Empowerment
BEEPS	EBRD–World Bank Business Environment and Enterprise Performance Survey
BJP	Bharatiya Janata Party
BLIHR	Business Leaders Initiative for Human Rights
C.A.F.E.	Coffee and Farmer Equity Practices
CAFTA	Central America Free Trade Agreement
CANISLAC	Cámara Nicaragüense del Sector Lácteo (*Nicaraguan Dairy Sector Chamber*)
CBU	completely built-up unit
CCI	Chamber of Commerce and Industry
CCP	Conservation Coffee Project
CEI	Confederation of Engineering Industry
CEO	chief executive officer
CI	Conservation International

CII	Confederation of Indian Industry
CITU	Centre of Indian Trade Unions
CMEs	coordinated market economies
CNI	Confederação Nacional da Indústria (*National Confederation of Industry*)
CNPA	Comisión Nacional de Productores de Azúcar (*National Commission for Sugar Producers*)
CONFIEP	Confederación Nacional de Instituciones Empresariales Privadas (*National Confederation of Private Business Associations of Peru*)
COSATU	Congress of South African Trade Unions
CPC	Confederación de la Producción y del Comercio
CPPDE	Consejo Publíco-Privado para el Desarrollo Exportador
CSO	civil society organization
CSR	corporate social responsibility
CSW	Corporate Social Welfare
CUT	Central Unitaria de Trabajo
DIRECON	General Directorate for International Economic Relations
DR–CAFTA	Dominican Republic–Central American Free Trade Agreement
DSA	developmental state approach
EBRD	European Bank for Reconstruction and Development
EFTA	European Free Trade Association
ESI	Employees' State Insurance
EU	European Union
FDI	foreign direct investment
FENACOOP	Federación Nacional de Cooperativas Agrícolas y Agroindustriales (*National Federation of Agricultural and Agroindustrial Cooperatives*)
FICCI	Federation of Indian Chambers of Commerce and Industry
FLG	Financial Leaders Group
FSLN	Frente Sandinista de Liberación Nacional (*Sandinista National Liberation Front*)
FTA	Free Trade Agreement
FTAA	Free Trade Area of the Americas
GATS	General Agreement on Trade in Services
GDP	gross domestic product
GEAR	Growth, Employment and Redistribution
GRI	Global Reporting Initiative
GSK	GlaxoSmithKline
GSP	General System of Preferences
IBIA	International Business Interest Association
IDA	Industrial Disputes Act

IFC	International Finance Corporation
IFI	international financial institution
IGO	intergovernmental organization
ILO	International Labour Organization
Iniciativa CID	Iniciativa de Comercio, Integración y Desarrollo (*Trade, Integration and Development Initiative*)
IME	international market exposure
IMF	International Monetary Fund
INGO	international non-governmental organization
IPE	Instituto Peruano de Economía (*Peruvian Institute of Economy*)
IPR	intellectual property rights
ISO	International Organization for Standardization
ITI	Information Technology Industries
ITI	Industrial Training Institute (India)
LEGISDATA	Database of the CNI
LQ	Leadership Questionnaire
LSAs	legal stability agreements
MEF	Ministerio de Economía y Finanzas (*Ministry of Economy and Finance*)
MERCOSUR	Mercado Comun del Sur
MIDC	Motor Industry Development Council
MIDP	Motor Industry Development Programme
MQ	membership questionnaire
MT	metric ton
NAFTA	North American Free Trade Agreement
NASSCOM	National Association of Software and Service Companies
NDA	National Democratic Alliance
NEDLAC	National Economic Development and Labour Advisory Council
NGO	non-governmental organization
NIRA	National Industrial Recovery Act
NRA	National Recovery Act
OECD	Organisation for Economic Co-operation and Development
OEM	original equipment manufacturer
P4	Trans-Pacific Strategic Economic Partnership Agreement (Brunei, Chile, New Zealand, Singapore)
PIM	public interest movement
PMTP	President's Management Training Programme
PPP	public–private partnership
PRA	power resources approach
PRSP	Poverty Reduction Strategy Paper
PSP	Preferred Supplier Program
R	Rand (currency of South Africa)

R&D	research and development
RDP	Reconstruction and Development Programme
RUIE	Russian Union of Industrialists and Entrepreneurs
S/.	nuevo sol (currency of Peru)
SC	Scheduled Caste
SCAA	Specialty Coffee Association of America
SCS	Scientific Certification Systems
SICON-SF	Database of the Brazilian Federal State
sme	square metre equivalent
SME	small and medium enterprise
SNA	Sociedad Nacional de Agricultura
SOFOFA	Sociedad de Fomento Fabril
SOMO	Centre for Research on Multinational Corporations
SONAPESCA	Sociedad Nacional de la Pesca
ST	Scheduled Tribe
SUNAT	Superintendencia Nacional de Administración Tributaria (*National Superintendency of Tax Administration of Peru*)
T&C	textile and clothing
TNC	transnational corporation
TPA	Trade Promotion Authority
TPL	trade preferential level
TRIPS	Trade-Related Aspects of Intellectual Property Rights
UK	United Kingdom
UN	United Nations
UPA	United Progressive Alliance
US	United States
VoC	varieties of capitalism
VRS	Voluntary Retirement Scheme
WHO	World Health Organization
WTO	World Trade Organization
WWF	World Wide Fund For Nature

Introduction: Understanding Business Power and Public Policy in a Development Context

José Carlos Marques and Peter Utting

Global trends and events in recent years – growing inequality, persistent poverty, climate change, food insecurity and the financial and economic crisis of 2008–9 – have called into question the development credentials and viability of a model of liberal capitalism that has been promoted by Northern governments and international financial institutions (IFIs), as well as business elites and technocrats from both the North and South. Core features of this model generated perverse distributional and social effects, particularly for developing countries. These included a low propensity for employment generation and decent work, the casualization of labour, the privatization of basic public services, financialization and a focus on short-term profitability and shareholder returns, economic concentration and the crowding out of smaller producers and enterprises, and the unlevel playing field for trade and investment that favoured some countries and business interests, and constrained others. Most problematic from the perspective adopted in this volume, however, are the rolling back of certain state functions and capacities, the residual status accorded to social policy and the disregard for power imbalances.

The pervasiveness of this model is typically explained with reference to its solid ideological foundation, namely neoliberalism, which arose in reaction to the perceived or real limits and contradictions of Keynesianism, socialism and developmentalism. Underpinning and reinforcing such a model, however, was a configuration of social forces and institutional arrangements that saw big business interests increase their power in a context where national states and other organized interests, notably labour, were losing ground in shaping the direction of economic and social development. The rise in business power was associated with the increasing mobility of capital worldwide, the rapid expansion of foreign direct investment (FDI) and international trade, financialization, privatization, as well as the structuring of production in global value chains.

Business power assumed multiple forms. A useful categorization refers to the structural, instrumental and discursive power of business (Fuchs 2005; Sell 2009). These different dimensions mean that the design and implementation of public policies are influenced, respectively, by 1) perceived or real threats of 'capital flight' or 'capital strikes', as well as competition among states at both national and subnational levels to create an investor-friendly environment; 2) lobbying, campaign financing, bribery, 'revolving doors', the provision of technical information and expertise, and other professional, as well as personal and family ties; and 3) cultivating a particular worldview or narrative concerning how development should be, and framing public and policy agendas and debates in ways that create blind spots related to particular issues and lines of argumentation.

While key aspects of business power and influence have been strengthened during the contemporary era of globalization and liberalization, it is also apparent that several 'varieties of neoliberalism' exist (Crouch 2010) and that numerous configurations of state–business–society relations are possible. Furthermore both states and business, like civil society, are highly heterogeneous entities with multiple interests[1] – the upshot of which may be very different types of alliances, coalitions and compromises.

This volume, and its companion volume, *Corporate Social Responsibility and Regulatory Governance: Towards Inclusive Development?* (Utting and Marques 2010), explore the complex dynamics of state–business–society relations and their implications for inclusive development, understood as patterns of growth and structural change associated with broad-based social wellbeing, equity and sustainable development. This volume addresses what constitutes a major blind spot in the mainstream literature on corporate social responsibility (CSR), namely how business interests influence public policy. If we are really to understand how business impacts inclusive development, it is necessary to analyse not only the more direct connections via the economic and social activities and performance of firms, notably in the fields of employment and CSR, but also how business interests interact with public policy. This volume examines the dynamics of business power and engagement with the public policy process in countries that have undergone the 'dual transitions' to democratic rule and economic liberalism in recent decades.[2] In addition to trying to open up the black box of business–state relations and understand their implications for inclusive development, it identifies various institutional arrangements and forms of collective action that can play a role in moderating business influence over public policy and crafting business responses more conducive to inclusive development.

Key questions addressed in the chapters that follow include:

- Can business–state relations be reconstituted in a manner conducive to inclusive development?
- Does the rise of big business fundamentally constrain inclusive development processes?
- Under what conditions might business support or accommodate progressive social policy?

- How should governments and regulatory institutions in developing countries respond and adapt to the increasing structural and lobbying power of business?

This introduction provides an overview of the chapters in this volume, summarizing their contributions and positioning them from both theoretical and policy perspectives. We argue that both the mainstream and 'alter-globalization' perspectives on neoliberal restructuring have been plagued by blind spots and misconceptions that have become particularly problematic in the current international policy environment. This is followed by a review of three streams of literature in comparative political economy and the welfare state tradition, which we propose provide a useful analytic framework for understanding how political processes have led to inclusive development in different contexts. We then summarize the individual chapters in this volume and the key contributions made by each of them. The final section reviews these contributions, using the analytic lens developed earlier, and reflects on some of the policy implications that might be drawn from the contents of this volume.

Blind spots and misconceptions

The analysis of state–business relations and the process by which public policies are crafted is crucial for understanding the nature and trajectory of contemporary development approaches and their distributional and social consequences. This section argues that both contemporary mainstream development thinking and the 'alter-globalization' perspective on how to deal with the failures of neoliberal restructuring have suffered from important blind spots and misconceptions.

Of particular concern is the question of business power and its influence on public policy, an issue for the most part ignored in international development circles. For example, in an inquiry into how to eliminate global poverty, Jeffrey Sachs calls on governments to reform policies and governance to facilitate aid, trade and investment, and urges the antiglobalization movement not to be overly concerned about big business, free trade and FDI (Sachs 2005). Such prescriptions give short shrift to the politics of contemporary policy processes. Situations where business tries to set the rules of the game are lamented, but few insights are offered into how the negative influence of big business on public policy might be curbed, or into the complex ways in which macroeconomic regimes and government policies are linked to actual or perceived business interests.

Similarly, the United Nations (UN), through the UN Global Compact and numerous other voluntary and partnership initiatives, has engineered a rapprochement with big business which pays scant attention to key questions of business power and influence in shaping public policy and regulatory regimes. Global corporations are now considered key partners in efforts to promote inclusive and sustainable development. Worrisome, however, is that in the process of crafting this new relationship with business, issues of institutional capture and the facilitation and legitimization of corporate capitalism are often ignored. Critical inquiry into the role of business elites in development and governance has been sidelined in mainstream international development circles (Utting and Zammit 2006).[3]

These constricted, apolitical approaches and prescriptions are characteristic of the way global elites have contributed and responded to the contradictions of 'neoliberalism'. The so-called 'Washington consensus' of the 1980s, which emphasized the need to downsize certain state institutions, 'get the prices right' and provide only minimal levels of social protection, failed to generate the promised levels of investment and growth for developing countries (Rodrik and Subramanian 2009) while exacerbating poverty and inequality. The response from the mainstream development community came largely in the form of the 'post-Washington consensus', that added 'good governance' and 'poverty reduction' to the original formula. Novel regulatory and managerial arrangements associated with CSR were perceived as a means to mitigate globalization's negative consequences and 're-embed liberalism' (Ruggie 2003). Since the early 1990s multilateral organizations such as the UN and the World Bank, as well as many non-governmental organizations (NGOs), crafted a proactive response centred on CSR. Encouraged by the development community to use their competencies and capacity for innovation in ways perceived to be more directly conducive to inclusive development, and facing new types of political risk and uncertainty in developing countries, transnational corporations (TNCs) responded positively.

The CSR agenda promoted an ever-widening range of reforms and voluntary initiatives. These included the setting of social and environmental standards; development of various monitoring, reporting and verification mechanisms; consultation and engagement with different stakeholders; and assistance to local communities. In recent years a growing number of global and national corporations have taken part in the new poverty reduction agenda, including the UN's Millennium Development Goals (MDGs). TNCs, in particular, are being urged to play a more proactive role, not only through CSR but also public–private partnerships (PPPs) and inclusive business models, that aim to connect 'the poor' or local communities to global value chains and markets as consumers, producers and service providers. They are also encouraged to play an increasingly prominent role in so-called epistemic communities or knowledge networks that shape international policy.

These reform agendas had major blind spots. The post-Washington consensus basically left unchanged the problematic macroeconomic agenda of the 1980s in the expectation that, in time, such policies would create the type of business-friendly environment that would attract FDI and facilitate export-oriented growth. The good governance agenda promoted multi-stakeholder dialogue and the participation of non-state actors in the policy process, but failed to address the gross imbalances in power relations among different 'stakeholders' and the problem of institutional or regulatory capture by business interests. The CSR agenda not only took for granted the rise of corporate power but also tended to place key issues off-limits. Employment generation, 'living wages', tax avoidance and evasion, lobbying for socially regressive policies, profit repatriation and the inequitable distribution of value within global production chains remained either off or at the very bottom of the CSR agenda. Given its focus on voluntarism, and the initial (if not ongoing) ideological suspicion of the state and trade unions, the CSR agenda largely ignored a fundamental political economy dimension of inclusive development, namely the nature of state–business relations and their implications for public policy. Little attention was paid to whether organized business interests support, accommodate or undermine government 'social policy', understood broadly in terms of diverse aspects of state policy – including not only traditional areas such as health, education and social security, but also those related to labour markets, taxation and small enterprise development – that impact social development and inclusive growth.[4]

If mainstream development agendas had some stark blind spots related to questions of power so too did those calling for more transformative patterns of development or 'alter-globalization'. Three, in particular, stand out. First, critics of voluntarism or private regulation often focus on the need for mandatory regulation of business. Such harder forms of regulation may indeed be key but what Newell (2008) has referred to as 'regulatory fetishism' runs the risk of ignoring the politics of regulatory change, as well as such aspects as the role of communities in regulating business at the local level (Newell 2008), and possible complementarities and synergies between voluntary and legalistic approaches (Utting 2005b). Second, critical perspectives on corporate capitalism and neoliberalism often emphasize the need to strengthen countervailing forces and reconfigure the balance of power among different social actors and the state to bring about a more transformative change.[5] Within this scenario, 'active citizenship and effective states' (Green 2008) play the key role in processes of institutional and policy change. If civil society can mobilize resources, access mainstream circuits of power and influence the policy process, then meaningful policy and institutional reform, it is assumed, will likely ensue. As several of the following chapters (and the companion volume) show, such dimensions of change are crucial. What this analysis often underestimates, however, is what is happening on the other side of the power equation both in terms of inertia and inbuilt resistance to progressive change within state institutions and their bureaucracies, the symbiotic relationship between government technocracies and business elites and the convergence of their interests and worldviews, as well as how business elites themselves are organizing and mobilizing to secure or enhance their power and influence (Levy and Newell 2002; Utting 2005a).

Third, alter-globalization perspectives have often paid insufficient attention to the potentially constructive role of big business in processes of inclusive development. Mobilizing the resources and competencies of business is an important part of the development equation. Indeed, this was a key feature of the Nordic and East Asian countries that managed to reduce poverty over relatively short periods of time. As explained in the following section, such contributions occurred in particular institutional and political contexts, where not only the correlation of forces but also the role of social pacts and compromises were key. So too were economic contexts where some segments of business had an interest in certain types of social policy. It is crucial therefore to differentiate business preferences: in practice, different firms and industries, large and small, operating in diverse economic, political and cultural contexts, may have quite different positions on public policies, in general, and social policy, in particular.

In contrast to the perspectives above, a more nuanced approach is essential for crafting inclusive development trajectories. Understanding state–business relations and public policy-making processes is particularly pertinent in the international policy context that has unfolded in recent years. A combination of circumstances, including democratization and growing recognition of the unacceptable social costs of neoliberal restructuring, has prompted some governments and IFIs to elevate the status of social policy and pay more attention to social programmes and active labour market policies. Global public policy and poverty reduction discourse is increasingly addressing the idea that social protection, employment protection legislation, and unionization may not be an impediment to high employment and productivity (World Bank 2005; OECD 2006). The supposed trade-off between social protection and economic growth, that was an ideational feature of the Washington consensus, is being reconsidered.

In assessing whether such reassessments are likely to translate into significant social policy changes, it is crucial to understand the position of organized business interests and the question of whether they are likely to resist or support such changes. Contemporary development thinking and those critical of it have largely ignored the empirical evidence provided by the development experiences of countries that have successfully followed socially inclusive development paths. The following section examines some of the rich and highly insightful literature on this topic, particularly how different schools of thought within the field of comparative political economy have analysed the relationship of business to social policy. It highlights the key theoretical contributions of these literatures, which we suggest provide the required analytical lens from which to analyse contemporary development concerns. It also highlights the limitations of these literatures, which the chapters in this volume seek to address.

Competing views on business and social policy

What does the broader literature that ventures beyond CSR to address business–state relations have to say concerning business positions on social policy? The extensive literatures on comparative capitalism and the emergence of the welfare state are highly relevant and provide critical theoretical and empirical–historical foundations from which to build. Three main strands of thinking can be discerned in this literature: the power resources approach (PRA), the developmental state approach (DSA) and the varieties of capitalism (VoC) approach. This section shall provide a brief overview of each, as well as how they relate to each other, before discussing the relevance of their contributions and their limitations in answering the questions posed at the beginning of this introduction.

Class-based distributional struggles – the power resources approach (PRA)

The strand of thinking referred to as the power resources approach (PRA), or power resources theory (PRT), is a class-based perspective that emerged in the mid-1970s as a reaction to the theories that held sway at the time. Whereas the pluralist, structural-functionalist and neo-Marxist theories assumed that the distribution of power in society was relatively stable and driven by either systemic requirements or elite preferences, PRA emphasized distributive politics, particularly the power of the working class as key to understanding social reform and the creation and expansion of Western European welfare states (Korpi 1983; Stephens 1979). It provided an explanation for the observed variance in welfare states and established a strong normative position, suggesting that the benefits and risks arising from the operation of the market can only be fairly distributed within society by a means of a welfare state driven by strong labour movements and their associated political coalitions and constituencies (Esping-Andersen and Korpi 1985; O'Connor and Olsen 1998).

Effective collective action in the form of unions, strong political organization and the parliamentary system provide labour with the means to counteract capitalist interests and achieve independence from the market and employers via a process of 'decommodication'[6] (Esping-Andersen 1990). The formation of coalitions with other groups that were either underprivileged or threatened, such as the agrarian class or the church, would increase political strength and shape social provisioning. In this view, the welfare state is not only the result of labour's political ability to mobilize against capital but the means by which labour is able to increase its power resources and maintain political leverage. Social provisioning and protection provides labour with greater and more egalitarian distribution of resources, leading to the elimination of social fragmentation and some of the barriers to concerted collective action.

Strong labour unions became a pivotal element of the postwar neo-corporatist system of governance in various countries in Western Europe (Esping-Andersen 1990). The resultant social partnerships between states, organized business groups and labour unions were characterized by 'political exchange' (Pizzorno 1978) and a sustained period of economic growth and low wage dispersion.

Re-emergence of the state – the developmental state approach (DSA)

In the mid-1980s, a state-centred perspective criticized the PRA for its excessive emphasis on labour and disregard for the role of the state. Rooted in Alexander Hamilton and Frederich List's infant industry theories,[7] the approach to business–state relations has been alternately referred to as 'statist', 'neo-Weberian' or 'developmental state'. The resurgence of the DSA in the 1980s was driven by the empirical observations of Japan's rapid economic and social development (Woo-Cumings 1999; Johnson 1982).

At the core of this approach is the idea that some states have the capacity to act autonomously and pursue goals that might be at odds with various social classes, including the capitalist class (Evans et al. 1985). The Asian postwar context demonstrated how a mix of geopolitical circumstances and economic nationalism granted some states the autonomy to intervene in the economy in order to promote national objectives, particularly economic advancement. Militarist–bureaucratic heritages as well as the reciprocal dependence of the state and a budding domestic capitalist sector provided the institutional capacity to do so effectively.[8] Social legitimacy was a prerequisite for holding on to power and although often corrupt, political actors also had an overriding commitment to build internationally competitive national industries (Gomez 2002).

One of the key points made by this literature is that what underlies successful instances of developmental states are corporatist structures within which highly institutionalized public–private cooperation took place (Doner and Schneider 2000).[9] These policy networks, frequently termed 'deliberation councils', were initially hailed by the World Bank as key to the 'East Asian Miracle.'[10] The statist account of East Asia highlights the need to provide economic rents to capitalists that would use it productively, and support policies and bureaucracies that would reinforce this process by disciplining unproductive rent-seekers through corporatist structures (Amsden 2001; Khan and Jomo 2000). Strong bureaucracies and deliberation councils did not eliminate rent-seeking and corruption. Rather, these ensured capital accumulation and developmental processes proceeded despite it. In the East Asian context, large-scale cronyism and corruption existed alongside economic development and the selective rent allocation process that spurred industrialization (Khan 2001).

This form of joint policy-making led to the instrumental use of social policy, an overlooked and poorly understood aspect of the developmental state in

East Asia. Social policy effectively provided both the legitimacy required for the economic project and enhanced the capital accumulation process itself (Mkandawire 2004). With regard to the former, expansion of social policy often coincided with a challenge to governments' legitimacy.[11] Concerning the latter, two specific elements stand out. First, an active social policy enabled the 'learning-by-doing' pattern of industrialization successfully pursued by East Asian firms. Second, social policies regarding pensions resulted in the creation of large state-directed investment funds that were used as leverage over capitalists (Amsden 2001). In sum, progressive social policies enabled dynamism in productivity and industrial progress, both directly through labour education, training and health initiatives and incentives, and indirectly as a means of ensuring more cooperative labour–management relations and a stable business environment.[12]

Firm-centred perspective – the varieties of capitalism (VoC)

In the late 1990s both the PRA and DSA explanations of progressive welfare reform were challenged by approaches based on neocorporatist lines of thinking that emphasized the role of companies as employers and the associated institutional complementarity of competitive systems of production (Hall and Soskice 2001; Hollingsworth and Boyer 1999; Mares 2003).[13] This literature, generally concedes that labour movements and states, particularly sociodemocratic governments, influence social policy but points to the salience of the firm and its social relations. It argues that the positive role employers played in the formation of welfare states was disregarded, particularly the important role played by cross-class alliances between employers and employees from the same sector (Swenson 1991).

Following a tradition of comparing different systems of capitalist production, Hall and Soskice's (2001) comparison of LMEs (liberal market economies) and CMEs (coordinated market economies)[14] argues that: 1) there is no ideal institutional arrangement for organizing economic activity and therefore the market should not be promoted as the basis for modern economic and social organization; and 2) social policy preferences on the part of employers will be determined by employee skill requirements for successful competition in different types of product markets. Together, these two points imply that social welfare can be perceived as an institutional complement to national production systems.

VoC's explanatory power lies in its ability to establish links between product market strategies, workforce skills and the divergence in welfare systems. Its main argument is that the welfare state in CMEs can be understood as a means of insuring employees against labour market risks inherent in developing the specialized skills firms require. The more specific an employee's skills are to the operations/processes of a particular firm, the less 'portable' those skills become within the marketplace, and therefore, the more dependent the employee becomes on that specific employer (Hall and Soskice 2001). Referring to 'welfare production regimes' as 'the set of product market strategies, employee skill trajectories, and social, political, economic institutions that support them',[15] Estevez-Abe et al. (2001: 180) argue that product-market competitiveness in CMEs requires access to a workforce with a mix of general, industry-specific and firm-specific skills. Whereas workers with general skills are not dependent on specific employers, workers investing in a narrow (and therefore not easily transferable) skillset are in effect restricting their employability options and increasing their risk exposure.

From this perspective, social welfare is the insurance required to lower employees' risks and provide firms with the skills required to compete in international markets. Not providing social guarantees would mean exposing themselves to the potential underprovision of the skills required for competitiveness. In this view the welfare state is not perceived as the result of capitalists' collective weakness in the face of strong labour, but rather of their ability to coordinate and overcome the collective action problem in pursuit of their own self-interest. As such, it provides an understanding of how welfare policies can be reconceptualized as an integral component of product-market competition and suggests a possible basis for understanding employer interests in social policies and influence in policy-making processes in developing countries.

Insights and limitations

While these three strands of thinking on welfare states and business–state relations place different weights on the roles of different actors in shaping social policy, they can be understood as complementary perspectives, which, when viewed holistically, provide an effective vantage point from which to contemplate inclusive development trajectories. Together these theories point to the fact that policy outcomes are a function of actors' policy preferences and the channels, mechanisms or institutions by which these are aggregated and mediated within policy-making structures. Three main analytic facets emerge: 1) the relative structural power and influence of different actors; 2) the collective action institutions that aggregate and mediate interests; and 3) the conditions under which these institutions engender a synergistic relationship between economic competitiveness and social policy.

These theories call attention to how the balance of power in society moderates the relationship between business and social policy. PRA suggests that capitalists have acquiesced to demands for expanded social policies when the working classes and their coalitions gained political strength, and the unions that represented them acquired negotiating power. The DSA proposes that states with the bureaucratic capacity and political autonomy to impose conditions upon capitalists have emphasized strong instrumental social policies and promoted economic development, in part as a means of legitimating their power. VoC, for its part, acknowledges the role of unions and the state but emphasizes the power dynamics within the business sector and firms' abilities to overcome divisions and conflicts over policy preferences.

All three theories direct our attention to the organizational aspects of how power is embedded and mediated. According to PRA, the expansion of social programmes was the result of social movements not only influencing policymakers but directly engaging the political process on an institutional level by forming political coalitions and parties that are elected to power and unions capable of calling for and enforcing strikes. Conversely, the VoC approach and DSA emphasize the role of powerful business associations, capable of facilitating and/or coercing compromises and sanctioning members that defect from agreements. The three theories converge in how they highlight the various deliberative institutions that permit actors to share information, negotiate and resolve issues relating to economic production and distributional concerns. PRA, DSA and VoC describe, in varied ways, how ongoing institutionalized interaction between the state and business, or between the state, business and unions, increases trust, resolves conflicts and mediates power. These negotiating structures, referred to as 'social pacts', 'deliberation councils' and 'neocorporatist institutions' in these literatures highlight the need for encompassing structures that represent broad segments of society.

These varied streams of thinking on welfare states also explain how such actor interactions produced production regimes that have simultaneously promoted economic growth and expanded social policies in a mutually reinforcing manner. VoC, in particular, focuses upon the institutional complementarity underpinning different political economies and the important role social policy can play in business product market strategies within CMEs. The DSA highlights how East Asian states used social policies in an instrumental fashion to promote economic growth. The PRA also suggests that the neocorporatist institutions resulting from business accommodation of labour power resulted in both economic growth and expanded social policies. Overall, these theories provide a strong argument for a more nuanced understanding of the structural reasons for employers' social policy preferences.

Despite their significant contribution to our understanding of the relationship between systems of political and economic governance, and social welfare, these literatures display certain shortcomings when applied to the contemporary developing country context. To some degree, they are each bound by time and space, meaning that they best explain a specific type of regime during a particular time period in history. 'Spatial' limitations include the fact that the unit of analysis of each of these literatures is at the regime or nation level, with attention focused on the advanced industrialized countries or the so-called 'late industrializers.'[16] The VoC perspective tends to focus on the OECD countries and suffers from a number of limitations when applied to developing countries. As it deals with ideal types, its explanatory power does not transfer well to economies where institutions are not well defined, undergoing rapid change, or of a hybrid nature. Furthermore, VoC's conceptualization is largely unconcerned with the origins of institutions, a point of importance to developing countries. Similarly, PRA's roots lie in the analysis of class-based partisan politics in Northern Europe's social democratic countries. Although it has been extended to countries where labour is weak, such as the United States, or to where labour unions are not dominant actors in the governing coalitions, such as European Christian democratic countries, its explanatory power is best suited to advanced capitalist societies.

In a similar vein, DSA has centred on East Asian developmental states, a narrow band of countries that began their development trajectory under unusual geopolitical and institutional circumstances. The confluence of factors that strongly shaped the nature of these states differs greatly from the circumstances most developing countries have encountered in recent decades. This developing–developed divide has seemingly determined whether issues relating to the detrimental effects of rent-seeking were addressed or sidestepped. While business–state research on developing countries examines the relationship between industrial policy and corruption, it gives short shrift to the role of social and labour policy in the development context. Similarly, the PRA and the VoC perspectives examine the welfare state but circumvent concerns relating to rent-seeking and political capture by special interest groups.

Regarding the 'temporal' limitations of these literatures, all three perspectives exhibit an inability to adequately model the dynamic nature of contemporary political economy scenarios. Their emphases upon the institutional structures of the postwar boom lead, in different degrees, to path-dependent explanations, ill-suited to considering the situation of today's developing countries affected by economic liberalization, democratization and the rise of new modes of policy-making and governance. Particularly pertinent with regard to the latter are the rise of 'technocratic governance', the premium placed on 'expert' knowledge and 'epistemic communities' (Haas 1992), as well as the emphasis on CSR and PPPs.

The three perspectives outlined above pay limited attention to business beyond national borders, TNCs operating in an international context, and the pressures exerted by financial capital. Whereas capital can now cross borders and access vast labour markets, labour unions are mostly confined to the national level, and have been undermined as a result of widespread casualization and informalization of labour. This has diminished their ability for collective action and power. As a result, the balance of power relations has generally shifted in the direction of business. In a global economy the labour-infused version of PRA may no longer be as relevant as it once was. Revising and updating PRA requires an understanding of what are the new power resources. Similarly, the neoliberal emphasis on rolling back the state or fostering the 'competition state' has constrained the scope for resurrecting new developmental states, the focus of the DSA literature.

What the chapters say

The 11 chapters that make up this volume begin to address the spatial and temporal limitations mentioned in the previous section. They do so by examining the dynamics of business–state relations and their implications for inclusive development in less developed economies. These chapters pay particular attention to political economy contexts characterized by weak labour movements, and curtailed state power and policy space. New modes of public and voluntary private regulation, as well as the rise of technocratic governance and systems of electoral competition where the differences between right and left have become more opaque, are also considered. As such, they provide a clearer understanding of how various business actors engage with social policy, an essential input into current policy concerns with moving beyond both past and current variants of the Washington consensus.

Chapter 1 by **José Carlos Marques** provides a historical and comparative perspective to understand the relationship of business to social policy. Drawing together insights from various streams of literature on the political economies of the United States, Northern Europe and East Asia, he examines the political, economic and institutional conditions under which business has contributed to progressive social policies and the promotion of more inclusive patterns of development. His analysis suggests that progressive social policies are prevalent when business has low structural power relative to other social actors; industrial production is heavily dependent on a highly skilled labour force; social pressures affect a large cross-section of the business community; and collaborative institutions, including encompassing business associations, facilitate social dialogue and policy-making.

Proposing that lightly regulated markets with minimalist social policies are inappropriate for developing country economies, **Kevin Farnsworth** argues in Chapter 2 that intergovernmental organizations and governments tend to selectively promote 'taken-for-granted' views of business, rather than responding to a broad range of business preferences and needs. Such preferences vary considerably, depending not only on types of firms and industries but also the institutional environment in which business operates. Furthermore, in relation to social policy, he notes that business actors often do not engage effectively in the policy process, given issues of complexity and uncertainty. Despite these conditions, the structural power of business is immensely important in shaping both fiscal and social policy. Key actors in such outcomes are intergovernmental organizations, international business associations and ministries of trade and industry, all of which promote generic assumptions about what 'business' needs and/or wants. The structural power of business is associated then not only with the perceived potential for investment strikes or capital flight, but the pressures states are under to compete for new investment in the context of globalization.

As a result, governments respond selectively to the structural pressures of certain types of firms and investors, thereby locking themselves into a social policy agenda that can harm the welfare of individuals, economic development and the interests of the business community as a whole.

Turning to the specific case of India, in Chapter 3 **Kanta Murali** outlines the evolution of business–government relations in the era of economic reforms in India, and the subsequent impact on public policy, particularly labour policy. Liberalization has resulted in competition for private capital among state governments, offering 'investor-friendly environments', and has provided a major impetus for collective action by business. As a result, the ability of the private sector to articulate common interests, and its channels of access to government, have increased significantly. Although the business reform lobby has been driven by competitiveness concerns, it has had mixed results, with few legislative changes and a trend of de facto reform in some areas, such as labour market flexibility that is optimal neither for labour nor for business. Murali proposes two factors that constrain the influence of business on labour policy liberalization: India's vibrant democracy, and the difficulty of policy reform posed by India's constantly shifting coalition politics at the national level. In effect, although the Indian state and political system struggle to respond to the needs of the masses, democratic politics provides an effective obstacle to the introduction of potentially harmful social policies.

The following two chapters examine the role of business actors in trade negotiations. In Chapter 4 **Benedicte Bull** explores how Chilean business has influenced, or attempted to influence, the way in which trade agreements regulate environmental conduct and respect for labour rights. Although trade negotiations have often been portrayed as a 'two-level' game in which governments have to bargain with domestic groups and foreign trading partners simultaneously, she argues that such a distinction fails to recognize the considerable symbiosis of technocratic and business opinion, and the fact that the state has delegated some regulatory authority to business actors. Active cooperation and participation on the part of the business community has provided Chilean negotiators with significant technical expertise (via revolving doors, feasibility studies, coordination of business input, provision of data and analysis, and so on), mitigating the antagonistic relationship that existed between the government and business after the return of democracy in 1990, as well as reducing domestic opposition to trade agreements. Against this backdrop, Bull affirms that the prominence of environmental and labour issues in trade negotiation and business association agendas varies significantly. She suggests that this variability is explained by the fact that norms and standards from trading partners and Northern consumers have been the most important factors behind the introduction of social and environmental concerns in discussions.

In Chapter 5 **Gloria Carrión** examines how business actors in Nicaragua, a small and low-income country, sought to influence the negotiations around the Dominican Republic–Central American Free Trade Agreement (DR–CAFTA). To understand the influence of business, however, the chapter also takes a closer look at the role of civil society actors and the state in the policy-making process. Asymmetrical power relations operated at two levels, both at the inter-state (United States versus Nicaragua) and national levels. Organized business interests heavily shaped the Nicaraguan government's negotiating position, as exemplified by the ample access to government negotiators granted to certain business associations and representatives with the financial resources and technical knowledge that technocrats needed. Meanwhile, civil society actors that were either opposed to the agreement or sought to secure safeguards related to labour and environmental issues and the situation of small producers remained divided and weak, and, as a result, were not influential. The chapter highlights the implications of DR–CAFTA for inclusive development, noting that a national alliance of business interests and technocrats enjoyed a degree of negotiating space on issues related to market access but could not confront the structural power of the United States and transnational capital. This ensured that any enhanced market access would come at the cost of more stringent commitments related to intellectual property rights and foreign investment. As a result, Nicaragua's policy space was further constrained.

In Chapter 6 **Bart Slob and Francis Weyzig** focus on the issue of lobbying. They provide an overview and assessment of the literature and debates on corporate lobbying and assert that the political strategies of firms can be grouped into two main types: information-oriented and pressure-oriented. Whereas information-oriented lobbying focuses on the provision of technical knowledge and support via research reports, data, analysis and opinions, pressure-oriented lobbying involves influencing policy-makers via advocacy campaigns, linking policy decisions to investment decisions and pushing for self-regulation. Referring to the rise of CSR discourse, they call attention to the fact that ethical aspects of corporate lobbying and efforts to systematically align corporate lobbying with CSR principles are lacking. Reporting systems that provide guidelines for companies on how to report about lobbying strategies and activities are seldom applied, comprehensive information on corporate lobbying strategies and activities is rarely provided to stakeholders, and companies often disregard the lobbying positions of the business associations of which they are members. Through an examination of specific cases, they argue that, from a development perspective, the current lack of coherent policies and disclosure is particularly worrying. Some of the most important lobbying channels and effects of lobbying, notably in developing countries, remain unaddressed by academics and policy-makers. Because of the difficulties of regulating lobbying through law and public policy, transparency, disclosure and aligning company CSR policy and lobbying practices constitute an important complementary approach. Lobbying must be included in CSR policies, and companies should have the obligation to report on all lobbying channels and positions.

The issue of political corruption following Peru's dual economic and political transitions is the focus of Chapter 7 by **Francisco Durand**. Drawing on data concerning the investigation by congressional committees of tax exoneration practices during and following President Fujimori's regime, he examines the changing nature of state capture. This evolved from a more extreme mode, during the authoritarian Fujimori administration, to a more moderate mode, in the post-Fujimori democratic and liberal context – a situation he refers to as 'stronger corporations operating within weaker states'. Corporations, the most powerful economic actors in the new liberalized democracy, obtained privileged access to, and undue influence over, the most important branches of the state apparatus. Specific conditions, such as revolving doors and control over the appointment process in key branches, allowed the concentration of economic power to persist, despite newly invigorated democratic institutions and a resurgent civil society. Calls for the elimination of corporate privileges made it more difficult, but not impossible, for both national and international corporations to defend economic rents, in the form of tax exonerations that amounted to billions of dollars and a significant share of the country's GDP.

State capture was a particularly acute problem in the former Soviet republics following the collapse of communism. In Chapter 8, an analysis of the rise of business associations in post-socialist Russia, **David O'Brien** depicts a situation where economic liberalization within a newly emergent democracy led to co-optation and capture of the state. The disproportionate voice of big business and its influence within the embryonic business associations operating across the countries of the former Soviet Union aggravated already deteriorating social circumstances and dismal government social policies. However, against this backdrop, O'Brien highlights how the implementation of a state-led national management training programme for young entrepreneurs provided unexpected impetus for the formation of local business associations that established links to local government officials as a means of influencing policy, including social concerns.

The black box of how business interests influence policy is opened up further in Chapter 9 dealing with Brazil. **Wagner Pralon Mancuso** examines the collective political strategies adopted by Brazilian industrial entrepreneurs in their campaign for reducing what is known as the 'Brazil cost' – factors perceived by the business community to be limiting the international competitiveness of domestic companies. These include excessive and poor-quality economic regulation; 'inadequate' labour legislation; a tax system that overburdens production; the high cost of financing productive activity; insufficient material infrastructure; and deficient social infrastructure. Mancuso describes how the National Confederation of Industry (Confederação Nacional da Indústria/CNI), Brazil's peak business association, has operated as a 'political entrepreneur', mobilizing the business community. The lobby group formed by the CNI in the mid-1990s has consistently exerted pressure on legislative decision-making processes and achieved a high degree of political success. Mancuso's research finds that the level of 'success' is particularly high in relation to legislative proposals emanating from the executive branch of the state, suggesting a symbiotic relationship between technocracy and business. He also suggests that Brazil's corporatist tradition is being replaced by forms of business–state relations normally associated with pluralist systems, such as those in the United States. This is particularly worrisome considering the absence of regulation of lobbying activities in Brazil.

The issue of PPPs is the focus of the final two chapters. In Chapter 10 **Martin Kaggwa's** investigation into the South African automotive industry provides sector-level insight into the nuances of institutional capture within a newly democratic and liberalizing state. He portrays a partnership between government, industry and labour where power relations and benefits were skewed in favour of business, and the partnership's social objectives were marginalized despite government efforts to address and prioritize them. Two key mechanisms that explain this bias relate to the considerable space that business actors and technocrats had been given in policy formulation and review when the government adopted a more neoliberal development strategy in the mid-1990s, and, more specifically, the resources that business could bring to the table in terms of information, analysis and expertise. In policy design, implementation, monitoring and review, business enjoyed greater access to knowledge, compared to both government and labour. The framing of industry performance appraisal came to centre very much on economic and financial aspects rather than social dimensions related to employment, empowerment and CSR. Government and labour also lacked the capacity to assess the partnership model and to propose alternatives. The resultant policy framework enabled local industry to successfully integrate into the global automotive value chain but resulted in poor social outcomes.

In Chapter 11 **Paola Perez-Aleman** provides insight into how standard-setting and TNC–NGO partnerships could, under specific conditions that include an important role for the state, foster the inclusion of the poorest small producers and micro-enterprises. She presents a case study on the specialty coffee global supply chain, in which small-scale producers in Mexico and Central America have an important presence due to their control over the limited areas where such beans can be harvested. Examining the evolution from standard-setting to implementation of the Starbucks and Conservation International (CI) alliance, she suggests that the elaboration and implementation of new standards through TNC–NGO partnerships reveal possible routes for fostering inclusive development. Active assistance approaches at the level of small-scale producers seem particularly important in building their capacity to meet standards and creating conditions that support development and sustainable business. Perez-Aleman points out how the Starbucks–CI alliance provides insight into how the state, a broadly representative private sector and NGOs have the potential to create policies that link social and economic development. While norms and principles can coordinate relations between actors, the standards emerging from partnerships can inform policy-making and government regulation. Sustainable improvement in the social and economic conditions of poor producers, however, requires supporting their collective organization, as a means to establish links with NGOs and governments, gain access to resources, and develop the ability to upgrade their products.

Key themes and findings

The three main themes that emerge from the analysis and related findings contained in the various chapters strongly parallel the analytic lens developed earlier. The first theme, social policy and competitiveness, concerns the relationship between business interests and social policy, particularly the implications for social policy of the changes occurring in business–state relations in contexts of globalization and liberalization. The second theme, power and influence, covers some suggested reasons why business engagement in social policy processes in some countries has been, and remains, quite restricted. The third theme, collective action, identifies structural, political and institutional conditions under which business interests might favour progressive social policies, and how regressive influences may be countered through subaltern collective action and the state's involvement and active provision of incentives.

Social policy and competitiveness

When examining business–state relations from the perspective of inclusive development, it is crucial to understand the relationship between business competitiveness and social policy. Whereas the CSR literature has largely ignored the link between the two, the neoliberal-era Washington consensus prescribed a residualist and targeted approach to social policy. Such an approach is clearly evident in the reforms many countries have undertaken in recent decades. Restraints on social spending, privatization or commercialization of basic public services, changes in tax regimes that favoured corporations and trade, deregulation or flexibilization of labour markets, and so forth, were all painted with the broad brush of being 'business-friendly'. Within such a frame it is generally assumed that there is a trade-off between business interests and progressive social policy. Several chapters in this volume however, highlight historical and contemporary empirical evidence that supports a different view – the considerable variation in business preferences towards social policy, as well as the importance of context in shaping the relationship.

Drawing a distinction between foreign TNCs, large domestic firms, small and medium enterprises (SMEs), and the industries in which they operate, this volume highlights the need to consider the variation and organization of private sector interests as an object of government policy. A main argument is that the suitability of minimal social policies for developing countries, and sweeping generalizations that assume business is inherently hostile to progressive social policy, are highly questionable. The reality or perception that the field of social policy is complex, that outcomes are uncertain and that some aspects of social policy are irrelevant for business may result in passive responses, rather than hostility, on the part of business.[17] However, various aspects of social policy can be conducive to both the short- and long-term interests of both business and society. This is particularly evident in relation to human capital formation, a healthy workforce, and social cohesion and stability. Globalization's effects upon business social policy preferences may also be much more nuanced than conventionally recognized. For example, in relation to trade agreements and related labour and environmental regulations, business may behave more as rule-takers rather than rule-makers in an effort to reduce barriers to market access.

An important insight emerging from the analysis in this volume is that inclusive development requires innovative policies that address and enable both increased competitiveness and rises in social welfare. This requires greater understanding of the complex relationship between fiscal, trade, labour and social policies rather than the marginalization of social policy and segregation of various policy-making spheres. The analysis by many of the contributors suggests the need for a programmatic approach that produces greater policy coherence across policy areas. However, the contemporary development context in many developing and transition countries continues to be dominated by policy approaches that aim primarily to enhance competitiveness in a manner that accommodates specific business interests and stifles the design and implementation of socioeconomic policies more amenable to broader segments of business and society. The next section examines this issue in greater detail.

Business power and influence

The second main theme addressed in this volume concerns the various mechanisms by which business influences public policy. The rise of large domestic corporations and TNCs has major implications for public policy in terms of lobbying and 'institutional capture', particularly where states and civil societies are incapable of constituting countervailing forces. Lobbying practices that frequently urge governments to adopt policies and laws that are socially and environmentally regressive often contradict CSR discourse. Several chapters consider the evolving nature of state–business relations – the manner in which business interests shape the fiscal, trade, labour market and social policies that determine national development trajectories.

The chapters concerned with Brazil, Chile, India, Nicaragua, Peru, Russia and South Africa examine how some business interests exercise considerable 'instrumental power' as a means of shaping policy in their favour. A variety of methods, including corruption and lobbying by both companies and business associations, are covered. Various cases in this volume, however, demonstrate that influence is often exercised via less overt channels, resulting from the reciprocal dependency between business and government and the shared interests of political and business elites. Stretched government bureaucracies often welcome and encourage business provision of technical expertise and its direct input into trade negotiations, in some cases even delegating trade negotiation and regulatory authority to the business sector. The rise of technocracies committed to free-market ideology and an overriding emphasis on FDI also facilitate corporate influence. Specific mechanisms, such as 'revolving doors',[18] further bind the interests of the two sectors together and reinforce patterns of business–state interaction that determine what type of expert knowledge is used and how it is transmitted to policy-makers. This can result in an exclusionary policy-making process that marginalizes social policy.

Also clearly evident in the case studies in this volume is how ideology and investment decisions reflect a form of 'structural power' associated with business interests that indirectly influences national policy priorities. It can restrict the policy options governments allow themselves and may therefore be equally influential in shaping policy as actual business voices or instrumental power, which attempts to influence government policy directly. Following conventional economic prescriptions on how to create 'investor-friendly' business environments as a means of attracting FDI, governments often accept broad generalizations concerning business needs based on the structural power of specific business actors. Such assumptions may distort fiscal, industrial and social policy in ways that benefit particular sectors of business to the detriment of the wider business community.

The chapters in this volume highlight how the structural conditions required to engender a scenario whereby some segments of business endorse progressive social policy directions are seemingly weak. In their absence, a more active state is essential to promoting the institutional reforms required for inclusive development in contexts of democratization and economic liberalization. Such reforms, relating to social protection, redistribution and regulation, require fostering various forms of collective action, including those involving organized business interests.

Collective action

A key analytical thread that runs throughout the book relates to the questions of which forms of collective action enhance inclusive development and how the state can promote these. Whereas neoliberal prescriptions frowned upon most forms of collective action, particularly labour unions, as 'market-distorting', various chapters in this book highlight the crucial role of collective action in various guises and at multiple levels: the local SME level, the level of business organizations, and the institutions of representative democracy. They also suggest that preventing state capture and successfully crafting innovative policies that benefit both business and society requires sustained collective action involving civil society organizations engaged in contestation, bargaining and advocacy[19] and a more active role for government than what has often been advocated in mainstream development circles in recent decades.

Pressures on global corporations that arise through collective action associated with subaltern groups and through the institutions of representative democracy are likely to increase. This is due not only to the ongoing – indeed, sharpening – contradictions between corporate capitalism and social and sustainable development, but also because the TNC is becoming an overt political actor. Large corporations are playing a more explicit role in global governance and are taking up various tasks of social protection, provisioning, inspection and standard-setting hitherto assumed by states. Indeed, in remote areas of the world, often where indigenous peoples reside, oil and mining companies may become de facto governments. Corporations therefore become legitimate targets of contestation that will likely respond through some form of co-optation or compromise (Crouch 2009). The growing 'corporate accountability movement', comprising myriad civil society groups and organizations, often with the support of particular mainstream political actors and institutions, is attempting to introduce various checks on business power and change corporate behaviour.

The state, however, clearly has a role to play in expanding business–state relations beyond narrow groups. While states are inevitably contradictory in their social and distributive orientation, a key role relates to enhancing collective needs. Catering to FDI or to a narrow band of domestic interests has been demonstrated to be a poor way of ensuring economic development and clearly does not promote inclusive development. Institutional innovation may require crafting broad coalitions with interests in promoting social policies. Economic and social concerns may be simultaneously addressed by strengthening the organizational capacity of business segments that support inclusive social policies and promoting deliberative institutions that generate the expertise required to craft innovative policies, facilitate interest representation and bargaining, and lead to social pacts. Although the specific form may well be different for each country, the function is the same. It is up to the state to foster the conditions required for these coalitions to emerge and develop the capacity to provide a countervailing force to narrow interests. This may require the development of forums for dialogue and deliberation on policies and contentious issues, or the provision of incentives to some business sectors, either because there is little business justification, too much risk involved in supporting more expansive social policies, or because of the collective-action problem. In other cases this may entail active state assistance and the provision of resources to smaller, disadvantaged groups and capacity-building measures for effective local participation.

Every developing and transition country is building from a different institutional and historical base. In some places, large corporations and business associations already play a significant role. Several chapters in this volume suggest that governments must seek to actively engage business associations and ensure that their ability to articulate common preferences is complemented by an ability to mediate differing interests and consider broader social needs. Under certain conditions 'encompassing' business associations, representing diverse sectors of business, can ensure that the voice of the business community is not only that of a narrow segment of corporate elites. Their ability to integrate and articulate the views and interests of diverse sectors is essential. The inclusion of SMEs, whose workforce often comprises the poorest and largest segments of society, may be essential to the promotion of more inclusive social policy. Business associations can also be harnessed in order to stimulate the state's capacity for co-regulation. Institutionalized dialogue between the state and encompassing associations usually provides a basis for understanding the competitive needs of different business sectors, sharing information and expectations, and establishing joint goals.

The research also shows how democratic processes and civil society can moderate institutional capture by business interests where the state is unwilling or unable to operate in this manner. Parliamentary oversight and other institutions of representative democracy can mitigate institutional capture or the deregulatory effects associated with the growing structural power of business, and ensure that the interests of weaker groups in society are defended or, at the very least, not further eroded.

Conclusion – prospects for inclusive development

Neoliberal-era policies related to economic liberalization, financialization, privatization, public sector reform and the associated rise of business power have had profound implications for social wellbeing, equity and democratic governance in developing countries. Mainstream development theory and policy in recent decades has been characterized by the promotion of a strategy that advocates the need to contain 'rigidities' such as business associations, labour unions, interventionist states and redistributionary welfare mechanisms – precisely the institutions many countries have relied upon for inclusive development. It has also advocated a set of macroeconomic policies that prioritized attracting FDI, export-orientation and economic stabilization that benefited a narrow subset of business, often at the cost of small and medium enterprises, and sustained growth. Such trade-offs and growing recognition of the relationship between such policy and institutional reforms and major social problems of un/underemployment, food insecurity, persistent poverty and growing inequality have called into question the stability and legitimacy of such a model of capitalism, even before the recent economic crisis.[20]

This volume considers what can be done to enhance the contribution of business to social development in contexts where the structural power of business has increased, where the rise of global value chains challenges or weakens the institutional environment regulating corporations, and where CSR and PPPs exhibit serious constraints on an effective approach to both business regulation and social development. Various case studies of countries that underwent the dual transitions of economic and political reforms during the height of the neoliberal era provide insights into the effects of neoliberal policies and the contemporary explanatory power of existing theory.

The PRA, DSA and VoC literatures reviewed above have to different degrees pointed to the mutually reinforcing nature of economic and social policy and the need to reconsider the definition, design and potential of social policy. They suggest that business competitiveness can occur in the context of diverse combinations of social policies and institutions. They also reveal the heterogeneity of business interests and how various groups or sectors of business may not necessarily be against progressive social policies. Various chapters in this volume confirm such views, but also suggest that in the context of developing and transitional economies, both instrumental and structural dimensions of business power, allied with technocracy, have skewed social policies towards generic prescriptions, thereby favouring a narrow business subgroup and reducing the potential for institutional and policy reforms capable of generating both widespread economic and social benefits. Furthermore, global trends associated with the casualization of labour, subcontracting, the intensification of international competition, and the disembedding of elites through FDI and globalization may also affect business preferences related to social policy in a regressive sense.

It remains to be seen if future historians will recognize this current period of global crisis as the end of a neoliberal experiment that poorly served many countries and a return to earlier development models and institutions. The need to 'bring the state back in', for greater 'policy space' and to shift the emphasis from corporate self-regulation to binding forms of business regulation seems to have moved on from theoretical argument to a stark necessity. Whether or not we will see the reassertion of developmental states is an open question, not least from a normative perspective, given ongoing authoritarian tendencies in countries like China and Vietnam.[21] In the current crisis context, the structural, instrumental and discursive power of TNCs, finance capital and international business associations may be somewhat weakened but there are signs that business interests have played a key role in 're-regulation' and the design of interventionist approaches.

At the time of writing, it is not clear whether this will result in a return to 'business-as-usual' or greater space for industrial policy, domestic-oriented production, public investment, social spending and countercyclical policies more generally. It also remains to be seen whether technocracies will significantly change their spots both in terms of their worldviews, their leaning towards certain types of business and investment, and the type of knowledge and 'experts' with which they choose to interact.

Regarding the role of the state, the challenge for many developing countries is how to increase state capacity following decades of downsizing and ongoing international pressures for fiscal constraint. This volume suggests that state action alone is necessary but insufficient for inclusive development – countervailing forces associated with civil society as well as a coalition of forces anchored in a clear and meaningful social pact between the state and business, and civil society, is required. This book, and its companion volume on CSR, emphasize the need to reconfigure social forces to bring about more transformative development agendas. However, social pressures 'from below' are often fragmented and lack the strength historically associated with the labour movement. Civil society activism is certainly alive but not particularly well in terms of how NGOs relate to both social movements and political parties, power imbalances within NGO networks, and a more comprehensive understanding of development and the politics of transformative change. As examined in the companion volume, however, certain developments associated with transnational or 'multi-scalar' activism suggest that activism is adapting in innovative and more effective ways to the realities of globalization and business power.

The recent re-emergence of buzzwords such as policy space, countercyclical policies, state capacity, re-regulation, food security and a global jobs pact suggest that at the ideational and normative level, the international development community has a better sense of what needs to be done. It is also the case that the fracturing of neoliberal hegemony opens up the space for so-called counter-hegemonic thinking. What is far less clear is whether we are seeing the emergence of a new politics that can translate alternative ideas into action.

Notes

1. The typology of Haggard et al. (1997), for example, refers to business as 'capital', business as 'sector', business as 'firm', business as 'association', and business as 'network'.
2. This volume pays particular attention to the dimensions of structural and instrumental power noted above. Aspects that relate to discursive power are addressed in more depth in the companion volume, where we examine, among other aspects, the effectiveness of CSR as a means of legitimizing contemporary forms of corporate capitalism.

3. Within the UN system there are some notable exceptions, including, for example, work carried out at the United Nations University–World Institute for Development Economics Research (UNU–WIDER) on the role of business elites, at the United Nations Research Institute for Social Development (UNRISD) on corporate accountability, and at the International Labour Organization (ILO) on labour rights and industrial relations.
4. UNRISD defines 'transformative social policy' as state intervention that aims to improve social welfare, social institutions and social relations. It involves overarching concerns with redistribution, production, reproduction and protection, and works in tandem with economic policy in pursuit of national social and economic goals. An important feature of transformative social policy is also the establishment and enforcement of standards and regulations that shape the role of non-state actors and markets in social provisioning and protection (UNRISD 2006).
5. See de Sousa Santos and Rodríguez-Garavito (2005); Martens (2007); Richter (2001); Klein (2000); Korten (1995); Reich (2007); Utting (2008).
6. 'De-commodification occurs when a service is rendered as a matter of right, and when a person can maintain a livelihood without reliance on the market' (Esping-Andersen 1990: 21–2).
7. The infant industry argument states that the theories of comparative advantage are not conducive to long-term development of countries with a low industrial base, due to their focus on the static efficiency in the allocation of resources (Sheffadin 2000: 2). As a result, the state should protect infant industries in order to promote industrialization rather than engage in unrestricted international trade (Chang 2002).
8. Evans (1995); Wade (1990); Amsden (1989).
9. There were of course differences in public–private cooperation. Some argue that Japan's form of corporatism differed from that of Taiwan and the Republic of Korea in the sense that it was more in line with democratic institutions and, as such, exhibited a form of corporatism that more closely resembled the neocorporatist institutions of Western Europe (Onis 1991).
10. However, subsequent to the Asian economic crises of the late 1990s, such close business–state relationships were relabelled 'crony capitalism' and demonized for contravening good governance principles. See World Bank (1993); Singh (1998); Woo (2007); Campos (1996).
11. For an overview of the Korean case, see Yi and Lee (2005).
12. Mkandawire (2007); Onis (1991); Chang (2004). In the case of the Republic of Korea, social programmes, such as Industrial Accident Insurance, National Health Insurance and the National Pension Programme, were available only to industrial labour (Kwon 2005).
13. Our focus is on VoC because of its focus on national-level institutions. The literature on social systems of production (SSP) addresses multiple levels, including the regional and local.
14. Germany and the United States are used as ideal types.
15. Estevez-Abe et al. (2001) identify four product-market strategies based upon the skill profile each requires: 1) Fordist mass production involving standardized tasks, mass production and requiring semi-skilled workers; 2) diversified mass production (DMP), a variation on mass production involving a varied range or products in large volumes, requiring highly firm-specific skills; 3) high quality product niche market strategy involving 'highly craft-intensive workshops' and requiring highly trained workers; and 4) a hybrid variant of the latter referred to

as 'diversified quality production', involving high-quality product lines and large production volumes and requiring craft and firm-specific skills.
16. Notable exceptions include Huber (2003) and Haggard and Kaufman (2008).
17. Business may adopt a neutral position vis-à-vis social policy or ignore it completely. Referring to Latin America, Schneider (2007) suggests that this position has arisen not only in contexts where low-skilled industries predominate. The difficulties of engaging with social policy processes, which tend to be protracted, and the cost-benefit implications of social policies, which are not always obvious, need to be considered.
18. A situation whereby conflicts of interest arise because of the appointment of civil servants or government officials previously employed in the private sector, and with potentially strong links to business interests, and vice versa.
19. This aspect is dealt with in more depth in our companion volume (Utting and Marques 2010).
20. Gill (2003); Beneria and Bisnath (2004); Bernstein and Pauly (2007); Held and Koenig-Archibugi (2003); United Nations (1995).
21. In the context of Latin America, some point to the re-emergence of the 'new Latin American developmental welfare state' (Riesco and Draibe 2007).

References

Amsden, Alice (1989) *Asia's Next Giant: South Korea and Late Industrialization* (Oxford: Oxford University Press).

——— (2001) *The Rise of 'the Rest': Challenges to the West from Late-Industrializing Economies* (Oxford: Oxford University Press).

Beneria, Lourdes and Savitri Bisnath (eds) (2004) *Global Tensions: Challenges and Opportunities in the World Economy* (London: Routledge).

Berger, Suzanne (2005) *How We Compete: What Companies around the World Are Doing to Make It in Today's Global Economy* (New York: Broadway Business).

Bernstein, Steven and Louis W. Pauly (eds) (2007) *Global Liberalism and Political Order: Toward a New Grand Compromise?* (Albany: State University of New York Press).

Campos, José Edgardo (1996) *The Key to the Asian Miracle: Making Shared Growth Credible* (Washington, DC: Brookings Institution Press).

Chang, Ha-Joon (2002) *Kicking away the Ladder: Development Strategy in Historical Perspective* (London: Anthem Press, 2002).

——— (2004) 'The Role of Social Policy in Economic Development: Some Theoretical Reflections and Lessons from East Asia', in T. Mkandawire (ed.), *Social Policy in a Development Context* (Basingstoke: UNRISD/Palgrave Macmillan).

Crouch, Colin (2010) 'CSR and Changing Modes of Governance: Toward Corporate *Noblesse Oblige?*', in Peter Utting and José Carlos Marques (eds), *Corporate Social Responsibility and Regulatory Governance: Towards Inclusive Development?* (Basingstoke: Palgrave Macmillan).

Doner, Richard and Ben Ross Schneider (2000), 'Business Associations and Economic Development: Why Some Associations Contribute More than Others', *Business and Politics*, 2 (3), 261–88.

Esping-Andersen, Gøsta (1990) *The Three Worlds of Welfare Capitalism* (Cambridge: Polity Press).

———, and Walter Korpi (1985) 'Social Policy as Class Politics in Post-War Capitalism', in J. H. Goldthorpe (ed.), *Order and Conflict in Contemporary Capitalism* (Oxford: Oxford University Press).

Estevez-Abe, Margarita, Torben Iversen and David Soskice (2001) 'Social Protection and the Formation of Skills: A Reinterpretation of the Welfare State', in A. Hall and D. Soskice (eds), *Varieties of Capitalism: The Institutional Foundations of Comparative Advantage* (Oxford: Oxford University Press).

Evans, Peter (1995) *Embedded Autonomy* (Princeton: Princeton University Press).

Evans, Peter B., Dietrich Rueschemeyer and Theda Skocpol (eds) (1985) *Bringing the State Back In* (Cambridge: Cambridge University Press).

Fuchs, Doris A. (2005) *Understanding Business Power in Global Governance* (Baden-Baden: Nomos).

Gill, Stephen (2003) *Power and Resistance in the New World Order* (New York: Palgrave Macmillan).

Gomez, Edmund Terence (2002) 'Introduction: Political Business in East Asia', in E. T. Gomez (ed.), *Political Business in East Asia* (London: Routledge).

Green, Duncan (2008) *From Poverty to Power: How Active Citizens and Effective States Can Change the World* (Oxford: Oxfam International).

Haas, Peter M. (1992) 'Introduction: Epistemic Communities and International Policy Coordination', *International Organization*, 46 (1), 1–35.

Haggard, Stephan and Robert R. Kaufman (2008) *Development, Democracy, and Welfare States: Latin America, East Asia, and Eastern Europe* (Princeton: Princeton University Press).

Haggard, Stephan, Sylvia Maxfield and Ben Ross Schneider (1997) 'Theories of Business and Business–State Relations', in S. Maxfield and B. R. Schneider (eds), *Business and the State in Developing Countries* (Ithaca: Cornell University Press).

Hall, Peter A. and David Soskice (2001) 'An Introduction to Varieties of Capitalism', in P. A. Hall and D. Soskice (eds), *Varieties of Capitalism: The Institutional Foundations of Comparative Advantage* (Oxford: Oxford University Press).

Held, David and Mathias Koenig-Archibugi (eds) (2003) *Taming Globalization: Frontiers of Governance* (Cambridge: Polity Press).

Hollingsworth, J. Rogers and Robert Boyer (eds) (1999) *Contemporary Capitalism: The Embeddedness of Institutions* (Cambridge: Cambridge University Press).

Huber, Evelyne (ed.) (2003) *Models of Capitalism: Lessons for Latin America* (University Park: Pennsylvania State University Press).

Johnson, Chalmers (1982) *Miti and the Japanese Miracle: The Growth of Industrial Policy, 1925–1975* (Palo Alto: Stanford University Press).

Khan, Mushtaq (2001) 'The New Political Economy of Corruption', in B. Fine, C. Lapavitsas and J. Pincus (eds), *Development Policy in the Twenty-First Century: Beyond the Post-Washington Consensus* (London: Routledge).

Khan, Mushtaq H. and Kwame Sundaram Jomo (eds) (2000) *Rents, Rent-Seeking and Economic Development. Theory and Evidence in Asia* (Singapore: Green Giant Press Pte. Ltd).

Klein, Naomi (2000) *No Logo* (London: Flamingo).

Korpi, Walter (1983) *The Democratic Class Struggle* (London: Routledge).

Korten, D. C. (1995) *When Corporations Rule the World* (San Francisco: Berette-Koehler).

Kwon, Huck-ju (ed.) (2005) *Transforming the Developmental Welfare State in East Asia* (Basingstoke: UNRISD/Palgrave).

Levy, David L. and Peter J. Newell (2002) 'Business Strategy and International Environmental Governance: Toward a Neo-Gramscian Synthesis', *Global Environmental Politics*, 2 (4), 84–101.

Mares, Isabela (2003) *The Politics of Social Risk: Business and Welfare State Development* (New York: Cambridge University Press).

Martens, Jens (2007) *Multistakeholder Partnerships – Future Models of Multilateralism?*, Dialogue on Globalization, Occasional Papers No. 29 (Berlin: Friedrich Ebert Stiftung).

Mkandawire, Thandika (2004) 'Social Policy in a Development Context: Introduction', in T. Mkandawire (ed.), *Social Policy in a Development Context* (New York: UNRISD/ Palgrave).

——— (2007) 'Transformative Social Policy and Innovation in Developing Countries', *European Journal of Development Research*, 19 (1), 13.

Newell, Peter (2008) 'CSR and the Limits of Capital', *Development and Change*, 39 (6), 1063–78.

O'Connor, Julia S. and Gregg M. Olsen (eds) (1998) *Power Resource Theory and the Welfare State: A Critical Approach* (Toronto: University of Toronto Press).

OECD (Organisation for Economic Co-operation and Development) (2006) *Boosting Jobs and Incomes, Policy Lessons from Reassessing the OECD Jobs Strategy* (Paris: OECD).

Onis, Ziya (1991) 'The Logic of the Developmental State', *Comparative Politics*, 24 (1), 109–26.

Pizzorno, Alessandro (1978) 'Political Exchange and Collective Identity in Industrial Conflict', in C. Crouch and A. Pizzorno (eds), *The Resurgence of Class Conflict in Western Europe* (London: Macmillan).

Reich, Robert (2007) *Supercapitalism: The Transformation of Business, Democracy and Everyday Life* (New York: Knopf).

Richter, Judith (2001) *Holding Corporations Accountable: Corporate Conduct, International Codes and Citizen Action* (London: Zed Books).

Riesco, Manuel and Sonia M. Draibe (2007) 'Latin America: A New Developmental Welfare State Model in the Making?', in Manuel Riesco (ed.), *Latin America: A New Developmental Welfare State Model in the Making?* (Basingstoke: UNRISD/Palgrave Macmillan).

Rodrik, Dani and A. Subramanian (2009) 'Why Did Financial Globalization Disappoint?', *IMF Staff Papers*, 56 (1), 112–38.

Ruggie, John Gerard (2003) 'Taking Embedded Liberalism Global: The Corporate Connection', in D. Held and M. Koenig-Archibugi (eds), *Taming Globalization: Frontiers of Governance* (Cambridge: Polity Press).

Sachs, Jeffrey D. (2005) *The End of Poverty: Economic Possibilities for Our Time* (New York: Penguin Books).

Sell, Susan (2009) 'Corporations, Seeds, and Intellectual Property Rights Governance', in Jennifer Clapp and Doris Fuchs (eds), *Corporate Power in Global Agrifood Governance (Food, Health, and the Environment)* (Cambridge MA: MIT Press).

Sheffadin, Mehdi (2000) *What Did Frederick List Actually Say? Some Clarifications on the Infant Industry Argument*, Discussion Paper 149 (Geneva: UNCTAD).

Singh, Ajit (1998) *'Asian Capitalism' and the Financial Crisis*, Working Paper Series III, International Capital Markets and the Future of Economic Policy, Working Paper No. 10 (New York: Center for Economic Policy Analysis/CEPA).

Stephens, John (1979) *The Transition from Capitalism to Socialism* (New York: Macmillan Press).

de Sousa Santos, Boaventura and César A. Rodríguez-Garavito (2005) 'Law, Politics and the Subaltern in Counter-Hegemonic Globalization', in B. de Sousa Santos and C. A. Rodríguez-Garavito (eds), *Law and Globalization from Below: Towards a Cosmopolitan Legality* (Cambridge: Cambridge University Press).

Swenson, Peter (1991) 'Bringing Capital Back In, or Social Democracy Reconsidered: Employer Power, Cross-Class Alliances, and Centralization of Industrial Relations in Denmark and Sweden', *World Politics*, 43 (4), 513–44.

——— (2002) *Capitalists against Markets: The Making of Labor Markets and Welfare States in the United States and Sweden* (New York: Oxford University Press).

United Nations (1995) *Report of the World Summit for Social Development*, 6–12 March (Copenhagen: United Nations).

UNRISD (United Nations Research Institute for Social Development) (2006) *Transformative Social Policy: Lessons from UNRISD Research*, UNRISD Research and Policy Brief 5 (Geneva: UNRISD).

Utting, Peter (2005a) 'Corporate Responsibility and the Movement of Business', *Development in Practice*, 15 (3/4), 375–88.

——— (2005b) *Rethinking Business Regulation: From Self-Regulation to Social Control*, Programme on Technology, Business and Society, Paper No. 15 (Geneva: UNRISD).

——— (2008), 'The Struggle for Corporate Accountability', *Development and Change*, 39 (6), 959–75.

———, and José Carlos Marques (eds) (2010) *Corporate Social Responsibility and Regulatory Governance: Towards Inclusive Development?* (Basingstoke: Palgrave Macmillan).

———, and Ann Zammit (2006) *Beyond Pragmatism: Appraising UN–Business Partnerships*, Programme on Markets, Business and Regulation, Paper No. 1 (Geneva: UNRISD).

Wade, Robert Hunter (1990) *Governing the Market: Economic Theory and the Role of Government in East Asian Industrialization* (Princeton: Princeton University Press).

Woo-Cumings, Meredith (ed.) (1999) *The Developmental State* (London: Cornell University Press).

Woo, Meredith Jung-En (2007) 'After the Miracle: Neoliberalism and Institutional Reform in East Asia', in M. J.-E. Woo (ed.), *After the Miracle: Neoliberalism and Institutional Reform in East Asia* (Basingstoke: UNRISD/Palgrave Macmillan).

World Bank (1993) *The East Asian Miracle: Economic Growth and Public Policy* (New York: Oxford University Press).

——— (2005) *Economic Growth in the 1990s: Learning from a Decade of Reform* (Washington, DC: World Bank).

Yi, Ilcheong and Byung-hee Lee (2005) 'Development Strategies and Unemployment Policies in Korea', in Huck-ju Kwon (ed.), *Transforming the Developmental Welfare State in East Asia* (Basingstoke: UNRISD/Palgrave Macmillan).

1
Organized Business and Social Policy in Comparative Perspective

José Carlos Marques

Introduction

In recent decades numerous governments and a host of multilateral institutions, such as the United Nations (UN), the Organisation for Economic Co-operation and Development (OECD) and the World Bank, have encouraged the private sector to engage in the development agenda. Non-state actors, including transnational corporations (TNCs), business networks and associations, have deepened their involvement in policy-making processes, institutional reform and the provision of public goods. More recently, economic stagnation and crisis, growing inequality, social tensions and the stability and legitimacy of the current form of capitalism have led to calls for more egalitarian development agendas and increased levels of social spending. Poverty reduction and social development have re-emerged as important development objectives and once-hollow calls to 'bring the state back in' have seemingly gained substance. The suggestion that public policy issues, including distributional concerns, could be dealt with by means of corporate self-regulation is being met with increasing scepticism.

How should we expect business actors to react to an agenda where liberal economic policies still hold sway but poverty and progressive social policy[1] are once again prominent issues? How has business responded in previous eras and in different countries to calls for social engagement? How do different literatures inform these questions? The aim of this chapter is to synthesize relevant findings from various streams of research that have dealt with these issues and interpret points of intersection that are relevant to the contemporary context. Referring to the historical experience of today's industrialized countries, this chapter will address the following question: Under what political, economic and institutional conditions has business contributed to progressive social policies and the promotion of more inclusive patterns of development?

Understanding such conditions requires a comparative and historical sociopolitical approach. As such, three political economies that most closely match three ideal 'regime' types are used as an organizing concept. The liberal United States (US) model is compared to two others that emphasize the coordination of actors – the neocorporatist Northern European model and the corporatist East Asian model.[2] The following sections will: 1) review the literature on pluralist forms of economic coordination and the resulting social policy in the American historical context; 2) contrast this literature to the literature on neocorporatist and corporatist forms of economic coordination and their associated welfare states in Northern Europe and East Asia; and 3) suggest an answer to the question being posed by contrasting the experiences of these different regime types.

The contents of this chapter cut across several bodies of literature from various fields and disciplines, including the welfare state, rent-seeking, collective action, (neo)corporatism, comparative capitalism, international relations, development studies and business studies. Keeping the contents manageable requires substantially compressing significant bodies of work, thereby omitting the explanatory richness and diversity of argument and perspective offered by these literatures. It is, however, hoped that the insights garnered by connecting these literatures will outweigh this obvious deficiency.

The American firm and the corporate social welfare state

The political economy of the United States is distinguished by its minimal welfare system, conflictual industrial relations, social inequality and a decentralized system of government. As the quintessential 'Anglo-Saxon' or neoliberal economy, the US experience was the model for both the contemporary Washington consensus and the corporate social responsibility (CSR) agendas. A holistic perspective of the origins and unique features of the American experience and its current issues is vital to understanding current global conceptions and prescriptions of development and business–state–society relations.

Industrialization in the new world

Incentives and opportunities to organize along class lines to overthrow an established ruling aristocracy and fight for collective economic and political rights – which led to the creation of socialist and social democratic parties in many European countries – were largely absent in the United States (Giddens 1973). The federated political system and civil war resulted in a pattern of conflict over wealth redistribution from the largely agricultural south to the industrializing north, rather than between capital and labour classes (Bensel 2000). The Lockean political ideals that led to the American Revolution inspired a strong embrace of individualism and individual rights and shaped a culture of entrepreneurial capitalism characterized by freedom of choice, distrust of government, and civic participation largely devoid of political class conflict (de Tocqueville 1835/40[2002]). Some strands of classical liberal ideology perceived the state as a corrupt, mercantilist regime that repressed human liberty (Esping-Andersen 1990). The intention to limit government power with a series of checks and balances is enshrined in the American constitution's design and the distrust of government and insistence on private-sector autonomy remains ingrained to this day (Vogel 1989).

As a result, the idea that markets were the surest path to equality, neutrality and freedom underpinned America's development trajectory, including its pattern of industrialization. The limited role that the US government played in regulating corporations is evidenced by the fact that up until the late nineteenth century the US Congress had yet to pass any laws regulating corporations, and that one of the first such acts of legislation by Congress, in 1890, was for the purposes of safeguarding market competition[3] (McQuaid 1994). Responding to the growth of informal railroad cartels and the rise of the 'Robber Barons', the Sherman Anti-Trust Act declared trusts and monopolistic behaviour illegal[4] (McCraw 1984). This proved to be a radical departure from the path followed by other countries at the time, which favoured collective solutions for the purposes of stabilizing industries that had expanded too quickly or whose market had become saturated. In fact, numerous governments during the nineteenth century promoted trade associations as a form of regulation in labour, product or raw materials markets for purposes of maintaining (that is, 'fixing') prices and therefore profits (Tedlow 1988).

The legislated prohibition of collaborative economic solutions triggered an unprecedented frenzy of horizontal and vertical merger activity intended to create large, integrated firms and achieve industry stability (Lamoreaux 1988). This trend was given added impetus when the urgency and massive scale of the military effort during the Second World War meant bypassing smaller firms for the sake of contractual and productive expediency. These conditions led to the significant expansion of firms using the 'American system of manufacturing', the standardized mass production methods that took root as early as the mid-nineteenth century (Chandler 1977). By 1945, a few hundred of the largest American firms were 'the source of half the total manufacturing output of the planet' (McQuaid 1994: 15).

Economic success resulting from this emphasis on economies of scale had significant consequences on American industrial and social models. Social relations in the industrial realm became characterized by the general lack of importance attributed to creating trust among transacting parties as many firms became fully integrated and therefore tended to be more self-sufficient (Hollingsworth 1997). Within the firm, the standardized system of production institutionalized the 'deskilling' of workers in the industries concerned, providing a disincentive for employers to invest in employee training or to enter into long-term employment contracts, and placing significant importance on the need for managerial, supervisory and technical skills required for monitoring semi-skilled labour and integrating machinery (Whitley

1999; Atack et al. 2004). The overriding concern of US industrialists in the late nineteenth century became the elimination of any unions of skilled workers in an effort to 'rationalize production and reduce dependence on skilled labour altogether through technological change, work reorganization, and product standardization' (Thelen 2004: 281). While at the beginning of the twentieth century, low- and semi-skilled labour became briefly associated with the high-earning welfare-conscious Fordist[5] production model, the slow decline of these traditional manufacturing industries and their associated unions since the Second World War has inevitably produced a wholesale reduction of labour costs and increased wage inequality that will be further discussed below (Freeman and Katz 1994).

A new deal?

Despite early and wildly successful industrialization, the American welfare state did not emerge until the Depression era and remained at the low end of the scale in terms of expenditure, with coverage remaining incomplete to the present day (Skocpol 1995).[6] Instead, 'Welfare Capitalism', or 'Corporate Social Welfare' (CSW) (the private provision of welfare by large corporations to their employees) has been the defining characteristic of US social policy. The likely causes of this 'American exceptionalism' has been the source of considerable academic debate and disagreement (Gordon 1998).

One of the main lines of argumentation provides a causal account of the social policy void during the pre-Depression era similar to the one that led to the growth of large integrated firms rather than collaborative multifirm exchanges. Competition in the private sector was paralleled by competition among American states to attract new business investment and provide an attractive business environment. Social policy initiatives by states were constrained by the inability to finance schemes – taxation or regulation proposals were countered by the fear of losing out to other states that did not impose such requirements on business.[7] Moreover, in a vein similar to the influence exerted by Congress on corporate collaboration and cartel activity, the Supreme Court 'sharply circumscribed federal interference with the "freedom" of workers and employers to settle contracts, regardless of how unequal the terms' (Hacker and Pierson 2002: 288), thereby virtually eliminating the possibility of a centralized national-level solution to the lack of social policy-making at the state level. Hacker and Pierson (2002) describe the situation as a collective action problem brought on by different states' conflicting interests and the federated structure of government that facilitated capital mobility.

In lieu of a national system, welfare capitalism emerged as the de facto mode of provision. Although it is undeniable that some employers likely provided social protection out of a sense of paternalistic obligation, numerous large corporations preferred a private system for business reasons. One was the belief that private provision was the best way to avoid industrial conflict, pre-empt government intervention and keep unions at bay, thereby exercising greater control over the terms of provision (Jacoby 1997). Similarly, the substantial and highly visible donations to public welfare by philanthropists, such as Rockefeller and Carnegie, at the beginning of the twentieth century were intended to keep government welfare regulations at bay (Bremner 1988; Friedman and McGarvie 2003). In some cases, corporate welfare was a means of keeping employees loyal to the company over the course of their lifetime and therefore a means of reducing hiring and training costs, retaining highly skilled employees and increasing overall productivity (Jacoby 1997).

The Great Depression significantly changed US sociopolitical circumstances. As the economy collapsed, so did CSW. Millions were plunged into unemployment and welfare programmes were shut down en masse, exposing the vulnerability of welfare capitalism and providing voters with a strong incentive to support the Democratic Party (Jacoby 1997). The extensive despair, depth and length of the Depression provided a window of opportunity for social policy reform by shifting the power base to the federal government, the only institution that would be able to provide a new social contract. 'Previously dominant business groups were forced to make peace with a vastly expanded federal social role and basic structure of U.S. welfare state was put in place' (Hacker and Pierson 2002: 287–97). Roosevelt's New Deal proved to be a radical departure from pre-Depression American political economy, with its initial social policy formulation proving to be as 'social democratic' as later welfare arrangements in Scandinavian countries (Esping-Andersen 1990: 28).

Yet in the end, and despite the seemingly strong labour and government activism during the post-Second World War decades, the New Deal ended up a 'faint echo' of other countries' responses to the Great Depression (Gordon 1998: 42).[8] Rather than centrally administered universal coverage, health insurance and pension programmes remained decentralized, and were eventually integrated into corporations' human resource management departments (Davis et al. 2006). Ruggie (1982: 394) suggests that 'the social and economic reforms of the New Deal had lacked ideological consistency and programmatic coherence, and opposition had remained firmly entrenched'. Explanations for the solid opposition and progressive 'erosion' of the American welfare state suggest the need to better understand business influence and instrumental power in the US policy-making context.

Policy-making in a pluralist context

In theory, the United States is a pluralist democracy in which numerous interest groups have similar access to, and influence upon, the state. Classic theories however suggest that business has a vested interest in the outcome of a political decision and will find a means of 'capturing' decision-makers (Bernstein 1955) or engage in 'rent-seeking' activities whereby regulation is pursued with the intent of benefiting specific business interests (Stigler

1971). Clearly, some groups have greater resources at their disposal with which to promote their interests at the expense of other groups (Domhoff 2001). Corporate political activities, such as campaign contributions, contracting or hiring professional lobbyists, sponsoring PACs (Political Action Committees), commissioning research on policy issues, writing and presenting technical briefs, and political advertising, are prohibitively costly to all but the biggest firms. Although lobbying activity is strongly believed to be engaged in mostly by interest groups, the majority of resources expended lobbying in Washington are in fact firm-specific[9] (Hart 2004: 8; OpenSecrets.org 2007). The resources large enterprises have at their disposal, the long legacy of operational independence and strong liberal political institutions make this fact somewhat inevitable.

However, shared policy-making and the granting of a 'representational monopoly', as practised in countries with neocorporatist institutions, runs counter to pluralist ideology based on a strict division between public and private interests and the belief that organized interests should have a voice but should be excluded from the policy-making process itself (Wilson 2003). Political and economic liberalism is based on safeguarding the individual's relationship with the state and the market and, as such, considers intermediaries undesirable (Streeck and Kenworthy 2003). Policy-making to a large degree adheres to market principles: 'To prevent "organized interests" from capturing the state, membership in them had to be strictly voluntary and their organizations preferably small, specialized, internally homogeneous, democratic, and in constant competition with each other and with other organizations undertaking to represent the same interests' (Truman 1951, cited in Streeck and Kenworthy 2003: 6). As a result, economic coordination is viewed as a matter of market signalling (Hayek 1945).[10]

Attempts at coordination, and even at forming cartel-like arrangements, have, however, taken place during exceptional periods in US history (Hollingsworth 1997). The most remarkable instance arose during the Great Depression under the auspices of the federal government's National Recovery Administration (NRA). A response by Roosevelt to private-sector demands for quotas and price fixing as a means of creating economic stability, the National Industrial Recovery Act (NIRA) effectively suspended anti-trust legislation and supported the creation of national trade associations and trade unions on a trial basis for the purposes of national economic survival. However, lacking the proper political context and institutional basis for effective collaboration, the exercise soon deteriorated into irresolvable disagreement and dissatisfaction, resulting in termination of the NIRA in 1935 only five years after business had lobbied government for it, and two years after it was passed (McQuaid 1994; Gordon 1998). Another major attempt took place decades later when Nixon turned to 'European-style' tripartite arrangements as a means to control inflation. The result was equally unsuccessful for much the same reasons (Salisbury 1979).

The lack of national coordination within different actor constituencies and among different social actors has been attributed by some to structural issues – the fact that the United States is a geographically large country with a complex economy, composed of varied groups and interests that render coordination much more problematic than in smaller countries[11] (Hollingsworth and Boyer 1999: 29; Salisbury 1979). This exceptional diversity and specificity of corporate interests in such a vast economy are essential to understanding the relationship between political activity and social policy. Martin (1999: 66) affirms that the 'history of social innovation in the U.S. reveals episodes of infighting between segments of capital over alternative views of social initiatives'. Similarly, Gordon (1998) alleges that the employers' response to the Wagner Act of 1935[12] was generally unfavourable, not because there was widespread resistance to the idea of collective bargaining but because they were unable to achieve consensus on policy design. Consequently, resistance to the act remained firmly entrenched after it was passed and later resulted in the passing of the Taft-Hartley Act (also referred to as the Labor-Management Relations Act) in 1947, effectively rolling back many aspects of the Wagner Act and significantly curtailing union power (Jacoby 1997; Abraham 1996).

The lack of a common base to unite businesses under peak representational structures reduces trade associations' legitimacy and effectiveness and, in turn, their membership and resources (Hart 2004; Olson 1965). The dearth of associational/representational structures and focus on firm-based policy advocacy and lobbying is believed to have far-ranging implications for social policy: 'The absence of any meaningful institutions of peak bargaining and representation . . . virtually devoid of substantial political debate, which strips the social contract of any sense of reciprocal civic obligation, and which is rarely able or willing to broker a cacophony of competing demands' (Gordon 1998: 40).

The social responsibility of disorganized business – post-welfare capitalism?

The 1960s and 1970s witnessed widespread postwar public support for business dissolve into distrust of corporations and the emergence of a vocal public interest movement (PIM)[13] that claimed business was profiting from the Vietnam war, exacerbating racism in the workplace and destroying the environment. Calling for greater government regulation and social responsibility on the part of corporations (Vogel 1986), these movements effectively targeted individual firms and focused the debate on the moral judgment of its managers (Vogel 2005). The public and academic discussion that ensued centred on whether managers could claim the mandate to engage in corporate philanthropy and other forms of social investment.[14] Initially surprised by the vehement opposition of these movements, corporations became acutely aware of the need to mitigate these social risks. The Business Roundtable's[15] *Statement on Corporate Responsibility* captured the business position at the time:

'some leading managers . . . believe that by giving enlightened consideration to balancing the legitimate claims of all its constituents, a corporation will best serve the interest of its shareholders. [. . .] the legitimate concerns of other constituencies (customers, employees, communities, suppliers, and society at large) also must have the appropriate attention' (Business Roundtable 1981).

The view of the corporation as an entity wielding social power that had to be legitimized through regulation and legislation eroded in the 1980s just as Reagan moved sharply towards an emphasis on voluntary social initiatives and corporate philanthropy (Hall 2000). Propounding that companies are responsible to all those individuals or groups who benefit from, or are harmed by, corporate actions and that, as a result, have a 'stake' in the corporation, stakeholder theory[16] firmly grounded the discussion in the individual firm's relationships (Freeman 1984). In 1990, the Business Roundtable issued its statement on *Corporate Governance and American Competitiveness* that revised its original position: 'It is important that all stakeholder interests be considered, but impossible to assure that all will be satisfied because competing claims may be mutually conflicting' (Business Roundtable 1990: 5).

The resurgence of the American economy in the 1990s exacerbated a labour market characterized by dualism, high wage dispersion and growing social inequality (Beattie 2006). Well paid 'new economy' jobs did not offset the large number of unskilled workers pushed into low-wage, increasingly transient and uncertain employment as a result of 'downsizing', 'reengineering' and 'outsourcing' and the decline in manufacturing (Davis et al. 2006).[17] In addition, large corporations began to shift social risks onto their employees, switching from defined-benefit pension schemes to defined-contributions plans and limiting overall health care contributions. The result has been an increasing number of people without adequate health care and the likelihood of inadequate pensions in the future (Roberts and Swann 2006). Growing inequality (McCarty et al. 2006) coincided with a mainstreaming of the CSR agenda, albeit with significantly altered boundaries. Management discretion for philanthropy and CSR expenditures, tolerated under the era of managerial capitalism, was sharply curtailed under shareholder market capitalism (O'Sullivan 2003). Once more, the Business Roundtable's *Statement on Corporate Governance* epitomized the change: 'The notion that the board must somehow balance the interests of stockholders against the interests of other stakeholders fundamentally misconstrues the role of directors. . . . It is, moreover, an unworkable notion because it would leave the board with no criterion for resolving conflicts between interests of stockholders and of other stakeholders or among different groups of stakeholders' (Business Roundtable 1997).

Thus CSR discourse has become synonymous with the financial benefits stemming from the hypothetical reciprocal nature of corporate social performance and corporate financial performance – often referred to as the 'business case' for corporate responsibility (Porter and Kramer 2006).[18] Yet, while the number of CSR-related shareholder resolutions and corporate CSR reporting initiatives documenting corporate benevolence increased significantly (Porter and Kramer 2006), charitable contributions by US companies failed to keep pace with profits[19] (Porter and Kramer 2002), and social inequality in the United States has continued rising.

Organized business[20] and the European welfare state

In contrast to America's economic woes, the competitive advantage of European-style institutional capitalism was celebrated in the academic literature and popular press throughout the 1970s and part of the 1980s (Crouch and Streeck 1997). The superior performance of countries in Northern Europe seemed to prove that cooperation could lead to competitiveness (Crouch and Streeck 1997). This socioeconomic model, sometimes referred to as the 'high road' to competitive capitalism, was based on a democratic system of neocorporatist interest representation and social compromise, resulting in low wage dispersion and a focus on competing in higher-end, quality-based markets.[21] As the next section will demonstrate, the Northern European experience has been characterized by 'social partnerships' between states, organized business groups and strong labour unions, whose joint governance processes have been both the driving factor behind social development and the product market strategies of numerous countries.

Industrialization of the craft tradition

A key component of the 'high road' model of social dialogue and compromise between organized groups can be traced back to feudal Europe. The existence of nobility, aristocracy and serfdom set the stage for organization along class lines and the impetus to fight for basic political rights in pre-industrial society. Industrialization in Northern Europe was based largely on the modernization of a craft tradition of production of high-end products, such as furniture, machine tools and specialty food items, that required high degrees of engineering skills or craftsmanship (Amsden and Hikino 1994). The availability of these skills was controlled by powerful guilds, responsible for upholding the quality of the particular craft through training and certification, which enabled the mobilization and cohesion of the employee interest groups (Whitley 1999). The new social risks associated with industrialization and wage labour (unemployment, workplace accidents and old-age security) prompted the effective political mobilization of these labour groups. The concentration of labour in cities – a result of industrial production – and the strength of the workers' guilds provided the organizational support required to solve the collective action problem, and gradually evolved into employee unions (Thelen 2004). These movements were strengthened by the formation of political coalitions (notably with agricultural interest groups) that developed into socialist and social democratic parties that became pivotal forces in numerous European parliaments. Political means resulted in the significant investment of public funds into technical and vocational education, thereby strengthening the support base of these social democratic parties and granting labour a strong voice in distributional struggles (Hollingsworth 1997; Esping-Andersen 1990).

Organized unions and post-Second World War sociopolitical conditions led to a 'postwar political settlement' of institutionalized political exchange and a social accord with a long-term horizon that equitably distributed the risks arising from the operation of markets (Harvey 2005; Ruggie 1982). The introduction of social security and universal health care tended to issues of poverty, retirement in old age, employment disability and unemployment, as well as publicly funded education, and increased people's life chances.[22] This deal fulfilled to a large degree Polanyi's (1944) call for 'national buffers' by which society could be protected from the shocks of participating in a global economy.[23] The national institutions that emerged across Europe as a result of this compromise are described by Esping-Andersen (1990: 172) as 'institutional rearrangements to accommodate labor's *novel* power: the emergence of "neo-corporatist" structures of interest-intermediation and concertation'.

The collaborative and welfare-based societies of Europe also had strong intellectual and religious roots. Prior to Polanyi, European intellectuals, such as Hegel and Durkheim, had signalled the importance of organized groups within society.[24] The Catholic church's doctrine of social groups' right to govern their affairs as a means of resisting the state's increasing encroachment into social provision and education provided further impetus to the acceptance of corporatist thinking and policy making[25] (Streeck and Kenworthy 2003: 4). Furthermore, the continent's tumultuous history, plagued by war and social conflict, provided ample evidence of the consequences of a failure to engage in social dialogue and compromise (Wilson 2003; Polanyi 1944). Together these elements resulted in the view that the organization and integration of various groups' interests strengthened policy-making, resulting in the acceptance of this mode of governance as the status quo.

Neocorporatist governance and the welfare state

This model of governance led to strong social and economic performance for most of the latter half of the twentieth century: the long-term competitiveness of Northern European companies was matched by a steady rise in living standards, including some of the highest wages and most generous welfare states in the world. In contrast to liberal countries where competition for representation occurs, governments in neocorporatist countries clearly established the desirability of strong unions and associations as policy-making partners, ensuring their unique representational authority within a process of 'political exchange' (Pizzorno 1978). At the heart of the neocorporatist form of governance are encompassing peak employer associations and labour unions engaged in cooperative negotiation. In effect, union and employer associations' close relationship with a facilitating state has resulted in shared policy development and implementation where market-regulating, quasi-public powers are granted to these groups.[26]

This collective bargaining structure and other neocorporatist institutions serve multiple objectives, often associated with risk reduction (Schmitter 1979; Olson 1982). Labour acquires greater job security due to the state's full employment policies, guarantees on the stability of purchasing power and a welfare state that provides social insurance and social services. Employers derive benefits associated with skilled employees and incentives to further invest in employee skills and maintain capital domestically. They are also provided with a more stable and predictable business environment, including restraint with regard to wage increases and strikes. In turn, the state benefits from greater social cohesion, access to, and assistance in, the management of macroeconomic policy, as well as assistance in devising, implementing and monitoring effective regulation: 'corporatist associations assume responsibility for the compliance of their members with public policies, they help the state overcome inherent limits of legal regulation and direct intervention' (Streeck and Kenworthy 2003: 11).

From the point of view of capital, tripartite bargaining institutions can be more than an arena for negotiation and political exchange with government and unions that lower the risk of strikes and provide a more stable environment for business operations. These institutions may also provide a regulatory framework that serves to facilitate the collaborative long-term nature of production, the safeguarding of skills-based investment and the basis for product-market competition. This critical link between the welfare state, risk reduction and business strategy has underpinned some of the literature on comparative capitalism, including the varieties of capitalism (VoC) literature.[27]

Post-neocorporatism

Descriptions of the European system as a superior economic and social model during much of the postwar period became a distant echo during the economic crises of the 1990s. Deep recessions and high levels of unemployment struck countries such as Germany, Sweden and Finland particularly hard but seemed to spare the United States and the United Kingdom, leading many to conclude that 'Eurosclerosis', brought on by rigid labour markets, corporatist structures and redistributive welfare policies, required a good dose of liberalization (Phelps 2002).

The welfare state's prospects in the face of pressures brought on by globalization has been greatly debated. The argument that the pressures of global economic competitiveness rendered retrenchment inevitable has been disputed by numerous scholars, who point to demographic shifts and other internal changes as the underlying causes of welfare reforms (Huber and Stephens 2001; Swank 2002). They also describe the changes taking place as adjustment rather than retrenchment (Kitschelt et al. 1999). The debate on the viability of social pacts has taken a similar turn. Recent years have led to some surprising changes and, with them, a resurgence in neocorporatist literature suggesting that tripartite institutions are not being dismantled but rather modernized and adapted to new circumstances while remaining underpinned by the same social principles (Pierson 2001). Some research suggests that, rather than an impediment, social pacts are the means by which new economic circumstances brought on by globalization are being successfully managed (Pontusson 2005; Perez 2000).

Nevertheless, there are strong indications that some form of transformation is taking place (Baccaro 2002). It has been described as moving away from organized capitalism and centralized bargaining towards a more pluralist system at the European Union (EU) level (Beyer and Höpner 2003), characterized by 'social dialogue' (as opposed to bargaining) and corporate self-regulation and other voluntary initiatives associated with CSR (Andersen and Mailand 2002; Utting and Marques 2009). In the midst of significant change and a strong emphasis on competitiveness, the EU has upheld Denmark's 'flexicurity' model, with its mix of flexible labour markets, strong social protection and emphasis on retraining, as an innovative example for all its members. However, scepticism concerning such institutional innovations runs high. Particular macroeconomic policies, unusually high unionization rates, institutional complementarities and path dependence pose serious challenges to replicating the Danish model elsewhere. Referring to the critical function of interest accommodation, Hyman (2001: 39) suggests that

> the notions of social partnership and social dialogue . . . are employed as little more than empty clichés, while at times they appear to function as a means of evading some of the difficult questions which beset any interpretation of the dynamics of industrial relations, or more generally of social processes directed towards the accommodations of conflicting interests.

Organized business and the developmental welfare state

The East Asian developmental state has been the source of a great deal of debate and conjecture. Explanations for the rapid industrial development witnessed by Japan, the Republic of Korea and Taiwan vary from cultural accounts (that is, a collective value system and/or Confucian philosophy) to market-based rationalizations (World Bank 1993). In turn, the political economy account of the Asian miracle points to the joint-policy-making processes of the highly organized and interdependent state and business sectors. Figuring prominently in this analysis is the particular mix of institutional arrangements and geopolitical circumstances that granted states the legitimacy required to carry out such rapid industrial and social transformation – a quasi-revolutionary, experimental, social project (Woo-Cumings 1999). These explanations move beyond the static market-or-state debate to analyse the organization of these economies and, in so doing, highlight the fact that although institutional origins were influenced by a distant past, they were shaped in a postwar era (Onis 1991). The following section situates the relationship between these corporatist governance structures and social policy within the wider developmental state literature.

Industrialization in the East Asian developmental state

Positioning Chalmers Johnson's pioneering account of Japan's industrialization 'in the context of the twin influences of social mobilization and economic nationalism', Woo-Cumings (1999) asserts that the wartime period in Asia is key to understanding the institutional origins of the developmental state and its relationship to society. Whereas Japan's experience was shaped by the postwar aspiration to catch up with Europe and the United States, Korean and Taiwanese industrial policy was forged in the context of civil war and ongoing geopolitical threats. 'Western humiliation and nationalism' legitimatized authoritarian political power and the developmental project (Woo-Cumings 1999: 9). The Japanese, Korean and Taiwanese people had one 'overriding objective' – economic development as a means of ensuring national survival (Onis 1991: 116).

However, economic development through technological innovation became untenable by the turn of the twentieth century for two reasons. First, the productivity gap between the least and most advanced countries had grown to the point where it was unbridgeable. Second, multinationals' institutionalized research and development (R&D) effectively created a barrier to entry at the 'technological frontier' (Amsden and Hikino 1994: 290). In response, Japan, the Republic of Korea and Taiwan were part of a group of countries that began their industrialization processes after the Second World War[28] by relying on borrowing and improving already existing technology developed by enterprises in developed countries – referred to as 'learning by doing'.[29] Amsden and Hikino (1994) attribute their success to three factors: 1) active government intervention and promotion of growth through numerous measures including state-controlled credit-based financing; 2) highly competitive enterprises focused on continuous improvement in the mid-tech industries as a means of differentiation from low-tech/low-wage and high-tech innovation countries; and 3) the use of business-group structures, such as the Japanese *zaibatsu* and Korean *chaebol* and, to a lesser degree, Taiwan's *guanxiqiye*[30] as a means of overcoming risk in entering mid-tech industries.

At the firm level, the focus became adopting, integrating and improving on foreign technology via process innovation on the shop floor (Amsden and Hikino 1994). Decentralized operations allowed product-market specific process and engineering experience to develop (often in the form of tacit knowledge) as close to the manufacturing process as possible. The social consequences of these production methods involved lower wage dispersion, the moulding of industrial groups' identities to their workplace rather than to their functional role, and an emphasis on life-long employment as a means of building and retaining the required skillsets (Whitley, 1999).

Associations and cartels were widely used as well. The Japanese government, for example, modelling its initiatives on Germany's successful 'rationalization cartels', promoted and helped organize sector-specific cartels as a means of enhancing productivity and monitoring compliance with agreed-upon objectives right up to the 1980s, despite the fact that cartels were theoretically illegal (Johnson 1982). It also had close relations with the *Keidanren*, Japan's peak employer association (Johnson 1982). Another example is how domestic private-sector Taiwanese firms were legally required to join government-structured industry associations, whose heads were selected from government-appointed former military or government officials and were often the main channels of communication between firms and government officials (Wade 1990).

Political settlements and the developmentalist welfare state

Although postwar poverty in the case of Japan, and extensive land reform in the Republic of Korea and Taiwan, resulted in an unusually egalitarian distribution of income prior to industrialization, thus somewhat easing distributional struggles and facilitating the transfer of agricultural surplus to manufacturing[31] (Kay 2002; Onis 1991), the significant economic and social changes taking place would still produce economic shocks, distributional struggles, winners and losers, and an inevitable resistance to change on the part of some groups (Khan and Jomo 2000). Although political stability is often assumed to be an outcome of East Asia's ethnic homogeneity and Asian cultures, in fact this region witnessed tremendous political upheaval in the latter part of the twentieth century (Chang 2004; Shin 2004). Overcoming opposition meant that although the regimes in East Asia relied on repression, coercion and control, they also demonstrated an understanding of the need to create social cohesion and gain social legitimacy via other means – a complementary 'soft authoritarianism' of sorts (Chang 2004).

Measured by the narrow Western yardstick of state expenditure, the social welfare state in East Asia is rather difficult to recognize. As a result, numerous observers declared that an East Asian welfare state was virtually nonexistent (Chang 2004). This view has, however, been contested by numerous researchers who have been better able to contextualize the role and forms of social welfare, and identify a number of Asian states that implemented an active social policy as a mechanism for promoting social and economic development (Mkandawire 2004; Kwon 2005). The pattern has been to introduce welfare programmes earlier in the development process, with broader coverage, focused on education and health, but spending proportionally less (as a percentage of gross domestic product/GDP) on provision. Although demographics may explain part of this difference,[32] it is also the result of a conscious policy to invest in the inputs required for rapid industrial development (Pierson 2004).

Social policy in East Asia focused less on redistribution, the hallmark of the European welfare state, and more on social investment through regulation, compulsory corporate welfare programmes, labour market participation and job security through lifetime employment or corporate regulation.[33] There was an explicit contract between employers and employees whereby employers agreed to more expansive social policies in return for employees' loyalty and agreement to wage moderation (Kwon 2005). These policies, permissible due to low wage levels, were purposely designed to develop a skills base as rapidly as possible, thereby permitting a learning-by-doing strategy, and reduce reliance on direct state 'provisioning'[34] (Chang 2004; Yi and Lee 2005). In sum, progressive social policies enabled dynamism in productivity and industrial progress, both directly through labour education, training and health initiatives and incentives, and indirectly as a means of ensuring more cooperative labour–management relations and a stable business environment (Mkandawire 2007).

Corporatist policy-making

Although the state–business nexus in each country's experience has been somewhat different,[35] institutional commonalities exist in how private sector interests were managed and how business was organized. The processes of consultation and cooperation between the state's elite bureaucracies and the private sector are a case in point. Institutionalized processes of information exchange and dialogue were crucial for agreement and joint goal-setting, ultimately serving as a basis for policy formulation and implementation and ensuring that the espoused policies reflected true developmental goals rather than narrower interests.

The developmental state was characterized early on as an authoritarian polity, commanding an unfettered and insulated Weberian bureaucracy. The state wielded control over policy-making, organizing and disciplining business, and displaying a tremendous ability to limit rent-seeking. The state's ability to maintain strong ties to, and control of, the private sector was the direct result of its ability to engineer the creation of business groups and associations (Gomez 2002; Wade 1990), and its concerted effort to inhibit business from organizing in opposition, instead creating dependent corporatist structures (Gomez 2002; Onis 1991). This formal, institutional corporatist framework ensured economic productivity and capital accumulation. However, when the capitalist sector grew stronger, this rigid authoritarianism gave way to a mutually dependent relationship between capitalists and the state. Johnson (1982: 311) identifies 'government-industrial' cooperation as a driving force behind Japan's successful mix of 'social goal-setting' and economic growth. Johnson (1999: 61) further elucidates that 'each side uses each other in a mutually advantageous relationship to achieve developmental goals and enterprise viability'. Wade (1990: 238) describes Japanese and Taiwanese business–state relations as 'institutionalized dialogue, joint formulation of goals, feedback and transparency as a means of circumventing rent-seeking behavior'. This form of close business–state cooperation and joint policy-making, sometimes referred to as 'deliberation councils', were upheld as proof of the benefits of public–private sector cooperation, and as a key element of the 'Asian Miracle' (World Bank 1993; Campos 1996).[36]

Clearly, social legitimacy via economic development was a prerequisite for holding on to power and, although often corrupt, political actors also had an overriding commitment to building internationally competitive national industries (Gomez 2002). They did not, however, determine policy in isolation. Instead, they recognized the need to provide rents to capitalists that would use it productively, and support policies and bureaucracies that would reinforce this process by disciplining unproductive rent-seekers through corporatist structures (Amsden 2001; Khan and Jomo 2000).

The role of business in the post-developmentalist welfare state

The nature of the business–state nexus in East Asia has undergone significant changes in recent decades. Most apparent is the state's inability to control the powerful capitalist class it created (Woo-Cumings 1999; Shafer 1997). Evans' (1997: 82) conjecture that 'developmental states may create the gravediggers of embedded autonomy in the form of [a] more economically and politically powerful, more internationally oriented business class' seems to have been largely proven right. Authoritarianism has also given way to democracy and healthy doses of social activism, labour rights and state welfare provision (Kwon 2005). Although life-long employment policies became unfeasible, Japan's welfare system expanded significantly throughout the 1990s (Peng 2005). The Republic of Korea, in turn, held its first elections in 1987, extended national health insurance to the entire population by 1989 and introduced the Employment Insurance Programme in 1995. In a similar vein, Taiwan relinquished control over labour unions when it lifted martial law in 1987, introduced a national health insurance scheme in 1995 and held its first elections in 1996. The Japanese welfare system expansion and the progressive changes in Korean and Taiwanese welfare policies have been largely attributed to intensified political competition and the strengthening of civil society, particularly advocacy coalitions permitted by the new democratic context[37] (Peng 2005; Kwon 2004). Once the restrictions on unions were lifted, labour's mobilization was swift and forceful (the

Republic of Korea's movement was particularly militant), demanding greater political freedom and higher wages (Kwon 2004).

Analysing the successful negotiations between social partners that led to this reform, Vartiainen (2007) suggests that the Republic of Korea and Taiwan will soon have all the components required for successful tripartite bargaining (neocorporatist) relationships similar to Western Europe: a highly organized business sector; the imminent centralization of labour unions with strong links to political parties; and a capable state with a strong bureaucratic tradition. Similarly, Kwon (2005) suggests that East Asia provides proof that economic development, social inclusion and democracy are mutually reinforcing. Other commentators are less sanguine about events, depicting the social partnership as a one-time event that occurred due to the exceptional circumstances brought on by the economic crisis (Baccaro and Lim 2006) and pointing out the urgent measures forced upon the Republic of Korea and Taiwan by the international financial institutions (IFIs), including labour market flexibilization (Yi and Lee 2005).

It is also argued that the mutual dependence characterizing the developmental state's business–state relations, and therefore its ability to promote productive rents and progressive social policies, eroded before democratic institutions capable of fulfilling the same function took hold (Lee 2002; Phongpaichit 2005). Highlighting the implications of the devolution of power to the private sector that has taken place over the last two decades, Gomez (2002: 10) stresses how the quality of East Asia's new democracies may be compromised by the accompanying rise in 'money politics' tied to big business attempts to exert greater influence over policy-making, and an increase in 'the scale – and form – of corruption'. Lastly, growing inequality has also afflicted East Asian countries. An Asian Development Bank report (ADB 2007) reveals substantial increases in inequality in both the Republic of Korea and Taiwan during the 1990s–2000s period and highlights possible implications for future economic growth and the need to further consider the effectiveness of redistribution mechanisms.

Under what conditions does business support progressive social policies?

Thus far, this chapter has reviewed the literature on the relationship between business and social policy from historical and comparative dimensions, revealing the different trajectories, configurations of social forces, pacts and contemporary challenges that define the American, Northern European and East Asian experiences. With the above in mind, we return to the question posed at the beginning of this chapter: Under what circumstances has business supported or at least not outwardly undermined progressive social policy? The remainder of this section identifies four key elements that must be considered in answering this question.

Structural power

The literature on business power has largely divided business power into two main forms: structural and instrumental. The literatures reviewed in this chapter point to the salience of structural power in the design of social policy. Two key insights emerge. First, the most impressive gains of progressive forces in numerous countries occurred precisely when corporate political influence was incontestably weak and social pressures were greatest relative to each other. Where social movements were capable of concerted collective action, or business was dependent on political patronage that, in turn, hinged on social legitimacy, social policy often made progressive strides. In many cases, a causal arrow can be traced from the balance of social forces and the resulting distribution of gains. In the early stages of industrialization, social policy outcomes are largely explained by reference to physical or social structural factors that led to specific patterns of resource concentration that, in turn, resulted in political leverage of some actors over others.

In the United States, the size of the country and its federated system of politics, together with the relative mobility of capital, resulted in intense competition between states to attract investment and a high degree of structural power for business. However, in Northern Europe, the powerful guild system, together with the congregation of labour in cities, facilitated political mobilization and organization into unions. Business faced few options other than to accommodate powerful labour groups' and their associated political parties' demands. In Asia, patterns of colonization and land reform led to the elimination of a landed aristocracy, facilitating the state's control of the labour force and budding capitalists. It can be argued that corporate paternalism, although contributing to productivity, may not have been so prevalent had the business–state nexus not been characterized by a mutual dependence that allowed for a *dirigiste* state to impose conditions and discipline firms that deviated from the implicit political agreements.

Second, business structural power, and therefore business willingness to accommodate the expansion of social programmes, is highly variable. The relative power of business expands and contracts depending on specific political, social and economic conditions, and is therefore best understood as a dynamic rather than a static variable (Hacker and Pierson 2002; Vogel 1989). The Second World War and the Great Depression dramatically altered structural power in the United States and in Europe, but with very different results. While many countries in Northern Europe went on to develop extensive social welfare systems, the liberal welfare state eroded to minimal levels of coverage. In the United States, the radical changes brought about by the New Deal proved a temporary window of opportunity rather than a deep structural change. Stimulated by mass-scale production and integration, American industry emerged from the Second World War more concentrated and powerful than ever. The structural reforms prompted by the Depression could not maintain momentum in the face of an American production regime that relied on low-skilled labour, lacked a strong, coordinated labour movement, and was driven by large firms.

These same events had much more severe consequences in Europe and Japan, destroying infrastructure and industry. In Europe, structural power was significantly altered and labour coalitions successfully institutionalized a postwar agreement that led to the introduction of an extensive welfare system. European states disciplined capitalist interests by integrating them, together with labour groups, into highly organized national representational structures, thereby negotiating social pacts. Geopolitical circumstances also played a fundamental role in East Asian states' ability to implement political projects that created, and for a time controlled, capitalist classes and transformed entire societies. Business groups eventually became too strong for state control but labour groups have in some circumstances proved to be an effective force for progressive reforms. For example, the post-crisis tripartite negotiations in the Republic of Korea were portrayed as being largely the result of a window of opportunity provided by the financial predicament gripping weakened *chaebols*.

Social risk mitigation

Another important consideration that comes through from this analysis is the nature and focus of social pressures. Social pressures affecting the state or a large cross-section of the business community make it difficult for individual firms or sectors to mitigate social risk on their own and provide an impetus for an aggregate response. Social reform has occurred when such broad pressures have focused on distributional issues, threatening the legitimacy of the state and capitalist system. Various literatures, including those providing accounts of the genesis of the welfare state itself, emphasize the legitimizing aspects of social policy. In many European countries, where a tradition of repression and class divisions fuelled social unrest, the guild system evolved into the institutional basis for the creation of strong labour unions and political coalitions, a pillar of the tripartite system, that granted labour a strong bargaining position. The welfare state fulfilled a social risk mitigation function for business, resulting in long-term 'industrial peace'. Likewise, in East Asia, the developmentalist welfare state served to build and maintain public support for the capitalist project and bolster the authoritarian regimes' legitimacy even as labour unions were forcefully repressed.

In the United States, welfare capitalism emerged in a context where the state and the liberal capitalist system were not threatened by widespread contestation along class lines. Voluntary welfare provision allowed firms to exercise greater control over resources expended on the delivery of social services. Social expenditures were sufficient to dissuade social support for government intervention and pre-empt government regulation, thereby maintaining private sector autonomy (Jacoby 1997). Likewise, large-scale philanthropic endeavours by the likes of Rockefeller and Carnegie are construed by some as part of an implicit political compromise – substantial social contributions from those who profit disproportionately from the market are a means of offsetting the social instabilities resulting from a lightly regulated capitalist system and a minimalist welfare state (Hall 2000; Friedman and McGarvie 2003). However, as US historical experience demonstrates, while corporate social welfare and corporate giving may be significant, the system overall is characterized by inequality and instability. CSW collapsed during the Great Depression when millions needed it most. Public pressure to provide social protection quickly resembled the widespread pattern of social pressures witnessed in Europe. In the end, a centralized solution involving government regulation was required for social stability.

Decades later, when broad-based social pressures resurfaced in the United States in the form of the 1970s' public interest movement (PIM), distributional issues, such as labour-driven wage or welfare demands, were not on the agenda. Major concerns included firm-level environment and consumer issues. CSR was largely a response to the social risk posed by the PIM and, as such, served much the same purpose as CSW, as exemplified by the evolution of the US Business Roundtable's various statements concerning the relationship between the firm and its stakeholders from the early 1980s to the late 1990s.[38] In response to social contention and 'explicit' calls for regulation, the Business Roundtable issued statements on the need to balance stakeholder interests (Business Roundtable 1981). When regulatory risk dissipated, it softened its legitimizing discourse to 'an attempt to balance interests' (Business Roundtable 1990), reversing its stance to prioritize shareholder interests when regulation became improbable (Business Roundtable 1997).

Collaborative institutions

Although widespread social pressures might trigger governmental and collective responses on the part of business, the shape and design of an effective response will depend on the presence and capacity of collaborative institutions to mediate the conflicting interests of different actor constellations. How conflict between firms, and between firms and other actors, is dealt with will be determined to a large degree by what has frequently been referred to as the firm's 'institutional embeddedness'. In a liberal market economy, the scenario is geared towards managing stakeholder demands and lobbying legislators and regulators – a transaction-based approach to corporate political action. In the case of the United States, some scholars have proposed that the strong opposition to specific social policies has been the result of a lack of collective action institutions required to facilitate consensus-building. As such, disagreement and opposition were in some cases based on particular policy design issues, a lack of trust in other actors, or opposition determined by a lack of information on how it would affect distributional outcomes. In the end, a tradition of corporate individualism, influential corporations, weak labour, and the resulting dearth of collective action and negotiation institutions, underpinned the opposition to government-provided welfare.

In a non-liberal institutional setting, diverging interests are dealt with by more relational forms of political action, heavily mediated by bipartite (business–state) or tripartite (business–state–labour) institutions. This form of coordinated policy-making has been a normal state of affairs in various countries at different times. In the EU, the tripartite system granted both labour and employer associations strong voices in policy-making. Rather than socially illegitimate special interests, organized groups, including business associations, are trusted parties that are granted quasi-public regulatory authority. In turn, these organizations play a critical role in reducing uncertainty via information exchange, negotiation, and/or mutual goal-setting, thereby building informed consensus within the private sector. In East Asia the developmental state created an 'encompassing organization', often directed by its own bureaucracy but encouraging joint policy-making. Based on goal-setting, dialogue and negotiation, this governance mechanism is construed by some as a bipartite version (without labour representation) of the tripartite neocorporatist structures prominent in Western Europe.

The case studies above clearly underline the fact that the positive contributions of national business associations are highly dependent on context. To different degrees, the social legitimacy and organizational strength of both neocorporatist and corporatist structures is granted by the state and via an institutional history that has evolved to provide trust among actors and clearly defined norms. The state compels private and public actors to work together (usually through the provision of selective benefits[39]) and facilitate integration across policy areas (budgetary and fiscal policy, wage and labour markets, social protection, trade policy). As such, when institutionally embedded in this manner, business associations perform a function not only of interest representation and mediation but also of actively shaping the collective interests of their members, including their social policy preferences. In many cases, consensus evolved to norms and/or standards enforceable by business associations. This specific aspect is remarkably consistent across countries – Wade's (1990: 328) description of industry associations in East Asia acting 'as a policeman on the practices of their own members' is similar to the regulatory functions performed by European counterparts.

These corporatist or neocorporatist institutions can be construed as conflict mediation approaches – negotiation and mutual compromise with a formal agreement (a social pact) that moves beyond dialogue. Consensus or political settlements are often negotiated groups of interests that straddle multiple actors and/or coalitions and include dependencies or trade-offs. The fact that actors will in some cases agree to the 'second-best option' demonstrates the value placed upon social stability and the leeway in policy design and interest formation at play in the development of some social policies. Key to understanding whether resistance persists or consensus is reached is the impact of policy reform upon firm competitiveness and profits. Policy reform is often accompanied by a great deal of uncertainty and, as such, will usually be opposed if it is perceived to be of a distributionary, 'zero-sum' nature (Rodrik 1996). As such, business associations can be construed as the means by which business adapts to the regulatory demands placed upon it.

Business preferences

Implicit in much of the literature that views capitalists as opposing social policy based on pure financial logic is the notion that lower costs improve profit margins. Empirical and theoretical evidence suggests this view may be an invalid generalization. In some cases, social 'costs' are believed to lower operational risk and/or become a source of competitive advantage. The idea that firms utilize social protection in a strategic manner, to build and retain a strong skill base, ensure stable industry relations, and lower employee turnover, staff and training costs has a long history.

When the 'balance of forces' has pushed business actors into pursuing a second-best position, business has adapted, in numerous cases integrating social concerns into business strategy, and a certain path dependence has ensued. In Northern Europe, the tradition of highly skilled craft production became incorporated into modern manufacturing techniques focused on mass production of quality goods that subsequently grew to be the basis for competition in global product markets and the source for financing generous social welfare systems. In East Asia, a competitive focus on global mid-tier industries required industrial productivity driven by intensive learning and skill-acquisition processes. Developmental states imposed an employee–employer compact of life-long employment (Japan) or compulsory, regulated CSW (Republic of Korea) in exchange for wage moderation.

Some strands of literature suggest that employers, recognizing the business benefits, were in fact not opposed to the introduction of progressive social policies. Firms' social policy preferences are influenced by several factors, including the employee skill profile a particular firm requires for competitiveness in specific product markets.[40] Different business groups or sectors may view social policies differently because of their skill or risk profiles. Firms dependent on skilled labour, such as those in Northern Europe, have a direct interest not only in education and training, but also in social protections such as unemployment and health insurance, and pension provisioning (Estevez-Abe et al. 2001). In the United States, however, large integrated firms generally thrived on economies of scale and mass production that required low-skilled work and therefore tended to see less benefit in social provisioning. Coverage was much more decentralized and unstable. Nevertheless, some employers provided CSW either out of a sense of paternalistic obligation, or for more instrumental reasons, such as the desire to avert industrial conflict, unionization of their workforce and government regulation.

Conclusion

Contemporary concerns with economic crises and growing inequalities suggest the need to better our understanding of the multiple paths to growth and development successful societies have taken, including the fact that some paths may lead to high levels of productivity, poverty reduction and equality. This chapter has reviewed several literatures providing insight into the conditions under which business has responded in previous eras and in different countries to calls for social engagement. What clearly emerges is the notion that social policy has been a vital component of an inclusive development agenda and an integral part of government policy-making in successful societies. Private and public interests have both shaped and been accommodated by social policies, particularly the provision of education, health care and social protection such as unemployment insurance, accident/sickness insurance and pensions (the main pillars of the welfare state), as well as labour market regulation.

The overall theme connecting these literatures is the emphasis upon the complementary nature and historical roots of various countries' political, social and economic institutions. The pattern of industrialization, and its structural context, critically shaped subsequent institutions, including the organization and constellation of social forces and sociopolitical agreements. More specifically, the above analysis suggests four key conditions that historically have led to both progressive social policy and economic progress: 1) business has low structural power; 2) social risk mitigation requires government regulation and collective business action; 3) collaborative institutions are part of the policy-making process; and 4) particular business preferences, usually driven by skills-based product market strategies, predominate.

The key point of contention between these literatures, as examined in the introductory chapter of this volume, is the question of which actors and institutions drive institutional innovation: the state, employer groups and labour unions have all been emphasized by different literatures as the agents responsible for bringing about institutional reform and progress. The broader perspective afforded by the juxtaposition of these literatures suggests that business social policy preferences varied and were strongly influenced by context and by other actors. Individual firms sometimes provided their own corporate welfare plans, or in coalition with other actors supported expansive public policies. The motives varied from instrumental reasons to a sense of paternalistic obligation (often both). In other scenarios, states had the capacity to regulate the corporate provision of welfare or labour unions and, in coalition with other groups, gained the political resources to expand the welfare state.

The discussion in this chapter, however, suggests that sustained, socially inclusive development occurred when dynamic sociopolitical processes resulted in institutions that enabled social risk management, collaborative learning and collective, consensus-based forms of bargaining and 'regulation'. A capable state, able to determine the mix of policies best suited to its context, social pressures and collective responses by business were key elements in forging socially inclusive forms of capitalism that generated long-term prosperity. Current development policy approaches and collaborative initiatives wishing to promote progressive systemic change could do more to consider the conditions that mediate the relationship between the economic and the social.

Notes

1. Progressive social policy refers to social policies purposely designed to engender greater social and distributive justice by focusing on the advancement of human rights, equality and social wellbeing.
2. Corporatism is a form of political governance that relies on economic organization and interest representation by representational groups, such as labour unions and business associations. The term 'neocorporatism', first used by Schmitter (1979), in reference to governance in democratic contexts of Northern Europe, was intended to expand political theory beyond pluralist thinking.
3. Although laissez-faire was accepted practice domestically, strongly protectionist and infant industry policies allowed US industry to thrive internationally. It was only following the Second World War, when the United States dominated numerous manufacturing industries, that it began promoting free-trade policies (Chang 2002).
4. Agricultural producers were exempted (Hollingsworth 1997).
5. Hirst and Zeitlin (1991: 2) define Fordist mass production as 'the manufacture of standardized products in high volumes using special-purpose machinery and predominantly unskilled labour'.
6. Skocpol (1995) points out, however, that in some ways the United States was a social policy pioneer – a large proportion of Civil War veterans, widows and orphans received generous pensions that accounted for a large share of the federal budget at the time.
7. For a full account of how the mobility of capital across states resulted in business's structural leverage and reduced social protection, see Hacker and Pierson (2002).
8. Jacoby (1997) writes that the strength of labour unions in the 1930s and 1940s was greatly exaggerated. In fact unions were strong in only a few sectors and regions and more than two-thirds of non-agricultural workers remained non-unionized
9. Although some of the largest lobbying expenditures are by public groups (for example, the American Medical Association) and business associations (for example, the US Chamber of Commerce and the Business Roundtable are the two largest), individual corporations are predominant – see opensecrets.org for a full listing.
10. Hayek (1945) argued that in a society with an extensive division of labour, only the 'marvel' of the market mechanism could be counted on to efficiently allocate scarce resources through price signalling.
11. Various literatures support this assumption. Reaching consensus, building trust, monitoring and enforcing agreements is easier within smaller groups (Ostrom 1990).

12. Included in Section 7a of the NIRA as federal law, the Wagner Act, also known as the 'National Labour Relations Act', granted labour the right to organize, be represented and bargain.
13. Vogel (1980: 607) describes how the movement 'consisted of a wide variety of law firms, research centers, lobbying groups, membership associations, and community organizations committed to public policies that attempted to reduce the power and privileges of business'.
14. This prompted Milton Friedman (1970) to famously argue that CSR was a 'subversive doctrine' and that the 'social responsibility of business is to increase its profits'.
15. The Business Roundtable is an influential association whose membership is composed of chief executive officers (CEOs) of American companies – see www.businessroundtable.org.
16. Based on Rawlsian liberal ideas of fairness, stakeholder theory proposes that each stakeholder would have agreed to the 'rules of the game', knowing that they had an equal chance of being any one of the stakeholders themselves (Rawls 1967).
17. The decline of manufacturing meant further deterioration of trade union power and well-paid jobs that provided health care and social protection (Pilat et al. 2006).
18. Despite significant research in this area, a clear link has proved elusive and the conclusions ambiguous (Margolis and Walsh 2001).
19. Porter and Kramer (2002: 5) write that, as a percentage of profits, corporate giving has fallen by 50 per cent over the past 15 years.
20. This refers to the collective action of firms, formally institutionalized in the form of business associations and business groups, or, more informally, as networks, alliances and communities (Hollingsworth and Boyer 1999; Haggard et al. 1997).
21. Countries where neocorporatism has existed in a form closest to the 'ideal type' include Austria, Denmark, the Netherlands, Norway and Sweden. Countries that have had neocorporatism at some point or in some form include Germany and the UK, and more recently Ireland, Italy and Portugal (Traxler 2004; Wilson 2003).
22. Many welfare states in Europe were based on the Bismarckian model. Bismarck is believed to have instituted the world's first welfare state in Germany in 1886 as a necessary tactic to appease social disquiet and fend off socialism's appeal to the masses (Esping-Andersen 1990).
23. Diametrically opposed to Hayek, Polanyi argued that the notion of a self-regulating market was utopian.
24. Streeck and Kenworthy (2003) mention Hegel's *Philosophy of Right* (1821[2005]) and Durkheim's *Division of Labour in Society* (1893[1984]) as particularly noteworthy.
25. In 1891, Pope Leo XIII, referring to the problems of working-class poverty and class struggle, suggested that the state should sanction associative arrangements as a means of resolving problems stemming from poor working conditions, health and safety (Molina and Miguez 2008).
26. Streeck (1997: 39) provides a description of how the process worked in Germany: 'Governance is delegated either to individual associations or to collective negotiations between them, with the state often awarding its outcome legally binding status. Associations performing quasi-public functions are typically granted some form of obligatory and quasi-obligatory membership, helping them overcome the free-rider problems associated with collective goods production.'

27. For an overview of this literature, see the introductory chapter to this volume.
28. The 'flying geese' model refers to the argument that as Japanese industry became more capital-intensive, production requiring low-skilled labour shifted to lower-wage Republic of Korea and Taiwan, followed by Thailand and Malaysia, and later on by China and Vietnam (Kasahara 2004).
29. Amsden and Hikino (1994) categorize late-industrializing countries into two main groups: 1) countries, such as Germany and the United States, that relied on manufacturing technology innovation to successfully 'catch up' with the UK; 2) countries diverse in history, culture and natural resources, including Brazil, Japan, Mexico, the Republic of Korea and Taiwan, that focused on specific product market targets and competitive industrial processes.
30. Taiwan's case is particular as its export-oriented economy is composed mostly of small and medium enterprises (SMEs) that are dependent on large upstream government-controlled suppliers and intermediate-sized private business groups (*guanxiqiye*) (Fields 1995).
31. The dependence of a weak manufacturing sector on the state has also been suggested as a factor (Amsden and Hikino 1994).
32. East Asia's population is on average younger than that of developed countries and is therefore more likely to result in comparatively higher expenses on health and lower spending on pensions, the most expensive component of welfare states (Pierson 2004).
33. Unlike Japan, the Republic of Korea did not have an official 'lifetime employment system' but regulation by the state and well-organized unions provided a functional equivalent (Woo 2007).
34. Compulsory savings were also used for the creation of large state-directed investment funds that were used as leverage over capitalists (Amsden 2001).
35. For example, smaller firms as opposed to large conglomerates played a far greater role in Taiwan's economy, as did democratization and 'neocorporatism' in Japan (Onis 1991; Doner and Schneider 2000; Wade 1990).
36. Following the Asian financial crisis of 1997, such institutions were referred to as 'crony capitalism' and depicted as a root cause of widespread corruption, which, in turn, was considered a main cause of the crisis (Singh 1998).
37. Urgent measures forced upon the Republic of Korea and Taiwan by international financial institutions (IFIs) included labour market flexibilization (Yi and Lee 2005).
38. Similarly, the significant uptake of contemporary CSR by many of the world's largest TNCs relates to risk mitigation strategies aimed at protecting brands from reputational damage by activists and consumers (Utting and Marques 2009).
39. See Doner and Schneider (2000) for examples.
40. Different corporate governance structures may also influence how firms relate to social policy: 'diffuse shareholder firms have limited incentives to invest in workers, while the blockholder system has more' (Gourevitch and Shinn 2005: 13).

References

Abraham, Steven E. (1996) 'The Impact of the Taft-Hartley Act on the Balance of Power in Industrial Relations', *American Business Law Journal*, 33 (3), 341–72.

ADB (Asian Development Bank) (2007) *Inequality in Asia – Key Indicators 2007 Special Chapter Highlights* (Manila: ADB).

Amsden, Alice (2001) *The Rise of 'The Rest': Challenges to the West from Late-Industrializing Economies* (Oxford: Oxford University Press).

———, and Takashi Hikino (1994) 'Staying Behind, Stumbling Back, Sneaking Up and Soaring Ahead: Late Industrialization in Historical Perspective', in W. Baumol, R. R. Nelson and E. Wolff (eds), *Convergence of Productivity: Cross-National Studies and Historical Evidence* (Oxford: Oxford University Press).

Andersen, Soren Kaj and Mikkel Mailand (2002) *The Role of Employers and Trade Unions in Multipartite Social Partnerships* (Copenhagen: The Copenhagen Centre).

Atack, Jeremy, Fred Bateman and Robert A. Margo (2004) 'Skill Intensity and Rising Wage Dispersion in Nineteenth-Century American Manufacturing', *The Journal of Economic History*, 64 (1), 172–92.

Baccaro, Lucio (2002) *What Is Dead and What Is Alive in the Theory of Corporatism* (Geneva: International Institute for Labour Studies).

———, and Sang-Hoon Lim (2006) *Social Pacts as Coalitions of 'Weak' and 'Moderate': Ireland, Italy and South Korea in Comparative Perspective* (Geneva: International Institute for Labour Studies).

Beattie, Alan (2006) 'Sans Safety Net, "Creative Destruction" Spurs America', *Financial Times*, 6 November.

Bensel, Richard Franklin (2000) *The Political Economy of American Industrialization, 1877–1900* (Cambridge: Cambridge University Press).

Bernstein, Marver H. (1955) *Regulating Business by Independent Commission* (Princeton: Princeton University Press).

Beyer, Jurgen and Martin Höpner (2003) 'The Disintegration of Organised Capitalism: German Corporate Governance in the 1990s', *West European Politics*, 26 (4), 179–98.

Bremner, Robert Hamlett (1988) *American Philanthropy* (London: University of Chicago Press).

Business Roundtable (1981) *Statement on Corporate Responsibility* (New York: Business Roundtable).

——— (1990) *Corporate Governance and American Competitiveness* (New York: Business Roundtable).

——— (1997) *Statement on Corporate Governance* (New York: Business Roundtable).

Campos, José Edgardo (1996) *The Key to the Asian Miracle: Making Shared Growth Credible* (Washington, DC: Brookings Institution Press).

Chandler, Alfred D. (1977) *The Visible Hand: The Managerial Revolution in American Business* (London: Belknap Press of Harvard University Press).

Chang, Ha-Joon (2002) *Kicking away the Ladder: Development Strategy in Historical Perspective* (London: Anthem Press).

——— (2004) 'The Role of Social Policy in Economic Development: Some Theoretical Reflections and Lessons from East Asia', in T. Mkandawire (ed.), *Social Policy in a Development Context* (Basingstoke: UNRISD/Palgrave Macmillan).

Crouch, Colin and Wolfgang Streeck (1997) 'Introduction: The Future of Capitalist Society', in C. Crouch and W. Streeck (eds), *Political Economy of Modern Capitalism: Mapping Convergence and Diversity* (London: Sage Publications).

Davis, Gerald F., Marina V. N. Whitman and Mayer Nathan Zald (2006) 'The Responsibility Paradox: Multinational Firms and Global Corporate Social Responsibility', Michigan Ross School of Business Working Paper Series, No. 1031 (Ann Arbor: University of Michigan), April.

Domhoff, G. William (2001) *Who Rules America? Power, Politics, and Social Change* (Columbus: McGraw-Hill).

Doner, Richard and Ben Ross Schneider (2000) 'Business Associations and Economic Development: Why Some Associations Contribute More Than Others', *Business and Politics* 2 (3), 261–88.

Durkheim, Émile (1893[1984]) *The Division of Labour in Society* (New York: Palgrave Macmillan).

Economist, The (2006) 'Denmark's Labour Market – Flexicurity', 7 September, at: www.economist.com/world/europe/displaystory.cfm?story_id=7880198 (accessed 27 August 2009).

Esping-Andersen, Gøsta (1990) *The Three Worlds of Welfare Capitalism* (Cambridge: Polity Press).

Estevez-Abe, Margarita, Torben Iversen and David Soskice (2001) 'Social Protection and the Formation of Skills: A Reinterpretation of the Welfare State', in P. A. Hall and D. Soskice (eds), *Varieties of Capitalism: The Institutional Foundations of Comparative Advantage* (Oxford: Oxford University Press).

Evans, Peter (1997) 'State Structures and Government-Business Relations', in S. Maxfield and B. R. Schneider (eds), *Business and the State in Developing Countries* (Ithaca: Cornell University Press).

Fields, Karl J. (1995) *Enterprise and the State in Korea and Taiwan* (Ithaca: Cornell University Press).

Ford, Henry (1926[1998]) *Today and Tomorrow* (University Park: Productivity Press).

Freeman, Edward R. (1984) *Strategic Management: A Stakeholder Approach* (Boston: Pitman).

Freeman, Richard and Lawrence F. Katz (1994) 'Rising Wage Inequality: The U.S. vs. Other Advanced ountries', in R. Freeman (ed.), *Working Under Different Rules* (New York: Russell Sage Foundation Publications).

Friedman, Lawrence Jacob and Mark Douglas McGarvie (eds) (2003) *Charity, Philanthropy, and Civility in American History* (Cambridge: Cambridge University Press).

Friedman, Milton (1970) 'The Social Responsibility of Business Is To Increase Its Profits', *The New York Times Magazine*, 13 September.

Giddens, Anthony (1973) *The Class Structure of the Advanced Societies* (New York: Harper & Row).

Gomez, Edmund Terence (2002) 'Introduction: Political Business in East Asia', in E. T. Gomez (ed.), *Political Business in East Asia* (London: Routledge).

Gordon, Colin (1998) 'Why No Corporatism in the United States? Business Disorganization and its Consequences', *Business and Economic History*, 27 (1), 29–46.

Gourevitch, Peter Alexis and James Shinn (2005) *Political Control and Corporate Power: The New Global Politics of Corporate Governance* (Princeton and Oxford: Princeton University Press).

Hacker, Jacob S. and Paul Pierson (2002) 'Business Power and Social Policy: Employers and the Formation of the American Welfare State', *Politics & Society*, 30 (2), 277–325.

Haggard, Stephan, Sylvia Maxfield and Ben Ross Schneider (1997) 'Theories of Business and Business–State Relations', in S. Maxfield and B. R. Schneider (eds), *Business and the State in Developing Countries* (Ithaca: Cornell University Press).

Hall, Peter Dobkin (2000) *Philanthropy, the Welfare State, and the Transformation of American Public and Private Institutions, 1945–2000* (Cambridge, MA: The Hauser Center for Nonprofit Organizations, Harvard University).

Hart, David M. (2004) '"Business" Is Not an Interest Group: On the Study of Companies in American National Politics', *Annual Review of Political Science*, 7 (1), 47–69.

Harvey, David (2005) *A Brief History of Neoliberalism* (Oxford: Oxford University Press).

Hayek, F. (1945) 'The Use of Knowledge in Society', *American Economic Review*, 35 (4), 519–30.

Hegel, Georg Wilhelm Friedrich (1821[2005]) *Philosophy of Right* (New York: Dover).

Hirst, Paul and Jonathan Zeitlin (1991) 'Flexible Specialization Versus Post-Fordism: Theory, Evidence and Policy Implications', *Economy and Society* 20 (1), 1–56.

Hollingsworth, J. Rogers (1997) 'The Institutional Embeddedness of American Capitalism', in C. Crouch and W. Streeck (eds), *Political Economy of Modern Capitalism: Mapping Convergence and Diversity* (London: Sage Publications).

Hollingsworth, J. Rogers and Robert Boyer (eds) (1999) *Contemporary Capitalism: The Embeddedness of Institutions* (Cambridge: Cambridge University Press).

Huber, Evelyne and John D. Stephens (eds) (2001) *Development and Crisis of the Welfare State: Parties and Policies in Global Markets* (London: University of Chicago Press).

Hyman, Richard (2001) 'Some Problems of Partnership and Dilemmas of Dialogue', in C. Kjärgaard and S.-Å. Westphalen (eds), *From Collective Bargaining to Social Partnerships: New Roles of the Social Partners in Europe* (Copenhagen: The Copenhagen Centre).

Jacoby, Sanford M. (1997) *Modern Manors: Welfare Capitalism since the New Deal* (Princeton: Princeton University Press).

Johnson, Chalmers (1982) *Miti and the Japanese Miracle: The Growth of Industrial Policy, 1925–1975* (Palo Alto: Stanford University Press).

——— (1999) 'The Developmental State: Odyssey of a Concept', in M. Woo-Cumings (ed.), *The Developmental State* (London: Cornell University Press).

Kasahara, Shigehisa (2004) *The Flying Geese Paradigm: A Critical Study of Its Application to East Asian Regional Development* (Geneva: UNCTAD).

Kay, Cristóbal (2002) 'Why East Asia Overtook Latin America: Agrarian Reform, Industrialisation and Development', *Third World Quarterly*, 23 (6), 1073–102.

Khan, Mushtaq H. and Kwame Sundaram Jomo (eds) (2000) *Rents, Rent-Seeking and Economic Development: Theory and Evidence in Asia* (Singapore: Green Giant Press Pte Ltd).

Khanna, Tarun and Raymond Fisman (2004) 'Facilitating Development: The Role of Business Groups', *World Development*, 32 (4), 609–28.

Kitschelt, Herbert, Peter Lange, Gary Marks and John D. Stephens (1999) *Continuity and Change in Contemporary Capitalism* (Cambridge: Cambridge University Press).

Kwon, Huck-ju (2004) 'The Economic Crisis and Politics of Welfare Reform in Korea', in T. Mkandawire (ed.), *Social Policy in a Development Context* (Basingstoke: UNRISD/Palgrave Macmillan).

——— (2005) 'The Developmental Welfare State and Policy Reforms in East Asia', in H.-j. Kwon (ed.), *Transforming the Developmental Welfare State in East Asia* (Basingstoke: UNRISD/Palgrave Macmillan).

Lamoreaux, Naomi R. (1988) *The Great Merger Movement in American Business, 1895–1904* (New York: Cambridge University Press).

Lee, Pei-Shan (2002) 'Democratization and the Demise of the Developmental State', paper presented at Challenges to Taiwan's Democracy in the Post-Hegemonic Era, Taipei, 7–8 June.

Margolis, Joshua D. and James P. Walsh (2001) *People and Profits?: The Search for a Link between a Company's Social and Financial Performance*, LEA Organization and Management Series (Mahwah: Lawrence Erlbaum Associates).

Martin, Cathie Jo (1999) *Stuck in Neutral: Business and the Politics of Human Capital Investment Policy*, Princeton Studies in American Politics (Princeton: Princeton University Press).

——— (2005) 'Corporatism from the Firm Perspective: Employers and Social Policy in Denmark and Britain', *British Journal of Political Science*, 35 (1), 127–48.

McCarty, Nolan, Keith T. Poole and Howard Rosenthal (2006) *Polarized America: The Dance of Ideology and Unequal Riches* (Boston: MIT Press).

McCraw, Thomas K. (1984) *Prophets of Regulation* (Cambridge, MA: Harvard University Press).

McQuaid, Kim (1994) *Uneasy Partners: Big Business in American Politics, 1945–1990* (London: Johns Hopkins University Press).

Mkandawire, Thandika (2004) 'Social Policy in a Development Context: Introduction', in Thandika Mkandawire (ed.), *Social Policy in a Development Context* (Basingstoke: UNRISD/Palgrave Macmillan).

——— (2007) 'Transformative Social Policy and Innovation in Developing Countries', *The European Journal of Development Research*, 19 (1), 13–29.

Molina, Fernando and Antonio Miguez (2008) 'The Origins of Mondragon: Catholic Co-Operativism and Social Movement in a Basque Valley (1941–1959)', *Social History*, 33 (3), 284–98.

O'Sullivan, Mary (2003) 'The Political Economy of Comparative Corporate Governance', *Review of International Political Economy*, 10 (1), 23–72.

Olson, Mancur (1965) *The Logic of Collective Action* (Cambridge, MA: Harvard University Press).

——— (1982) *The Rise and Decline of Nations: Economic Growth, Stagflation and Social Rigidities* (New York: Yale University Press).

Onis, Ziya (1991) 'The Logic of the Developmental State', *Comparative Politics*, 24 (1), 109–26.

OpenSecrets.org. (2007) Center for Responsive Politics, Lobbying Overview, Lobbying Database, *Top Spenders 1998–2006*, at: http://opensecrets.org/lobbyists/ (accessed 9 August 2007).

Ostrom, Elinor (1990) *Governing the Commons: The Evolution of Institutions for Collective Action* (Cambridge: Cambridge University Press).

Peng, Ito (2005) 'The New Politics of the Welfare State in a Developmental Context: Explaining the 1990s Social Care Expansion in Japan', in H.-j. Kwon (ed.), *Transforming the Developmental Welfare State in East Asia* (Basingstoke: UNRISD/Palgrave Macmillan).

Perez, Sofia A. (2000) 'From Decentralization to Reorganization: Explaining the Return to National Bargaining in Italy and Spain', *Comparative Politics* 32 (4), 437–58.

Phelps, Edmund S. (2002) *European Myths, European Realities* (Project Syndicate, November), at: www.project-syndicate.org/commentary/phelps4 (accessed 27 August 2009).

Phongpaichit, Pasuk (2005) 'Money Politics and Its Impact Keynote Address', paper presented at Political Economy Center's Annual Seminar on Money Politics, Chulalongkorn University, 7 December.

Pierson, Chris (2004) 'Late Industrializers' and the Development of the Welfare State', in T. Mkandawire (ed.), *Social Policy in a Development Context* (Basingstoke: UNRISD/Palgrave Macmillan).

Pierson, Paul (ed.) (2001) *The New Politics of the Welfare State* (Oxford: Oxford University Press).

Pilat, Dirk, Agnès Cimper, Karsten Bjerring Olsen and Colin Webb (2006) 'The Changing Nature of Manufacturing in OECD Economies', Working Paper 2006/9 (Paris: OECD, Directorate for Science, Technology and Industry).

Pizzorno, Alessandro (1978) 'Political Exchange and Collective Identity in Industrial Conflict', in C. Crouch and A. Pizzorno (eds), *The Resurgence of Class Conflict in Western Europe* (London: Macmillan).

Polanyi, Karl (1944) *The Great Transformation: The Political and Economic Origins of Our Time* (Boston: Beacon Press).

Pontusson, Jonas (2005) *Inequality and Prosperity: Social Europe vs. Liberal America* (Ithaca: Cornell University Press).

Porter, Michael E. and Mark R. Kramer (2002) 'The Competitive Advantage of Corporate Philanthropy', *Harvard Business Review*, 80 (12), 57–68.

——— (2006) 'Strategy & Society: The Link Between Competitive Advantage and Corporate Social Responsibility', *Harvard Business Review*, 84 (12), 78–92.

Rawls, John (1967) 'Distributive Justice', in P. Laslett and W. C. Runciman (eds), *Philosophy, Politics and Society* (Oxford: Basil Blackwell).

Roberts, Dan and Christopher Swann (2006) 'America's Dilemma: As Business Retreats From Its Welfare Role, Who Will Take Up the Burden?', *Financial Times*, 13 January.

Rodrik, Dani (1996) 'Understanding Economic Policy Reform', *Journal of Economic Literature*, 34 (1), 9–41.

Ruggie, John Gerard (1982) 'International Regimes, Transactions, and Change: Embedded Liberalism in the Postwar Economic Order', *International Organization*, 36 (2) (International Regimes), 379–415.

Salisbury, Robert H. (1979) 'Why No Corporatism in America?', in P. Schmitter and G. Lehmbruch (eds), *Trends toward Corporatist Intermediation* (London: Sage Publications).

Schmitter, Philippe (1979) 'Modes of Interest Intermediation and Models of Societal Change in Western Europe', in P. Schmitter and G. Lehmbruch (eds), *Trends toward Corporatist Intermediation* (London: Sage Publications).

Schnabel, Claus and Joachim Wagner (2007) 'Union Density and Determinants of Union Membership in 18 EU Countries: Evidence From Micro data, 2002/031', *Industrial Relations Journal*, 38 (1), 5–32.

Schneider, Ben Ross (2007) 'Business Politics and Social Policy in Latin America: Sources of Disconnect', paper presented at the Conference on Business, Social Policy and Corporate Political Influence in Developing Countries, Geneva, 12–13 November (Geneva: UNRISD).

Shafer, Michael, 'The Political Economy of Sectors and Sectoral Change: Korea Then and Now', in S. Maxfield and B. R. Schneider (eds), *Business and the State in Developing Countries* (Ithaca: Cornell University Press).

Shin, Myung-Soon (2004) 'The Effectiveness of Political Protest in Korean Politics', in Korean National Commission for UNESCO (ed.), *Korean Politics: Striving for Democracy and Unification* (Seoul: Hollym).

Singh, Ajit (1998) '"Asian Capitalism" and the Financial Crisis', Working Paper Series III, *International Capital Markets and the Future of Economic Policy*, Working Paper No. 10 (New York: Center for Economic Policy Analysis/CEPA).

Skocpol, Theda (1995) *Social Policy in the United States* (Princeton: Princeton University Press).

Stigler, George J. (1971) 'The Theory of Economic Regulation', *The Bell Journal of Economics and Management Science*, 2 (1), 3–21.

Streeck, Wolfgang (1997) 'German Capitalism: Does It Exist? Can It Survive?', in C. Crouch and W. Streeck (eds), *Political Economy of Modern Capitalism: Mapping Convergence and Diversity* (London: Sage Publications).

Streeck, Wolfgang and Lane Kenworthy (2003) 'Theories and Practices of Neo-Corporatism', in Thomas Janoski, Robert Alford, Alexander Hicks and Mildred

A. Schwartz (eds), *A Handbook of Political Sociology: States, Civil Societies and Globalization* (New York: Cambridge University Press).

Swank, Duane (2002) *Global Capital, Political Institutions, and Policy Change in Developed Welfare States* (Cambridge: Cambridge University Press).

Tedlow, R. S. (1988) 'Trade Associations and Public Relations', in M. Miyamoto and H. Yamazaki (eds), *Trade Associations in Business History – International Conference on Business History: Proceedings of the Fuji Conference* (Tokyo: University of Tokyo Press).

Thelen, Kathleen (2004) *How Institutions Evolve: The Political Economy of Skills in Germany, Britain, Japan and the United States* (Cambridge: Cambridge University Press).

de Tocqueville, Alexis (1835/40[2002]) *Democracy in America*, Penn State Electronic Classics (University Park, PA: Pennsylvania State University – orig. pub. 1835 [Vol. I] and 1840 [Vol. II]), at: www.docin.com/p-12026366.html (accessed 27 August 2009).

Traxler, Franz (2004) 'The Metamorphoses of Corporatism: From Classical to Lean Patterns', *European Journal of Political Research*, 43 (4), 571–98.

Truman, David B. (1951) *The Governmental Process. Political Interests and Public Opinion* (New York: Knopf).

UNRISD (United Nations Research Institute for Social Development) (2008) *Business, Social Policy and Corporate Political Influence in Developing Countries* (Geneva, 12–13 November 2007), *Conference News*, No. 22.

Utting, Peter and José Carlos Marques (eds) (2009) *Corporate Social Responsibility and Regulatory Governance: Towards Inclusive Development?* (Basingstoke: UNRISD/ Palgrave Macmillan).

Vartiainen, Juhana (2007) 'Asian Regimes and the Labour Contract', in M. J.-E. Woo (ed.), *After the Miracle: Neoliberalism and Institutional Reform in East Asia* (Basingstoke: UNRISD/Palgrave Macmillan).

Vogel, David (1980) 'The Public-Interest Movement and the American Reform Tradition', *Political Science Quarterly*, 95 (4), 607–27.

——— (1986) *Kindred Strangers: The Uneasy Relationship between Politics and Business in America* (Princeton: Princeton University Press).

——— (1989) *Fluctuating Fortunes: The Political Power of Business in America* (New York: Basic Books).

——— (2005) *The Market for Virtue: The Potential and Limits of Corporate Social Responsibility* (Washington, DC: The Brookings Institution).

Wade, Robert Hunter (1990) *Governing the Market: Economic Theory and the Role of Government in East Asian Industrialization* (Princeton: Princeton University Press).

Wallace, Michael and Craig Jenkins (1995) 'The New Class, Postindustrialism, and Neocorporatism: Three Images of Social Protest in the Western Democracies', in C. Jenkins and B. Klandermans (eds), *The Politics of Social Protest* (Minneapolis: University of Minnesota Press).

Whitley, Richard (1999) *Divergent Capitalisms: The Social Structuring and Change of Business Systems* (Oxford: Oxford University Press).

Wilson, Graham K. (2003) *Business and Politics: A Comparative Introduction* (New York: Palgrave Macmillan).

Woo, Meredith Jung-En (2007) 'After the Miracle: Neoliberalism and Institutional Reform in East Asia', in M. J.-E. Woo (ed.), *After the Miracle: Neoliberalism and Institutional Reform in East Asia* (Basingstoke: UNRISD/Palgrave Macmillan).

Woo-Cumings, Meredith (1999) 'Introduction: Chalmers Johnson and the Politics of Nationalism and Development', in M. Woo-Cumings (ed.), *The Developmental State* (London: Cornell University Press).

World Bank (1993) *The East Asian Miracle: Economic Growth and Public Policy* (New York: Oxford University Press).

Yi, Ilcheong and Byung-hee Lee (2005) 'Development Strategies and Unemployment Policies in Korea', in H.-j. Kwon (ed.), *Transforming the Developmental Welfare State in East Asia* (Basingstoke: UNRISD/Palgrave Macmillan).

2
Business Power, Social Policy Preferences and Development

Kevin Farnsworth

Introduction

Business influenced the evolution of social policies within the developed welfare states and it is just as important in the context of economically developing countries. Policy-makers everywhere respond to powerful structural signals, business lobbying and business engagement in social provision. Meanwhile citizens are the victims or benefactors of corporate activities within the various spheres of production, distribution and consumption. However, the context within which states and citizens engage and respond to business in developing economies is different to that which spurred social policy development in the West. In addition to facing a different playing field, where contemporary corporations are internationally more significant and more powerful, international governance is also more important and more prescriptive in terms of how states engage with the international economy. Even with evidence of the softening of neoliberal prescriptions at the international level, intergovernmental organizations (IGOs) and governments alike promote taken-for-granted views that corporations both need and favour lightly regulated economies with minimalist social policies.

Upon closer examination, however, it becomes clear that different firms require different policies and that the power balance between competing business interests can have a significant impact upon corporations' social policy needs. The prioritization of certain business preferences at the international level, this chapter argues, risks distorting the development of good social policy solutions in the context of development. This, in turn, risks harming both the welfare of individuals and the interests of business as a whole. Key here is the size and nature of inward investment and the significance of markets within developing countries and national policy responses to such investment. While some companies actively seek out low tax and low wage regimes for exported goods, for instance, others will be attracted by productive and skilled labour, stability in labour markets, and access to growing consumer markets. For their part, national governments may approach foreign investment in various ways, but important as a factor are the policies of IGOs.

This chapter investigates the dynamics at play here in four parts. First, it examines the implications of business power and influence over social policy in developing economies. Second, it examines, as a proxy for gauging structural signals, the various ways in which developing economies 'sell' themselves to international capital through Trade and Industry ministries. It is argued that states, in responding selectively to structural pressures and certain larger and international business voices, risk gearing policies towards the narrow policy preferences of certain businesses rather than broader economic and social needs. Third, it examines the impact of business on human welfare. Fourth, it reflects on how such narrow policy solutions risk locking developing states into a social policy agenda that is neither in the best interests of businesses nor citizens, especially the poorest and most vulnerable within societies.

Theorizing business power

Business is able to exert influence on social policy through both agency and structural mechanisms.[1] Both mechanisms are important to welfare state outcomes, but both are variable in terms of their impact within different contexts and settings. Structural theory is concerned with indirect influence – the ability of business to shape policy without having to place direct pressure on the state through the actions of actors. Rather, political and economic structures restrict the policy options available to governments to those that are, on balance, favourable to business in one way or another. The primary source of business structural power is its monopoly control over existing and future private investments. Its investment decisions and subsequent profitability have long-lasting and far-reaching consequences, impacting on future production, employment and consumption. Governments raise revenues from taxation levied on corporate profits and employee wages, therefore depending on continuing profitability and investment for their own survival.

However, a firm's investment decisions are privately made on the basis of potential profits, and as such are beyond the direct control of either states or employees (Lindblom 1977; Przeworski and Wallerstein 1988). Although governments and employees can try to induce companies to invest, they cannot compel them. And it is because of this dependence on future private investment and profitability, over which they have no control, that governments and employees ultimately have to prioritize the wishes and demands of private firms (Offe and Ronge 1984).

The other form of structural power lies in the ideological domain. A group may exercise ideological hegemony if its interests can be legitimized as the 'common interest'. Because of the foregoing arguments, this is precisely the position that business is in. The dependence of society and state on capital profitability and accumulation acts as a gravitational tug on the 'volitions' of the population, according to both Lindblom (1977) and the dominant ideology thesis within Marxist theory. The notion that most social and economic activities depend on the freedom of private enterprises to pursue and maximize profits is taken for granted. Neither is ideological power restricted to the national context: pro-capitalist ideas are also propagated at the international level (Cox 1983). National and international governments play a key role in reinforcing a pro-business ideology, which serves to further increase the power of business by preventing or neutralizing opposition to it. The implication here, then, is that business or capitalist power translates into ideological power, and this helps to shape values and interests within capitalist societies, including those of labour and the state. Viewed in this way, structural power defines the context for agency engagement.

Two key forms of agency power are commonly identified in the literature. First, business is able to exert influence through its political lobbying activities. Individual firms or business associations apply political pressure on policy-makers or, alternatively, employ one of a growing number of professional lobby organizations to do so on their behalf (see Jordan 1991). Such is the size and importance of many firms and business organizations that they are seldom denied an audience with even the most senior politicians (Bonnet 1985; Offe and Weisenthal 1980).

The second mechanism of business agency power is achieved through its command over vast resources. Business is able to use its access to financial resources to fund business-centred interest groups, boost the electoral standing of sympathetic political parties and gain access to politicians or help prevent the election of unsympathetic political parties.

These, then, are the various theoretical mechanisms through which business is able to influence policy-making. As the following section illustrates, however, in practice, power and its application are seldom uniform and straightforward.

Making sense of business power within the context of development

Business is clearly an important and powerful interest in market economies; but the actual impact of business on social policies is widely variable. Structural signals vary in their strength and business demands are not always met. Moreover, different states appear to succeed with widely variable state–business relations, varying levels of state social provision, and with varying levels of human wellbeing.[2] This section outlines the various ways in which the potential for business influence on social policy development is boosted or limited.

First, the global is increasingly important to business power at the national level. Business priorities are institutionally embedded within the major

IGOs; the World Bank, the International Monetary Fund (IMF), the World Trade Organization (WTO) and the United Nations (UN) exist in order to help promote economic cooperation, growth, stability and development. The World Bank and the IMF, through various strategies, from structural adjustment policies and its Poverty Reduction Strategy Papers (PRSPs), have also placed pressure on developing states to open up their economies and services to the private sector, including international capital (Moen 2003). Pressure to prioritize business interests in international policy-making, which in turn has an impact on national politics, also stems from nation-states. Because structural pressures steer national governments towards prioritizing economic development and new investment, states transfer these concerns to the international level. Governments often lobby IGOs on behalf of their own national business interests in response to the structural pressures they face, stemming not from the specific representations of firms or business organizations to national governments, but from a desire to defend their own national and party political interests. Of course, the most powerful governments are most likely to succeed in this objective.

Internationally organized business has also been more successful than other interests in organizing and exploiting new openings beyond the level of the nation-state and has been able to present a relatively united front across borders and form linkages with important non-economic elites within IGOs (Sklair 2001). Organized business has also been boosted at the international level since the 1980s by the increasing number of opportunities afforded to it for institutional engagement by IGOs, including the United Nations.[3] Business dominance has been further aided by the historical dominance of senior positions within IGOs, especially the World Bank and IMF, by senior economists and politicians with links to the business community. This has created a revolving door between business, the World Bank and the IMF, according to Stiglitz (2002), which ensures that they 'naturally see the world through the eyes of the financial community.'[4]

Second, the extent to which business can relocate investment is a key factor in determining structural power and influence. Yet, the conditions for capital mobility shift and vary over time and between spaces. For some firms, relocation may not be an option at all because they are tied to specific locations by production or access to markets and, despite the processes of globalization, as Hirst and Thompson (1996) have demonstrated, increased trade and investment flows since the 1970s have been, for the most part, restricted to the triad of North America, Japan and Europe, although this is less and less the case with the phenomenal growth of China and India. Yeates (1999) also reminds us that even the most transnational companies still have identifiable national bases and that relocation is expensive and entails greater logistical problems than is often assumed, especially for firms that require access to raw materials or markets. However, it is equally true to state that certain countries have been more successful in attracting certain firms and that, depending on the starting point of economic development, even relatively small levels of inward investment may be extremely important within a region or a country. This notwithstanding, as outlined above, the extent of structural power is shaped, in part, by investment options and levels of mobility.

Third, the state form is important to the realization of business power. The development and openness of state institutions and economies, the spaces occupied by business and other actors and the neutrality and independence of ruling parties are all important determinants of the relative power of business and state actors (Skocpol 1979). The extent to which business is embedded within policy-making or delivery can create important veto-points for business and entrench or maintain powerful business agendas at the heart of services (Thelen and Steinmo 1992). State rules and regulations define the basis of business involvement in state services, not to mention the provision of occupational and community-based provision.

Fourth, those who maintain that business is no more privileged than other interests tend to point to divisions within the business community that prevent it from putting forward clear and coherent policy proposals (Dahl 1961). Cleavages exist at various levels, and may be even greater in the context of development: between the international and national; the national and local; the local and micro; between sectors; between organizations of different sizes, for example, large versus small business, and between firms within different national bases (Mann 1993).

While such divisions and policy incoherence may reduce business power in some instances, they do not altogether negate business power and influence. As already noted, at the international level divisions are not deeply embedded. In fact, research into business engagement tends to illustrate that there are relatively few issues that lead to deep divisions within the business community (Coates 1984; Miliband 1969). Rather, it is the smaller and ultimately less controversial issues that tend to divide business. Deliberate strategies on the part of the state often help to ensure unity. In areas that are particularly controversial, governments will often engage business representatives in policy-making, even where existing corporatist structures do not exist, in order to avoid direct conflict with powerful actors. Even where business is divided, or where business lacks a coordinated or coherent approach in a particular area, this does not mean that business is unable to exert influence. Where divisions emerge, the most powerful business organizations, representing big business, international firms or financial capital, will often win the day.

Fifth, the activities and relative power of rival interests, particularly the labour movement, are important counters to the power of business. Non-governmental organizations (NGOs) and the wider labour movement are capable of offsetting and challenging the power and dominance of business either through democratic or non-institutionalized challenges, including civil disobedience and popular uprisings (Korpi 1983; Piven and Cloward

1971). International NGOs (INGOs) certainly play an important role in monitoring and publicizing poor corporate behaviour in various parts of the world. Hence, various non-business interests are often able to extract favourable policy outcomes which do not directly serve the interests of business, especially in the sphere of social policy and employment regulations (Esping-Andersen 1990; Korpi 1989) and governments have been able to follow distinct pathways in managing capitalism (Esping-Andersen 1990; Hall and Soskice 2001).

Together, these various factors combine to define particular sets of institutions and policy settings. What is clear is that institutions matter; the particular constellations and configurations of state institutions, the various opportunities for political engagement and exchange, and the particular opportunities for firms to meet their particular needs to satisfy their drive towards profit help to define development regimes in a similar way to how theorists increasingly categorize welfare and capitalist systems. Esping-Anderson (1990), for instance, identified three distinct 'worlds of welfare'. Gough (2004) identified welfare regimes in various developing countries based on welfare outcomes, and Hall and Soskice (2001) categorized two distinct types of capitalism associated with different systems of welfare. These various works are important because they allow us to more clearly understand why different states respond in different ways to similar types of external and internal pressures. The key to understanding different state responses is to be found in distinct national institutional arrangements. These help to mediate conflicting interests and help to define the parameters and basis of social policy solutions to problems confronting citizens and firms. In certain nations, the state provides opportunities for diverse interests to come together, exchange views and help to formulate binding agreements on a range of policies. Different regulatory regimes also create different demands and pressures on businesses which must evolve to maximize market opportunities. Thus, corporations adopt different competition policies, production methods, financing and marketing strategies, and work to various timeframes, within different states.

Regime analysis literature suggests that different political and economic histories, including previous and ongoing political struggles, the extent of political accountability, economic strengths and weaknesses, historical patterns of trade and industrial output, and so on, play important roles in shaping business power, business needs and business preferences in social policy development.

The business–social policy nexus in the context of development

It is often assumed in accounts of social history that business is always against welfare expansion and labour is always for it. Power resources theory, for instance, suggests that welfare settlements reflect the relative balance of power between these two actors. However, social policy-making is often rather more nuanced and less straightforward than this dichotomy suggests, and the preferences of business and labour are more malleable. A key reason for this is that different social policies impact in different ways on various parties. As far as business is concerned, certain social policies contribute directly, and others contribute indirectly, to the fulfilment of business needs. In fact, certain business activities are directly dependent on state social policy. Whether and how social policies make a positive contribution to business activities, however, depends on the form they take and how they are funded.

Economic development models of welfare growth link socioeconomic factors with the evolution of social policy. Wilensky (1975) posits that the most important determinant of the extensiveness of social provision is economic development and accompanying political and bureaucratic development. As economies develop, so former political and economic settlements break down, and previous institutions of care and welfare collapse. Social problems and dislocation that inevitably arise from major transformations in production require state solutions to poverty, disease and cyclical unemployment. Developing-market logic has also tended to demand better disciplined, more healthy and educated workforces. Moreover, because industrialization processes tended to undermine social capital, state provision is increasingly required and relied upon, and as state institutions develop, so too does their capacity to provide more ambitious solutions to social problems. Because these developments apply to every industrialized and industrializing country, welfare states should, accordingly, converge, and social policy should develop in tandem with economic development.

Those working within a neo-Marxist framework similarly emphasize the importance of economic development to social policy, although theirs is a more functionalist account which suggests that the motor behind welfare development is the role that welfare states play in supporting capitalist development by assisting the accumulation process and legitimizing social relations. According to O'Connor (1973), a major function of state expenditure is to increase labour productivity and lower reproduction costs on the one hand, and to maintain social harmony and stability on the other. Thus, social policy has to be compatible with or fulfil, in one way or another, the needs of business.

The needs of business are reducible to the simple pursuit of ever greater profits (Gough 2000; Wetherly 1995). In order to realize this fundamental need, firms require adequate sales and turnover, facilitated primarily through a legal and monetary system, social stability, a sufficiently skilled, appropriately priced, reliable supply of labour power and adequate infrastructure. State services, such as education, training, health care, housing and social protection, are all capable of contributing positively to business productivity and sales levels. State education, training and health care, for instance, help to create more highly skilled, healthy and therefore productive employees (Estevez-Abe et al. 2001). Education again plays a role here by indoctrinating students into accepting the status quo, while social protection benefits help to sweeten the pill of forced redundancy or retirement. Social housing helps to increase the mobility and, in some instances, the supply of employees, particularly where high housing costs are a barrier to labour supply.

When we transpose these various accounts of welfare state evolution to the developing contexts, the issue of social policy growth becomes even more complex. Theories of social policy development tend to focus on states and neglect the wider welfare mix, including occupational and voluntary provision, which are both important to human welfare in the absence of comprehensive state provision (Gough 2004). While economic development may shape the capacity for states to enact social policies, it does not shape occupational and voluntary provision, nor do all states of similar levels of economic development provide comparable levels of social provision. Most importantly, in terms of the link between business needs and social policies, mobile firms feature more heavily within the context of contemporary economic development, making it even more difficult for policy-makers to take account of the various needs of companies operating within their economies. Although IGOs tend to emphasize the developmental potential of education and training, for instance, whether large businesses invest in new locations in order to make use of such services is in doubt (Schneider 2007), and whether they 'need' highly, or even moderately, trained workers varies between firms and regions. In fact, firms often rely on their own in-house training rather than the state (Schneider 2007). Business actors, including business organizations, meanwhile, often do not engage effectively in social policy-making since: 1) social policy is a complex and sprawling policy arena; 2) social policy has both long-term goals and uncertain outcomes; and 3) many social policies do not have clear and obvious benefits for businesses (Farnsworth 2004; Schneider 2007). These problems are increased, of course, where business organization and engagement with policy-makers is poor and business demands are unclear or contradictory.

Given that the needs of business are sensitive to policy context, it is not surprising to find that business preferences are highly variable. Although it is possible to extract a 'class-representative' view of general business preferences (Farnsworth 2005), different manufacturing and trading conditions and competing ideas within firms translate into different preferences when it comes to specific social policies.

The international context

In so far as it is possible to determine a common business view, it is that only those social policies that contribute to economic stability and growth are defensible and affordable (Farnsworth 2005). But whether and how far social policy contributes to economic stability and growth, and how affordable it is, depends on overriding economic concerns. Thus, the priority of International Business Interest Associations (IBIAs) from the 1980s has been to place pressure on governments to reduce expenditure and taxation (especially on corporations) and to utilize social provision to reduce disincentives to work, halt the propensity towards early retirement and increase the productivity of workers. IBIAs have also lobbied hard to ensure that governments pay particular attention to the generic needs and concerns of employers in formulating social policy, especially regarding skills, flexibility and adaptability within the labour force (BIAC 2002), with the idea being that the specific needs of national capital can be fought over locally. In general terms, IBIAs have tended to promote what, on the face of it, are generic economic growth models that, in theory, would fit with all economies: the prioritization of human capital formation policies and training provision that have been prioritized and vigorously defended as key strategies to improving employability; liberalized labour markets; and work-focused social provision. Social protection benefits have been defended in instances where they might function to smooth out employment markets, but they are considered to be viable only under certain circumstances (BIAC 1998). High social security costs and accompanying administrative burdens, business argues, undermine profitability and increase unemployment (BIAC 1998); hence strict qualifying conditions, time limitations, the retention of work incentives and conditionality based on the acceptance of employment are all viewed as essential.

The opinions of INGOs echo international business perspectives (Farnsworth 2008). Perhaps paradoxically, the World Bank was less positive about social policy than was international business during the 1980s and 1990s, but it has since become more positive about the capacity for state social policies to bring economic benefits to economies so that it has moved closer towards the views of international business. A recent pronouncement on social policy was embodied in the so-called Arusha initiative[5] and the resulting statement which speaks of the 'growing international consensus about the complementarity between social and economic development' and the 'interrelationship between social policy and economic policy'. The World Bank appears to have accepted the broad thrust of the Arusha statement, even though it was agreed by 'social policy experts' who generally were not connected directly with the World Bank. However, a better representation of World Bank policy is probably found in its annual *World Development Reports*. Again evidence of positive endorsements of social policy can be found in many of the most recent reports, especially those published after the mid-1990s, but the general message is that poverty eradication and welfare services are only possible if positive business environments are promoted. The objective, according to the 2005 *World Development Report* (World Bank 2004: xiii) is about

> creating opportunities for people to escape from poverty and improve their living standards. It is about creating a climate in which firms and entrepreneurs of all types – from farmers and microenterprises to local manufacturing concerns and multinationals – have opportunities and incentives to invest productively, create jobs, and expand, and thereby contribute to growth and poverty reduction.

The policy prescriptions that flow from this objective are primarily concerned with boosting business interests by creating improved investment environments so that more wealth is generated. The key difference from previous World Bank policy is that crude free market idealism has been replaced by a more pragmatic stance which accepts the need for state intervention provided it results in more positive investment climates for business. Within the Bank and other IGOs, there has been a realization that strong, reliable and stable investment is promoted best within stable states with higher levels of social harmony. Market liberalization is still promoted by the Bank, especially within its satellite organizations, but it also accepts the need for adequate regulation, corporate taxation, education and some forms of (targeted) social protection in order to promote the best possible investment climates for business.

> The investment climate should benefit society as a whole, not only firms. Well-designed regulation and taxation are thus an important part of a good investment climate. And the investment climate should embrace firms of all types, not just large or influential firms. . . . [E]fforts to improve the investment climate need to go beyond just reducing business costs. Those costs can indeed be extraordinary in many countries, amounting to several times what firms pay in taxes. But policy-related risks dominate firms' concerns in developing countries and can cripple incentives to invest. And barriers to competition remain pervasive, dulling incentives for firms to innovate and increase productivity . . . [P]rogress requires governments to address important constraints in ways that give firms the confidence to invest – and to sustain a process of ongoing improvements. (World Bank 2004: xiii–xiv)

This apparent change in World Bank thinking has been facilitated as much by the opportunities created by institutional changes within the institution as by lobbying by business. Indeed, the Bank is divided, according to Wade (2002), between its financial and civil society wings. In many ways, the neoliberal financial wing of the Bank is following broadly structural constraints in setting economic policy while the social welfare wing is paying greater heed to the arguments of various political lobbies, including civil society and internationally organized business. While parts of the World Bank have embraced the need for state intervention in social welfare, other sectors of the Bank continue to emphasize market liberalization, especially through the Bank's other arms. Its Private Sector Development Strategies (PSDS), alongside its private finance arms, the International Finance Corporation (IFC) and its Multilateral Investment Guarantee Agency (MIGA), continue to promote privatization, including in education and health care (Mehrotra and Delamonica 2005). Moreover, the IMF and the World Bank Group continue to promote privatization through conditionality rules attached to lending and other policy initiatives. Its PRSPs are as prescriptive in terms of opening up markets and forcing privatization deals as were the previous structural adjustment programmes (Mehrotra and Delamonica 2005).

Although the Bank's more positive endorsement of social policy is to be welcomed, there is some danger in its promotion of business and economic needs within its social policies, for two reasons. First, social policies complement economic growth in less obvious ways than is often recognized by governments. Social protection and health provision may be just as important as education, for instance, in supporting productive workers. Second, as already indicated, business needs and priorities are highly variable. They are also partly created by states. If the economic setting is such that firms can only extract competitive advantage through cost factors, so that they are unable to rely on higher skill levels, stable employment relations and higher levels of stability and flexibility afforded by welfare systems, they are more likely to push for reductions in regulations, taxation and public provision. If, on the other hand, business is able to extract added value from more highly skilled and productive workers, it is less likely to demand such reforms from the government (Hall and Soskice 2001: 55–6). The key here is how, and to what extent, a country has 'sold' itself to investors in the past, and how quickly the economy is able to readjust to different ways of securing future investments.

Business and social policy within developing economies

The international context within which states operate is important to shaping the power and influence of business within national settings and local institutional arrangements help to mediate power and influence in determining the shape of national social policies. Developing economies have to contend with a more powerful global business class, a more competitive environment for capturing foreign investment, predominantly pro-business IGOs and international pro-business prescriptions and/or recommendations on local policies. At the same time, IGOs offer little in the way of global regulation of corporate behaviour which could offer some protection from competitor nations prepared to reduce national social protections in order to capture new foreign investment. The international promotion of business-centred social policy is also unhelpful since those economies that are likely to benefit most from the pursuit of such policies are likely to be already highly developed. Economies dependent on, for example, agricultural exports, mineral extraction or low-skilled and low-cost labour will not benefit from the prioritization of education or training unless it develops at a similar pace to more comprehensive social protection. The key problem is that business needs themselves are shaped by social and other policies; gearing social policy towards business needs could therefore lock states into low levels of social provision. Table 2.1 attempts to capture the relationship between social policies and economic structures. It distinguishes five categories of developing state according to their international market exposure to foreign investment. This is important since it reveals a great deal about the likely external demands and pressures they face from international governmental bodies and from transnational business interests.

As already noted above, states compete in various ways to capture inward investment and they face different pressures from international governmental organizations, with the highest level of external governmental pressure applied to those economies that are more heavily indebted or dependent on foreign aid. Transnational corporations (TNCs), meanwhile, are attracted to different economies for various reasons, from mineral extraction opportunities to cheap labour to new market opportunities. Countries thus face different forms of structural pressure and may need to compete differently as a result. The problem comes when states face the same kinds of prescriptive policies, especially from international actors, to steer public policies towards 'universal' business needs, generally informed by some flavour of neoliberalism, as highlighted below, regardless of the nature of their economies and their particular state of development. While business factors will likely help to shape social policy development, they may either promote or restrict the expansion of social policy depending on the particular conditions, including structural pressures and subsequent policy responses on the ground.

Thus, the current state of play with regards to investment, and the state's response to the investment environment, helps to shape social policy possibilities. The relative size of state versus private investment will be important, but the most important determinant of social policy is likely to depend on the volume and type of inward investment sought by states. Several issues are important here.

First, all states control a portion of annual investment, with some states undertaking the majority of total investment each year or controlling investment within particular sectors. While states may depend on private investment, the extent of this dependence varies from state to state. Most economies today are moving towards greater liberalization and greater dependence on indigenous and foreign investment, but some states continue to impose

Table 2.1 Investment regimes and social policies

	Lower international market exposure (IME)	**Medium IME**	**High IME**	**Highest IME**	**Managed IME**
Dominant sectors	Mineral extraction Agriculture	Agriculture Mineral extraction Apparel industry	Agriculture Apparel industry Technology Telecommunications	Higher technology Information Technology Industries (ITI) Research and development (R&D)	Agriculture Apparel industry Higher technology ITI R&D
Labour market requirements	Lower cost Lower skills	Lower cost Lower skills	Lower cost Mixed abilities High productivity	Higher literacy Technology	Mixed abilities
Main 'pull' for investors	Access to mineral reserves Ability to shape agricultural production	Raw materials Low-cost labour	Low-cost moderately skilled labour Consumer markets	High-skilled labour Consumer markets	Low-cost or high-skilled labour Access to new markets
Dependence on conditional foreign flows and aid	High	High	Low	–	–
Social welfare functions	Some education for human capital development	Some education for human capital development	Higher dependence on education High dependence on state-sponsored training	High dependence on state education and training for human capital development Some social protection	Human capital development as growth strategy

(*Continued*)

Table 2.1 Continued

	Lower international market exposure (IME)	**Medium IME**	**High IME**	**Highest IME**	**Managed IME**
Labour market regulations/ protection	Low	Low	Low-medium	Medium-high	–
Economies	Nigeria	Kenya Uganda	Mexico India	Czech Republic	China

Source: Compiled using World Bank data (2006, 2007).

tight controls on the shape and size of investment, especially with the mineral extraction industry. Control over lucrative oil markets has been used by some states to reduce their dependence on generating higher private investment and, in some instances, they have used the resources to boost some aspects of public provision. Hence, the extent to which states are limited by external foreign investment markets depends both on access and control over raw materials and policies shaping the pursuit of new investment. Also important here will be external pressures from IGOs and other governments, especially where conditionality is applied to grants and loans.

Second, the nature of inward investment is important. Inward investment designed to capture cheap, unskilled labour places downward pressures on social policy. On the other hand, policies to tap into lower cost but more highly skilled labour places upward pressure on states to invest in, and boost, educational programmes, at least to a sufficient degree to meet demand. Similarly, investment to extract raw materials and mineral reserves places different pressures on states, and different concerns for corporations, than investment to target new markets. To put it simply, investing in consumer markets requires the firm to embed itself socially and economically within communities for long-term gain; investing to export oil requires only legal protections to extract reserves for as long as they exist.

Third, the compatibility of social welfare provision with economic growth is largely determined by evolving business needs; yet for the reasons outlined above, business needs are themselves shaped by their political and economic contexts. For instance, businesses that are attracted to a region in order to exploit cheap labour require little in the way of skills. Firms that are attracted by market opportunities may become directly tied into the development or privatization of public services. They may also be boosted by some degree of economic redistribution and growing prosperity within an economy. Those that are attracted by access to low-cost but highly skilled labour will depend on good educational systems but relatively low-level labour regulations.

Thus, a nation's investment strategies help to shape corporate structural power *and* reveal a great deal about its ability to reconcile the need for investment with the promotion of social goals. This is confirmed if we examine how states themselves try to 'sell' themselves on the international stage. For this part of the analysis, a spread of countries that fit into the five different categories in Table 2.1 above were chosen: Uganda, Kenya, India, Mexico, the Czech Republic and China.

Each of these countries has well-developed bureaux designed to 'sell' their economies to outside investors. All six countries have witnessed an increase in foreign direct investment (FDI) since 1990, and each of them has a growing dependence on foreign investment.

If we take these six countries together, we clearly see the impact of the globalization of investment. While the emphasis is slightly different in each case, each of these economies tries hard to persuade potential investors that it offers the most cost-effective, advantageous, productive workforce. All of these countries have made efforts to liberalize their economies in order to capture greater levels of inward investment.

We can further investigate these issues if we consider the investment strategies of different economies. The importance of international investment flows to national economic growth strategies is illustrated clearly by the fact that the vast majority of governments have, since the early 1990s, set up investment bureaux which advertise investment opportunities to foreign capital.

Investment regimes

A common theme that runs through all the investment bureaux is the range of financial incentives offered by governments. Governments commonly provide tax breaks and some states openly advertise the subsidies on offer to inward investors. Because of the dominance of oil exploration within its economy, Nigeria places most emphasis on the continued scope for expansion within its oil fields and the incentives it provides to exporters. Uganda and Kenya also stress their unexploited mineral resources as an area for potential investment, but seek to emphasize other opportunities, for example, within manufacturing and newly privatized services. China and India emphasize their potential as growing consumer markets as well as relatively low-cost, high-skilled employment markets. Mexico and the Czech Republic, meanwhile, emphasize their locations as gateways to wealthy markets in the United States (US) and the European Union (EU) respectively. Most interesting here are the differences in emphasis placed on market liberalization and labour power, which are discussed below.

Economic liberalization

All of the economies examined here stress their liberalizing credentials and tendencies. The government of Nigeria states that it

> accepts the private sector as the engine of growth and the creator of wealth, while the government's major responsibility is to provide the enabling environment for the private investors to operate. In this regard, laws which had hitherto hindered private sector investments have been either amended or repealed and a national council on privatisation has been established to oversee orderly divestment to private operators in vital areas of the economy such as mining, transportation, electricity, telecommunications, petroleum and gas. (Embassy of the Federal Republic of Nigeria 2009)

The government of India, through its Investment Commission of India (ICI 2009), is similarly at pains to demonstrate its more liberal approach to FDI:

> The reform process has deregulated the economy and stimulated domestic and foreign investments, taking India firmly into the forefront of investment destinations. The Government, keen to promote investment in the country, has radically simplified and rationalised policies, procedures and regulatory aspects. Foreign investment is welcome in almost all sectors, except those of strategic concern (for instance, defence and atomic energy).

The government of Uganda states that:

> Most economic activities are fully liberalized and open to foreign investment. There are no restrictions to 100% foreign ownership of investments and no barriers to remittance of dividends. Uganda's shilling is fully convertible and has remained stable over the last years. The foreign exchange market is now wholly liberalized. [...] Uganda is now one of about only five countries in the whole of Africa that have no restrictions on capital amount transfers. (Uganda Investment Authority 2003)

And the government of Kenya

> has now fully liberalised its economy by removing all obstacles that previously hampered the free flow of trade and foreign private investment. (Kenya Investment Authority 2009a)

Sensing concerns about economic instability, the governments of Uganda and Kenya are also at pains to stress their long-term commitments to the private sector:

> The Uganda Government's economic strategy is to modernize the economy through relying on markets and the efforts of entrepreneurs as the basis for efficient and productive economic activity. Government's major role in Uganda's private sector driven economy is mainly to provide the necessary legal policy and physical infrastructure for private investment to flourish. (Uganda Investment Authority 2003)

> By African standards, Kenya has a very substantial private sector, including a significant number of foreign investors ... and is touted as one of the most resilient in the world. The country has always been a market economy, and it escaped both the dislocation caused in Uganda by the expulsion of the Asians in the late 1970s and the problems created by the socialist experiment in Tanzania. (Kenya Investment Authority 2009b)

China, in contrast, stresses the continued important role of the public sector:

> In line with the requirements of releasing and developing the productive forces, we must uphold and improve the basic economic system, with public ownership playing a dominant role. (NPC 2002)

China is clearly in a different position than most other countries in that it holds key advantages for foreign investors that other economies do not. An increasingly skilled, low-cost labour market, a rapidly expanding economy with one-tenth of the world's consumers, continuing political and economic stability despite the lack of democracy, and an important 'bridge', in the form of Hong Kong, between China's evolving market economy and the liberalized global economy. In recent years, quite uniquely, investors have been falling over themselves to gain access to relatively tightly (in global terms) controlled markets.

As an economy within the EU, the Czech Republic offers an altogether safer and more predictable investment environment. Here, concerns are not so much over the country's commitment to market liberalism, but market opportunities within the world's largest free-trade area.

Labour markets

The cost and quality of labour power are central to national investment strategies. Depending on the nature of potential investors, states place different emphases on costs, flexibility and skills. Nigeria, for instance, keen to increase the number of people employed within historically low employing investment sectors, including mineral extraction, offers significant tax relief, of up to 15 per cent, for those with more than 1,000 employees. India, with its eye on developing its high-tech sectors, places greater emphasis on its 'competitively' priced, highly skilled, English-speaking workforce and management. The Mexican government's pro-investment bureau, Pro México, states that its workforce, in keeping with its strategy of maintaining cost advantages for exporting US firms, is:

> Young, abundant, skilled, well educated and fast to learn new skills, as well as eager to fulfill any labor requirement. (Pro México 2009)

Pro México also promotes the flexibility and high productivity of its workforce and the eagerness of local states to fully equip workers for employment with foreign investors:

> The working population in Mexico has consistently demonstrated that it can perform any job it has being asked to do by foreign investors. The

> local authorities are fully aware of the specialized labor needs of companies, and they have therefore helped satisfy such requirements by structuring and funding training programs and working in coordination with business. Mexican workers perform the specific jobs they are trained for successfully and often surpass the expectations of their employers, achieving higher levels of productivity than the workers of these companies in their original locations. [. . .] Mexico places its biggest and best asset at the disposal of all foreign investors, namely its people. (Pro México 2009)

The Kenyan bureau also emphasizes its

> large pool of professional workers . . . fluent in English and highly trained in various fields. Kenya holds the distinction of having the highest number of university and college educated English speaking professionals in East Africa. (Kenya Investment Authority 2009b)

Again, emphasizing its desire to capture higher-tech industries within the EU, the Czech Republic emphasizes its move away from low-cost, low-skilled labour markets:

> Gone are the days when the Czech Republic attracted foreign investors primarily due to the country's inexpensive labour. Investors' interest [in technology] is underpinned primarily by the effective labour market, job applicants' level of education, and high-quality universities and their ability to responds to companies' real-world needs. The country's developed education system, a component part of which is comprised of universities with histories dating back several centuries, guarantees that companies in the Czech Republic have an abundant supply of graduates from the technical, economic and other fields. (CzechInvest 2008)

> The Czech Republic is interested in advancing from the stage at which it was attractive mainly for setting up primary production and assembly plants, to projects that place strong emphasis on top-quality specialists and a stable business environment. (CzechInvest 2008)

Few countries highlight the importance of social policies other than education, in utilizing or attracting investment, although China stated that one of its economic goals, alongside economic development, was to 'steadily uplift the people's living standards' (NPC 2002).

More typical is the Thai bureau's highlighting of education and health services in order to outline how services would benefit foreign investors:

> A great number of international schools and colleges offer world-class education. In terms of healthcare, the country has developed a good

> reputation globally, due to its internationally qualified doctors and medical staff, and modern facilities and equipment. It is so good that one of the fastest-rising tourism sectors is medical tourism, with international patients visiting Thailand to take advantage of Thailand's world-class and extremely affordable health care system. (Thailand Board of Investment 2009)

Business investment and provision: opportunities and harms

For the reasons already discussed, one of the key reasons why business is powerful is because businesses are so central to economic growth and development. Social policy, in turn, is highly dependent on economic growth. Hence, business investment brings a great many opportunities. This is even more the case where individuals do not have access to state welfare. In such instances, the behaviour of corporations, including their provision of services to their employees and impact on their local communities, is extremely important. For this reason, a great deal of the discussion of business and social policy within developing countries has tended to focus on the social as well as economic roles and responsibilities of firms (see UNRISD 2008), generally referred to as corporate social responsibility (CSR). CSR describes a range of business initiatives and policies that contribute positively to the welfare of a company's stakeholders, whether employees, consumers or their communities, while maintaining the interests of another set of corporate stakeholders – its shareholders. International business organizations have encouraged companies to promote themselves as socially responsible organizations in order to foster 'peaceful conditions, legal certainty and good human relations' (ICC 2002) and 'credibility and trust amongst stakeholders' (ERT 2001) as they have played a key role in negotiating international agreements that define good corporate citizenship (Farnsworth 2005). Moreover, some companies and 'philanthropists' (most notably, Bill Gates, Warren Buffet and George Soros) have donated billions of pounds through global philanthropic trusts to fund various 'good' causes. While CSR garners support from a number of business and non-business actors, however, it also attracts a strong degree of scepticism for being little more than a corporate public relations stunt. Moreover, levels of CSR are highly dependent on profitability and are undermined by economic slowdowns. As a result, CSR is not a credible alternative to appropriate levels of state regulation and good quality public provision.

What the CSR debate has done is point to the various ways in which firms benefit or harm their various stakeholders. While some have argued that corporations are inherently harmful (Bakan 2004), others take a more moderate view, arguing that the extent to which business organizations are harmful depends on a number of variables: the regulatory regime in which they operate; the ownership of the firm (whether it is a publicly floated company and faces shareholder pressure to boost sales and profits or whether it is a private business following its own internal logic); prevailing sector standards and practices; the national regulations imposed by the host country; the relative strength of trade unions and other activist groups; and the extent of public scrutiny. A firm's options are also shaped by its brands and the particular niche they occupy within given markets.

All of this is important, of course, to the experiences of employees and various other 'stakeholders' within developing economies. The terms and conditions of employment within the context of development, for instance, can be more important to overall levels of wellbeing than minimal provision by the state. The activities of corporations within local areas can also have a large impact on health and wellbeing, both positive and negative. The existence of relatively weak international regulations on corporate behaviour, coupled with more open economies, has, for many, increased the harmful effects of business activities. Hence, there is a tension between the very real benefits brought to a country or region by investing TNCs – by way of increased employment, incomes, tax revenues, improvements to infrastructure and the provision of goods and services – and the risks they present, especially where political environments fail to adequately regulate corporate behaviour. Moreover, in environments that fail to adequately regulate their competitors, other firms face greater incentives to drive down their own standards.

Opposition to the production and trading practices of TNCs commonly fall into four categories. First, TNCs are accused of driving down employment standards. A number of exposés of the employment practices of large corporate clothing manufacturers and retailers, including Nike and The Gap, and Walmart and other large supermarkets, have accused TNCs of exploiting low labour regulations in developing countries and paying poverty wages to vulnerable employees, including young women and children. The exploitation of workers is made worse by the fact that desperate workers often reside many miles from home and know that they can be easily replaced if they refuse to work as requested. Already weak regulations governing working ages, working hours and pay rates are therefore tested to the limits and are frequently flouted.

Second, corporations that invest in corrupt and/or undemocratic states are accused of undermining workers' rights and colluding with regimes that systematically torture and kill opposition groups, including trade unionists. Just as the withdrawal of capital can 'punish' states that fail to deliver favourable policies, so new or continued investment can signal corporate approval for the policies of a state. Shell, Coca-Cola and Nestlé, among others, have been accused of colluding with governments that systematically torture and murder their own citizens, including those that have protested against these same companies. In Colombia, an investigation by Amnesty International in 2007 reported death threats and assassinations of trade unionists, and members of their families, who worked in bottling plants owned by Coca-Cola. Amnesty reported that a total of eight union leaders from four separate Coca-Cola bottling sites in Colombia were assassinated between 1994 and 2002 (Amnesty International 2007).

Third, the pursuit of sales or new markets can lead corporations to engage in inappropriate or illegal practices. Corruption, in the form of corporate bribes to government officials, has been considered to be such a problem in the past that it triggered moves at the international level to impose effective controls on them. Nevertheless, BAE Systems has recently been accused of giving multi-million pound bribes to the government of Saudi Arabia in order to secure major arms deals (Leigh and Evans 2007). Not only do such practices perpetuate similar practices and help to support corrupt regimes, they also undermine the interests of other corporations.

In some instances, products have been inappropriately extended to new areas to the detriment of consumers. The most obvious case here is the example of baby milk formula. A lack of access to the clean water necessary to make formula milk directly contributes to the deaths of some 105 million babies each year, according to UNICEF (2001). The outcry as a result of these avoidable deaths has led to an international ban on the marketing of baby milk formula and one of the longest international corporate boycotts against Nestlé, which is accused of repeatedly engaging in questionable marketing campaigns in a number of developing countries (Richter 2001).

TNCs are also accused of seeking to profit from the inappropriate privatization of certain services. Most controversially, water privatization has led to the denial of fresh water to many of the poorest consumers, restrictions on water gathering and higher charges for access to water.

Fourth, TNCs are accused of dangerous and environmentally damaging practices resulting from cost-cutting and neglect. The most oft-cited example here, and still the most significant, is the Bhopal disaster in India in 1984.

The issue of CSR is a very interesting one because it firmly ties production and sales practices within developing economies to policies and practices within developed ones. While globalization appears to increase the incentives for corporations and governments to undervalue the health and safety of people and the environment, the weight of pressure felt by corporations to cut corners and ill-treat workers depends, however, to a great extent on the firm in question: whether it is a publicly floated company and faces shareholder pressure to boost sales and profits or whether it is a private business following its own internal logic; prevailing sectoral standards and practices; the national regulations imposed by the host country; the relative strength of trade unions and other activist groups; and the extent of public scrutiny. A firm's options are also shaped by its brands and the particular niche they occupy within given markets. Ethical brands, for instance, trade on the fact that they engage in more socially responsible production. Yet, even where corporations do assert their ethical credentials, they are rather selective in their choice of 'good' causes. Company policies on the environment and instances of company giving tend to be highlighted most enthusiastically; in contrast, the employment conditions of those that help to make or sell their products are seldom discussed.

Conclusions

This chapter has examined business power and influence and its implications for the evolution of social policy in developing countries, outlining how and why business is especially important to social welfare within developing countries. Transformations in the global economy, including the rise in the importance of TNCs, and growing state dependency on corporate investment, are important but context-specific factors in human welfare and the capacity for states to develop welfare solutions. The international community plays an important role here as well.

While issues such as business power, influence, the needs of capital and social welfare are widely variable and often ambiguous in terms of their impact, some issues seem clear. First, the international context is increasingly important to developing discourse on social policy, and business needs are argued to require greater consideration in social policy formation according to global social policy prescriptions. Yet, international social policy discourse actually serves to strengthen corporate structural power and stall the development of domestic social policies within the context of development. Weak international regulations on corporate behaviour add to corporate harm within nations and place greater downward pressure on states, especially those in a weaker bargaining position when it comes to inward investment.

Second, generic business preferences for social policy appear to be clear enough – but the specifics are more variable. Moreover, business social policy needs are, this chapter argues, partly manufactured by state institutions and existing social policies (or the lack of them). Structural theories often focus on the power of the 'investment strike' for states currently holding investment. However, there is another dimension to structural power: the pressures states are under when they compete for new investment. States compete in different ways, and on the basis of different 'offerings'. Where states compete on the basis of cheap labour or mineral reserves, a different set of pressures stems from this for future policy-making than if a state competes on the basis of higher skills, productivity or labour market stability. Similarly, a corporation investing for short-term access to mineral reserves will clearly approach its 'investment' differently from one investing to access new markets.

Third, structural influences tend to steer governments and IGOs, towards taken-for-granted views of what is in the interests of business – but national economic systems require more nuanced approaches to social and economic policy design. Developing economies need control and room for manoeuvre so that social policy can respond to diverse human and business needs within an economy. The dominance of foreign or big business needs in social policy considerations does not necessarily foster social policies which are best suited to social protection or best fit with the needs of domestic capital. The risk is that developing economies become locked into particular investment regimes that, in turn, lock them into particular social policy regimes. Further work is needed, however, if we are to more fully get to grips with the impact of business on social policy in developing countries. In particular, we need to further investigate the divergent needs of capital, the impact and sustainability of social policy within different investment regimes and the needs of local business people and business organizations in relation to social policy formation on the ground.

Notes

1. Farnsworth (2004); Farnsworth and Holden (2006); Hacker and Pierson (2002); Vogel (1989).
2. Gough (2004); Pierson (1995); Vogel (1989).
3. Korten (1997); O'Brien (2002); Stiglitz (2002, 1998); Tesner (2000); Utting (2006).
4. See Chapter 7 by Durand in this volume for an analysis of a revolving-door scenario in the national context of Peru.
5. In collaboration with several bilateral agencies, the World Bank organized the conference on 'New Frontiers of Social Policy: Development in a Globalizing World' in Arusha, Tanzania, on 12–15 December 2005.

References

Amnesty International (2007) *Colombia: Killings, Arbitrary Detentions, and Death Threats – The Reality of Trade Unionism in Colombia AMR 23/001/2007* (London: Amnesty International).

Bakan, J. (2004) *The Corporation* (New York: Free Press).

BIAC (Business and Industry Advisory Committee to the OECD) (1998) *Meeting of the Employment, Labour and Social Affairs Committee at Ministerial Level on Social Policy* (Paris: BIAC).

——— (2002), *Employment and Learning Challenges for the 21st Century* (Paris: BIAC).

Bonnet, K. (1985) 'Corporatism and Industrial Policy', in A. Cawson (ed.), *Organised Interests and the State: Studies in Meso Corporatism* (London: Sage).

Coates, D. (1984) 'The Political Power of Capital', in D. Coates (ed.), *The Context of British Politics* (London: Hutchinson).

Cox, R. (1983) 'Gramsci, Hegemony and International Relations: An Essay in Method', *Millennium*, 12 (2), 162–75.

CzechInvest (2008) *Investment Climate in the Czech Republic* (Prague: Ministry of Industry and Trade of the Czech Republic).

Dahl, R. (1961) *Who Governs? Democracy and Power in an American City* (New Haven: Yale University Press).

Embassy of the Federal Republic of Nigeria (2009) *Investment Incentives in Nigeria* (Washington, DC: Embassy of the Federal Republic of Nigeria), available at www.nigeriaembassyusa.org/invest_incent.shtml (accessed 20 May 2009).

ERT (European Round Table of Industrialists) (2001) *ERT Position on Corporate Social Responsibility and Response to Commission Green Paper 'Promoting a European Framework for Corporate Social Responsibility'* (Brussels: European Round Table of Industrialists).

Esping-Andersen, G. (1990) *The Three Worlds of Welfare Capitalism* (Cambridge: Polity Press).

Estevez-Abe, M., T. Iversen and D. Soskice (2001) 'Social Protection and the Formation of Skills: A Reinterpretation of the Welfare State', in P. A. Hall and D. Vogel (eds), *Varieties of Capitalism: The Institutional Foundations of Comparative Advantage* (Oxford: Oxford University Press).

Farnsworth, K. (2004) *Corporate Power and Social Policy in a Global Economy: British Welfare under the Influence* (Bristol: The Policy Press).

——— (2005) 'International Class Conflict and Social Policy', *Social Policy and Society*, 4 (2), 217–26.

——— (2008) 'Business and Global Social Policy Formation', in N. Yeates (ed.), *Understanding Global Social Policy* (Bristol: Policy Press).

Farnsworth, K. and C. Holden (2006) 'The Business-Social Policy Nexus: Corporate Power and Corporate Inputs into Social Policy', *Journal of Social Policy*, 35 (3), July, 473–94.

Gough, I. (2000) *Global Capital, Human Needs and Social Policies* (Basingstoke: Palgrave Macmillan, 2000).

——— (2004) 'Welfare Regimes in Development Contexts: A Global and Regional Analysis', in I. Gough and G. Wood (eds), *Insecurity and Welfare Regimes in Asia, Africa and Latin America* (Cambridge: Cambridge University Press).

Hacker, J. S. and P. Pierson (2002) 'Business Power and Social Policy: Employers and the Formation of the American Welfare State', *Politics and Society*, 30 (2), 277–325.

Hall, P. A. and D. Soskice (eds) (2001) *Varieties of Capitalism: The Institutional Foundations of Comparative Advantage* (Oxford: Oxford University Press).

Hirst, P. and G. Thompson (1996) *Globalisation in Question: The International Economy and the Possibilities of Governance* (Cambridge, Polity Press).

ICC (International Chamber of Commerce) (2002) *Business in Society: Making a Positive and Responsible Contribution* (Paris: International Chamber of Commerce).

ICI (Investment Commission of India) (2009) *Investment Opportunities and Incentives* (New Delhi: Investment Commission of India), at: http://business.gov.in/outerwin.htm?id=http://www.investmentcommission.in/index.html (accessed 8 April 2009).

Jordan, G. (1991) *The Commercial Lobbyists: Politics for Profit in Britain* (Aberdeen: Aberdeen University Press).

Kenya Investment Authority (2009a) *Fully Liberalised Economy* (Nairobi: Kenya Investment Authority), at: www.investmentkenya.com/index.php?option=com_content&task=view&id=42&Itemid=38 (accessed 8 April 2009).

——— (2009b) *Why Kenya?* (Nairobi: Kenya Investment Authority), at: www.investmentkenya.com/index.php?option=com_content&task=blogcategory&id=15&Itemid=38 (accessed 8 March 2009).

Korpi, W. (1983) *The Democratic Class Struggle* (London: Routledge and Kegan Paul).

——— (1989) 'Power, Politics and State Autonomy in the Development of Social Citizenship: Social Rights During Sickness in Eighteen OECD Countries since 1930', *American Sociological Review*, 54 (3), 309–28.

Korten, D. (1997) *The United Nations and the Corporate Agenda*, at www.pcdf.org/1997/PKortenUNcorporate.htm (accessed 22 May 2009).

Leigh, David and Rob Evans (2007) 'BAE Accused of Secretly Paying £1bn to Saudi Prince', *The Guardian*, at: www.guardian.co.uk/world/2007/jun/07/bae1 (accessed June 2007).

Lindblom, C. E. (1977) *Politics and Markets* (New York: Basic Books).

Mann, M. (1993) *The Sources of Social Power: Vol. II: The Rise of Classes and Nation-States, 1760–1914* (Cambridge: Cambridge University Press).

Mehrotra, S. and E. Delamonica (2005) 'The Private Sector and Privatization in Social Services: Is the Washington Consensus "Dead"?', *Global Social Policy*, 5 (2), 141–74.

Miliband, R. (1969) *The State in Capitalist Society* (London: Quartet Books).

Moen, E. (2003) *Private Sector Involvement in Policy Making in a Poverty Stricken Liberal Democracy* (Oslo: Centre for Development and the Environment, University of Oslo).

NPC (National People's Congress) (2002) *Jiang Zemin's Report to the 16th CPC National Congress* (Beijing: National Congress of the Communist Party of China), at: http://news.xinhuanet.com/english/2002-11/18/content_632554.htm (accessed 6 April 2009).

O'Brien, R. (2002) 'Organizational Politics, Multilateral Economic Organizations And Social Policy', *Global Social Policy*, 2 (2) (2002) 141–61.

O'Connor, J. (1973) *The Fiscal Crisis of the State* (New York: St Martins Press).

Offe, C. and V. Ronge (1984) 'Theses on the Theory of the State', in C. Offe (ed.), *Contradictions of the Welfare State* (London: Hutchinson).

Offe, C. and H. Wiesenthal (1980) 'Two Logics of Collective Action: Theoretical Notes on Social Class and Organizational Form', in M. Zeitlin (ed.), *Political Power and Social Theory*, Volume 1 (Greenwich, CT: JAI Press).

Pierson, P. (1995) *The Scope and Nature of Business Power: Employers and the American Welfare State, 1900–1935*, mimeo.

Piven, F. F. and R. A. Cloward (1971) *Regulating the Poor: The Functions of Public Welfare* (New York: Pantheon Books).

Pro México (2009) *Why Mexico?* (Mexico City: Pro México), at: www.promexico.gob.mx/wb/Promexico/why_mexico (accessed 20 May 2009).

Przeworski, A. and M. Wallerstein (1988) 'Structural Dependence of the State on Capital', *American Political Science Review*, 82 (1), 11–29.

Richter, J. (2001) *Holding Corporations Accountable: Corporate Conduct, International Codes and Citizen Action* (London: Zed Books).

Schneider, B. R. (2007) 'Business Politics and Social Policy in Latin America', paper presented at the Conference on Business, Social Policy and Corporate Political Influence in Developing Countries, Geneva, 12–13 November.

Sklair, L. (2001) *The Transnational Capitalist Class* (Oxford: Blackwell Publishers).

Skocpol, T. (1979) *States and Social Revolutions* (Cambridge: Cambridge University Press).

Stiglitz, J. (1998) *More Instruments and Broader Goals: Moving Towards the Post-Washington Consensus*, WIDER Annual Lecture (Helsinki: UNU–WIDER).

——— (2002) *Globalization and its Discontents* (London: Norton House).

Tesner, S., with the collaboration of Georg Kell (1990) *The United Nations and Business: A Partnership Recovered* (Basingstoke: Palgrave Macmillan).

Thailand Board of Investment (2009) *Why Thailand?* (Bangkok: Thailand Board of Investment), at:. www.boi.go.th/english/why/reasons_to_invest_here.asp (accessed 8 April 2009).

Thelen, K. and S. Steinmo (1992) 'Historical Institutionalism in Comparative Politics', in S. Steinmo, K. Thelen and F. Longstreth (eds), *Structuring Politics: Historical Institutionalism in Comparative Analysis* (Cambridge: Cambridge University Press).

Uganda Investment Authority (2003) *An Investment Guide to Uganda* (Kampala: Uganda Investment Authority), at: www.ugandainvest.com/guide.htm (accessed 8 April 2009).

UNICEF (United Nations Children's Fund) (2001) *The State of the World's Children* (New York: UNICEF).

UNRISD (United Nations Research Institute for Social Development) (2008) *Business, Social Policy and Corporate Political Influence in Developing Countries*, Conference News No. 22 (Geneva: UNRISD).

Utting, P. (ed.) (2006) *Reclaiming Development Agendas: Knowledge, Power and International Policy Making* (Basingstoke: Palgrave Macmillan).

Vogel, D. (1989) *Fluctuating Fortunes: The Political Power of Business in America* (New York: Basic Books).

Wade, R. H. (2002) 'US Hegemony and the World Bank: The Fight over People and Ideas', *Review of International Political Economy*, 9 (2), 215–43.

Wetherly, P. (1995) *Marxism, History and the State: A Critical Examination of Marxist Theory with Particular Reference to Functional Explanation* (Middlesbrough: University of Teesside).

Wilensky, W. (1975) *The Welfare State and Equality: Structural and Ideological Roots of Public Expenditure* (Berkeley: University of California Press).

World Bank (2004) *World Development Report 2005: A Better Investment Climate for Everyone* (Washington, DC: World Bank).

——— (2006) *World Development Indicators* (Washington, DC: World Bank).

——— (2007) *World Development Report 2008: Agriculture for Development* (Washington, DC: World Bank).

Yeates, N. (1999) 'Social Politics and Policy in an Era of Globalisation: Critical Reflections', *Social Policy and Administration*, 33 (4), 372–93.

3

Liberalization, Business–State Relations and Labour Policy in India

Kanta Murali[1]

Introduction

India's adoption of market reforms in 1991 signalled a major shift in its development strategy. An interventionist, inward orientation gave way to a more external outlook and a decentralized policy-making structure. Private investment displaced public investment as the engine of growth and this, in turn, had considerable consequences for the nature and content of policy making in the country. While the reforms of 1991 were far-reaching, authors such as Kohli (2004, 2006a, 2006b) and Rodrik and Subramanian (2005) suggest that the initial signs of a shift in India's development strategy were noticeable in the 1980s. Whatever the specific timeline of India's economic liberalization, there is little doubt that the process has had major economic and political ramifications. One area that has undergone a striking transformation since 1991 has been the relationship between the state and business. In broad terms, this chapter is an attempt to understand the evolution of business–government relations in the era of economic liberalization in India and its subsequent impact on one area of public policy – labour policy. Specifically it tries to answer the following questions: How have economic reforms affected business–state relations? What impact has this had on policy-making more generally and labour policy more specifically? What constrains corporate influence in these policy spheres and what is required to bring business preferences in line with the goal of inclusive development?

For authors such as Kohli (2006a: 1251), the Indian state since 1980 has 'slowly but surely embraced Indian capital as its main ruling ally'. The 1991 market reforms served to strengthen this alliance further and both the degree and nature of business influence differ considerably when compared with the licensing era. Subnational competition for private investment has resulted in greater pressure on regional[2] governments to create investor-friendly environments. In addition, the scope of business collective action, its organizational capacity and channels of access to the government have all increased considerably since 1991. Driven largely by concerns of competitiveness, business has lobbied for several reforms in the sphere of labour policy but has enjoyed mixed results. The findings of this chapter reinforce the conclusion that authors such as Jenkins (2004), Anant et al. (2006), Nagaraj (2004) and Bhattacharjea (2006) have drawn in terms of labour policy. While formal legislative changes in labour laws have largely been absent in the liberalization era, a process of de facto reform in some areas has been taking place and this has provided firms with more flexibility than a simple reading of the law would suggest.

What accounts for this variable outcome? On the one hand, business's structural and instrumental power has expanded since 1991 and has pushed governments in the direction of more pro-business measures. On the other, explicit labour reform has faced political obstacles. This chapter identifies India's electoral politics as the main source of constraints to business influence. While labour reform has appeared on the policy agenda of several governments at the centre, the nature of coalition politics at the national level has prevented a consensus on more pro-business measures from developing. There has also been a trend in Indian politics where parties increasingly espouse divergent views when in power and in opposition. High levels of electoral competition since the early 1990s have meant that parties are wary of alienating key constituencies, particularly those that inhabit what Varshney (1999) refers to as the realm of 'mass politics'. While organized labour is a relatively privileged section of the total workforce, issues pertaining to it have historically fallen into the 'mass politics' category (Jenkins 2004). In a poor, vibrant democracy such as India, it is unlikely that governments can *overtly* ignore mass concerns and act solely at the behest of business interests. One point needs to be highlighted. While electoral politics serves as a check on the growing influence of business, it does not necessarily act as a catalyst for more inclusive developments where groups such as labour are concerned. It is the tension[3] then between growing business power and electoral politics that largely explains the current situation, which is optimal neither for labour nor for business.

The second section outlines the broader economic policy regime in the licensing and liberalization eras and then describes the changes in various aspects of the business–government relationship. The third section looks at this influence specifically on labour policy. The fourth section concludes by evaluating the role of business in labour policy, identifying constraints to its influence and examining the policy implications that arise from this analysis. This chapter is primarily based on interviews[4] conducted with business and labour representatives, as well as archival research on several Indian newspapers and magazines and documents of business associations. Secondary sources were used to supplement this material.

The reforms process in India and its impact on business[5]–government relations

Any attempt to trace the evolution of business–government relations in India first necessitates a broader understanding of the policy environment. After independence in 1947, India chose an inward-looking economic strategy based on import-substitution and a preference for heavy industry. The state would occupy the 'commanding heights' of the economy and the private sector was to be controlled, regulated and protected by the state, primarily through the industrial licensing system – the 'licence-permit raj'. While India was relatively unique among developing countries at the time in that it had a fairly developed indigenous business class that had been incorporated into the nationalist movement, the espoused ideological proclivity of India's ruling elite to socialism led to a distrust of business in general and made for difficult relations with private entrepreneurs (Kochanek 1996; Kohli 2004). Despite these ambiguities, economic achievements in the Nehruvian period were marked by commendable levels of industrial growth as well as considerable industrial diversification (Panagariya 2008).

The relatively solid economic performance in the first 15 years after independence gave way to a sharp slowdown in overall levels of growth and public investment by the mid-1960s. It was against this economic background and general political uncertainty that Indira Gandhi came to power in 1967 and, for various political imperatives, chose to heighten the socialist and populist rhetoric and pursue policies that increased state control of the private sector. Average gross domestic product (GDP) growth between 1965 and 1981 declined to under 3.2 per cent, the infamous 'Hindu rate of growth' (Panagariya 2008). In part, inability to deliver on economic promises created a tremendously volatile political situation, and Indira Gandhi's response was to resort to an even more dictatorial style, which would reach its culmination in the Emergency of 1975–77. The Congress was subsequently unseated from power in New Delhi for the first time in 1977, but the fractious Janata coalition that replaced it was short-lived.

Rodrik and Subramanian (2005) and Kohli (2006a) have suggested that, on returning to power in 1980, Indira Gandhi instituted a pro-business policy shift. She toned down her populist rhetoric and implemented measures aimed at improving private sector efficiency (Kohli 1990, 2006a). After his mother's assassination in 1984, Rajiv Gandhi came to power and began by claiming a shift away from the old system. He inducted several new ministers and a group of economic advisers who were in favour of decreasing state control in the economy. One of the biggest breaks with the past was the 1985 budget, which, by delicensing 25 sectors, allowing 'broad-banding' or diversification in select industries and easing restrictions on large firms, introduced an element of internal competition. However, Rajiv Gandhi's economic policies soon met with strong opposition and by 1987 the reform process was virtually abandoned (Kohli 1990).

Despite the reform setbacks, India exhibited strong growth rates in the 1980s. This was, however, accompanied by a steady decline in its fiscal position. In the midst of the precarious political situation in 1991, the balance of payments went into freefall. The first Gulf War dealt a dual blow in the form of increased oil prices and decreased overseas remittances. India's credit ratings were downgraded, leading to short-term capital flight. The assassination of Rajiv Gandhi in May 1991 resulted in more political uncertainty and, by June 1991, the country had foreign exchange reserves sufficient for only two weeks of imports. It was at this point that the newly elected minority government of Narasimha Rao, under then Finance Minister Manmohan Singh, approached the International Monetary Fund (IMF) for a standby loan and announced broad reform measures that would come to have a defining impact on India's political economy.

The reforms of 1991 virtually abolished the industrial licensing system, and this meant that the central government effectively ceded control of private investment decisions. State governments became major players in the economy, competing with each other for both foreign and domestic private investment. Sectors of the economy where the public sector had enjoyed a monopoly were opened to the private sector. Measures of import substitution were eliminated. Ideologically one of the biggest changes involved easing the entry of foreign investment. Financial reforms were also far-reaching and in accordance with India's accession to the World Trade Organization (WTO), quantitative restrictions were dismantled. The import policy regime was also rationalized.

The evolution of business–government relations

Having laid out the broad post-independence policy framework, this section will trace the evolution of business–government relations. Following the theoretical approaches used by Haggard et al. (1997),[6] this section will show that business's role 'as firm' as well as individual connections between entrepreneurs and politicians were most influential before 1991. In the post-1991 environment, the focus has shifted to business's role 'as capital' and 'as association'. Business leverage in public policy has been enhanced both through its collective engagement in the policy process, as well as through the need for governments to attract private investment.

Business and the state in the licensing era – 1947 to 1991

Arguably, the most publicized aspect of the business–government connection prior to liberalization was the state's micromanagement of investment decisions through the licensing system. In addition, India's policy-makers at the time of independence decided to place the public sector at the forefront of the economy. While it would appear that the private sector was completely marginalized during the 'licence-permit raj', India's *dirigisme* effectively shielded domestic industry from both external and internal competition.

After independence, business interaction with government occurred both at the collective level and the firm level. At the collective level, it was represented by numerous chambers of commerce, trade and industry associations and employers' associations. There were two peak associations until the 1990s – the Federation of Indian Chambers of Commerce and Industry (FICCI) and the Associated Chambers of Commerce and Industry of India (ASSOCHAM), which were both established prior to independence. FICCI and ASSOCHAM were autonomous from political parties and, by the standards of the developing world in the postwar period, could be considered as well-organized and well-funded examples of interest group articulation (Kochanek 1974). In addition to FICCI and ASSOCHAM, a third peak association – the Confederation of Indian Industry (CII) – emerged in 1992.

In terms of their formal policy role, business associations participated in a consultative capacity in various forums, such as government committees and advisory groups, but their function in these spheres was largely symbolic prior to liberalization. The strength of collective business activity prior to 1991 was restricted for many reasons, including low incentives to invest in collective associations due to private sector dependence on the government to maintain monopoly profits, the prevalence of widespread sector-wise lobbying and the government's control of the policy agenda. The role of business was reactive and its influence on the broader direction and content of public policy was substantially constrained (Kochanek 1996).

Compared to its collective role, business was much more effective in individual lobbying, and firms were successful in using resources and personal connections for particularistic benefits under the 'licence-quota raj'. One of the tactics most frequently used to gain a competitive advantage was pre-emption where industrial licenses would be applied for but, once granted, these would remain unused. Kochanek (1996) suggests there were distinct phases in the system of particularistic lobbying. Business had numerous opportunities to expand under Nehru, despite the state's socialist rhetoric. Indira Gandhi's first three terms in office were characterized by a tightening of restrictions on the private sector and 'briefcase politics'. For Kochanek, this implied a patron–client relationship where funds from industry (often black money) were exchanged with the Congress party in return for licences and permits. The third phase for Kochanek began in the late 1970s when 'briefcase politics' spread beyond the licensing system to public sector civilian contracts, military contracts and infrastructure projects.

The transformation of the role of business in public policy

The economic liberalization process received a fillip under Rajiv Gandhi, though the measures enacted under him were short-lived. The sentiment within the business community itself is that Rajiv Gandhi left a lasting impact in terms of government attitude to business.[7] His direct encouragement also saw the Association of Indian Engineering Industry (AIEI) transform itself into a broader industry organization (the Confederation of Engineering Industry/CEI), which began to serve as an apex association for the manufacturing industry. In 1992, CEI became an all-industry apex body – the CII, which arguably has come to be the most influential industry body.

The scope and coherence of business collective action The three apex associations of big business, CII, FICCI and ASSOCHAM, along with the information technology industry trade association – the National Association of Software and Services Companies (NASSCOM) – have grown in visibility and influence since the mid-1990s. In terms of membership, the three peak organizations are predominantly organs of large and medium-sized firms but also include small firms, multinationals, as well as some public sector enterprises. These bodies are autonomous and industry-financed through various categories of membership. Currently, FICCI has over 1,500 corporate entities and 500 chambers of commerce and business associations as its members, accounting directly or indirectly for more than 250,000 business units.[8] CII has 7,576 direct members in its ranks and indirectly accounts for 83,000 members.[9] ASSOCHAM represents over 200,000 units through direct and indirect membership.[10] NASSCOM in 2007 had over 1,200 direct members.[11]

The transformation in collective action is most evident in the expansion of the scope of activities that business associations now perform. This has prompted authors such as Sinha (2005a) to term India's apex associations as 'developmental' in nature. As the demands of a liberalizing economy grew, business associations began providing their members with collective goods targeted to improving their competitiveness. These have included training and consultancy on a variety of aspects, such as quality management, logistic support systems, energy issues and environmental assessments. As discussed in the section below 'Skill Development', the shortage of suitably skilled workers has also prompted business associations to focus on skills development.

The information function of business associations has also rapidly proliferated since 1991. Major business associations now include policy briefs, market research surveys, seminars and trade fairs in their repertoire and there is greater exchange of information between the government and industry associations than in the past. Government is also more responsive in ascertaining industry feedback in certain policy areas.[12] There is a conscious effort on the part of government and industry to try to create an image of 'India Inc.' to the outside world. A highly publicized example of this type of campaign was the 'India Everywhere' brand-building exercise at the Davos World Economic Forum in 2006, undertaken jointly by the Ministry of Commerce and Industry and the CII.

The Davos campaign also signifies the broader role business has been playing in the international realm. Since the early 1990s business groups have been included as part of India's official foreign delegations accompanying the Prime Minister and President to various countries – a stark change from the previous era when non-governmental actors barring the media were largely ignored. There are indications that business played an active role in some instances – for example, as part of official delegations in several WTO rounds and in 'Track II' diplomacy with China and Pakistan in the 1990s.

In various areas of infrastructure, public–private partnerships (PPP) are becoming a common model of service delivery. Industry has been increasingly lobbying for the PPP model in infrastructure delivery and international donors have also been partial to this model. Business representatives argue that it is the poor quality of government delivery systems and local bureaucracy that was the motivating factor behind business involvement in PPPs.[13] Governments at the state and central levels have, in recent times, responded to industry's demands by creating pockets of high quality infrastructure known as the Special Economic Zones (SEZs).

While the involvement of business associations in a range of activities has expanded, how united is business as a collective entity in the liberalization era? In the past, both sector-based lobbying and individual lobbying undermined the efforts of business to articulate a common platform. The pay-off to sector-based and individual lobbying has reduced considerably since 1991, though both types of lobbying have not been eliminated entirely. Demands such as tax concessions and subsidies for certain areas are still prevalent. With simultaneous improvement in the internal capacities of these organizations, business has become much more proactive and coherent in articulating its demands and this has occurred alongside greater plurality within the business power structure. New economy and service sector firms have become more prominent while older industrial houses held complete sway under the 'licence-permit raj'. This in part reflected in the prominent role of associations such as CII and NASSCOM. While business associations are definitely more united than in the past, differences in orientation, style and strategy between the major associations continue to place limits on the degree of unity within business. Of the three apex organizations, CII is considered to have firms that are more 'modern' and 'outward-looking' (Kohli 2006b; Sinha 2005a). NASSCOM, which represents a new-economy sector that is significantly dependent on external markets, is even more outward-looking. In sum, differences between business associations arise periodically, but the level of unity within business is significantly higher than in the past and its demands are more coherent and consistent at a collective level.

Individual lobbying By eliminating the need for licences, the market reforms process vastly reduced individual lobbying but it would be naïve to suggest that such lobbying is entirely a thing of the past. In the early stages of liberalization, there were considerable policy ambiguities and lack of transparency in sectors such as infrastructure and this opened up avenues for individual lobbying (Kochanek 1996; Jenkins 1999). Governments at the state level have used tax concessions and land allocation as tools to attract private investment and there is little transparency surrounding such subsidies, leaving room for firm-level efforts. In addition, business representatives argue that those in charge continue to find various ways by which firms are required to approach individual ministers for permission and are 'taxed' for such approval.[14] Various central and state governments have also demonstrated the willingness to lobby for individual companies, particularly in the international realm, and this is best exemplified by the Indian government's efforts during Mittal Steel's takeover of Arcelor in 2006 and Tata Steel's acquisition of the Anglo-Dutch giant Corus.

Patterns of access and information exchange The tremendous growth in business association activity has provided new avenues for the state and collective organizations of capital to interact, potentially giving industry more channels to influence policy. Business associations are more proactive in articulating their policy demands and now produce a considerable volume of reports and communiqués. Information is also disseminated through trade fairs, summits and annual meetings, and attendance by high-ranking cabinet ministers and even prime ministers at such events is now commonplace. In what is seen as a break with the past, industry representatives interviewed for this study felt that there was a sea change in the government's attitude towards interacting with business in various forums. While events such as trade fairs and summits have increased visibility of business–government relations on the one hand, informal channels of access continue to be highly relevant. Representatives of one business association indicated that they met officials as high as the Prime Minister on a periodic basis to discuss various policy issues informally. In addition, associations admit that they maintain regular contact with Members of Parliament and bureaucrats. While the relative advantage of business in access to government compared with other interest groups is not new, this phenomenon seems to have intensified in the liberalization era.

Political funding The connection between business and the state in terms of political funding remains particularly opaque. Indira Gandhi banned company contributions to political parties in 1969, ushering in the 'briefcase politics' era (Kochanek 1996). There have since been some policy amendments but there continues to be little transparency. Parties were exempt from income and wealth tax in 1979, provided they filed annual returns including audited accounts with identities of their donors (Sridharan 2001). Sridharan points out that, in 1996, the Supreme Court noted that no major political party had filed annual returns since 1979 despite the fact they were required to do so. Rajiv Gandhi overturned the policy banning company contributions in 1985 and an amendment in the Companies Act was made to that effect. In theory, both the need for parties to file annual returns and the amendment to the Companies Act should have ensured some transparency. In practice, Sridharan points out that the overwhelming majority of contributions continue to be made through the black money route in order to protect identity and to circumvent the need for shareholder approval. Industry associations have made recommendations, such as state funding of elections, a common industry pool from which parties would receive funds and making contributions tax deductible, but none of these have been implemented so far. Industry associations have also chosen not to regulate any aspect of political funding of their members (Muralidharan and Mahalingam 1999; Venkatesan 1999). Prior to the 1998 general elections certain industrial conglomerates, such as the Tatas, the Aditya Birla group and the Mahindras, set up election trusts where a common pool of funds was distributed to all qualifying parties that met certain criteria. However, none of these measures seems to have had an impact.

The federal dimension of business–government relations While the central government dominated economic policy-making in the licensing era, states now play a major role. One of the most publicized aspects of liberalization is that states compete to attract foreign and domestic private investment.[15] Performances of states in terms of growth have been markedly dissimilar in the liberalization era (Ahluwalia 2000; Kohli 2006b). Several authors, including Ahluwalia (2000), Kohli (2006b) and Sinha (2005b), suggest that interstate growth differences are driven in large part by variation in levels of private investment and this in turn was due to both initial structural and institutional conditions as well as contrasting behaviour of state governments. Perceptions of business representatives interviewed in this chapter strongly confirmed differences in pro-business inclinations as well as investment climate factors across states. Factors suggested as important in location decisions include levels of infrastructure, human resource quality and availability, tax concessions and subsidies, the policy environment and levels of governance. When asked how states varied in pro-business attitudes, the dimensions that were most often identified as being relevant were 'responsiveness to business needs', efficiency and capability in policy implementation, and levels of corruption. In terms of responsiveness, a few interviewees, particularly in manufacturing, pointed to examples that some states were more proactive in allocating land than others.

Business–government relations and labour policy in India

This section of the chapter will analyse the impact of the changing nature of business–state relations on labour policy.

Key background features of labour markets and labour policy

The Indian labour market is characterized by considerable segmentation and dualism. Anant et al. (2006) suggest that it is useful to divide the labour market into three broad segments: 1) an agriculture sector that accounts for 60 per cent of total employment and about 25 per cent of total domestic output; 2) a formal or organized sector, which employs less than 8 per cent of the labour force and produces approximately 40 per cent of total domestic output; and 3) an urban informal or unorganized sector, which is engaged in a variety of consumer and producer goods and services. Wages and working conditions tend to be markedly worse in the unorganized sectors. The scope of this chapter is almost entirely restricted to the formal or organized sector since business influence largely pertains to this area.

In addition, it is the formal sector that falls under the purview of organized labour in India. By some estimates there are 50,000 trade unions in India and of these 10,000 are affiliated to 10 major trade union federations (Khan 2005). One key feature of labour politics in India is that the major trade union federations are all affiliated to political parties and this has led to considerable fragmentation and competition within the union movement. At the national level, the polarization is particularly evident between the unions associated with the communist parties (Centre of Indian Trade Unions/CITU, and the All-India Trade Union Congress/AITUC), the Congress party-affiliated Indian National Trade Union Congress (INTUC) and the Bharatiya Janata Party's (BJP) wing, the Bharatiya Mazdoor Sangh (BMS). At the state level, the fragmentation is even greater and a multiplicity of unions often exists within the same firm. In part, this can be linked to the low threshold for union formation and lack of clear procedures for union recognition under the Trade Union Act. Links to political parties have also led to a scenario where no political party at the national level is willing to undertake a major revision of labour laws (Venkata Ratnam 2004).

Labour is a concurrent subject under the Indian constitution and both the centre and the states enjoy jurisdictional authority in this area. The involvement of the centre and the states has led to a multiplicity of laws that are often overlapping and sometimes contradictory (Debroy 2005). Despite extensive legislation, enforcement of labour laws in India has been particularly weak.[16] Within the vast collection of laws related to labour in India, some are of particular importance to this chapter. These include the Industrial Disputes Act, Contract Labour (Regulation and Prohibition) Act and some laws relating to social security provision in the organized sector (Workmen's Compensation Act, Employees' Provident Fund (EPF) Act, Employees State Insurance Act and Payment of Gratuity Act). Details of labour legislation and social security provisions are not included in the chapter but thorough overviews of labour legislation can be found in Anant et al. (2006), Debroy (2005) and Venkata Ratnam (2005).

Business preferences and influence on labour policy

Labour market flexibility and business demands

Business has repeatedly called for increased labour flexibility since the start of the liberalization process. Efforts have been aimed at three aspects of labour market flexibility – an 'exit policy', removal of restrictions on contract labour and non-interference of the government in relation to working hours and firing decisions on the basis of indiscipline and productivity. One long-standing demand of business with relation to labour policy and politically, perhaps, the most intractable area of reform has been the call for an 'exit policy' or amendments to section V-B of the Industrial Disputes Act (IDA). This section mandates that firms employing more than 100 workers obtain state government permission before closure, lay-offs or retrenchment. The main point of contention of business is that historically state governments have rarely granted permission for closure and in fact there are numerous cases where firms had stopped production but were not allowed to close or lay off workers. Business claims that such labour laws have served to undermine competitiveness in an increasingly global economy, especially when rival firms in countries operate in favourable labour environments. Business has also argued that the rigidity of labour laws in this aspect has had a perverse effect on employment generation in the organized private sector and has also resulted in growing use of contract labour and apprentices in several business operations.

Various governments since 1991 have appeared sympathetic to calls from business for labour market flexibility but, politically, reform in this area has proved to be intractable. Starting with the Congress under Narasimha Rao to the BJP-led National Democratic Alliance (NDA) (1999–2004), governments have set up committees and formulated proposals for the amendment of section V-B of the IDA as well as the Contract Labour Act. In each case efforts have been met with staunch resistance, particularly from unions, and have had to be abandoned. Realizing the political impossibility of a hire and fire policy, business demands in the area have over time increasingly shifted to asking for a removal of restrictions on contract labour. Business representatives willingly admit that they have resorted to subcontracting in the liberalization era. While the Contract Labour Act contains stipulations on the use of contract labour in core and perennial activities of the firm, in practice the government has turned a blind eye to many violations. In sectors such as textiles, there are estimates that almost 75 per cent of the workers in most firms are employed on a contract basis.[17] Businessmen argue that demand in a global market tends to be cyclical and they should be allowed the flexibility to hire more workers during peak periods and shed staff at other times. The third major demand of business in relation to labour market flexibility involves the non-interference of government in matters related to work hours and termination decisions relating to discipline or productivity-related causes. Recently there appears to be more support for business on this front. Both business and labour unions suggest that the judiciary has become increasingly favourable to employers, particularly in relation to discipline-related issues.

De facto reform and labour market flexibility While the call for flexibility in hiring and firing decisions has been long-standing, there have been virtually no changes in the actual laws. There are rare instances where states have managed to amend laws – Andhra Pradesh, for example, passed a law in 2003 permitting temporary contract labour employment in core activities of firms and broadening the definition of non-core activities. Such cases remain an exception. However, the absence of legislative change may not be as strong a deterrent to competitiveness as business suggests – a process of de facto reform that has been underway since 1991 has provided firms with more flexibility than a formal reading of the law would suggest.[18] Enforcement of existing laws is extremely weak. Furthermore, the widespread use of contract labour and apprentices in the liberalization period coupled with poor enforcement has led to the 'casualization' of the work force. While the retrenchment of even a single worker in large firms requires state government permission, Tendulkar and Bhavani (2007) suggest that such permission appears to be more forthcoming in recent years compared with the past. Companies in both the private and public sectors have also managed to downsize directly in the liberalization era, primarily through the use of the Voluntary Retirement Scheme (VRS). The VRS in effect is a 'golden handshake' paying the employee a lump-sum amount for voluntary retirement and has in practice acted as a substitute for an exit policy.[19] While companies have not been forthcoming in publicizing VRS figures, one interviewee estimated that members of the peak association he belonged to retrenched close to half a million workers between 1997 and 2000.

Social security provisions

Business representatives overwhelmingly accept that social security provisions are inadequate. Many representatives of business, both of large and medium-size firms, claim that the quality of government-run social security services, particularly related to Employees' State Insurance (ESI) Act, is very poor. The problem of weak delivery is considered to be exacerbated by widespread corruption and leakage in the ESI system. Business suggestions for improving ESI include allowing employees a choice of insurance providers, expanding the range of hospitals covered and providing vouchers that would allow employees to go to a medical provider of their choice while offsetting this against the contributions made under the act. One study finds that there is a trend for companies to gain exemption from the ESI by providing a greater level of benefits than that is mandated by the act (Venkata Ratnam 2003). Business believes that the lack of a strong social security mechanism in part hinders attempts at making labour laws more flexible. While industry claims to be willing to accept increased social security if it is exchanged for labour market flexibility, it must be kept in mind that business is overwhelmingly in favour of social security provisions at the unit or industry level.

Skills development

Business representatives claim that though India produces a vast number of graduates every year, the majority lack suitable skills for employment. Representatives of the Information Technology–Business Process Outsourcing (IT–BPO) industry, for example, suggest that, among the pool of graduates with the requisite educational qualification, 30 per cent at best have sufficient skills to enter the industry.[20] Further representatives in manufacturing point out that information technology has increasingly tapped into the resource pool of engineers and science graduates who would have typically entered their sector in the past. Most large firms in India now have in-house training programmes. In addition, some firms have also tied up with universities to create internship programmes, revise curricula, identify suitable talent and are involved in faculty development programmes. Business associations are supplementing firm-level efforts. NASSCOM has set up 'finishing' schools and certification courses and has created a centralized database – the national skills registry (NASSCOM 2006) – of educational backgrounds and employment records of professionals working in the IT-enabled services and business process outsourcing sectors. CII too performs similar training and certification tasks and is involved in the upgrading of the country's Industrial Training Institutes (ITIs).

Industry is also increasingly lobbying for greater privatization of higher education and a more 'market-responsive' system. Business justifies this call by arguing that de facto privatization at various levels has already taken place. For its part, government policy with regard to higher education has been ambiguous and there has been a general reluctance to bring about major education reform.

Affirmative action in the private sector

In its 2004 election manifesto, the Congress proposed the idea of reserving[21] private sector jobs for Scheduled Castes (SCs) and Scheduled Tribes (STs). The proposal was then incorporated into the Common Minimum Programme of the ruling United Progressive Alliance (UPA). In late 2004, Prime Minister Manmohan Singh suggested that reservation in the private sector would be a national policy but the preference of the government was that it was 'done voluntarily by industry' (*The Hindu*, 7 October 2004). The initial reaction of both industry bodies as well as numerous individual industrialists was strong opposition. FICCI, CII and NASSCOM all articulated views against the proposals. Business then began to formulate its response differently and, by

2005, several leading industrialists signed a joint letter supporting the idea of increased opportunities for SCs and STs on a voluntary basis (*The Hindu*, 1 June 2005). Subsequently, CII and ASSOCHAM formulated an action plan on affirmative action, which included a voluntary code of conduct for its members, training of SC/ST entrepreneurs, tutorials for SC/ST students in colleges and entrance examinations, scholarships for SC/ST students in various colleges and vocational training. The official position of business was that it was against any legislative provisions, as these would contradict meritocratic, performance-based hiring and impinge on competitiveness, but would support voluntary measures.

Discussion

Two key questions emerge from what has been presented so far. First, what factors serve to circumscribe business influence? Second, what policy implications arise in terms of labour policy? Business leverage in public policy in the liberalization era has been enhanced both through its engagement in the policy process and as well as through the need for governments to attract private investment. While it would be naïve to suggest that business influence in Indian policy-making is solely an artefact of the liberalization era,[22] this chapter nevertheless shows that changes in India's broader policy environment as well as the shift in the nature of the ruling alliance at the top (Kohli 2006a, 2006b) have led to a scenario where both the degree and nature of business influence differ considerably when compared with the licensing era. It is clear that the reforms have ushered in a closer relationship between business and government.

The suggestion of growing business leverage would lead us to expect that policy is considerably skewed in favour of business. However, as seen in the discussion of labour policy, business lobbying has achieved mixed results. In the old regime, a compact existed between business, government and labour, where business accepted laws that encouraged employment for life in return for a steady stream of rents from the licensing system (Anant et al. 2006). The liberalization era has seen business attempting to change the terms of this compact, with varying degrees of success. While formal legislative changes in labour laws have not been forthcoming because of political reasons, a system of de facto reform has taken place in some areas of labour policy. Yet one overarching fact remains – formal changes to the law have largely been absent and this is an important indicator that business influence is circumscribed. What factors account for this? The main constraints to business influence in public policy, more generally, and specifically in labour policy, arise from the domain of electoral politics. In particular, three main dynamics are identified here as constituting the checks on business power – first, the imperatives of coalition politics; second, what can be termed as the 'politics of opposition'; and third, the dichotomy between 'mass'[23] and 'elite' politics in India. In large part the obstacles to business influence are an example of what Kohli (2007, 2006b) and Chatterjee (2008) identify as the inherent tension between a narrow ruling business–state alliance and a poor but mobilized electorate in the liberalization era.

The first constraint on business influence is coalition politics. Since 1989, no party has managed to gain an electoral majority at the national level and several states have also seen a fragmentation of the vote. Coalition politics has meant that decision-making is fragmented and subject to the veto power of coalition members. In the case of labour policy, several governments, at both the centre and state levels, have demonstrated an inclination towards more pro-business legislative changes but a consensus across coalition partners has been difficult to construct. The difficulty in policy-making in coalition governments has been particularly evident in the case of the Congress-led UPA coalition, which came to power in 2004. The UPA government depended on the outside support of the Communist parties for most of its term, and these parties have consistently opposed various reform measures, at least at the national level. The shifting nature of Indian politics is well demonstrated by the Congress–Left parties in the UPA government. The Congress competes against the Left parties in West Bengal and Kerala, two major states where the latter is a force, but this did not prevent the UPA from receiving outside support from the communists for more than four years. The Left's opposition at the central level to various liberalization measures also stands in contrast to West Bengal's attempt to reinvent itself along business-friendly lines. Recent elections provide little evidence to suggest that India is likely to move away from coalition politics anytime in the near future.

A second key difficulty in governments enacting pro-business policies in the last decade or so has been what can be described as the 'politics of opposition'. The discontinuity between party stance when in opposition and in power is constantly reiterated through various contexts, including labour policy. At the national level, both the Congress during Narasimha Rao's term (1991–96) and the BJP-led NDA coalition in Vajpayee's second stint (1999–2004) tried to initiate the process of labour reform when in power but then shifted their position when in opposition. Venkata Ratnam (2004) argues: 'Regardless of the colour and identity of the party, if it is the ruling party or part of the ruling coalition, it is in favour of investor-friendly labour market reforms. If it is in opposition, it is more cautious, if not opposed outright to such reforms.'

Another conclusion that arises from the analysis of labour policy is that business influence varies across policies. On what policies is business more likely to have an effect? Varshney (1999) differentiates the Indian political arena into the spheres of 'mass' and 'elite' politics, a distinction which is useful in this context. The former is influenced by policies such as inflation that affect areas of mass concern, while the latter, which consists of many aspects of industrial, financial market and trade policy, is confined to elite-level discourse. For the most part, the first-generation reforms that began in 1991, such as the removal of industrial licensing, trade liberalization and financial reforms, have had little salience for the masses, but second-generation reforms, such as labour, tend to fall within the purview of mass interest (Jenkins 2004). The fact that several dimensions of labour policy have been formulated as being of mass concern, even though organized labour enjoys a relatively privileged position, provides a degree of insulation from business demands. Governments cannot be completely oblivious to mass demands and act solely at the behest of business. This might also explain why the Indian state has undertaken reforms largely by 'stealth' (Jenkins 1999, 2004). In the words of a union leader:

> One difference between India and other developing countries is that the trade union movement is still alive here and the democratic system is still playing a major part. Democracy is a so-called hurdle for them [the government] because every five years they have to come to us. That too with the assembly and parliamentary election coming alternately, they usually get only three years.[24]

However, this does not mean that governments will be responsive to mass demands or that the nature of Indian democracy will ensure inclusive development. Indeed, historical evidence in India points squarely to governmental neglect of various mass concerns such as health and education. The larger point that is being made here is that India's electoral politics currently act as a check on business influence but not necessarily as force for inclusion of less powerful groups such as labour. This is amply evident in the trend of de facto labour reform. How much of a constraint democracy is to business power remains to be seen but the call for inclusive development and the proposed legislation in areas such as affirmative action seems to affect business, rhetorically at least. When asked whether business recognized the urgency of inclusive development, one interviewee had this to say:

> Industry is acting out of fear. The sword that is hanging is that the government will pass legislation . . . If we want to prevent that from happening, we have to do two things. One is to concur with the government's idea of inclusive growth and two, act on it as well. Help in causes of education, hire a more diverse group of people into the organization, train them, develop them and prove to the world that you are part of that inclusive growth story. That recognition is there – not out of any conviction – but out of fear.

Conclusion – policy implications

What are the policy implications that arise from this analysis? First, as has been suggested by numerous authors, there is a need to rationalize labour laws (see, for example, Debroy 2005 and Anant et al. 2006). Multiple laws and their cross-cutting scope pose an automatic problem for enforcement. Combined with the weakening of the state's labour enforcement capacity, such laws offer very little actual protection to labour. Second, there is considerable scope for improving the position of both labour and business if the government chose not to rely on de facto reform but instituted legal changes instead. It could then regulate conditions more effectively and business would also benefit from the easing of restrictions. Third, there is a need to reform the social security mechanism. Business is increasingly calling for unit-level measures and some large firms have offered benefits greater than what is available under current government-run schemes. While enhancements to current social security mechanisms are welcome, a sole reliance on unit-level social security and self-certification in the area would be detrimental. The fourth policy recommendation is based on similar concerns with voluntary business action in the area of affirmative action. There is currently no mechanism to hold business to its voluntary promises. Given that business has typically responded to tax breaks and subsidies, one immediate solution might be to tie affirmative action measures to such concessions. Various state governments already offer a plethora of concessions and these could be linked to concrete affirmative action outcomes of firms.

Finally, are institutional arrangements, for example, European-style corporatist arrangements, which ensure direct representation of labour, viable in the Indian context? Several factors suggest this is unlikely. Interest group representation in India has historically drawn on British liberal traditions of pluralism rather than European corporatism (Kochanek 1996). Rudolph and Rudolph (1987) have suggested that the Indian system of interest representation is unique – state domination in the licensing era co-existed with a multiplicity and plurality of societal interests. It is also highly unlikely that the state would voluntarily create more effective channels of labour representation, given that its interests are now closely linked to those of capital. Political fragmentation within the labour movement also acts as a major barrier to the articulation of a united platform. Indeed it is difficult to characterize the union movement in India as a single entity. The best hope for inclusive representation of labour is unified mobilization from below, but currently the prospects for such a movement at the national level appear dim.

Notes

1. I would like to thank José Carlos Marques and Peter Utting for useful comments on an earlier draft.
2. The term 'state' is used in two contexts in this paper. The state or the Indian state is used to refer to the general concept of political and bureaucratic institutions of a country. Regional or provincial governments below the central level are also referred to as states in India's federal system.

3. Recent work by Kohli (2007) on the politics of redistribution in India also identifies this inherent tension between a narrow business–state alliance at the apex and an electorate where the poor and near-poor constitute a majority.
4. I have not included names or other background information in those cases where the interviewee preferred confidentiality.
5. Many authors, including Schneider and Maxfield (1997), have pointed out that there is a need to disaggregate the term 'business'. This chapter will focus primarily on 'big business' in a variety of sectors. Large and mid-sized firms and their representative associations are primarily analysed here. Concerns of small firms are not entirely excluded and indeed many relevant issues cut across firm size. However, this chapter suggests that 'big business' has been the primary actor involved in the transformation of business–government relations and, as such, this chapter concentrates on this section.
6. This approach is referred to in note 1 of the Introduction to this volume.
7. Interviews with various businesspersons, July–August 2007.
8. www.ficci.com/about-us/brief-profile.htm (accessed on 20 July 2008).
9. http://cii.in (accessed on 20 July 2008).
10. www.assocham.org/about/mission.php (accessed on 20 July 2008).
11. www.nasscom.in (accessed on 20 July 2008).
12. Numerous interviews confirmed the fact that government elicited feedback from industry. However, as will be discussed later, business has more influence and interaction with the government in some policy areas than others.
13. Interview with Tarun Das, chief mentor, CII, 28 August 2007.
14. Interviews with various businesspersons, July–August 2007.
15. Rudolph and Rudolph (2001); Ahluwalia (2000); Singh and Srinivasan (2006).
16. This was strongly expressed in interviews with labour union representatives and is also noted by several authors, including Anant et al. (2006); Nagaraj (2004); Bhattacharjea (2006); and Tendulkar and Bhavani (2007).
17. Interview, 23 August 2007.
18. Anant et al. (2006); Nagaraj (2004); Bhattacharjea (2006); Tendulkar and Bhavani (2007).
19. Various interviews, July–August 2007.
20. Interview with Kiran Karnik, president of NASSCOM (2001–08), 29 August 2007.
21. India has pursued caste-based reservation since its independence. This policy has included the reservation of seats for Scheduled Castes (SCs) and Scheduled Tribes (STs) in institutions of higher education as well as reservation of public sector jobs both at the central and state levels. Reservations were originally aimed at SCs and STs but were later expanded to include the Other Backward Classes (OBCs).
22. See, for example, Bardhan (1984), Chatterjee (2008), Corbridge and Harriss (2000) and Chibber (2003).
23. As will be discussed later in this section, the mass–elite distinction is made by Varshney (1999).
24. Interview with A. K. Padmanabhan, secretary-general of CITU, 8 August 2007.

References

Ahluwalia, M. S. (2000) 'Economic Performance of States in the Post-Reform Period', *Economic and Political Weekly*, 35 (19), May, 1637–48.

Anant, T. C. A., R. Hasan, P. Mohapatra, R. Nagaraj and S. K. Sasikumar (2006) 'Labour Markets in India: Issues and Perspectives', in J. Felipe and R. Hasan (eds), *Labour Markets in Asia: Issues and Perspectives* (Basingstoke: Palgrave Macmillan).

Bardhan, P. (1984) *The Political Economy of Development in India* (New Delhi: Oxford University Press).

Bhattacharjea, A. (2006) *Labour Market Regulation and Industrial Performance in India: A Critical Review of the Empirical Evidence*, Working Paper No. 141 (Delhi: Centre for Development Economics, Delhi School of Economics).

Chatterjee, P. (2008) 'Democracy and Economic Transformation in India', *Economic and Political Weekly*, 43 (16), April, 53–62.

Chibber, V. (2003) *Locked in Place: State-Building and Industrialization in India* (Princeton: Princeton University Press).

Corbridge, S. and J. Harriss (2000) *Reinventing India: Liberalisation, Hindu Nationalism and Popular Democracy* (Cambridge: Polity Press).

Debroy, B. (2005) 'Issues in Labour Law Reform', in B. Debroy and P. D. Kaushik, *Reforming the Labour Market* (New Delhi: Academic Foundation).

Haggard, S., S. Maxfield and B. R. Schneider (1997) 'Theories of Business and Business-State Relations', in S. Maxfield and B. R. Schneider (eds), *Business and the State in Developing Countries* (Ithaca: Cornell University Press).

Jenkins, R. (1999) *Democratic Politics and Economic Reform in India* (Cambridge: Cambridge University Press).

——— (2004) 'Labour Policy and the Second Generation of Economic Reform in India', *India Review*, 3. (4), 333–63.

Khan, A. U. (2005) 'Regulating Labour Markets', in B. Debroy and P. D. Kaushik (eds), *Reforming the Labour Market* (New Delhi: Academic Foundation).

Kochanek, S. (1974) *Business and Politics in India* (Berkeley and Los Angeles: University of California Press).

Kochanek, S. A. (1996) 'Liberalization and Business Lobbying in India', *Journal of Commonwealth and Comparative Politics*, 34 (3) 155–173.

Kohli, A. (1990) *Democracy and Discontent: India's Growing Crisis of Governability* (Cambridge: Cambridge University Press).

——— (1996) 'Liberalization and Business Lobbying in India', *Journal of Commonwealth and Comparative Politics*, 34 (3), 155–73.

——— (2004) *State-Directed Development: Political Power and Industrialization in the Global Periphery* (Cambridge: Cambridge University Press).

——— (2006a) 'Politics of Economic Growth in India, 1980–2005, Part I', *Economic and Political Weekly*, 41 (13), April, 1251–9.

——— (2006b) 'Politics of Economic Growth in India, 1980–2005, Part II', *Economic and Political Weekly*, 41 (14), April, l1361–70.

——— (2007) 'State and Redistributive Development in India', paper written for the UNRISD project on Poverty Reduction and Policy Regimes, mimeo (Geneva: UNRISD).

Muralidharan, S. and S. Mahalingam (1999) 'Big Business and Elections', *Frontline*, 16 (16), 31 July–13 August (1999), at: www.flonnet.com/fl1616/16160040.htm (accessed 9 August 2007).

Nagaraj, R. (2004) 'Fall in Organized Manufacturing Employment: A Brief Note', *Economic and Political Weekly*, 39 (30), July, 3387–90.

NASSCOM (National Association of Software and Service Companies) (2006) *NASSCOM: Annual Report 2005–06* (New Delhi: NASSCOM), at: www.nasscom.in/upload/41527/Annual_report.pdf (accessed 28 August 2007).

Panagariya, A. (2008) *India: The Emerging Giant* (Oxford: Oxford University Press).
Rodrik, D. and A. Subramanian (2005) *From Hindu Growth to Productivity Surge: The Mystery of the Indian Growth Transition*, IMF Staff Working Papers, 52 (2).
Rudolph, L. and S. H. Rudolph (1987) *In Pursuit of Lakshmi: The Political Economy of the Indian State* (Chicago: University of Chicago Press).
——— (2001) 'Iconisation of Chandrababu: Sharing Sovereignty in India's Federal Market Economy', *Economic and Political Weekly*, 36 (18), May, 1541–51.
Schneider, B. R. and S. Maxfield (1997) 'Business, the State and Economic Performance in Developing Countries', in S. Maxfield and B. R. Schneider (eds), *Business and the State in Developing Countries* (Ithaca: Cornell University Press).
Singh, N. and T. N. Srinivasan (2006) 'Indian Federalism, Economic Reform and Globalization', in J. Wallack and T. N. Srinivasan (eds), *Federalism and Economic Reform* (Cambridge: Cambridge University Press).
Sinha, A. (2005a) 'Understanding the Rise and Transformation of Business Collective Action in India', *Business and Politics*, 7 (2), 1–34.
——— (2005b) *The Regional Roots of Developmental Politics in India* (Bloomington: Indiana University Press).
Sridharan, E. (2001) 'Reforming Political Finance', *Seminar*, 506, October, at: www.india-seminar.com/cd8899/cd_frame8899.html (accessed 28 October 2007).
Tendulkar, S. D. and T. A. Bhavani (2007) *Understanding Reforms: Post 1991 India* (New Delhi: Oxford University Press).
The Hindu (2004) 'Manmohan for Voluntary Quota in Industry', 7 October.
——— (2005) 'Industry Backs Plan for SCs, STs', 1 June.
Varshney, A. (1999) 'Mass Politics or Elite Politics? India's Reforms in Comparative Perspective', in J. Sachs, A. Varshney and N. Bajpai (eds), *India in the Era of Economic Reforms* (New Delhi: Oxford University Press).
Venkata Ratnam, C. S. (2003) *Negotiated Change: Collective Bargaining, Liberalization and Restructuring in India* (New Delhi: Response Books).
——— (2004) 'The Politics of Labour Reforms in India', in B. Debroy and R. Mukherji (eds), *India – The Political Economy of Reforms* (New Delhi: Bookwell).
——— (2005) 'Labour Market in India', in B. Debroy and P. D. Kaushik (eds), *Reforming the Labour Market* (New Delhi: Academic Foundation).
Venkatesan, V. (1999) 'Chequered Relations', *Frontline*, 16 (16), 31 July–13 August, at: www.flonnet.com/fl1616/16160100.htm (accessed 9 August 2007).

4

Business Participation in Free Trade Negotiations in Chile: Impacts on Environmental and Labour Regulation

Benedicte Bull

Introduction

Business is among the main stakeholders in trade negotiations. It is therefore common practice for business associations as well as individual companies to lobby their governments to make them pursue trade agreements that suit their interests. Thus, trade negotiations have often been envisaged as a 'two-level' game in which governments have to bargain with domestic groups and trading partners simultaneously (Putnam 1988, Intal-ITD-STA 2002). Recently many governments have involved business so closely in trade negotiations and delegated such authority to it that the sharp distinction between the two levels of the game has become blurred.

Chile is one country where business has been intimately involved in free trade negotiations (V. Silva 2000; Sáez 2002; Porras 2003; Bull 2008). Chile has pursued a free trade strategy for a longer period of time and more consistently than any other Latin American country. Since 1990 it has followed a liberalization strategy, negotiating and signing numerous bilateral and regional free trade agreements. Chile now has free trade agreements with most Latin American countries (including MERCOSUR/the Common Market of the South), as well as the United States (US), the European Union (EU), the European Free Trade Area (EFTA) and, more recently, with several Asian countries, including China and Japan (see Table 4.1). Business participation has provided Chilean negotiators with significant expertise as well as reduced domestic opposition to the agreements. It has also contributed to greatly improving the antagonistic relationship that existed between the government and business after the return of democracy in 1990 (Silva 1996a, 2002; Campero 2003).

However, these trade negotiations are not only about market access; they also encompass complex regulatory measures, including new mechanisms to regulate business practice (Woll and Artigas 2007).[1] Among the most controversial issues related to trade agreements are measures to regulate environmental and labour conduct. Such measures have traditionally been strongly opposed by business in developing countries. However, recent literature suggests that competitive business actors in developing countries that aim to gain access to highly regulated markets may favour such regulations as they contribute to levelling the playing field. Thus, rule-making under trade agreements may indirectly contribute to strengthen standards.

The free trade agreements signed by Chile include a variety of measures to regulate labour and the environment. This chapter explores the role of business in negotiating these measures. The shock therapy and subsequent economic transformation experienced by Chile in the 1980s has resulted in businesses with offensive interests largely outnumbering those with defensive interests. However, although Chile currently cannot be considered a 'lax regulation' country, Chilean business has forcefully resisted regulation related to labour rights. Respect for labour rights and standards is not yet culturally ingrained, and there is strong evidence of severe violations.[2] The questions explored in this paper are therefore: What were Chilean business preferences regarding labour and environmental rules related to free trade agreements? How has business attempted to influence the regulatory aspects of trade agreements in the areas of labour and the environment? How has the intimate public–private collaboration affected business's attitude towards environmental and labour regulation? Answers to these questions are sought through the analysis of the positions and strategies of business representatives towards the negotiations over such regulatory measures, the positions and strategies of counterparts and the outcome of the negotiations.

The chapter is based on fieldwork in Chile during the first half of 2006. This included approximately 60 in-depth interviews with representatives of most major business associations, public officials, labour unions and other civil society representatives. The chapter is structured as follows. The first section discusses literature on business preferences and strategies towards rule-making in developing countries. The second section introduces Chile's trade agreements and the context for business participation in terms of major business associations and their relationship to the state. The third section analyses the positions and strategies of business towards labour and environmental clauses in three free trade negotiations: with Canada, with the United States and with the EU. The concluding section discusses what general lessons may be drawn from this case in terms of the dynamics of corporate influence on trade policy and social regulation.

The trade–labour–environment debates: competing predictions of business preferences

In the literature, there are competing predictions regarding business's preferences towards regulation of environmental and labour issues in trade agreements. A common distinction is made between business from lax and strict regulatory countries, often thought to coincide with the distinction between developing and developed countries. In the debate about the linkage between trade agreements and environment and labour regulations, business in developing countries has been characterized as staunchly opposed. Utilizing trade agreements for regulating environmental and labour conduct was pioneered by the North American Free Trade Agreement (NAFTA) as will be discussed below. In multilateral negotiations, the shift towards regulation occurred with the Uruguay Round of the World Trade Organization (WTO), where the policy focus moved from border barriers to domestic regulatory and legal systems. However, the attention in the Uruguay Round was clearly on *economic* regulation: the legislation and institutions required for ensuring competition, protecting intellectual property rights and protecting investments (Ostry 2004, 2005). The negotiations on social regulation either received little attention or were relegated to other United Nations (UN) organizations with weaker authority than the WTO (the International Labour Organization/ILO, the United Nations Environment Programme/UNEP, and so on). One of the main reasons for this approach was opposition from developing countries that saw such regulatory measures as possible instruments for protectionism.

However, the two major actors – the United States and the EU – have continued to pursue these issues in bilateral and regional trade agreements (RTAs). Social regulation has received more attention in these agreements than in the multilateral talks, possibly because developing country resistance to them has been less coordinated and powerful. In general, developing country business is viewed as opposing such measures, but lacking the power to avoid them.

Stephen Woolcock (2006) has developed specific predictions about business preferences towards trade-related regulation. He argues that rule-making in trade agreements varies according to coverage, principles, transparency, cooperation, regulatory safeguards and implementation as well as substantive measures. Regarding substantive measures of rule-making included in such agreements he distinguishes between 1) harmonization (of legal framework); 2) partial harmonization; 3) approximation as a general aim; 4) equivalence; and 5) mutual recognition of regulations or test results (Woolcock 2006: 14–15).[3]

Regarding business preferences Woolcock distinguishes between sectors that have 'offensive' and 'defensive' interests in trade agreements and argues that the interests regarding scope and content of rules negotiated in trade agreements will vary between them. Defensive interests are likely to oppose any policy approximation or convergence. Offensive sectors, on the other hand, will favour greater coverage because they wish to have greater transparency or predictability in rule-making. They may also seek deeper integration in terms of policy approximation, harmonization or mutual recognition in order to ensure *de facto* non-discrimination and create a 'level playing field' (Woolcock 2006: 16).

This view on business preferences in trade negotiations provides a twist to the argument of the 'California effect' (Vogel 2000). Vogel's argument was a response to the pessimistic hypotheses about a regulatory 'race to the bottom'; increased trade integration was argued to lead to a lowering of environmental and labour standards in poor countries through 'industrial flight' and 'social dumping'. Vogel argued that contrary to these predictions evidence could show that regulatory competition may also lead to a 'race to the top' resulting from what Vogel has called a California effect: that standards are raised overall as firms from less regulated markets attempt to penetrate relatively large, highly regulated markets in the world's richest countries. For those firms to get access to these markets, they have to meet the latter's relatively strict environmental and consumer standards, and they may in turn create demand for stricter regulations at home (Vogel 2000).

While Vogel did not speak directly of trade negotiations, one could hypothesize that the same companies that are exposed to higher standards in highly regulated markets will also seek to include such regulations in trade agreements. However, whether they choose to do that depends on the degree to which they view this as an efficient way of 'levelling the playing field', or whether there are other means of regulation that are more attractive to business.

In all of the above, regulation is considered to be mainly formal regulation that is included in a written agreement between governmental entities and that is enforced by states and intergovernmental institutions. Business is viewed as a 'rule-taker', albeit one that intends to influence the rules that it subsequently will be subject to. However, regulation may also occur through 'soft' measures resulting from the exchange of information, the encouragement of social dialogue and networks.[4] There is at present a tendency to replace hierarchical patterns of interaction between governments and private actors and coercive forms of regulation with relations of cooperation between states and business.[5] Moreover, regulation is no more strictly national, as domestic state institutions and agencies become enmeshed within a system of transnational regulation, consisting of networks relying on formal standards rather than rules, and in which both public and private actors take part (Djelic and Sahlin-Anderson 2006; Jayasuriya 2004). Business is in this perspective at the same time a 'rule maker' and a 'rule-taker'

Many trade agreements include soft rather than hard regulatory measures, such as the establishment of participatory councils aiming, for example, to exchange experiences and discuss 'best practices', in which business participates along with governments and other civil society actors. These trade negotiations may also be arenas for interaction between parties that result in learning and mutual influence of preferences. If business collaborates closely with governments in trade negotiations, one may hypothesize that both develop new loyalties and may be susceptible to mutual influence. Thus, one may have to reconsider the assumption that business comes to the negotiations with fixed preferences. As argued by Odell (2006), in international trade negotiations officials demonstrate uncertainties, biases and heuristics that can channel learning and thus subsequent interactions in particular directions. Although Odell is mainly referring to interaction between different governments, the increasing involvement of business may also set off processes of learning between governments and business actors. This is supported by the findings of Woll and Artigas (2007) who argue that, due to the high level of complexity in current trade negotiations, business often finds it hard to really grasp the implications of specific regulations and may demonstrate uncertainties.

There are two other implications of the perspective above on the relationship between business, trade agreements and rule-making on environment and labour issues. The first is the fact that because business and governments are jointly involved in discussing these issues at the international level, 'spill-over effects' may result at the domestic level, that is, a close relationship may also lead to better business compliance with environmental and labour regulations at home.

The second relates to the partial reliance on private authority in forms of 'soft regulation'. Compliance with standards increasingly depends on a degree of business self-regulation and voluntarism, and significant authority is vested in the private actors themselves (Cutler et al. 1999; Hall and Biersteker 2002). There is a considerable literature about private standards, norms and regimes, particularly in global environmental governance (see, for example, Clapp 1998; Newell 2004). Such standards, although often developed on the basis of intergovernmentally established norms, may provide an alternative for business in the pursuit of creating a 'level playing field'. In other words, instead of seeking international trade related measures or stricter domestic regulation, businesses may adopt private standards or negotiate directly with business associations to get easier access to highly regulated markets. As such, they may engage in a kind of 'forum shopping' wherein intergovernmental negotiations are but one possibility. Business in this perspective is considered to be mainly a 'rule-maker'.

In sum, different predictions are made regarding business preferences, strategies and engagement in trade negotiations and their implications for regulation of environment and labour. While it is common to regard business from developing countries as strictly opposing the linkage between trade and environmental and labour regulation, the literature on trade-related rule-making suggests that preferences may differ between offensive and defensive business, and that the latter may favour regulations in order to create a level playing field. Drawing on the lessons from the 'race to the top versus race to the bottom' debate, one may further hypothesize that business favours stricter regulations in order to gain access to strictly regulated countries. The lessons from the 'soft' regulation debate add nuance to the picture in two ways: first, it reminds us that preferences are not always fixed but are subject to influence through processes such as learning, and secondly, it suggests that social interaction between business and government at the international level may have positive spill-over effects at the domestic level. Finally, the literature on private authority points to an alternative strategy for business that aims to create a 'level playing field': namely to emphasize private standards and agreements.

In the following section, I will analyse the positions of Chilean business related to social regulation in trade accords, the extent to which they have influenced Chile's position and the outcome of the agreements. However, I will first provide some background to the state–business relationship and how it has evolved following the return of democracy.

Trade negotiations, business and the government in Chile

For almost 30 years Chile has pursued a strategy of trade liberalization. Although the roots of this path date back before the dictatorship of Augusto Pinochet (1973–90), under his rule a drastic unilateral reduction in tariffs was introduced. By 1979, Chile's tariffs had been reduced to a flat 10 per cent. The governments of the elected centre-left coalition (Concertación) that ruled Chile from the reinstitution of democracy to 2010 have continued the export-led strategy but complemented unilateralism with trade agreements. By the end of the third Concertación government (of Ricardo Lagos, 2000–6), tariff levels were reduced from 17.6 per cent in 1990 (Ffrench-Davis 2005),[6] to 6 per cent in 2004, but due to trade agreements the effective average was about 2 per cent. Its export to gross domestic product (GDP) ratio had reached 69 per cent, and 66 per cent of exports were carried out through preferential agreements (Mesquita Moreira and Blyde 2006).

Throughout these 30 years, the relationship between the state and business has changed significantly. During the first phase of the Pinochet dictatorship, business associations were generally excluded from policy-making. After the economic crisis of 1982–3, they were selectively included, although leaders of the largest companies and conglomerates were equally or more influential (Silva 1996a). Nevertheless, as Pinochet was viewed as the main guarantee for avoiding the return of a socialist government, organized business stayed united behind the regime. Business organizations supported Pinochet's candidate in the 1989 election, and mostly opposed the incoming Concertación government in 1990 (Campero 2003). A majority of the business organizations have also since then directly or indirectly supported the opposition.

At the same time, a cordial relationship evolved between the Concertación governments and organized business. The governments consciously pursued a strategy of involving business in policy-making. In this they gave priority to business associations rather than individual business leaders, and attempted to institutionalize the government–business relationship (Foxley 1994; P. Silva 2000). Related to free trade negotiations, the government set up a number of institutions to facilitate business input. During

Table 4.1 Trade agreements signed by Chile

Country(ies)	Year of signing	Effective
ALADI countries*	1983	1983
Mexico	1991/1999	1991/2003
Venezuela	1993	1993
Bolivia	1993	1993
Colombia	1994	1994
Ecuador	1994	1995
MERCOSUR	1996	1996
Canada	1996	1997
Cuba	1998	2008
Peru	1998/2006	1999/2009
Costa Rica	1999	2002
El Salvador	1999	2002
EU	2002	2003
Republic of Korea	2003	2004
United States	2003	2004
EFTA**	2003	2004
P4***	2005	2006
China	2005	2006
India	2006	2007
Panama	2006	2008
Colombia****	2006	—
Japan	2007	2007
Australia	2008	2009

Notes: *The members of the Asociación Latino Americana de Integración/ALADI (Latin American Integration Association) were at this point Argentina, Bolivia, Brazil, Chile, Colombia, Mexico, Paraguay, Peru, Uruguay and Venezuela. ** EFTA (Iceland, Norway, Switzerland and Lichtenstein). *** Trans-Pacific Strategic Economic Partnership Agreement (Brunei Darussalam, Chile, New Zealand and Singapore). **** Signed, but not yet ratified.
Source: Bull (2008): Table 1, updated with data from DIRECON, no date (accessed on 17 March 2009).

the government of Patricio Aylwin (1990–4) it set up a Bilateral Council for Trade and Investment with participation from business and the labour unions in 1990, and in 1992 it formed the Business Advisory Committee as a permanent consultative body to the government in trade negotiations. During the following government of Eduardo Frei (1994–2000), the practice of always bringing business representatives in official delegations to other countries started and the institution of the 'room next door' where business associations and labour representatives are invited to follow the negotiations, in order to get briefings and provide advice to the government negotiators, was created (Porras 2003). President Lagos expanded the 'room next door' to three 'rooms next door': one for business, one for labour and one for medium-sized, small and micro industries. He also established the Consejo Publico-Privado para el Desarrollo Exportador/CPPDE (Public-Private Council for Export Development) with representatives of business and several branches of the government to discuss trade related issues.

In the strategy to include business, the government was aided by the existence of relatively strong business associations. Along with Mexico and sometimes Colombia, Chile is listed among the cases of relatively strong business associations in Latin America (Schneider 2004). The main economy-wide business association in Chile is the Confederación de la Producción y del Comercio/CPC (Confederation of Production and Commerce). CPC encompasses six sector peak organizations; the Sociedad Nacional de Agricultura/SNA (National Agricultural Association), the industrialist association (the Sociedad de Fomento Fabril/SOFOFA – Society for Industrial Promotion), the Sociedad Nacional de Minería/SONAMI (National Mining Association), the Cámara Nacional de Comercio/CNC (National Chamber of Commerce), the Cámara Chilena de la Construcción/CChC (Chilean Construction Chamber) and the Asociación de Bancos e Instituciones Financieras/ABIF (Association of Banks and Financial Institutions). Related to trade issues, the Asociación de Exportadores de Manufacturas y Servicios/ASEXMA (Association of Manufacture Exporters), established in 1985 to defend the interests of medium-sized export-oriented manufacturing enterprises, has also been influential. It is a member of SOFOFA but was initially critical of what it viewed as SOFOFA's reluctant support for free trade and export interests.

The restructuring of business resulting from the introduction of neoliberalism and export orientation of the economy from the 1970s on has weakened sectors dominated by small- and medium-sized manufacturing enterprises, but at the same time given rise to large conglomerates and groups with transnational linkages that are now active investors in neighbouring countries (Fernández Jilberto 2004; Fazio 2004). In turn this has engendered a turnaround in the preferences of SOFOFA related to trade issues. Whereas traditionally it was the SNA that was most pro-free trade and SOFOFA jealously guarded protection of industry sectors, with the transnationalization of the economy after the restructuring of the 1980s, SOFOFA has become a staunch defender of trade liberalization and trade agreements.[7] It has also contributed to a strengthening of SOFOFA that now represents the major conglomerates and groups. It is now the strongest and most well-funded of the sectoral peak associations, and it encompasses 88 per cent of Chilean business.

SOFOFA has also been the main actor related to trade negotiations. In 1993, it hired a former director of the office in charge of trade negotiations in the Ministry of Foreign Affairs (General Directorate for International Economic Relations/DIRECON) with nine years of experience with trade negotiations, to lead a newly formed Department of Foreign Trade, along with an expert on the WTO from the same institution. Later SOFOFA hired a former director of the 'twin-institution' of DIRECON with responsibility for trade promotion, ProChile, as a second general manager of SOFOFA with responsibility for strategic issues. SOFOFA's trade department became the technical secretariat for the International Commission on Foreign Trade established soon after by the CPC. From the late 1990s, SOFOFA's trade department started to coordinate the inputs to trade negotiations by all the other organizations. During the Lagos government, the CPPDE meetings were held at SOFOFA's headquarters and it was delegated increasing authority from the government, including representing it in exploratory negotiations with neighbouring countries.

By the time of the Lagos presidency a close and cordial relationship between governmental officials, SOFOFA representatives, and representatives of other business associations had developed concerning trade negotiations (Bull 2008). This was premised on a basic consensus about offensive free trade strategies; the pursuit of increased market access for Chilean products abroad and limited need for protection at home.[8]

However, regarding environmental and labour regulation, there was no such basic consensus. Indeed labour reform has been the most divisive issue between the government and business after 1990. The Concertación governments have met strong opposition from business associations in their efforts to reform Pinochet's labour legislation that sought to increase 'the flexibility' of the labour market and severely curtailed labour protection and rights (Schurman 2001; Frank 2002). The first set of reforms was passed in 1994 under Patricio Aylwin. Eduardo Frei attempted a new set of reforms, but due to pressure from business associations and the business-backed right-wing opposition parties, they were not adopted until the Lagos presidency, which could rely on a majority in Congress (Durán-Palma et al. 2005). In 2002, against a blistering campaign from the CPC, the Concertación-controlled Congress passed a new law which strengthened the labour inspectorate and improved worker protection. Nevertheless, it failed to reflect the promised changes in the right to dismiss striking workers or the extension of rights to collective bargaining (Murillo and Schrank 2005; Silva 2002). Furthermore, it did not encompass the growing number of independent or sub-contracted workers in Chile. Improving protection of this group of workers was proposed already in 2002, but opposed by the major business associations. It resurged during the Lagos presidency, and became a major topic during the election campaign in 2005. A law finally was passed in May 2006. By this time, business associations, led by the CPC, had come to accept a law, but still opposed several elements of it (see CPC n.d.).

Environmental issues have not been divisive to the same extent. Whereas the legislation aimed at disempowering labour had been part of a conscious and highly prioritized strategy under Pinochet, environmental issues had simply been ignored (Silva 1996b). In 1994, Chile got its first environmental law (Ley sobre Bases Generales del medio Ambiente). Under this law the Comisión Nacional del Medio Ambiente/CONAMA (National Environmental

Commission) was created as a cross-departmental organization reporting directly to the Ministry of the Presidency. Although some of the environmental initiatives that have arisen since have provoked debate, environmental issues have not caused the same kind of conflicts as labour issues.

Nevertheless, in comparison to issues of market access, labour and environmental issues provoked much more controversy between the government and organized business. In the following, I will analyse how this played out in practice.

Negotiations of trade agreements and business positions on labour and environmental regulation

Among the trade agreements listed above, three in particular have dealt with the issues of labour and the environment: the agreements with Canada, the EU and the United States.

The negotiations with Canada

When President George H. W. Bush launched the 'Initiative for the Americas' in 1990, Chile was among the first countries to express interest in a free trade agreement with the United States (Ramos and Urrutia 2003). In 1994, Chile received a surprise invitation to become a member of NAFTA. However, due to the political costs incurred by NAFTA for the US administration, the door was closed again in 1995. Instead, Chile entered negotiations with Canada and deepened the agreement with Mexico into a full Free Trade Agreement (FTA),[9] thus entering NAFTA 'through the back door'.[10] The Mexico agreement was negotiated under the framework of ALADI and environmental and labour issues were never on the table. Thus, the first experience of including labour and environmental issues in a trade agreement for Chile was the agreement with Canada.

It was clear from the start that labour and environmental issues would be a part of the agreement with Canada as it had been in NAFTA. NAFTA broke new ground as it included side agreements on the environment and labour issues and a model of regulation characterized by minimal regional institution-building, and rejection of 'common minimum standards' in the areas of labour and the environment. Rather, it recognizes the rights of each Party to adopt its own legislation and standards and creates a dispute resolution mechanism to deal with cases of failure to enforce these. The mechanism can only be used, however, if lax enforcement can be shown to impact on trade between the parties. Failure to enforce environmental and labour laws may result in monetary penalty, but since the labour and environmental provisions are part of side agreements only and not the main agreement, it can not result in trade sanctions.

The Canadians wanted to go further than NAFTA and called for a harmonization of legislation not only mutual recognition of existing domestic regulation. Furthermore, they proposed that any failure of a party to enforce its own environmental or labour laws may be brought to the resolution mechanism, not only in the case that it impacts directly on bilateral trade. According to one of the Chilean chief negotiators, the Chileans were also eager to bring these issues into the agreement (Lagos Weber 2004). However, they wanted the agreement to be based on existing national legislation, and they were particularly concerned to avoid the outcome that a failure to comply with specific labour or environmental standards could result in trade sanctions.

In general, the initiative to negotiate with Canada provoked only lukewarm interest in the business community. Although Canadian investors had become important in the Chilean mining industry, Canada was a small market for Chilean exports.[11] Regarding environmental and labour issues, the main priority for business was to ensure that trade-related rules could not be used to accuse Chileans of social or environmental 'dumping'. Business opposed harmonization on the grounds that it would impinge upon domestic sovereignty. But it also opposed 'mutual recognition', particularly on environmental issues. The reason was that Chile at this point had a deficient and outdated environmental legislation.[12] SOFOFA's review of Chile's legislation discovered 2,160 laws that could be interpreted as 'environmental', but that were old and 'sleeping'. SOFOFA thus worried that a trade agreement would result in their being held accountable to such laws.[13]

The mining industry had suffered significantly from the 1988 exclusion from the General System of Preferences (GSP) due to accusations of social dumping and it had a motive for supporting higher standards.[14] However, the mining associations had little faith in the ability of such clauses to alleviate the risk of such accusations.[15]

Generally, with some exceptions, the business community did not participate very eagerly in the negotiations with Canada.[16] The environmental and labour agreements were negotiated separately from the main trade agreement and the business community was even less involved in these negotiations than in those related to market access. The main reason given in interviews was that business trusted the government to take care of their interests. And indeed, the joint concerns about protecting Chilean sovereignty and avoiding jeopardizing market access overshadowed differences between the government and business regarding, for example, domestic labour legislation.

As well, the labour unions were quite passive in these negotiations. The reason was twofold. First, the unions had still not recuperated from the persecution suffered during the 17 years of dictatorship and were both numerically and organizationally weak. Second, although there was no consensus regarding the desirability of trade agreements among the unions, largely for idiosyncratic reasons, the agreement with Canada did not provoke the same kind of opposition as the coming agreement with the United States.[17] Thus, although the unions, represented by the Central Unitaria de Trabajo de

Chile/CUT (Chile's National Labour Centre), were informed and participated in certain meetings, they had no strong, unified position on the issues.

The result of the negotiations was an agreement that could be interpreted as a replica of NAFTA, adjusted to Chilean and Canadian preferences. As with NAFTA, it is based on 'mutual recognition' of domestic legislation, and an obligation to enforce it. It furthermore sets up a similar institutional structure as NAFTA, and stipulates a mechanism for dispute resolution. This is specific to the different areas, and the cases are not in the final instance referred to the general dispute resolution mechanism of the agreement. Thus, there is no mention of trade sanctions as a part of the dispute resolution of environmental and labour issues, but rather penalties in dollar amounts. However, as opposed to NAFTA it outlines 11 specific principles for good conduct in the case of labour relations and a series of corresponding responsibilities in the case of the environment. Although this does not result in harmonization, it is intended to move the parties towards approximation. The agreement further lists areas for collaboration and sets up a series of committees and procedures to strengthen it, reflecting partly Canadian preferences for voluntarism, public participation, empowerment of advisory committees and a belief in deliberation (Hockin 2004).

When negotiated, the agreement met major opposition from the SNA, which mobilized to avoid it being ratified in the Chilean congress. However, SNAs opposition was based on the perception that the agreement gave unnecessary concessions regarding liberalization of agriculture and that the benefits it had achieved were little more than what Chile already had through the GSP (Porras 2003). The business community as well as the government was relatively pleased with the labour and environmental aspects of the agreement and their worries about potential negative impact of international trade agreements on Chile's market access were eased. That would only last until the negotiations with the United States returned to the agenda.

The negotiations with the United States

Negotiations with the United States remained pending after 1995 primarily due to the failure of President Clinton to renew the trade promotion authority (TPA). In spite of this, in 2000, President-elect Ricardo Lagos agreed with President Clinton to start negotiations for a FTA with or without TPA. One round of negotiations was conducted before President Clinton left office, and the process progressed with the incoming Bush administration. When the TPA was renewed it was premised on the inclusion of labour and environmental clauses in trade agreements – not in a side agreement as in NAFTA.

When negotiations started, the United States brought 'blueprints' for the chapters on labour and the environment based on a recently signed agreement with Singapore. The 'blueprints' included an obligation that each party should make its labour and environmental legislation compatible with international standards, and that that each party's failure to enforce its own domestic environmental or labour laws could be brought before the trade agreement's general dispute resolution mechanism if such lax enforcement could be shown to impact on trade between the parties. This would essentially mean that trade sanctions could be imposed in any area in the case of non-compliance with domestic labour or environmental law.

The Chilean negotiators wanted instead the agreement to be based on the agreement they already had with Canada. Partly because the Bush administration did not seem particularly eager to insist on a strict interpretation of the TPA, there was room for negotiation.[18] A compromise agreement was reached which is in principle similar to NAFTA with its conflict resolution mechanism and lack of specific standards.[19] However, the agreement establishes that any allegation of failure to adhere to domestic labour or environmental legislation would first have to pass through a complicated and time-consuming process, including the use of monetary penalties, before any trade sanctions could be considered. The use of penalties was based upon the Canada agreement as proposed by the Chilean negotiators. The agreement also sets up an institutional structure with a Labour Affairs Council and an Environmental Affairs Council at ministerial level and a consultative Labour Affairs Committee and Environmental Affairs Committee with wide public participation. It also lists eight concrete collaborative projects in the areas of labour and the environment respectively.

In the process towards reaching this agreement, Chilean business played a particularly active role. In general, the business community was highly supportive of an agreement with the United States, in spite of opposition from ASEXMA (that always had preferred deeper integration with the Latin American region) and the SNA, that feared inflow of cheap agricultural products. Moreover, led by CPC and SOFOFA, and the bilateral American Chamber of Commerce (AmCham), business engaged strongly in making the agreement a reality. AmCham and SOFOFA had set up an office specifically to work on ensuring that a Chile–US FTA would become a reality, it made visits to the US Congress in Washington and invited US Congressmen to Chile.[20]

Business also participated actively in the different rounds of negotiation. Although participation was coordinated by SOFOFA, sectoral peak associations and more specialized producer organizations (particularly in agroindustry and agriculture) followed the negotiations closely from the room next door and established a cordial relationship with governmental negotiators. Close friendships and a sense of having a common project developed across the public–private divide (Bull 2008). This was of great value when difficult issues of market access were negotiated, for example on chicken, avocado, corn and wheat.

Among the main issues of concern to the business community were the requirements for environmental and labour regulation that the US negotiators demanded. The business community worried, first, that they would be held accountable to standards other than the domestic Chilean legislation. Again, the worries related mainly to a possible lack of compatibility between Chilean environmental laws and international standards because of the perceived immaturity of Chilean legislation, and that stricter standards could thus be imposed. There was less concern with labour legislation as business felt that domestic laws were extremely strict and thus there was little concern that a suspension of benefits such as had happened in 1988 was a risk. In general, however, business rejected the idea that trade sanctions against any products could be used if failure to comply with domestic legislation could be established.

There was remarkably little disagreement within business, or between business and other Chilean actors, on the points about labour and the environment. Indeed, the strong pressure from US domestic actors – particularly Congress and the main labour union – seemed to have united forces on the Chilean side. Governmental negotiators and business actors were equally opposed to the use of trade sanctions to handle failure to comply with domestic legislation on environmental and labour issues.

Labour also rejected imposition of legislation and any weakening of Chilean sovereignty. The labour central CUT was deeply split regarding strategies towards the agreement with the United States. In the early phase of the negotiation, CUT allied with the American Federation of Labor and Congress of Industrial Organizations (AFL–CIO) in the demands that a condition for supporting a possible agreement was that it included strong measures to protect labour (see CUT and AFL-CIO 2002). However, CUT later split into two factions; one led by the International Secretary Diego Olivares that wanted active participation in order to secure a deal that was as good as possible for the workers, and another faction, led by the President, Arturo Martínez, rejecting the agreement altogether. Olivares continued to participate actively in the negotiations, but mid-way through the negotiations he broke with CUT and established his own labour central. The one thing that labour did agree upon was that it wanted labour laws and compliance to be settled in Chile and not be directed by the United States.

As for the environmental organizations, these were not allowed any 'room next door' as they were not perceived as representative of anybody.[21] To the extent that they contributed to the debate (many were outright opposed to the agreement and did not participate), they were concerned with the investment rules (that are similar to NAFTA's Chapter 11 and might impinge upon ability to regulate transnational companies) and the strengthening of the export model based on exploitation of natural resources that the agreement would signify. They did not express strong viewpoints on the environmental mechanisms, as they viewed trade agreements as relatively weak instruments for ensuring compliance with environmental regulations.[22]

As soon as it became clear that there would be no direct linkage between labour and environmental conduct and potential use of trade sanctions, the business community felt less threatened. According to the Chilean chief negotiator:

> As soon as the business community got convinced that the only thing that would be in the agreement was that they would have to comply with the domestic legislation and that the domestic legislation still would be a topic of national autonomy – that we as a sovereign country would decide what to do with that, but of course there would be a compromise that we would not go back on the national legislation – then they calmed down.[23]

Thus, Chilean business was mainly defensive regarding these issues. There was little real interest in promoting any form of regulation, be it harmonization or mutual recognition. As noted by one key negotiator in response to a question about whether Chilean business was really interested in these topics:

> Business, no. I mean they were concerned with the idea of having sanctions, but they were concerned not because what it meant for their own labour practices but for what it would mean in terms of lack of access. So in the end, it was an issue of market access.[24]

Business not only participated in the intergovernmental negotiations, it also pursued parallel strategies of negotiating directly with US private counterparts in order to prepare the ground for an intergovernmental agreement. However, these concerned mainly sanitary and phyto-sanitary standards and detailed issues of market access.[25] They did not encompass environmental and labour legislation. However, this defensive and passive attitude changed somewhat in the negotiations with the EU.

The negotiations with the EU

At the same time as Chile negotiated with the United States it intensified negotiations with the EU. Contact with the EU had already started in the early 1990s, largely for political reasons. However, Chilean business eagerly promoted a more concrete and binding economic agreement that would allow it to access the EU market with a broader set of products and under more stable conditions. The EU is Chile's largest single market, receiving 24.6 per cent of its exports, and the Chileans had strong interests in securing stable market access for, among other goods, fish and agricultural products.

The Chileans were well informed of the European preference for including social issues in the agreement, and increasingly worried about the European non-governmental organizations' (NGOs) linking of trade and environmental issues and wanted to ensure that they did not campaign against an agreement with Chile (Van Klaveren 2006). Thus the Chilean negotiators proposed to include strong commitments on environmental and labour rights, backed by sanctions largely on the model of the Canada agreement.

The negotiators' proposals were backed by key business associations. Although SOFOFA was the main coordinating body, negotiations with the EU also included some specialized associations – notably the Sociedad Nacional de la Pesca/SONAPESCA (National Fishing Association) and the Association of Vineyards – that were very active in attempting to secure a deal. In particular SONAPESCA was worried about exclusion from the European market due to allegations of failure to adhere to environmental standards and it was eager to include a predictable framework and a mechanism for resolution of conflicts in the agreement.

This was however rejected by the European negotiators who instead pressured for the adoption of institutions of dialogue similar to those that had been adopted within the EU.[26] The European position reflected on the one hand the long-standing strategy of rejecting a sanctions-based approach, particularly in relation to labour standards in trade agreements (Mandelson 2006). On the other hand, it reflected emerging 'soft' regulatory approaches to social regulation at the EU level (Borrás and Jacobsen 2004). The result was an agreement which envisages cooperation on social issues, defined more broadly than labour rights and the environment, and focusing on social dialogue, human rights, labour rights and gender issues as well as poverty reduction. Quite paradoxically, the agreement with the EU is most ambitious when it comes to requiring institutional changes, but it includes the shortest formal statement about such matters, stating only that the Parties should promote the participation of the social interlocutors in questions related to living conditions and social integration. The agreement also stipulates a conflict resolution mechanism, but this is set up to resolve commercial disputes and there are no provisions for bringing conflicts on social issues before the conflict resolution mechanism. Moreover, it places significant emphasis on support for Chilean adherence to standards, and recognizes Chilean certifiers as authorities in this area.

In sum, Chilean businesses were positive towards including regulatory mechanisms in the agreement, mainly because they had already felt the pressure for rising standards from consumers and EU institutions. Thus, their main preference was for creating mechanisms enhancing predictability on these issues. However, the agreement only partly reflected their preferences in this respect.

Spill-over effects and forum shopping

The case studies above show that Chilean business preferences and strategies towards labour and environmental rules in trade negotiations have differed depending on the market in question. Related to the Canadian market, they were not very important for Chilean business when the agreement was negotiated and the business community was relatively indifferent, but to the degree that they were engaged they were concerned about the possibilities of imposition of stricter regulations. Related to the United States, business acted defensively against the possible threats of trade sanctions as well as of stronger regulations. Only when negotiating with the heavily regulated European market did Chilean business show offensive interests and push for strong regulations as a means of creating a level playing field.

As well, the strategies differed somewhat, particularly the pursuit of alternative strategies to the intergovernmental negotiations. Related to the United States, significant emphasis was placed on negotiating with private sector counterparts, that is, private associations with the power to hinder market access due to failure to comply with, for example, sanitary and phytosanitary standards. In the case of the EU, emphasis was more strongly placed on complying with private or public–private voluntary standards. Businesses representing about half of Chile's GDP are now involved in voluntary environmental schemes (OECD/ECLAC 2005a). They include several different measures. One important measure is the Acuerdos de Producción Limpia/APL (Agreements for Clean Production) – a multi-actor initiative in which Chilean businesses enter into agreements about certain environmental standards in production that are developed and monitored jointly by public and private agencies. By 2002, 600 individual businesses had such agreements, and they have now been developed for 25 product groups. These include all the major export products, including mining, which constitutes 42 per cent of Chile's export value.[27] The main motivation for establishing this system was to secure access for Chilean businesses to OECD markets (OECD/ECLAC 2005a). Furthermore, according to the International Organization for Standardization (ISO) 2005 survey, 277 Chilean businesses were ISO 14001 certified. This includes the 14 largest mining companies, among them the world's largest producer of copper, the Chilean state-owned Corporación Nacional del Cobre de Chile/CODELCO (National Copper Corporation of Chile). Chilean businesses have recently been active in various initiatives to improve their corporate social responsibility (CSR) conduct and respect for labour rights, and to participate in the development of the new ISO 26000 on social responsibility. Yet, this does not match the importance Chilean business has accorded to standards in the area of the environment.

It is difficult to judge whether this constitutes an alternative to formal regulations. It is, however, clear that attempts to penetrate the EU market has made Chilean business more concerned with adhering to, in particular, environmental standards. The question is whether this has also – as hypothesized by Vogel – led to business demands for stricter national regulations on environment and labour issues. This effect seems to have been limited due to the very different interpretation by business, governmental and other social representatives over the actual state of affairs regarding regulation.

A final issue to consider is whether there at least have been some 'spillover effects' from the intimate relationship developed between business and government in trade negotiations towards creating a more positive, collaborative relationship related to environment and labour regulation.

Across the different actors, everybody seems to emphasize that the relationship between public and private representatives improved significantly through the process of negotiation. This was the case not only between actors negotiating market access, but also between actors focusing on labour issues. According to one representative of the Ministry of Labour:

> What happens is that after the whole process, travelling together and so on, a very good relationship was developed with labour organizations and business associations. With all this we have maintained a type of agreement, a compromise. It has produced a better knowledge about the counterparts and very close relations, more personal.[28]

This cordial relationship does seem to have facilitated somewhat the implementation of the labour and environmental aspects of the trade agreement, but it does not seem to have 'spilled over' to collaboration on labour and environmental issues in general. One of the reasons is that there are different actors included in the two processes, and that the close and cordial relationships occurred mainly at the personal level; it was not an institutional *rapprochement*. The public officials who are in charge of implementing the labour and environment aspects of the agreement differ from those who negotiated them, and they have limited contact with the domestic business associations that were involved in trade negotiations. On the business side, the highly favourable evaluation that most business associations make of the agencies responsible for negotiating free trade agreements does not spill over into a more favourable evaluation of the conduct of the government in relation to issues of the environment and labour. Most representatives for business associations express that Chilean labour legislation is excessively protective of workers, and that the strict enforcement of its rules is to their competitive disadvantage in the global marketplace.

Conclusion

In the 1990s, Chilean business, particularly export-oriented business, was celebrated as the new agent of development (Montero 1997). While previously business had been viewed with suspicion by large parts of the population, it was now perceived as the group best suited to bringing the country forward. In the same period, there is ample evidence that business, and particularly business associations, have increased their influence on public policy in Chile. Business associations in particular have taken on more of a public leadership role. For example, the launch of the joint government-SOFOFA for Growth Agenda by the SOFOFA president Juan Claro in 2001 signalled a new role for business in Chilean development. The question is whether this increased business influence has worked to the detriment of socially inclusive policies. Looking at social and environmental clauses in trade agreements provides a small piece of that picture. In trade negotiations, business has not proved to be particularly interested in issues other than market access, and to the extent they have been preoccupied with social issues it has been to overcome possible barriers to market access.

The study of Chilean business may have bearings on the general debate about the desirability of linking trade and environmental and labour governance, as well as about the role of business in policy-making. As argued strongly by Stephen Woolcock (2006), the current developments at the regional and bilateral levels in terms of making rules to govern trade and investments have ramifications for the entire global trade framework. This is where there is currently most dynamism, considering the relative deadlock of the WTO. It is also at this level that there currently is a great deal of competition between conflicting regulatory models proposed by the various strong powers. Chile has been exposed to both major models: the one proposed by the United States and the one proposed by the EU. The former is characterized by 'mutual recognition' of domestic law backed by international sanctions, whereas the latter, based more on a 'soft' law approach, aims towards approximation and harmonization in legal frameworks, and strong internal regulations that can motivate potential exporters. The lessons from the Chilean case is that the US model created strong opposition for reasons of national sovereignty and worked to unify forces against what was considered imposition from the United States. The EU model has to a greater extent encouraged business to voluntarily take on commitments and it has made business more offensive regarding, in particular, environmental standards.

What does this tell us about the role of business in policy-making? Chilean business has played a significant role in the negotiation of the many FTAs that Chile has signed with other countries. The strong role played by SOFOFA helped business overcome sectoral differences and play an active and supportive role in the general negotiations. However, related to environmental and labour regulations, it has been a 'rule-taker' rather than an active 'rule-maker' and it has been more defensive than offensive. As well, the possible indirect impact of the close involvement of business in discussions of these regulatory aspects in trade agreements, the possible 'spill-over effect' locally, has been limited. One should believe that the establishment of relationships of trust and loyalty across the public–private divide during international negotiations would prepare the ground for forms of 'soft' regulation or 'co-regulation' at the national level. However, this study has shown such effects to be limited by institutional barriers between those who make and those who implement labour and environmental policy. In the future, it is expected that business from emerging markets will gain increasing influence in global policy-making due to their increasing economic strength and global reach. This study shows that these may have an incentive to press for stronger regulations on labour and the environment mainly as way of 'levelling the playing field' in the pursuit of gaining market shares in heavily regulated markets. However, in practice, in the case of Chile, business has mainly behaved in a defensive way and has acted as a reluctant 'rule-taker' rather than a 'rule-maker'.

Notes

1. The definition of regulation adopted in the article is 'mechanisms of social control' (Baldwin et al. 1998). This definition allows for the inclusion of formal as well as informal rules, and multiple regulatory actors, and national as well as international and transnational regulatory forms.
2. See, for example, the collection of articles in Winn (2004).
3. Regarding social regulation in Latin America more specifically, I have shown elsewhere how competing models that combine different features of Woolcock's list coexist. The United States promotes what I have called a 'supranational regulation enforcement' that is weak on harmonization, including instead a measure of mutual recognition of national regulation, but is strong on implementation provisions and cooperation. The EU promotes a form of collective national regulation that has approximation as a general aim, and is strong on cooperation in terms of technical cooperation and capacity-building, but has few intergovernmental decision-making bodies and is weak on implementation measures (Bull 2007).
4. There is an enormous literature on this. Majone (1997) and Kirton and Trebilcock (2004) are some good examples.
5. The early literature on this subject emerges out of domestic studies of changes in legal regulation. See Ayres and Braithwaite (1992). Later contributions have been focused on transnational and international relations between business and governments. See, for example, Elsig (2007); Levy and Newell (2005).
6. The tariffs had increased after the 1982–3 economic crisis in Chile.
7. For a good expression of SOFOFA's position on trade agreements, see the speech given by SOFOFA President Juan Claro at the annual industry dinner, 9 November 2004, at: www.sofofa.cl/mantenedor/detalle.asp?n=12534 (accessed on 15 September 2007).
8. There were two major exceptions to this rule. One was the opposition launched by small and micro enterprises. The other, as emphasized by Leight (2008), was the opposition from traditional agriculture against possible threats against the price bands from trade agreements.
9. A free trade agreement is characterized by a 'negative list approach': the goal is full free trade and the parties negotiate about exceptions. This differs from the more limited Economic Complementation Agreement (ECA) in which tariff reduction is negotiated for specific products based on a 'positive list approach'. An Association Agreement (AA) is more encompassing and also includes political collaboration.
10. Interview, Representative ProChile, Embassy of Chile, Washington, DC, 23 February 2006.
11. In 2006, 2.6 per cent of Chilean exports went to Canada.
12. Interview, Manager, Environmental Department, SOFOFA, Santiago, 7 March 2005.

13. Interview, Manager, Environmental Department, SOFOFA, Santiago, 7 March 2005.
14. The regular abuse of worker rights under the Pinochet dictatorship prompted the United States to suspend trade benefits under the GSP in 1988 (US Department of Labor 2003).
15. Interview, Manager, National Society of Mining, Santiago, 23 June 2006.
16. The most important exception was perhaps the Chilean associations of poultry and pork producers (Asociación de Productores Avícolas de Chile/APA and Asociación Gremial de Productores de Cerdos de Chile/APROCER, respectively). Both the poultry and the pork producers are traditionally protectionist sectors in Chile, and as Canada is a significant pork producer with significant offensive interests in Chile, it had reason to worry. However, instead of opposing the agreement, APROCER's strategy was to accompany the government, and it achieved an agreement that it was reasonably happy with. Interview, President of APA and APROCER, Juan Miguel Ovalle, 15 March 2006.
17. Interview, labour specialist, DIRECON, former ILO, Chile, and negotiator for Ministry of Labour, Santiago, 26 February 2006.
18. This statement is based on interviews with several of the key negotiators.
19. Any citizen of a Party can bring in the other Party for lack of enforcement of its own environmental or labour laws *if* this is seen to have direct impact on bilateral trade between the two countries. The ultimate sanction envisaged if such a complaint is found to be justified is to set aside the benefits under the commercial part of the agreement. However, a long procedure is stipulated before such sanctions may be put into effect, including the issuing of fines of up to US$15 million annually.
20. Interview, former President of AmCham, Santiago, 20 March 2006.
21. Interview, Responsible for civil society interaction, DIRECON, Santiago, 3 March 2006.
22. Interview, president of environmental organization, Santiago, 11 April 2006.
23. Interview, former DIRECON director and chief negotiator, Santiago, 3 April 2006.
24. Interview, ProChile representative, Embassy of Chile, Washington, DC, 23 February 2006.
25. The most successful of these was APA, that justifiably had feared that US poultry producers would dump chicken legs on the Chilean market as only chicken breasts are commercially viable in the United States. In order to resolve this, APA negotiated an agreement with the US National Broiler Council that included a 25 per cent rise in tariffs on chicken legs and that formed the basis of the final agreement between the two governments. Interview, Juan Miguel Ovalle, President of APA, 15 March 2006.
26. Interview, Director of Europe relations, DIRECON, Chilean Ministry of Foreign Affairs, Santiago, 27 June 2006.
27. For information on what sectors this includes, see the website for the Consejo Nacional de Producción Limpia (www.pl.cl).
28. Interview, former Director of the International Department, Ministry of Labour, Santiago, 27 June 2006.

References

Ayres, Ian and John Braithwaite (1992) *Responsive Regulation: Transcending the Deregulation Debate* (Oxford: Oxford University Press).

Baldwin, Robert, Colin Scott and Christopher Hood (eds) (1998) *A Reader on Regulation* (Oxford: Oxford University Press).

Borrás, Susana and Kerstin Jacobsson (2004) 'The Open Method of Co-ordination and New Governance Patterns in the EU', *Journal of European Public Policy*, 11 (29), 185–208.

Bull, Benedicte (2007) 'Trade Liberalization and the Spread of Regulatory Institutions: The Case of Chile', *Regulation & Governance*, 2 (4), 372–84.

——— (2008) 'Policy Networks and Business Participation in Free Trade Negotiations in Chile', *Journal of Latin American Studies*, 40 (2), 195–224.

Campero, Guillermo (2003) 'La relación entre el Gobierno y los grupos de presión: El proceso de la acción de bloques a la acción segmentada', *Revista de Ciencia Política*, XXIII (2), 159–76.

Clapp, Jennifer (1998) 'The Privatization of Global Environmental Governance: ISO 14000 and the Developing World', *Global Governance*, 3 (4), 295–316.

CPC (Confederación de la Producción y del Comercio) (n.d.) *Proyecto de Ley sobre Subcontratación y Empresas de Servicios Transitorios: Observaciones Principales de la CPC*, at: www.cpc.cl/pdfs/Proyecto%20sobre%20Subcontrataci%F3n.pdf (accessed 11 March 2009).

CUT (Central Unitaria de Trabajo) and AFL-CIO (American Federation of Labor and Congress of Industrial Organizations) (2002) *The Declaration of the CUT/Chile and of the AFL-CIO Concerning the Proposed Free Trade Agreement between Chile and the United States*, August (2002), at: www.union-network.org/uniflashes.nsf/0/173a99c02ce845edc1256c2100584054?OpenDocument (accessed 18 March 2009).

Cutler, A. Claire, Virginia Haufler and Tony Porter (eds) (1999) *Private Authority and International Affairs* (New York: State University of New York Press).

DIRECON (General Directorate for International Economic Affairs, Ministry of Foreign Affairs, Chile) (n.d.) *Summary Chart: Free Trade Agreements,* at: www.direcon.cl/cuadro_resumen_en.html (accessed 17 March 2009).

Djelic, Marie Laure and Kerstin Sahlin-Anderson (eds) (2006) *Transnational Governance: Institutional Dynamics of Regulation* (Cambridge: Cambridge University Press).

Durán-Palma, Fernando, Adrian Wilkinson and Marek Korczynski (2005) 'Labour Reform in a Neo-Liberal "Protected" Democracy: Chile 1990–2001', *International Journal of Human Resource Management*, 16 (1), 65–89.

Elsig, Manfred (2007) 'Business and Public–Private Regulation Arrangements: Beyond Corporate Social Responsibility', paper presented to the conference Non-State Actors as Standard Setters: The Erosion of the Public-Private Divide, Hotel Hilton, Basel, 8–9 February.

Fazio, Hugo (2004) *Mapeo Empresarial Chile. Enero del 2004* (Santiago: Centro de Estudios Nacionales de Desarrollo Alternativo/CENDA).

Fernández Jilberto, Alex E. (2004) 'Neoliberal Restructuring: The Origin and Formation of Economic Groups in Chile', *Journal of Developing Societies*, 20 (3–4), 189–206.

Ffrench-Davis, Ricardo (2005) *Entre el neoliberalismo y el crecimiento con equidad: Tres décadas de política económica en Chile* (Santiago de Chile: J.C. Sáez).

Foxley, Alejandro (1994) *La economía política de la transición: El camino del diálogo* (Santiago de Chile: Dolmen).

Frank, Volker (2002) 'The Elusive Goal in Democratic Chile: Reforming the Pinochet Labor Legislation', *Latin American Politics and Society*, 44 (1), 35–68.

Hall, Bruce and Thomas J. Biersteker (2002) *The Emergence of Private Authority in Global Governance* (Cambridge: Cambridge University Press).

Hockin, Thomas A. (2004) 'The World Trade Organization, the North American Free Trade Agreement and the Challenge of Sustainable Development', in John J. Kirton and Michael J. Trebilock (eds), *Hard Choices, Soft Law: Voluntary Standards in Global Trade, Environment and Social Governance* (Aldershot: Ashgate).

Intal-ITD-STA (Institute for the Integration of Latin America and the Caribbean – Integration, Trade and Hemispheric Issues Division – Statistics and Quantitative Analysis Unit) (2002) 'The Trade Policy-Making Process. Level One of the Two Level Game: Country Studies in the Western Hemisphere', Intal-ITD-STA Occasional Paper 13 (Buenos Aires: Inter-American Development Bank/Inter-American Dialogue/ University of Toronto, Munk Centre for International Studies at Trinity College).

Jayasuriya, Kanishka (2004) 'The New Regulatory State and Relational Capacity', *Policy & Politics*, 32 (4), 487–501.

Kirton, John J. and Michael J. Trebilcock (2004) *Hard Choices, Soft Law: Voluntary Standards in Global Trade, Environment and Social Governance* (Aldershot: Ashgate).

Lagos Weber, Ricardo (2004) Untitled article in *Tratados de Libre Comercio: Desafíos para las relaciones laborales*, Seminario interno (Santiago: Dirección del Trabajo, October).

Leight, Jessica (2008) 'The Political Dynamics of Agricultural Liberalisation in the US-Chile Free Trade Agreement', *Journal of Latin American Studies*, 40 (2), 225–49.

Levy, David and Peter Newell (eds) (2005) *The Business of Global Environmental Governance* (Cambridge, MA: MIT Press).

Mesquita Moreira, Mauricio and J. Juan Blyde (2006) *Chile's Integration Strategy: Is There Room for Improvement?*, IADB-INTAL-ITD Working Paper No. 21 (Buenos Aires: Intal).

Majone, Giandomenico (1997) 'The New European Agencies: Regulation by Information', *Journal of European Public Policy*, 4 (2), 262–75.

Mandelson, Peter (2006) 'Trade Policy and Decent Work Intervention', speech to the EU Decent Work Conference, 5 December, at: http://ec.europa.eu/commission_barroso/ashton/speeches_articles/sppm134_en.htm (accessed 17 March 2009).

Montero, Cecilia (1997) *La revolución empresarial chilena* (Santiago de Chile: Cieplan/ Dolmen Ediciones).

Murillo, Maria Victoria and Andrew Schrank (2005) 'With a Little Help from My Friends: Partisan Politics, Transnational Alliances, and Labor Rights in Latin America', *Comparative Political Studies*, 38 (8), 971–99.

Newell, Peter (2004) 'Business and International Environmental Governance: The State of the Art', in David Levy and Peter Newell (eds), *The Business of Global Environmental Governance* (Cambridge, MA: MIT Press).

Odell, John (2006) 'Introduction', in John S. Odell, *Negotiating Trade: Developing Countries in the WTO and NAFTA* (Cambridge: Cambridge University Press).

OECD/ECLAC (Organisation for Economic Co-operation and Development/Economic Commission for Latin America and the Caribbean) (2005a) *Evaluaciones del desempeño ambiental: Chile* (Santiago de Chile: ECLAC).

——— (2005b) 'The Multilateral Agenda: General Overview of the Negotiations', paper presented to the Inter-American Development Bank, Trade and Integration Network, Regional Policy Dialogue, 5–6 October.

Ostry, Sylvia (2004) 'The Future of the World Trading System: Beyond Doha', in John J. Kirton and Michael J. Trebilcock (eds), *Hard Choices, Soft Law: Voluntary Standards in Global Trade, Environment and Social Governance* (Aldershot: Ashgate).

Porras, José Ignacio (2003) *La estrategia chilena de acuerdos comerciales: Un análisis político*, Serie Comercio Internacional 36 (Santiago: ECLAC).

Putnam, Robert D. (1988) 'Diplomacy and Domestic Politics: The Logic of Two Level Games', *International Organization*, 42 (3), 427–60.

Ramos, José and Alfil Ulloa Urrutia (2003) 'El tratado de libre comercio entre Chile y Estados Unidos', *Revista de Estudios Internacionales*, XXXVI (141), 45–65.

Sáez, Sebastian (2002) 'Making Trade Policy in Chile: An Assessment', in Intal-ITD-STA, *The Trade Policy-Making Process Level One of the Two Level Game: Country Studies in the Western Hemisphere*, Occasional Paper 13 (Inter-American Dialogue/University of Toronto: Munk Centre for International Studies at Trinity College).

Schneider, Ben Ross (2004) *Business Politics and the State in Twentieth-Century Latin America* (Cambridge: Cambridge University Press).

Schurman, Rachel (2001) 'Uncertain Gains: Labor in Chile's New Export Sectors', *Latin American Research Review*, 36 (2), 3–30.

Silva, Eduardo (1996a) *The State and Capital in Chile: Business Elites, Technocrats and Market Economics* (Boulder: Westview Press).

——— (1996b) 'Democracy, Market Economics, and Environmental Policy in Chile', *Journal of Interamerican Studies and World Affairs*, 38 (4), 1–33.

——— (2002) 'Capital and the Lagos Presidency: Business as Usual?', *Bulletin of Latin American Research*, 21 (3), 339–57.

Silva, Patricio (2000) *State Capacity, Technocratic Insulation, and Government-Business Relations in South Korea and Chile* (Santiago de Chile: FLACSO).

Silva, Verónica (2000) 'Política comercial y la relación público-privada en Chile durante los años noventa', in Oscar Muñoz Gomá (ed.), *El Estado y El Sector Privado: Construyendo una nueva economía en los años 90* (Santiago: FLACSO/Dolmen – Economía y Gestión).

US Department of Labor (2003) *Labor Rights: Chile*, at: www.dol.gov/ilab/media/reports/usfta/HR2738ChileLaborRights.pdf (accessed 18 March 2009).

Van Klaveren, Alberto (2006) 'América Latina y la Unión Europea: La otra relación transatlántica, *Revista de Estudios Internacionales*, 39 (153), 53–67.

Vogel, David (2000) 'Environmental Regulation and Economic Integration', *Journal of International Economic Law*, 3 (2), 265–79.

Winn, Peter (2004) *Victims of the Chilean Miracle: Workers and Neoliberalism in the Pinochet Era, 1973–2002* (Durham, NC and London: Duke University Press).

Woll, Cornelia and Alvaro Artigas (2007) 'When Trade Liberalization Turns into Regulatory Reform: The Impact on Business-Government Relations in International Trade Politics', *Regulation & Governance*, 1 (2), 121–38.

Woolcock, Stephen (2006) 'Introduction: The Interaction Between Levels of Rule-Making in International Trade and Investment', in Stephen Woolcock (ed.), *Trade and Investment Rule-Making: The Role of Regional and Bilateral Agreements* (Tokyo, New York and Paris: United Nations University Press).

5

Business, Politics and Free Trade Negotiations in Nicaragua: Who Were the Winners and Losers?

Gloria Carrión

> *We were waiting in Washington to find out what was going to happen. At this time, the negotiations were not in hotels, but in the offices of the United States Trade Representative. DR–CAFTA had been finalized, the official picture had been taken and the celebrations began without an agreement on the sugar quota*
>
> Mario Amador, president, National Commission for Sugar Producers (CNPA).

Introduction

Business and other non-state actors like non-governmental organizations (NGOs) and social movements have proliferated in the crafting of international trade regimes at the bilateral, regional and multilateral levels. In an increasingly technical, legalistic and complex international trade policy-making environment, expertise and financial resources take a leading role. These actors, however, differ in their degrees of access to knowledge and resources, and, ultimately, in the exercise of power.

Both gains and losses in the context of free trade agreement negotiations will be determined by the amount of power that different actors wield at the national, regional and transnational level. In the case of small and low-income countries like Nicaragua, however, both negotiating space – the ability to shape outcomes in a trade agreement[1] – and the results obtained will be further demarcated by power relations vis-à-vis stronger negotiating partners like the United States. In the case of the Dominican Republic–Central American Free Trade Agreement (DR–CAFTA), Amador's depiction of events (see above) during the final round of negotiations conveys the extent to which Nicaragua negotiated that agreement from an unequal footing with the United States.

International relations literature has focused on a two-level bargain model (Putnam 1988) to explain the outcomes of international negotiations. However, the political economy of DR–CAFTA shows that current changes in global governance structures are increasingly empowering particular economic actors within and beyond the boundaries of the nation-state and transforming trade policy-making into a more complex and multilevelled process in which power dynamics take a decisive role in shaping final outcomes. This will bear profound implications for inclusive development – understood as development that is both participatory and social – in small and low-income countries like Nicaragua.

Furthermore, the inherent political economic trade-off that bilateral and regional trade agreements entail in relation to multilateral agreements – greater market access into developed countries in exchange for commitments on intellectual property rights, services, government procurement, investment and so on, more stringent than those at the World Trade Organization (WTO) (Shadlen 2005) – will also greatly impact policy space.[2]

This chapter is based on 16 in-depth interviews with Nicaraguan government officials, private sector, NGO and social movements' representatives conducted throughout the first half of 2007, as well as the analysis of relevant literature,[3] including key negotiating documents kindly provided by negotiators from the Ministerio de Fomento, Industria y Comercio (MIFIC/the Nicaraguan Ministry of Development, Industry and Trade). Furthermore, it is also based on one in-depth interview the author conducted in 2005 with the former Nicaraguan director for international trade and one phone interview with a civil society representative in 2008.

This chapter explores three main questions:

1. How do business and other non-state actors shape trade policy-making and national preferences in the context of a regional trade agreement like DR–CAFTA?
2. How does business collective action and social mobilization impact the trade policy-making process?
3. What significance does this have for inclusive development?

This chapter shows how business actors shape and influence trade policy-making in a small and low-income country like Nicaragua in the context of asymmetrical power relations and the potential implications for inclusive development. To understand the relative influence of business, however, a closer look at civil society actors and the state is fundamental. Thus, this chapter also explores the role of these actors in trade policy-making. As such, the objective of this chapter is to contribute to the information gap that Ventura-Dias and Lengyel (2004) have identified with respect to Latin American domestic trade policy-making.[4]

The structure is as follows. The first section contains the relevant concepts and debates. The second section maps the actors (business and civil society). The third section exposes the mechanisms of business influence in DR–CAFTA negotiations. The fourth section analyses business's proposals and outcomes in

DR–CAFTA. The fifth section discusses NGOs' and social movements' outcomes in the negotiations and the extent to which business influence was counteracted by these actors. The sixth section develops the main conclusions.

Relevant concepts and debates

Economic globalization – understood as 'rising economic openness and integration of national economies' (Wade 2004) – along with free movement of capital, investment flows and strategic transnational business alliances are core elements of the current international political economy. As neoliberal ideology has spread globally, international trade flows have become increasingly important to national economies. According to neoclassical economists, this is overwhelmingly positive as 'free' trade, growth and development are causally linked.

At the core, regional trade regimes entail a level of policy harmonization that can facilitate the flow and exchange of goods and services. States and their policy-makers play a crucial role in this process. Given that policy-making is still the realm of national state bureaucracies, it is important to highlight its inherent political nature. By picking 'winners' and 'losers', policy-makers are involved in a highly political process that, as Keeley and Scoones (2003: 21) argue, 'both reflects and shapes particular institutional and political practices and ways of describing the world'.

Traditional international relations literature focuses on a two-level interface between international negotiations and domestic politics in order to explain preference formation in the context of international trade regime creation. According to Putnam (1988), in Level I (international) bargaining takes place among representatives of states in order to conclude an agreement. In Level II (domestic), bargaining involves attempts to gain support from domestic constituencies which must concur with the terms of the agreement if it is to be ratified. The interaction between the two levels is highly dynamic.

Within this conception, Level II interests usually shape the bargaining positions and strategies of negotiators and demarcate the possibility of an agreement at Level I. Expectations by Level I actors about prospects for ratification also determine the parameters within which potential agreements are considered. Conversely, Level I developments can affect politics at Level II, sometimes increasing the prospects for ratification and at other times diminishing them. According to Putnam (1988: 434), domestic groups at the national level will pressure the government to 'adopt favourable policies, and politicians seek power by constructing coalitions among those groups. At the international level, national governments seek to maximise their own ability to satisfy domestic pressures, while minimizing the adverse consequences of foreign developments'.

The increasing involvement of powerful economic actors within and beyond the nation-state in regime formation, however, is deeply challenging traditional notions of what actually constitutes the 'domestic' level, introducing new levels of governance whose impact on national decision-making processes and development we are only beginning to grasp. This will therefore require new ways of understanding preference and interest formation, which increasingly and effectively take into account current changes in global economic governance and move beyond the fluidity and linearity this model is based on.

Some authors (Ventura-Dias and Lengyel 2004; Singh 2003) have directed our attention to the potential limitations of this model and are showing both how structural conditions of particular world regions may interfere with a straightforward causality between the international and domestic bargain and what role the negotiating *process* plays in preference and interest formation. Other scholars have noted that the political, economic and social conjuncture during the process of negotiations is crucial in actively shaping outcomes and, in many cases, forming and contesting actors' interests. In this view, interests are socially constructed and, as such, are in constant creation, alteration or disposal (Singh 2003). Interests, previously formulated, can, and do, change in the context of international negotiations as 'power structures may shape initial preferences and negotiations, but negotiations shape the interests and outcomes and, therefore, the exercise of power' (Singh 2003: 2). Thus, potential changes in preferences and power of business constituencies across issues and sectors and in different fora may account for 'the uneven and fragmented nature of the resulting system' (Levy and Prakash 2003: 147).

These frameworks highlight, and rightly so, the malleability of actors' interests. However they may ignore the particular experiences of low-income countries in negotiations with *hegemonic* players, which seem to be introducing further complexity. For these countries, changes in preferences and the negotiating *process* itself are seldom disentangled from power structures that define the boundaries for national preferences and the scope of these countries' negotiating space. Hence, contrary to what new international negotiations theory argues (Singh 2003), strategic use of negotiating space (that is, negotiating tactics such as coalition building and agenda-setting) may not be sufficient in the case of these countries to secure outcomes in the context of deep power imbalances. Negotiating tactics can get these countries only so far; outcomes will be shaped to a large extent by the *hegemon*'s preferences and interests.

Far from arguing for a return to structural determinism in which only the powerful actor obtained gains in negotiations, the experiences of these countries signal the importance of rescuing notions of power within trade-negotiation theory that are closer to the Gramscian and Foucauldian traditions. Gramsci's work on hegemony highlights the crucial role ideology plays in the exercise of power in a non-coercive way while Foucault's stresses the inescapable ubiquity of power relations. It is precisely these notions of power that trade-negotiation theory needs to rescue in order to account for the negotiating experiences of small and low-income countries like Nicaragua.

New state and society relations: the rise of business and other non-state actors in international trade regimes

Markets do not operate in a vacuum of rules and power (Ventura-Dias and Lengyel 2004: 1). Instead, they are embedded in complex state–society relations. The boundaries between the spheres of state, society and markets are becoming increasingly porous, and each sphere is intricately tied into the structures of the others (Riain 2000: 190). As such, spaces are created for social and political action within and between these connections. In the context of economic globalization, new multilayered and multiplayer forms of governance have emerged, profoundly changing traditional conceptions of the 'nation-state'. Indeed, transnational business is increasingly exerting power in policy-making processes through both formal (that is, business associations) and informal (that is, personal relations) mechanisms. In response to these actors' political and economic expansion, however, new forms and expressions of national and transnational social contention (Giugni et al. 2006) in the form of NGOs and social movements have arisen, clearly echoing Polanyi's (1944) metaphor of the 'double movement'.

The increasing uncertainty and complexity of issues accompanying the restructuring of economic, political and social life has placed crucial emphasis on the interactions between interest groups and policy-making in the developed and developing world. Several authors (for example, Utting 2006; Sell 2000) have directed attention to the intricate workings of knowledge and power in determining policy outcomes at the national and international level. Peter Haas (1992) first introduced the concept of 'epistemic community' in order to illustrate this interaction. Epistemic communities can be understood as a 'network of professionals with recognised expertise and competence in a particular domain and an authoritative claim to policy-relevant knowledge within that domain or issue-area' (Haas 1992: 3). Through their expertise, ability to frame the issues, and access to negotiators and policy-makers, epistemic communities can, and do, exert power in international negotiations. Business constituencies and NGOs with 'expert' knowledge can thus be understood under the premise of epistemic communities.

Business constituencies can take the form of 'national and transnational business associations, such as industry, trade associations, and business lobbying organisations representing the interests of a group of firms' (Haufler 2000: 123). As the 'structural power' of the private sector increases as a result of the restructuring of the global economy, some argue, states become ever more open to their influence to the point where business interests become national priorities. Andrew Walter (2000: 51) refers to this as the 'convergence hypothesis', which claims that 'enhanced mobility of transnational corporations (TNCs) in the world economy confers structural power upon firms, resulting in a process of convergence of national policy regimes upon TNC policy preferences'. Although such causality is still highly debated (Walter 2000: 54), the truth is that both business constituencies and states, particularly from developed countries, commonly envision and lobby for increased policy harmonization.

Business motivations for deep integration, Haufler (2000: 123) argues, are driven by the desire to achieve efficiency, stability and security of transactions, as well as power and autonomy. Indeed, Levy and Prakash (2003: 139) add:

> TNCs might find that fewer resources are needed to resolve an issue in a single international forum than to negotiate the issue on a country-by-country basis. International forums offer TNCs the opportunity to share the costs of political activity with firms based in other countries.

Furthermore, for Woll and Artigas (2007), deep integration inherent to current international trade negotiations, require 'deep' knowledge and expertise, which business associations are in a position to provide and in turn shape the policy-making process. Direct access to 'policy networks', agency and 'framing' are crucial to ensuring such influence.

'Policy networks' refer to the emergence of close personal networks with international ties that have become central to public policy formulation and implementation (Teichman 2001). In Latin America these policy networks have been characterized by the increasing inclusion of business representatives into the policy-making process, either informally through chats over lunch and so on, or formal relations granted to trade associations or chambers (Bull 2004). The ideological 'authority' the Washington consensus gave to business may partly explain this, but so does the ability of business to influence public policy through its agency and framing ability.

Business constituencies have been actively engaged in framing their interests in ways that are compatible with national state priorities and consistent with 'a public sense of legitimacy' (Sell 2003: 182). Furthermore, they have also heavily relied on their agency – businesses' own actions. Business constituencies take advantage of power structures through their agency. As such, agency is highly and dynamically linked to structure. 'Structured agency', Sell (2003: 180) argues, highlights the manner in which 'structural factors condition agency, by examining the way that structure identifies and creates agents and distributes resources of vested interests and bargaining power.'

The form in which business constituencies strategically use power structures is thus crucial to reaching goals, but so is the interaction with 'other' (civil society[5] – NGOs and social movements) actors. As DR–CAFTA negotiations show, the different levels of power that each of these actors wield at the national and regional level plays a crucial role in determining the winners and losers from a free trade agreement (FTA). It is, thus, to a closer look of both Nicaraguan business and civil society actors that we now turn our attention to.

Mapping the actors: business and civil society

Nicaraguan business is a central player in national economic policy-making, and it has organized, more or less effectively, to strengthen and expand its role. The privatization of national industries, the deregulation of capital investment, and growth in export-oriented activities in the context of neo-liberal reforms were fundamental in increasing the political prominence of business.

Indeed, one of the most transformative reforms of the 1990s was the transfer of economic power from workers, obtained during the previous decade,[6] to the national business elite through the process of privatization. The government of Violeta Barrios created the General *Junta* of the National Public Sector Corporation to lead the privatization of state-owned and confiscated property. Although the government agreed to leave up to 25 per cent of ownership of each of the privatized enterprises in the hands of the workers in order to ensure political stability and promote entrepreneurship among small- and medium-sized economic actors, this seldom materialized. Many of the agricultural lands and agroindustrial plants producing cotton, coffee and meat, among other commodities, were returned to their former owners. In contrast, the lands given to the workers during the Sandinista Revolution were rarely legalized (Equipo Envío 1991), making it extremely difficult for workers to be eligible for loans and credit.[7]

Moreover, the government granted licenses to the economic elite for the establishment of private banks and insurance companies, and for the development of investment banking. By 1991, the banks, which currently account for 92 per cent of the assets of the national financial system (Equipo Envío 1991: 70), emerged. Large banks such as the Banco de América Central (BAC/Central American Bank), Banco de la Producción (BANPRO), Banco de Finanzas (BDF), Banco de Crédito Centroamericano (BANCENTRO/Central American Credit Bank), and Banco UNO,[8] gave rise to the national business groups that now hold strong power over the economic and political realms. Indeed, the restitution of the financial system and the licences granted to private individuals proved fundamental for the repositioning of national economic actors.

Since then, the growth of regional and transnational economic ties has been particularly central to creating a new political dynamic that greatly accentuates the sway of business, but also redefines the players. In the context of globalization and regional integration, Central American business groups have expanded their activities beyond national state boundaries. Some of these groups include the *Grupo Gutiérrez* in Guatemala which owns large food chains, the Salvadorean *Grupo Poma* and *Grupo TACA*, with investments in tourism and hotels and regional airlines, and the Nicaraguan *Grupo Pellas*, with financial services, among others (Bull 2004). These groups have become more integrated at the regional level through joint ventures, direct investment and buying competitors, particularly in areas such as finance, real estate projects like housing, business and shopping centres, and car sales (Segovia 2005).

Parallel to the integration of Central American business, transnational capital has also emerged as a powerful player. Indeed, foreign direct investment (FDI) in the region has increased[9] since 1990, with particular emphasis on the services sector (including energy, telecommunications and *maquiladoras*). In the case of Nicaragua, FDI in the tertiary sector increased from $20.3 million[10] in 1991 to $207 million in 2000 (UNCTAD 2007). The United States remains the country's major trade and investment partner even though countries like Spain, Taiwan and Korea have also become important FDI providers.

TNCs are increasingly buying regional and national businesses or have become important shareholders of locally owned companies. Retailing giants like Ahold (the Netherlands), Walmart (US) and Carrefour (France) have bought many supermarket chains in the region and are centralizing the commercialization of agricultural products. La Fragua, a Guatemalan supermarket bought by Ahold, fused with Corporación de Supermercados Unidos (CSU/Corporation of United Supermarkets) – another locally owned supermarket – to become the Central American Retail Hold Company, making $2 billion in sales in 2003 (Dugger 2004). In Nicaragua, General Electric bought, in 2005, 50 per cent of the shares of Banco de América Central, owned by the powerful Grupo Pellas (Segovia 2005: 74). The increasing economic prominence of these actors has also strengthened their political leverage. National, regional and transnational business actors are indeed highly influential in the economic and political arenas. Given the region's increased dependence on FDI and exports, the role of these actors in financing political parties' campaigns and their influence over the media[11] has granted them direct access to policy networks and public spheres of decision-making like trade negotiations.

In the context of DR–CAFTA, Nicaraguan business, particularly large business, organized itself into industry-specific associations through which it exerted direct influence. Some of the major players during the negotiations were the Asociación Nicaragüense de la Industria Textil y Confección (ANITEC/Nicaraguan Apparel and Textile Manufacturers' Association) – mainly comprised of large national enterprises and United States (US), Taiwanese, and South Korean TNCs' subsidiaries under the Free Trade Zones Regime[12] and the Comisión Nacional de Productores de Azúcar (CNPA/National Committee for Sugar Producers) that represents the four sugar mills established in the country. Two of those mills belong to the powerful Nicaraguan Pellas Group and the Guatemalan Pantaleon Group. Two individuals, Fernando Traversari, vice-president of ANITEC, and Mario Amador, president of the CNPA, were powerful advocates of business interests in the negotiations.

Moreover, beef producers were important players. However, since beef exports are in the hands of three local medium to large abattoirs, they have not yet created an association and lobbying has fallen under the responsibility of the individual owners. During DR–CAFTA negotiations, Alfredo Marín, the president of Matadero San Martín, the largest abattoir in the country, personally attended all the rounds of negotiations.[13] Dairy producers organized under the Cámara Nicaragüense del Sector Lácteo (CANISLAC/Nicaraguan Dairy Sector Chamber), also engaged in the negotiations. CANISLAC represents mainly small and medium dairy producers. Wilmer Fernández, vice-president of CANISLAC, was their main spokesperson. However, as we will see, CANISLAC's negotiating position led to a clash between Fernández and the negotiating team.

Nicaraguan business has thus been highly successful in repositioning itself at the economic and political level. Changes in economic governance have granted business actors unprecedented structural power to influence policy-making processes vis-à-vis civil society actors. An understanding of the composition and characteristics of Nicaraguan social actors is thus fundamental to grasp how this asymmetry permeated DR–CAFTA negotiations and its implications for inclusive development.

Civil society actors

Nicaraguan civil society is highly diversified, disaggregated and fragmented. Its recent history along with the 1990s neoliberal reforms and the rise of business partly explain this. The emergence and increasing importance of aid donors and development agencies in developing countries, the downsizing of the state and the disillusionment of many Frente Sandinista de Liberación Nacional (FSLN/Sandinista National Liberation Front) members with the party leadership, however, played particularly determining roles. They have, to a large extent, been the drivers behind the increasing NGO-ization[14] of Nicaraguan civil society. Moreover, civil society actors have diversified and comprise old and new social movements as well as NGOs.

As the state rolled back from areas that had traditionally been its realm and international aid donors and development agencies gained a preeminent role in development discourse, the composition of civil society changed (Utting 2006). According to Utting (2006: 2), 'Development agencies positioned themselves as "knowledge agencies", attempting to enhance their role as intellectual actors and to be more responsive to "local knowledge" and the "voices of the poor" and the needs and realities of developing countries.' In Nicaragua, this translated into wide availability of donor funds for local organizations that worked on 'social' issues and projects. NGOs flourished. Indeed, the number of organizations formally registered increased from 150 in the 1980s to approximately 300–400 in 2006[15] (Borchgrevink 2006: 22).

NGOs became important professional spaces for former Sandinista government employees who in 1990 lost their jobs and were looking for continued altruistic activities. Likewise, for those who in the context of the 1994 division of the FSLN – that gave rise to the Movimiento Renovador Sandinista (MRS/Sandinista Renovation Movement) – wanted to distance themselves from the party, but still maintain a presence in national non-partisan political processes. NGOs rapidly gained space in the Nicaraguan political and organizational landscape as mass organizations and grassroots movements (that is, peasant movements and workers' unions) weakened.

New social movements have since also emerged. Particularly relevant are the Movimiento Maria Elena Cuadra, working mainly on women's labour rights in export processing zones, the Red de Mujeres por la Salud (network of women for health), the Red de Mujeres contra la Violencia (network of women against violence), and the Movimiento Ambientalista Nicaragüense (Nicaraguan environmental movement). During DR–CAFTA negotiations, the Movimiento Maria Elena Cuadra, along with other movements and organizations, joined one of the blocs that emerged. Indeed, in DR–CAFTA, Nicaraguan civil society divided into two camps: the Iniciativa de Comercio, Integración y Desarrollo (Initiativa CID/Trade, Integration and Development Initiative),[16] which participated and lobbied the government during the negotiating process, and the *Anti*-CAFTA movement. This division, along with the lack of resources for mobilization and weaker political leverage vis-à-vis business actors, would ultimately limit the influence social actors exerted in the negotiations.

Business influence, the 'room next door' and DR–CAFTA negotiations

DR–CAFTA negotiations officially began on 8 January 2003. Since the onset, business actors influenced the negotiating agenda both formally and informally through what Alvaro Porta[17] refers to as the 'room next door'. This consisted of a room for both business and civil society next to the space where negotiations were being held. Negotiating teams and non-state actors could thus have constant access to each other's inputs throughout the negotiations, although some were more successful than others at seeing their interests reflected in negotiating strategies.

The differing levels of power among the actors involved underlined the limits of both Central American states' negotiating space and non-state actors' policy influence. From the start, the pace of the negotiations dictated by the US delegation reinforced the inherent trade-off between more stringent intellectual property rights (IPR) and investment commitments for enhanced market access. The first few rounds of negotiations were mostly dedicated to the revision of pre-agreement texts on issues of key interest to the United States, such as IPRs, investment, services and government procurement, among others (Cáceres 2003). These texts had been drafted based on previous US FTA negotiations with Chile and the general framework was not open for negotiation (Cáceres 2003). Thus, the negotiating space that Nicaragua and the rest of the Central American countries had in DR–CAFTA negotiations existed mostly on the market access pillar.

In this context, the government turned to business associations, representatives and technical experts to obtain direct information on how to strengthen and support the country's offensive and defensive negotiating strategy, creating a sort of symbiosis.[18] Negotiators gained vital technical information they may not have obtained otherwise and, in turn, business ensured that their interests were reflected in the national negotiating strategy and eventually in the results of DR–CAFTA. Meetings between business actors and negotiators would generally take place in the evenings after negotiations had been finalized for the day. Meetings to brief business representatives and discuss potential strategies were usually held bilaterally, sector by sector.[19]

Information was presented to the negotiating team both formally (for example, written proposals, a consultation forum, the 'room next door') and informally (for example, over lunches, in corridors, hotel lobbies, telephone conversations, and so on).[20] In some cases, however, both the business associations and the negotiating team jointly discussed and crafted the negotiating strategy for the sector, which became a 'national' negotiating priority (for example, textiles and clothing negotiations).

Nicaraguan business actors had ample access to financial resources, technical knowledge and policy circles. In the case of ANITEC, the association hired two Washington-based consultancy firms to draft the sector's proposal, which was then adopted by the Nicaraguan government as the negotiating strategy for the textile and clothing sector.[21] Likewise, the CNPA hired experts from Louisiana State University in order to run simulations of different negotiating scenarios, which ended up informing CNPA's proposal, which became Nicaragua's proposal on sugar. Furthermore, Mario Amador states that during the Managua Round of Negotiations, the CNPA, along with other regional sugar associations, presented and discussed the sector's priorities and demands at national and regional levels with Central American trade ministers.[22]

Likewise, the CNPA maintained a fluid relationship with Nicaraguan National Assembly representatives from the two main political parties (the FSLN and the Constitutionalist Liberal Party) that dealt with DR–CAFTA issues. Additionally, the CNPA had direct and privileged access to US policy circles. During and after the rounds of negotiations, Mario Amador met with influential US Congressmen and Senators 'approximately ten times',[23] as well as with key negotiators like Allen Johnson, the Chief Agriculture Negotiator. The purpose was to lobby the US Congress and Senate, and the Department of Agriculture and the State Department, regarding CNPA's interests in sugar access quotas into the United States.

In contrast, rice, dairy, poultry and other producers who consider themselves ill-prepared to compete with US companies' economies of scale, technology and structural advantages, such as subsidies, advocated longer transition periods from the status quo to complete trade liberalization (for example, dairy producers). Although some of the associations that represented these sectors also had access to the negotiators, their levels of influence varied vis-à-vis the more powerful business associations. Indeed, CANISLAC, the Nicaraguan Dairy Sector Chamber, clashed with the negotiators with what the government considered a 'rather excessive defensive approach'.[24] CANISLAC was arguing for small dairy export quotas into the United States even though their current export capacity was quite good.[25]

Small and medium dairy producers are highly vulnerable to milk powder imports from the United States since, by adding water, milk powder can be returned to its fluid state and thus enter into unfair competition (that is, due to US subsidies) with domestic dairy producers. Since DR–CAFTA was based on reciprocity, CANISLAC figured that a small export quota into the US market would translate into a small import quota into Nicaragua.[26] Thus, for CANISLAC this was the best strategy to salvage its members' interests. However, this placed the association 'at odds' ideologically with the negotiating team, which made the relationship less smooth than it was with CANISLAC's counterparts.

Business actors strongly differed in their access to financial resources to participate and hire international trade experts. In the case of CANISLAC, Wilmer Fernández states that he personally financed his participation in some of the rounds due to CANISLAC's financial resource constraints regarding lobbying,[27] whereas the CNPA's participation was fully funded by its members.[28] Moreover, international trade negotiations were a new milieu for business actors like CANISLAC (with approximately 200–300 affiliates). According to Fernández, 'We [CANISLAC] did not have the technical knowledge or the experience to make proposals and bargain.'[29]

Finally, many other small and medium producers and entrepreneurs lacked the resources and technical capacity to even organize and articulate a particular negotiating position during the consultation process and negotiations (Cáceres 2005). NGOs and other civil society representatives were thus highly instrumental in voicing potential threats to the Nicaraguan peasant economy. Orlando Nuñez, Executive Director of the Centro para la Promoción, la Investigación, y el Desarrollo Rural y Social (CIPRES/Centre for Promotion, Research, and Rural and Social Development) and others, for instance, argued for the importance of protecting white corn production in the context of the FTA, given this product's importance for rural livelihoods.[30]

Business proposals and outcomes in DR–CAFTA negotiations

Business proposals were generally sector-specific and in tune with the interests of the associations' members. The majority of these were clearly reflected in Nicaragua's negotiating strategy. However, the extent to which DR–CAFTA outcomes addressed those interests ultimately depended on the structural power and interests of the United States.

During DR–CAFTA negotiations, ANITEC's objective was 'to strengthen the most powerful branch of its membership', consisting of large assembling plants within the Export Processing Zone Regime. According to Traversari, 'We [ANITEC] were not necessarily excluding other sectors, but we decided that these companies would be the spearhead of the industry's future strategies.'[31] ANITEC presented its negotiating proposal bilaterally to the US delegation based on the simulations conducted by the Washington-based consultants. The strategy consisted of demanding trade preferential levels (TPLs) – an export quota to the US market using fabric originating from countries outside of DR–CAFTA (hence, at lower costs). Countries in FTAs or trade preferential schemes with the United States with similar low development profiles had also received TPLs, notably Jordan and sub-Saharan countries. ANITEC wanted to emulate the concessions granted under those agreements and the initial proposal was set at 500 million square metres equivalent (sme).[32]

Given the higher prices of US textile fabric and inputs, the possibility of buying these at lesser costs in countries outside of the DR–CAFTA region would enhance, according to ANITEC, the industry's competitive stance at a regional and international level. Upon the US delegation's refusal of the initial amount, however, ANITEC counter-proposed a TPL total of 300 million sme. This was also rejected based on the argument that the US textile industry could be harmed under these conditions. In the end, both delegations settled for TPLs at 100 million sme for a period of 10 years. For ANITEC this was a real victory as only Nicaragua would be eligible for this.[33]

When DR-CAFTA reached the US Congress for approval, however, the 'unofficial negotiations' began. Faced with political pressures from the powerful Southern textile lobbyists, US Congressmen and negotiators reopened the textile and clothing (T&C) chapter for negotiations. According to Traversari, US jeans producers felt particularly threatened since 60 per cent of Nicaragua's textile manufacturing production concentrates on trousers. Traversari thus visited Southern Congressmen to strike a deal that would ensure the 20 votes, which according to US negotiators were not secure at that point to pass DR–CAFTA. Both national delegations demanded that the T&C associations in each country negotiate and agree on new terms in a deal for the sector. As a result, the special and differential treatment Nicaragua had obtained in the official DR–CAFTA negotiations was eroded through the inclusion of a 'one-to-one rule'.[34]

In the case of sugar, another 'winning' product according to Nicaraguan negotiators,[35] the CNPA and its counterparts organized under the Central American Isthmus Sugar Association. They proposed a regional quota starting at 350,000 metric tons (MT), which was, however, rejected. Subsequently, the CNPA counter-proposed a regional market access quota equivalent to 25,000 MT annually, which, it was calculated, based on the simulations conducted by the experts from the University of Louisiana, would affect sugar prices in the United States by only 10 per cent.[36] For the CNPA, nonetheless, it became clear that the US delegation would never accept that. Currently, sugar represents one of Nicaragua's highly competitive exports[37] and sugar producers have according to the CNPA the infrastructure and export capacity to take immediate advantage of DR–CAFTA. A high market access quota was thus crucial for the sector. Although under DR–CAFTA the United States doubled Nicaragua's sugar market access quota at the WTO,[38] for Amador this was not nearly as ambitious as the CNPA had previously expected.

In agricultural negotiations, business positions at the national and regional level were sometimes at odds. According to Marín, Nicaraguan negotiators were more inclined to protect poultry from US imports than beef, as poultry is part of the national food basket. For Marín, however, the government made a mistake prioritizing the protection of poultry over beef since 'beef production creates around 300,000 jobs whereas poultry only creates 1,500 jobs.'[39] Early on in the negotiations, Nicaraguan beef exporters demanded a regional export quota of 650,000 MT, knowing that Nicaragua is a major exporter in the region.[40] Central American delegations, however, opposed this. For Marín, this was mainly due to national rivalries among Central American countries. In the end, each country obtained export quotas even though Guatemala and El Salvador are beef-importing countries.

The beef quota Nicaragua obtained under DR–CAFTA (10,500 MT), however, does not match the country's current export capacity, which according to Marín is approximately 25,000 MT a year.[41] For him, the lack of cohesion among beef producers, and their small number, inhibited them from lobbying the government more successfully and largely explain these results. The US beef producers, on the contrary, have a powerful farm lobby and hired economists to draft the beef proposal, which, according to Marín, ended up informing the final agreement.[42] The most important products for the US beef industry are the Prime and Choice cuts, which obtained immediate tariff elimination in the six countries (FAS 2005).

Dairy producers, for their part, decided to actively engage in the negotiations in order to avoid being 'traded-off' against beef or sugar quotas.[43] Contrary to the other associations, CANISLAC had a rockier relationship with the negotiators. For the large dairy processing and pasteurizing plant, run by the Italian Parmalat company, milk powder is of key interest, given its lower cost. To preserve its members' interests, however, CANISLAC argued for a small import quota of US milk.[44] Nicaragua did obtain a small dairy export quota (1,500 MT), which was nonetheless the highest in the region. The quota the US delegation obtained for milk powder in Nicaragua, however, was the highest in the region. These results have already caused negative impacts in domestic dairy production. Magda Lanuza, from the Hijas e Hijos del Maíz (Children of Corn) cooperative, states that 'Parmalat used to pay local dairy farmers $0.45 a litre for fresh milk. But now they are buying more US milk powder and asking Nicaraguan farmers to supply milk for only $0.25 a litre' (Ricker 2004).

The limits of civil society actors in DR–CAFTA negotiations

Divisions within civil society, the power differentials vis-à-vis Nicaraguan business and the United States, and the lack of expertise and lobbying capacity, limited the influence of both Iniciativa CID actors and the *Anti*-CAFTA movement. Iniciativa CID organizations made a series of proposals on most of the pillars[45] of the negotiations along with a 'complementary agenda' that aimed to secure certain benefits for small producers and protect traditional knowledge and access to generic drugs.

At the end of the day, however, only a rather 'watered-down' version of these proposals made it into the final text.[46] Furthermore, a strong media campaign led by the Nicaraguan government largely weakened the *Anti*-CAFTA movement. The campaign was called: 'CAFTA, our bridge to progress'. Its strategy rested on creating short slogans linking DR–CAFTA to positive ideas like 'DR–CAFTA = more FDI, more exports, more employment, more quality products, and more opportunities for SMEs [small and medium enterprises]' (Fonseca-López 2007).

Once DR–CAFTA reached the Nicaraguan National Assembly, the Iniciativa CID actors presented the elements for a legally binding national complementary agenda. Formal political backing for civil society demands, however, was rather weak, even from an apparent natural ally like the Sandinista party, which adopted a 'pragmatic' stance on DR–CAFTA. Such pragmatism derived partly from a desire to lock in trading arrangements that could not be destabilized so easily for ideological reasons, should the Sandinistas return to power, as indeed they did a few months later.

But pragmatism also related to the fact that DR–CAFTA became part of a political game where support for or against the agreement became entangled with the issue of political alliances and divisions in the run-up to the elections. It was also facilitated by the considerable property and other business interests that some party officials or their families had developed in the previous decade (Rodgers 2008), precisely in areas that stood to benefit from DR–CAFTA, such as textile and clothing *maquilas* and agroindustry. Ultimately, business interests prevailed over more socially and environmentally oriented proposals made by civil society actors.

Business, the complementary agenda, and the labour and environmental chapters

The complementary agenda was a legally binding instrument proposed by the Iniciativa CID to deal with structural issues and constraints the FTA did not take into account. Proposals centred on a range of binding tools and monitoring and compliance mechanisms in relation to labour and environmental standards; TNC regulation and performance evaluations of foreign direct investment; and effective protection mechanisms for biodiversity and traditional knowledge, as well as access to generic drugs (CST–JBE 2003; Iniciativa CID 2004).

CST-JBE[47] (2003: 2), for instance, proposed the introduction of economic sanctions to address potential foreign investors' violations of International Labour Organization (ILO) Conventions, the National Labour Legislation, and the Constitutional Rights. Similarly, Iniciativa CID representatives proposed a law to defend and preserve biodiversity and natural resources and ecosystems in FTAs (CST–JBE 2003: 7) in order to tackle biopiracy and address traditional knowledge issues and drug patents.

Moreover, they proposed the creation of a state-owned Development Bank to increase and ensure access to credit for SMEs and farmers and the introduction of state-run cohesion funds to help them withstand unfair competition from US agricultural subsidies (CST–JBE 2003). Mechanisms for effective technology transfer of foreign direct investment (that is, performance requirements and tax breaks granted to companies that transferred knowledge and technology to local producers and entrepreneurs), the creation of backward linkages with other productive sectors of the economy like SMEs, and value-addition were also structural parts of their proposals.[48]

The complementary agenda these actors envisioned was both comprehensive and legally binding. When the Nicaraguan National Assembly ratified DR–CAFTA, however, the complementary agenda annexed to the official publication of DR–CAFTA texts had significantly lost its 'teeth'. According to Mario Quintana, the complementary agenda gave the government the possibility to 'speak the language of NGOs and social movements' regarding the need to tackle national structural constraints and the defence of national interests (that is, traditional knowledge, access to generic drugs, and so on).[49] However, in practice the scope of the agenda, which social movements and Iniciativa CID actors had proposed, was reduced to a few laws and general statements.[50]

Business positions regarding the complementary agenda proposed by the Iniciativa CID differed between big business associations and representatives of small and medium producers and entrepreneurs. The most powerful business associations remained, in general, neutral. They did not oppose the complementary agenda per se, but did not facilitate its adoption either. The most important legally binding instruments proposed by the Iniciativa CID were highly focused on TNCs, which could potentially explain this apparent neutrality. Although some of these legally binding elements regarding fines and technology transfer, among others, could eventually touch national investors, business associations did not perceive any particular threat to their interests. According to Orlando Valverde, it was the government and national legislators who in the end diluted the Iniciativa CID's proposals.[51]

For small and medium producers and entrepreneurs, however, the complementary agenda was crucial to address their particular supply-side constraints such as credit, technology, quality and economies of scale. Thus they fully supported, and were highly involved in, the agenda's conception. They also envisioned it as a useful instrument to safeguard labour rights and promote a sustainable use of the environment.[52] According to Valverde, however, large business associations strongly opposed increasing labour and environmental standards. They wanted, instead, to maintain the status quo (that is, the national constitution). Large business associations argued that any increase in labour and environmental standards would be detrimental to the economic viability of their businesses.[53]

In DR–CAFTA, labour and environmental issues are in separate chapters, as social actors argued for.[54] However, instead of putting the 'burden of proof' on investors or employers, the labour chapter in DR–CAFTA places it on the government and its ability to comply with its national labour legislation (Office of the United States Trade Representative 2004). Furthermore, given that DR–CAFTA is an intergovernmental agreement, the introduction of economic sanctions (that is, fines) would only target the state and not the potential national and/or foreign investors who violate labour and environmental standards. These provisions do not capture the increasing influence and involvement of business in economic planning and activity and the role it plays in the shaping and setting up of those standards.

Furthermore, the chapters clearly address US fears of potential relaxation of labour and environmental standards by Central American governments to attract foreign direct investment, since it is ultimately the state which will be monitored and held accountable. Thus, in terms of what Iniciativa CID actors had previously proposed regarding binding instruments for both states and investors, these chapters and other DR–CAFTA outcomes were not as fully encompassing as these actors had wished for.

Conclusions

Business and other non-state actors clearly influenced DR–CAFTA negotiations. The extent of their influence and the distribution of gains and losses, however, were directly related to the level of power these actors wielded at the national level. The privatization processes and structural adjustment programmes of the 1990s strengthened business actors in relation to civil society (NGOs and social movements). In DR–CAFTA negotiations, business had ample access to negotiators, financial resources and knowledge, which granted them an important advantage over weakened and divided civil society actors. This clearly shaped the outcomes obtained in the negotiations.

DR–CAFTA outcomes, however, can only be ultimately understood in the context of US structural power. In fact the space for influence for both business and civil society actors was further constricted by the US delegation's positions. The erosion of Nicaragua's only concession on textiles and clothing; the fact that non-tariff barriers (that is, sanitary and phyto-sanitary measures) distorting agricultural subsidies, and structural bottlenecks in Central America, were out of the reach of DR–CAFTA; and the 'extra-official' negotiations, clearly illustrate this.

The case of Nicaragua in DR–CAFTA negotiations shows that low-income countries can, and do, use their negotiating space in the formation of international trade regimes. However, their strategies and tactics, as well as the power differentials in relation to other players, will deeply dictate the boundaries of this negotiating space. In these negotiations, Nicaragua's and other Central American countries' space was limited to the market access pillar. The other pillars were out of reach of the Central American players for agenda-setting purposes. Instead, they were central to the political-economic bargain of DR–CAFTA – enhanced market access in exchange for more stringent commitments in IPRs and investment rules.

This therefore suggests that a closer study of the role of power, in particular, *asymmetrical* power, plays in trade regime formation is needed in order to better understand the dynamics at play and the potential implications for policy space and inclusive development for weaker players in the international economic system. Furthermore, the increasingly direct involvement of business actors in international trade negotiations has blurred the distinction between the 'two' levels proposed by the 'two-level' bargain model. Indeed, new ways of understanding preference and interest formation will be required in order to move beyond the fluidity and linearity implicit in this model.

DR–CAFTA negotiations constricted Central American countries' policy space. Indeed, Central American countries committed to more stringent standards than they had at the WTO, with important implications for inclusive development. In the case of IPRs, the agreement further limited the definition of what constitutes a 'national health threat' in relation to the Trade-Related Aspects of Intellectual Property Rights (TRIPS) Agreement, potentially curtailing the autonomy of Central American governments to allow parallel imports of generic drugs in case of need. Likewise, it allowed for the patenting of plant varieties as well as crucial genetic material (that is, the International Union for the Protection of New Varieties of Plants/UPOV, and the Budapest Agreement on the Patenting of Microorganisms). This could in the future lead to the 'privatization' of Central America's rich biodiversity resources and traditional knowledge, which have until now been a 'common good'.

In the case of investment, host countries can no longer use some of the tools that have been central to East Asian countries' development. These include local content (the ability of host governments to demand a certain percentage of locally produced inputs in the production process of foreign investors), performance requirements of FDI in order to receive incentives and tax breaks granted to national economic actors, and technology transfer. This will thus bear clear implications for the ability of Central American governments and policy-makers to foster creative 'state-crafting' in the future and for the use of policy space to generate the synergies from industrial and other supply-side policies responsible for the growth levels that developed and that more advanced developing countries have experienced.

Moreover, in terms of labour and environmental rights and standards, DR–CAFTA stresses that parties enforce their own national labour legislations. However, criticisms have arisen regarding the capacity of the region to safeguard labour rights and environmental standards in the long term based on the provisions of these particular chapters. Indeed, in DR–CAFTA only governments bear the burden of proof and costs of potential sanctions and fines for potential violations of labour and environmental standards. Although trade agreements are ultimately agreed upon and implemented by states, these provisions do not capture the increasing influence and involvement of business in economic planning and activity.

Indeed, states are the only actors to be monitored and potentially sanctioned for labour and environmental standards violations, even though business actors play a key role in shaping and implementing such standards. These actors, however, do not bear any direct liability for labour and environmental violations in the context of international trade regimes. Furthermore, the existing differences between dispute resolution procedures and remedies between commercial and labour and environmental issues in DR–CAFTA may in the future render their enforcement more difficult.

Although identifying impacts of DR–CAFTA could be a premature and potentially difficult exercise given methodological limitations (that is, general equilibrium models, and so on) and heterogeneity among actors and sectors (Jansen et al. 2007), DR–CAFTA's one-year implementation period and current political economic dynamics suggest certain trends for inclusive development in Nicaragua and the region. According to the Ministry for Development, Industry and Trade, the market access exporting quotas obtained under DR–CAFTA have not yet been fully utilized by Nicaraguan producers, excepting sugar and T&C producers. Dairy producers have in general been able to fully use their quotas, but these are, as a result of the negotiations, very low. Their performance should thus be analysed within that context. Indeed, several small and medium dairy producers still face severe infrastructural and productive challenges to transform and add value to milk production as well as non-tariff barriers that curtail real access to the US market. For both regional economic groups with a fully established export capacity and TNCs export and import quotas have been largely utilized.

Structural constraints are, however, by no means only relevant to dairy SMEs. This is a cross-cutting national and regional reality for many Nicaraguan SMEs. Access to roads, technology and innovation, credit and productive inputs are a profound challenge to SMEs' participation in national and international markets. Likewise, the lack of productive structures that inhibits the creation of economies of scale among Nicaraguan SMEs clearly limits their ability to compete with other regional and international players and respond to potential product and quality demands from international partners and importers. It is thus essential to deal with supply-side constraints at the national and regional level to enhance the competitiveness of Central American SMEs and address objectives for inclusive development.

A '*macro* complementary agenda' geared towards strengthening the potential 'losers' from trade liberalization is hence key to ensure a more equal distribution of costs and benefits between business and civil society actors. Moreover, it is crucial that such an agenda tackles national and regional supply-side constraints to fully benefit from the opportunities that international trade regimes create. Indeed, without the domestic and regional capacity to connect trade regimes with inclusive and sustainable development policies, linking to the world economy on better terms will remain an elusive challenge for small and low-income countries.

Notes

1. Author's definition.
2. This refers to the right of democratic national states to craft a development strategy through policies that are in tune with national priorities and realities, rather than kowtowing to the perspectives, priorities and conditionality associated with international financial institutions (IFIs) and donor governments. The concept is grounded in three principles of international law and policy: namely, the sovereignty and self-determination of nation-states; the right to development; and the principle of special and differential treatment for developing countries (South Centre 2005). Two crucial interrelated elements of policy space are thus the autonomy of governments to resort to a diverse range of policy instruments to enhance sustainable development outcomes in the future and the ability of the state to orchestrate the development process (that is, state capacity). In the particular context of trade and other international negotiations, the notion of policy space can also be understood as being highly interlinked to 'negotiating space', that is, the ability of developing country governments to have a voice at the bargaining table and to shape the final outcomes (Utting et al. 2008).
3. Roberto Fonseca Lopez assisted the author through the data collection process and interviews.
4. Ventura-Dias and Lengyel (2004: 4) argue that 'the subordinated role of Latin American countries in the international system together with weak or highly ineffective political and legal institutions, and an opaque economic decision-making process suggest that more information should be provided on the domestic trade policy-making process in Latin America before a model of reciprocal causation could be devised [referring to Putnam's two-level bargain – see the first section].'
5. Civil society is defined as 'the associational sector between family, market and the state' (Borchgrevink 2006: 13).
6. The Sandinista Revolution in Nicaragua (1979–90) distributed land and economic assets to social and more disadvantaged economic actors, such as workers, peasants, farmers and so on. During this period, the relations between the government and business (particularly the sectors represented by the elite) were greatly at odds, partly due to land and property confiscations and the revolution's popular-leaning policies.
7. Furthermore, public financing directed to agricultural small and medium production through the Banco Nacional de Desarrollo (BANADES/National Development

Bank) was discontinued during this time, greatly weakening the economic and political position of these actors. Between 1990 and 1992, the number of peasant families that received credit dropped from 97,217 to only 34,684, excluding most small producers (Spoor 2000: 19).

8. By the end of 2005, the total assets of these banks were: BANPRO, US$775.8 million; BANCENTRO, US$623.1 million; BAC, US$519.3 million; Banco UNO, US$247.2 million; and BDF, US$368.7 million (Mayorga 2007: 70).
9. From 1990 to 1994, FDI in Central America averaged US$577 million, but between 1995 and 1999 it increased dramatically to US$2,039 million (ECLAC 2002). Between 1997 and 2001, the annual average of FDI in Costa Rica, El Salvador, Guatemala, Honduras and Nicaragua was US$1.6 billion. That average increased to US$1.9 billion between 2002 and 2006, but the upward trend was acute; in 2005 those countries received US$2.2 billion and in 2006 they received US$2.6 billion (ECLAC 2006).
10. All references to $ in the main text are to US dollars.
11. In 2000, the Grupo Pellas provided US$490,000 in order to finance the electoral campaign of President Enrique Bolaños (2002–7). Furthermore, the regionalized private sector and transnational business actors have used media to frame their particular interests as 'national' interests and back political and economic reforms and integration schemes in the region (Segovia 2005).
12. Free Trade Zone refers to a tax-break regime to attract foreign direct investment. In Nicaragua, this is linked to textile and clothing production.
13. Interview with Alfredo Marín, president, *Matadero San Martin*.
14. Montenegro (2002) states that NGO-ization refers to 'the replacement of activism with the professional tasks entrusted by an NGO'.
15. This is only a conservative estimate since several other NGOs have not formally registered or been given a formal status.
16. The Mesoamerican Trade and Development Civil Society Platform. In Nicaragua, Iniciativa CID actors included the Federación Nacional de Cooperativas Agrícolas y Agroindustriales (FENACOOP/National Federation of Agricultural and Agro-industrial Cooperatives); the Unión Nacional de Agricultores y Ganaderos (UNAG/National Union of Farmers and Ranchers); the Centro Humboldt, an environmental NGO; the Central Sandinista de Trabajadores–José Benito Escobar (CST–JBE/Sandinista Workers' Union–José Benito Escobar).
17. Interview with Alvaro Porta, former Nicaraguan director general of international trade.
18. Interview with Fernando Traversari, vice-president, ANITEC.
19. Interview with Mario Amador, president, CNPA.
20. Interview with Fernando Traversari and Alfredo Marín.
21. Interview with Fernando Traversari.
22. Interview with Mario Amador.
23. Interview with Mario Amador.
24. Interview with Wilmer Fernández, vice-president, CANISLAC.
25. In 2001, dairy exports reached US$15 million, whereas in 2006 they rose to US$57.6 million (Corrales 2007).
26. Interview with Wilmer Fernández.
27. Interview with Wilmer Fernández.
28. Mario Amador states that not all business representatives were able to attend the rounds. For instance, flight tickets and hotels costs were around US$600 and US$200/night respectively for the Washington rounds.

29. Interview with Wilmer Fernández.
30. Interview with Alvaro Porta.
31. Interview with Fernando Traversari.
32. Interview with Fernando Traversari.
33. In exchange for ANITEC's concession, Honduras obtained an article in the agreement that allowed for flexible entrance of fabric for T-shirt production while Costa Rica demanded an additional market access quota for its wool production. According to Traversari, the US delegation agreed to this, but instead of creating a new quota for Costa Rica, it took away the wool quota concession previously granted to Nicaragua.
34. This rule will prevail from years five through ten for all Nicaraguan cotton trousers entering the US market under the TPL (NCTO 2005). Under this rule, if a company needs 100,000 sme, on year five, it will be allowed to buy only 50,000 sme of fabric from China or other origin, as the other 50,000 sme will need to originate from the United States (NCTO 2005). Given, however, that the bulk of Nicaragua's textile production falls under categories 3–47 and 3–48 (cotton trousers), this 'new deal' clearly eroded Nicaragua's major concession in DR–CAFTA, potentially harming Nicaragua's current and future competitiveness in the production of cotton trousers.
35. Nicaragua obtained the third largest quota (22,000 MT, which will grow yearly by 2 per cent) after Guatemala and El Salvador.
36. Ibid.
37. Between 1999 and 2001, sugar exports increased from US$30.4 million to US$49.1 million (López 2003: 30). Subsequently, in 2004 exports reached US$36,757,70 million and in 2005 they increased to US$60,305,07 million (MIFIC 2006).
38. Under WTO agreements, Nicaragua has a market access quota of 22,000 MT into the United States. As a result of DR–CAFTA, Nicaragua obtained an additional quota of 22,000 MT, growing by 2 per cent yearly.
39. Interview with Alfredo Marín.
40. Interview with Alfredo Marín.
41. Interview with Alfredo Marín.
42. Interview with Alfredo Marín.
43. Interview with Wilmer Fernández.
44. According to Fernández, 'If CANISLAC had accepted the 8,000 MT export quota the US delegation was offering to us, we would have been invaded with 8,000 MT of milk powder imports and our industry would have been wiped out. For instance, 8,000 MT of exported Nicaraguan cheese would not threaten the US dairy industry, but 8,000 MT of imported US milk powder would have substituted our domestic milk production. Indeed, US producers would not have to face the NTBs [non-tariff barriers] or the capacity constraints that Nicaraguan producers face if they want to export the United States. Hence we could not accept this proposal and instead we proposed a smaller quota with a 5 per cent increase through time.'
45. Inciativa CID (2004) argued for subsidy elimination, special and differential treatment in tariff and non-tariff barriers (for example, sanitary and phyto-sanitary measures), value-addition, technology transfer, and so on.
46. White corn, crucial for Central American peasants' livelihoods, was exempted from tariff liberalization (that is, white corn's tariff will never reach zero). However, the US delegation still managed to obtain an export quota of white corn into Central America.

47. Central Sandinista de Trabajadores – José Benito Escobar (Workers' union).
48. Central Sandinista de Trabajadores – José Benito Escobar (Workers' union).
49. Interview with Mario Quintana, national coordinator, Coordinadora Civil (a civil society forum).
50. The complementary agenda that national legislators agreed upon included a number of laws to promote access to credit for SMEs, foster free competition, and safeguard natural resources such as water. The regulation and implementation of these laws, however, are still pending in the National Assembly. As for the rest, the Agenda contains a series of general statements with little specificity on how to implement them – for example, 'V. On Intellectual Property Matters: In a period of time no later than twelve months, the Executive shall define the mechanism to ensure access to generic medicines in cases where a national emergency emerges or health priorities that may arise from the national health plan, taking into consideration the commitments at the WTO and the Doha Round' (*La Gaceta* 2005: 6556). This and other similar commitments, however, are yet to be met.
51. Interview with Orlando Valverde, coordinator of the Project on Rural Policy Influence in FENACOOP.
52. Interview with Orlando Valverde.
53. Interview with Orlando Valverde.
54. Interview with Mario Quintana.

References

Borchgrevink, A. (2005) *A Study of Civil Society in Nicaragua: A Report Commissioned by Norad*, NUPI Working Paper, No. 699 (Oslo: NUPI).

Bull, B. (2004) *Business Regionalization and the Complex Transnationalization of the Latin American States*, Working Paper No. 2004/02 (Oslo: Centre for Development and the Environment, University of Oslo).

Cáceres, S. (2003) 'Nicaragua: En el TLC definimos si nos suicidamos o si morimos de muerte natural', *Envío*, October, No. 259.

——— (2005) 'El CAFTA será como un huracán Mitch con nombre comercial', *Envío*, September, No. 282.

Corrales, G. (2007) 'El dinamismo del sector lácteo nicaragüense', *La Prensa*, No. 23851, 28 March, at: www.laprensa.com.ni/archivo/2007/marzo/28/suplementos/negocios/181230.shtml (accessed 4 September 2007).

CST–JBE (Central Sandinista de Trabajadores – José Benito Escobar) (2003) *Declaración de Principios Fundamentales del Movimiento Sindical Nicaragüense en Torno al Tratado de Libre Comercio con Estados Unidos*, mimeo.

Dugger, C. (2004) 'The Food Chain-Survival of The Biggest: Supermarket Giants Crush Central American Farmers', *The New York Times*, 28 December.

ECLAC (Economic Commission for Latin America and the Caribbean) (2002), 'Regional Overview: Recent Trends in Foreign Direct Investment in Latin America and the Caribbean', in ECLAC, *Foreign Investment in Latin America and the Caribbean*, ECLAC Series (Santiago de Chile: ECLAC).

——— (2006) 'Foreign Direct Investment and Transnational Corporations in Latin America and the Caribbean', in ECLAC, *Foreign Investment in Latin America and the Caribbean*, ECLAC Series (Santiago de Chile: ECLAC).

Equipo Envío (1991) 'Privatizacion: Tres puntos de vista', *Envío*, October, No. 120, at: www.envio.org.ni/688 (accessed 21 March 2007).

FAS (Foreign Agricultural Service) (2005) *Central American–Dominican Republic–United States–Free Trade Agreement: Overall Agriculture Fact Sheet, US Foreign Agricultural Service*, March, at: www.fas.usda.gov/info/factsheets/CAFTA/overall021105a.html (accessed 8 December 2007).

Fonseca-López, R. (2007) *CAFTA–DR: El Reto del Gobierno en Materia de Comunicación*, mimeo.

Giugni, M., M. Bandler and N. Eggert (2006) *The Global Justice Movement: How Far Does the Classic Social Movement Agenda Go in Explaining Transnational Contention?* Programme on Civil Society and Social Movements, Paper No. 24 (Geneva: UNRISD).

Haas, P. (1992) 'Introduction: Epistemic Communities and International Policy Coordination', *International Organization*, 14 (1), 1–36.

Haufler, V. (2000) 'Private Sector International Regimes', in A. Higgot, G. Underhill and A. Bieler (eds), *Non-State Actors and Authority in the Global System* (London: Routledge).

Iniciativa CID (Iniciativa Mesoamericana sobre Comercio, Integracion y Desarrollo) (2004) *Desafíos y Propuestas para Sector Ambiental, Laboral, y Agropecuario de Nicaragua ante la Firma del CAFTA*, mimeo (Managua: Iniciativa CID), at: www.iniciativacid.org/filer/desafiosypropuestascidnicaragua.doc (accessed 25 June 2009).

Jansen, Hans G. P., Sam Morley and Máximo Torero (2007) *Impacto del Tratado de Libre Comercio de Centroamérica en la Agricultura y el Sector Rural de Cinco Países Centroamericanos*, Executive Summary (San José: Proyecto RUTA–Regional Unit for Technical Assistance/IFPRI–International Food Policy Research Institute/ECLAC–United Nations Economic Commission for Latin America and the Caribbean).

Keeley, J. and I. Scoones (2003) 'Understanding Environmental Policy Processes: A Conceptual Map', in J. Keeley and I. Scoones (eds), *Understanding Environmental Policy Processes: Cases from Africa* (London: Earthscan Publications).

La Gaceta (2005) 'Agenda complementaria de país para el mejor aprovechamiento del CAFTA-DR', *La Gaceta Diario Oficial*, 199, 14 October, 6554–6.

Levy, D. and A. Prakash (2003) 'Bargains Old and New: Multinational Corporations in Global Governance', *Business and Politics*, 5 (2), 131–50.

López, G. (2003) *Comercialización de la Caña de Azúcar en Nicaragua, Casos Comparativos con Honduras y Costa Rica*, mimeo (Managua: Proyecto IICA–Instituto Interamericano de Cooperación para la Agricultura/EPAD–Economic Policy and Agribusiness Development).

Mayorga, F. (2007) *Megacapitales de Nicaragua*, second edition (Managua: Ediciones Albertus).

Ministerio de Fomento, Industria y Comercio (MIFIC) (2006) *Comercio Exterior: Anuario Estadístico 2004–2005*, at: www.mific.gob.ni/Anua0405/Portada.pdf (accessed 26 August 2008).

Montenegro, S. (2002) 'Our Weak Civil Society Has Been Weakened Further', *Envío*, No. 250, May.

NCTO (National Council of Textile Organizations) (2005) *NCTO Applauds Major Improvements in CAFTA That Will Promote Textile Exports and Protect Textile Jobs: U.S. Pocketings and Trouser Fabric Makers to Benefit*, at:. www.ncto.org/newsroom/pr200526.asp (accessed 29 January 2008).

Office of the United States Trade Representative (2004) Executive Office of the President, Free Trade Agreements, Final Text, at: www.ustr.gov/trade-agreements/free-trade-agreements/cafta-dr-dominican-republic-central-america-fta/final-text (accessed 24 June 2009).

Polanyi, K. (1944) *The Great Transformation: The Political and Economic Origins of Our Time* (Boston: Beacon Press).

Putnam, R. (1988) 'Diplomacy and Domestic Politics: The Logic of Two-Level Games', *International Organization*, 42 (3), 427–60.

Riain, O. (2000) 'States and Markets in an Era of Globalization', *Annual Review of Sociology*, 26, 187–213.

Ricker, T. (2004) 'Competition or Massacre? Central American Farmers' Dismal Prospects under CAFTA', *The Multinational Monitor*, 25 (4), at: http://multinationalmonitor.org/mm2004/04012004/april04corp1.html (accessed 15 April 2007).

Rodgers, Dennis (2008) 'A Symptom Called Managua', *New Left Review*, 49, January–February, 103–20.

Segovia, A. (2005) *Integración Real y Grupos de Poder Económico en América Central: Implicaciones para el Desarrollo y la Democracia de la Región* (San Jose: Friedrich Ebert Stiftung).

Sell, S. (2000) 'Structures, Agents and Institutions: Private Corporate Power and the Globalization of Intellectual Property Rights', in A. Higgot, G. Underhill and A. Bieler (eds), *Non-State Actors and Authority in the Global System* (London: Routledge).

——— (2003) *Private Power, Public Law: The Globalization of Intellectual Property Rights* (Cambridge: Cambridge University Press).

Shadlen, K. (2005) 'Exchanging Development for Market Access? Deep Integration and Industrial Policy under Multilateral and Regional-Bilateral Trade Agreements', *Review of International Political Economy*, 12 (5), December, 750–75.

Singh, J. (2003) 'Wiggle Rooms: New Issues and North–South Negotiations during the Uruguay Round', paper presented at the Conference on Developing Countries and the Trade Negotiation Process, 6–7 November (Geneva: UNCTAD).

South Centre (2005) 'Policy Space for the Development of the South', *T.R.A.D.E. Policy Brief*, No. 1 (Geneva: South Centre).

Spoor, M. (2000) *Two Decades of Adjustment and Agricultural Development in Latin America and the Caribbean*, Series Reformas Económicas (Santiago de Chile: ECLAC).

Teichman, Judith A. (2001) *The Politics of Freeing Markets in Latin America: Chile, Argentina and Mexico* (Chapel Hill: University of North Carolina Press, 2001).

United Nations Conference on Trade and Development (UNCTAD) (2007) *World Investment Directory: Nicaragua Country Profile*, at: www.unctad.org/Templates/Page.asp?intItemID=3198&lang=1 (accessed 17 April 2007).

Utting, P. (2006) *Reclaiming Development Agendas: Knowledge, Power and International Policy Making* (Basingstoke: Palgrave Macmillan).

Utting, P., M. Mejido and G. Carrión (2008) *The Changing Coordinates of Trade and Development in Latin America: Implications for Policy Space and Policy Coherence*, mimeo (Geneva: UNRISD).

Ventura-Dias, V. and Lengyel, M. (2004) *Trade Policy Reforms in Latin America: Multilateral Rules and Domestic Institutions* (Basingstoke: Palgrave Macmillan).

Wade, R. (2004) 'On the Causes of Increasing World Poverty and Inequality, or Why the Matthew Effect Prevails', *New Political Economy*, 9 (2), 163–88.

Walter, A. (2000) 'Globalisation and Policy Convergence: The Case of Direct Investment Rules', in A. Higgot, G. Underhill and A. Bieler (eds), *Non-State Actors and Authority in the Global System* (London: Routledge).

Woll, Cornelia and Alvaro Artigas (2007) 'When Trade Liberalization Turns into Regulatory Reform: The Impact on Business-Government Relations in International Trade Politics', *Regulation & Governance*, 1 (2), 121–38.

Interviews

Mario Amador, president, Comité Nacional de Productores de Azúcar (CNPA), 3 August 2007.

Wilmer Fernández, vice-president, Cámara Nicaragüense del Sector Lácteo, 28 August 2007.

Alfredo Marín, president, Matadero San Martín, 8 August 2007.

Alvaro Porta, former Nicaraguan director general of international trade, 21 July 2005.

Mario Quintana, national coordinator for the Coordinadora Civil, 14 August 2007.

Fernando Traversari, vice-president, Asociación Nicaragüense de la Industria Textil y de Confección, 20 August 2007.

Orlando Valverde, Project on Rural Policy Influence, FENACOOP, 21 October 2008.

6

Corporate Lobbying and Corporate Social Responsibility: Aligning Contradictory Agendas

Bart Slob and Francis Weyzig

Introduction

Although many transnational corporations (TNCs) have developed comprehensive corporate social responsibility (CSR) policies in the past ten years, most of these companies do not refer to ethical aspects of corporate lobbying in their business principles or codes of conduct. Whereas political donations (OECD 2000) and policy influence to support human rights are sometimes recognized as CSR issues (Holme and Watts 2000), efforts to systematically align corporate lobbying with CSR principles are often lacking (Blowfield 2005). While various CSR reporting frameworks, such as the Global Reporting Initiative (GRI), provide guidance for reporting on lobbying strategies and activities, apart from a few exceptions, TNCs do not provide comprehensive information to stakeholders on their corporate lobbying strategies and activities (SustainAbility and WWF–UK 2005; Blueprint et al. 2007; Lascelles 2005). As others have pointed out, this lack of coherent company policies is extremely worrisome for developing countries (for example, Blowfield 2004; Dharanajan 2005; Utting 2000).

In this chapter we argue that effective systems to avoid inconsistencies between direct corporate lobbying activities and CSR policy are relatively easy to develop, but that indirect lobbying channels, such as those provided by business associations and chambers of commerce, are more difficult to address. It is however imperative that these channels be aligned with CSR policy as well. We suggest that current disclosure practices are insufficient to hold companies to account for their lobbying activities.

The aim of this chapter is to provide a more detailed analysis on the relation between corporate lobbying and CSR policies than what can currently be found in the literature. The focus will be on corporate influence on legislation and government policies in both developed and developing countries, as well as on international policy and agreements affecting developing countries. The chapter starts by outlining a theoretical framework that distinguishes the targets, strategies and channels of policy influence. The proposed framework also discusses the two main options for regulating lobbying – government regulation and business self-regulation. Taking into account the relative importance of different lobbying channels, the chapter then assesses the effectiveness of both regulatory approaches. Both the theoretical framework and the analysis are illustrated with several corporate lobbying case studies. The chapter ends with conclusions and recommendations.

Understanding corporate political influence

While there is no commonly accepted definition of lobbying, both general and specific aspects are pertinent (Anastasiadis 2006). The definition of lobbying for the purpose of this chapter is a very broad one, based on a paper by the European Commission: 'lobbying' means all activities carried out 'with the objective of influencing the policy formulation and decision-making process' (Commission of the European Communities 2006: 5). Some of the literature refers to these activities as corporate political activity instead, and regards lobbying as a specific component of corporate political activity, limited to direct interactions with politicians or civil servants to discuss legislative proposals. In Europe, however, the term lobbying is generally used to refer to a broad range of activities aimed at influencing policy (Hillman 2003). This chapter follows the European practice and uses the terms 'corporate lobbying', 'corporate policy influence' and 'corporate political activity' interchangeably. Depending on the context companies may refer to the same sets of activities as 'public affairs', 'public relations' or 'government affairs'.

Debates concerning the influence and privileged status of special interest groups within society were the focus of a classic theoretical literature on the subject (Olson 1982; Dahl 1983; Lindblom 1977). However, empirical studies of interest group influence are notoriously difficult because of the complexities associated with operationalizing the concept, obtaining data on corporate practices and measuring successful influence (Mahoney 2007).[1]

Within the management literature, the majority of contemporary academic research on corporate lobbying focuses on the study of corporations' alternatives regarding lobbying strategies.[2] Moreover, while some researchers seek to analyse lobbying in high-income countries and in international policy-making contexts, such as the World Trade Organization (WTO) negotiations, few academic studies address corporate lobbying in developing countries (Utting 2007). Nevertheless, the existing literature provides a useful basis to develop a theoretical framework to analyse corporate lobbying within a developing-country context. The remainder of this section reviews the targets, strategies and channels of policy influence.

Targets of policy influence

Lobbying usually refers to the practice of trying to influence one or more of the various branches of government. While lobbying efforts often centre on attempts to influence the legislature and the framing of laws, great efforts can also be expended on the executive and the judiciary branches of government. According to Henriques (2007: 149), 'the classic function of lobbying is to influence specific legislation or regulation'. He specifies how lobbying may extend to efforts influencing the way the judiciary will interpret legislation before or after it is in force. Although many analysts also consider donations to political parties as lobbying, there is less control over the specific policies which may be supported as a result.

Besides practising these conventional forms of lobbying, companies also try to influence stakeholders other than the legislative authorities. These include customers, other companies, the media, non-governmental organizations (NGOs) and other civil society organizations (CSOs) (Henriques 2007). However, as this chapter deals with public policy influence, it focuses mainly on corporate lobbying of legislative authorities.

Apart from the ultimate actors targeted by corporate lobbying, a distinction can also be made according to the type of policy that is targeted. From a CSR perspective, it is important to distinguish between corporate lobbying directly related to CSR, for instance, against binding regulation on CSR, and lobbying practices related to other relevant and adjacent areas, such as trade and investment agreements, government contracts, public procurement regulation, regulation of business incentives, advertising and subsidies for public–private partnerships. Both types of policies are considered below.

Corporate lobbying directly related to CSR can be illustrated by Shell's lobbying campaign against an initiative by the United Nations (UN) to define the human rights responsibilities of companies. This initiative, known as the UN Norms on the Responsibilities of Transnational Corporations and Other Business Enterprises with Regard to Human Rights, is widely supported by international NGOs (INGOs) and has also received the support of some corporations. Shell, along with the International Chamber of Commerce, the International Organisation of Employers (IOE), the United States (US) Council of International Business, and the United Kingdom (UK) Confederation of Business and Industry, actively opposed the UN Norms. Asserting that the UN Norms sought to impose inappropriate responsibilities on businesses, Shell argued that human rights standards should be voluntary for businesses rather than mandated by law. The company further asserted that it was already implementing human rights standards and that, as a result, the UN Norms offered little added value (Global Policy Forum 2004). Shell's reputation suffered greatly as a result of the debate on the UN Norms, particularly when a senior executive, Robin Aram, took a public position against the Norms in his role as representative of the International Chamber of Commerce (Webb 2004).

Shell's position contrasted sharply with that of a group of 10 companies, including ABB, Barclays Plc, Gap Inc., Hewlett Packard, MTV Networks Europe, National Grid Transco, Novartis, Novo Nordisk, Statoil and The Body

Shop International, which joined the Business Leaders Initiative for Human Rights (BLIHR) and agreed to test the application of the UN Norms (BLIHR 2004). In a report launched in 2003, the BLIHR called for a single universal framework for corporate responsibility based on internationally recognized human rights standards, and noted that the UN Norms provided a useful starting point for developing such a framework (BLIHR 2003).

An example of a lobbying target not directly related to CSR itself, but to a related area that has consequences for responsible business in developing countries, is the liberalization of financial services that took place under the General Agreement on Trade in Services (GATS). Large banks, insurance companies and other financial service providers from the United States and the European Union (EU) have had a significant influence on GATS negotiations. Their highly effective lobbying efforts were closely coordinated by the Financial Leaders Group (FLG), which was established for this purpose in 1996. The EU Trade Commissioner even called business lobbyists during the negotiations to consult them directly on the issues at stake (Vander Stichele et al. 2006). The resulting EU negotiation positions are relatively well documented due to a series of leaked bilateral liberalization requests. To many developing countries, the European Union requested to remove all limitations on the commercial presence of foreign companies for a range of financial services, including the removal of limitations on full foreign ownership. In some cases, the European Union also requested to end specific government requirements intended to enhance financial stability or to stimulate access to financial services for poorer clients and smaller companies (Vander Stichele 2005). The resulting market liberalization has contributed to foreign firms' domination of financial markets in developing countries and increased competition only in the most profitable high-end market segments. Empirical research shows that this has reduced access to financial services for the poor (Detragiache et al. 2006), which contradicts the CSR policies of many financial companies. In addition, in some countries the market liberalization that many companies were pushing for may have contributed to increased financial instability (Bird and Rajan 2001).

Strategies and channels of policy influence

Hillman and Hitt (1999) provide a useful framework for the analysis of the different strategies and channels of policy influence. The model distinguishes three dimensions: 1) the approach to political strategy; 2) the participation level; and 3) the type of political strategy. Each of these is reviewed below.

The first dimension, the approach to political strategy, can be either transactional, meaning it is aimed at specific issues, or relational, that is, aimed at building lasting relationships. 'Revolving door' practices are an important example of a relational approach. These practices refer to government officials, staff of international organizations or members of parliament becoming professional lobbyists, or vice versa, when company executives join relevant government bodies. Apart from revolving doors, the focus of this chapter is mainly on transactional aspects, because relationship-building facilitates policy influence in general, but concrete acts of policy influence always involve a transactional approach as well.

The revolving door strategy is rarely identified as an explicit lobbying strategy in academic literature,[3] but has been a central issue in several analyses by CSOs (Public Citizen 2005). The specific nature of revolving door practices is most apparent when previous company executives become employed or current executives are seconded as policy advisors by public policy institutions, be they national governments or international organizations. For example, a past chairman of Pfizer, the world's largest pharmaceutical company, was appointed as a special representative to the US Trade Representative (Oxfam 2001).

The relations between Cisco and the administration of George W. Bush provide a more elaborate illustration of revolving doors. The company's central lobbying department, Cisco Worldwide Government Affairs, 'seeks to drive public policies that grow and protect the use of technology through traditional means and by using the Internet' (Cisco 2008). The company's declared top worldwide policy issues include increasing broadband deployment, promoting wireless technology, supporting Voice over Internet Protocol (VoIP) services, improving Internet security and advocating better education through technology. In the United States, Cisco employs at least two in-house lobbyists for this purpose, in addition to the private lobby firms it contracts. In the first half of 2007, this amounted to $680,000[4] of lobbying expenditures on various issues in the Senate, the House of Representatives and other sections of the US federal government (US Senate Office of Public Records 2007). Moreover, some of Cisco's ex-employees have become important government officials. A former lobbyist for Cisco was appointed assistant secretary of commerce for the US Department of Commerce during the first George W. Bush administration (Brown 2001). In 2004, when President Bush was re-elected, that same official resigned and returned to lobbying. Clients seeking his consulting services included the Technology CEO Council, then a new organization founded by nine leaders in the high-tech industry, as well as health care companies, Walmart and other firms with strong interests in free trade and global offshore outsourcing (Cummings 2007).

The level of participation, the second dimension of Hillman and Hitt's model, refers to individual lobbying versus collective action by a group of companies. While the former may involve competition between companies or companies with a shared policy objective that do not coordinate their activities, the latter is characterized by cooperation between companies, for example via industry associations and chambers of commerce.

The lobbying activities of the FLG for liberalization of financial services, referred to above, provide an illustration of collective action. The lobby of

US agribusiness TNCs in defence of in-kind food aid by donor countries provides an example of direct lobby by executives of individual companies. In-kind food aid is a form of tied aid and may harm farming livelihoods in developing countries because it has an effect similar to the dumping of agricultural products (Eagleton 2006). However, a few major US companies have a significant interest in continuing the practice. During the negotiations preceding the WTO ministerial meeting in Hong Kong in 2005, the US Trade Representative organized a series of meetings in Geneva with developing country representatives and lobbyists of individual companies, despite the fact that such meetings normally take place between governments only (Eagleton 2006). Thus, company representatives were directly involved in trade negotiations between the United States and developing countries. Similar to the financial industry lobby for market liberalization of financial services, the lobbyists had privileged access to policy-makers. This increases the opportunities for large corporations to promote their business interests, including where these conflict with the interests of poor communities in developing countries.

The third dimension of the theoretical model, namely the type of political strategy, can be subdivided into informational strategies, financial incentives and constituency building (Hillman and Hitt 1999). Informational strategies are intended to inform and persuade decision-makers by providing research reports (Kolk and Pinske 2007) and other specific data, analysis and opinions. Provided by business executives themselves or by professional lobbyists, such information is welcome to some extent, because of limitations to the expertise and resources of government departments and international organizations. Although the provision of information appears to be a neutral business practice, lobbyists may provide biased, incomplete, misleading, or sometimes even false, information in support of their own policy preferences.

Although financial incentives often take the form of political donations (the case of illegal payments is not considered here), such incentives may be interpreted more broadly to include, for example, charitable donations in support of specific social goals. These, however, need not necessarily be confined to transactional strategies. For example, it has been observed that there is a melding between corporate political activity and corporate social performance. As Hillman et al. (2004: 252) explain: 'A firm with a history of sponsoring community projects most likely realizes easier access to and a better hearing from local politicians.' Alternatively, companies sometimes hint that they will link decisions about the location of production sites that generate jobs and government revenues to public policy outcomes. This may even involve speculative threats to relocate production or suspend new investments in order to put pressure on a government, while in reality a company may not implement such strategies even in the case of unfavourable policy changes.

The last political strategy, constituency building, refers to the encouragement of company stakeholders, such as employees, suppliers, clients, consumers and community members, to voice the public policy concerns of the company (Lord 2000). Other examples of this type of political strategy include the funding of think tanks, research programmes and interest organizations that, knowingly or unknowingly, support the lobbying efforts of a company. A more aggressive strategy is to set up front groups that appear not to be linked to the company, but whose sole purpose is to promote its policy goals. Constituency building is sometimes referred to as 'grassroots campaigning' because it involves the mobilization of non-business actors. The strategy is more indirect, and therefore less visible, than other types.

At a more basic level, political strategies may also be thought of as either information-oriented or pressure-oriented (Getz 1997). In this case, the latter category includes financial incentives and constituency building as well as more direct forms of public campaigning, such as public advertising. Bonardi and Keim (2005) argue that widely salient issues, which receive a lot of public scrutiny, require different types of strategies from those mentioned above. If a company wants to influence policy-makers in a way that goes against public opinion, it may employ more subtle strategies. In early stages of policy formulation, it could be more effective to influence experts, opinion leaders and reporters than to influence policy-makers directly. In later stages, self-regulation is suggested as the most appropriate strategy (Bonardi and Keim 2005). However, self-regulation can be part of a corporate political strategy only for specific types of policies. In the context of CSR, self-regulation is often employed to pre-empt the tightening of legal regulation of corporate behaviour. Influencing experts, on the other hand, can also be used to lobby for policy changes that are the opposite of tightening legislation or that are not directly related to CSR, such as market liberalization.

The funding provided by ExxonMobil to think tanks and researchers, with the aim of influencing policies on climate change, is an example of policy influence through external experts. According to the US Union of Concerned Scientists, ExxonMobil funded 29 climate change denial groups in 2004 alone. Since 1990, the company has spent more than $19 million on financial resources for groups that promote the company's views through publications and web sites. Research undertaken by the Royal Society in the United Kingdom indicates that, in 2005, ExxonMobil provided more than $2.9 million to organizations in the United States that misinformed the public about climate change (Ward 2006). In the same year, the *Guardian* newspaper revealed that US State Department papers showed that the US government's conservative position on climate change partly resulted from input from the Global Climate Coalition, of which ExxonMobil was a prominent member (Vidal 2005; Kolk and Pinske 2007).

In October 2006, two US Senators wrote to ExxonMobil's chairman and chief executive officer (CEO), asking the company to 'end any further financial assistance' to groups 'whose public advocacy has contributed to the small but unfortunately effective climate change denial myth' (Sandell 2006). The Senators singled out the Competitive Enterprise Institute and Tech Central Station as such groups. They wrote that they were convinced that ExxonMobil's long-standing support of a small cadre of global climate change sceptics, and those sceptics' access to and influence on government policy-makers, had made it increasingly difficult for the United States to demonstrate the moral clarity it needed across all facets of its diplomacy (Sandell 2006).

Exerting influence by disseminating information and providing expert knowledge is a common strategy employed in the field of public health. This strategy has been well documented in relation to the World Health Organization (WHO) (Richter 2004). At one of WHO's collaborating centres, the International Agency for Research on Cancer, half the experts on a review committee that was established to look into the carcinogenicity of saccharin included persons affiliated with food and chemical companies who were known for their 'pro-saccharin' position. A drug manufacturer was also deemed to have exerted excessive influence in the drafting of the Guidelines for the Management of Hypertension, which reportedly resulted in the increased use of anti-hypertensive drugs with little regard for the significant costs and limited benefits. Concerns also arose in relation to the secondment of an employee of Merck, Sharp and Dohme to WHO's Tobacco Free Initiative. Such influences were documented more systematically in relation to the strategies of tobacco companies to undermine tobacco control activities at the WHO. An in-depth report by a committee of experts documented various ways in which companies sought to 'contain, neutralize and reorient' such activities (Richter 2004: 23).[5]

A combined framework for analysis

Table 6.1 identifies and summarizes the elements of the model that are most important for the purpose of this chapter. The first column distinguishes relational and transactional approaches. As explained above, the focus is on transactional approaches, which are subdivided into mainly information-oriented and pressure-oriented strategies. Thus, the first column combines the first and second dimension of Hillman and Hitt's model. The second column identifies main direct target groups, and as policy-makers are always the ultimate target group, it also indicates which strategy types are indirect in nature. The third column lists the different types of lobbying strategies discussed above. The last two columns mention the alternative participation levels of different strategy types, adding the third dimension of Hillman and Hitt's model. As some strategy types are relatively uncommon at the individual or collective level, a few cells in the table have been left blank.

The framework for analysis outlined above is largely based on analyses of corporations based in high-income countries lobbying international institutions and the governments of EU countries and the United States. However,

Table 6.1 Combined framework for analysis of channels of influence

Approach and orientation	Main direct target group	Type of lobbying strategy	Participation level	
			Individual	**Collective**
Relational approach	Policy-makers	Revolving doors	Government officials becoming company executives or lobbyists and vice versa	Government officials becoming representatives or lobbyists of associations and vice versa
Transactional approach, mainly information-oriented	Policy-makers	Direct lobbying	Lobbying by company executives and lobbyists hired by companies	Lobbying by representatives of associations and lobbyists hired by associations
	Experts and opinion leaders	Influencing experts and opinion leaders	Lobbying by company executives and lobbyists hired by companies	Lobbying by representatives of associations and lobbyists hired by associations
Transactional approach, mainly pressure-oriented	Policy-makers	Political donations, charity	Donations and charity by companies	
		Promises and threats	Linking company investment decisions to policy outcomes	
		Self-regulation		Industry initiative to pre-empt stricter legal regulation
	Stakeholders and grassroots organizations	Constituency building	Mobilization and funding by companies	
	General public	Advocacy advertising	Campaigns sponsored by companies	Campaigns sponsored by associations

Source: Authors' analysis.

the lobbying strategies employed in emerging economies can be assumed to be quite similar, if not identical. Support for this assertion is provided by a study on corporate political activity in China (Kennedy 2007). It finds that, although government relations usually fall under the responsibility of the firm's country manager, most large TNCs also have government affairs staff in China and a representative office in Beijing for lobbying purposes. In addition, when executives from the global corporate headquarters visit China, they usually meet with senior government officials because relational strategies, aimed at building trust, are an essential part of corporate lobbying in China. Similar to revolving door practices in the United States and the European Union, TNCs often hire former officials of the Chinese government to lobby the department where they were previously employed. Companies use the services of global public relations and lobbying firms as well, several of which have substantial operations in China. Furthermore, TNCs act both individually and collectively through business associations.

When domestic strategies are inadequate, foreign companies may request their home governments put pressure on the host country on their behalf (Kennedy 2007), thereby adding an important additional channel to the international lobbying efforts of TNCs. It is likely that this particular channel is more influential when lobbying developing country governments, because the power imbalance between the home and host countries is often larger if the latter is a developing country, although major variations in the relative power of host states exist.

As we have seen in the previous sections, a variety of different channels exist for exerting policy influence. However, not all are equal in importance and effectiveness. In this section, we will analyse the relative importance of different channels. Returning to the developed country context, Lord (2000) conducted a large survey among corporate executives and congressional aides to assess what types of lobbying strategies were most successful in influencing US federal legislation. Results indicated that constituency building was identified as the most effective strategy to get a proposed law passed or defeated, but to influence the content of legislation itself, lobbying by business executives or hired professionals was considered most effective. In contrast, advocacy advertising and political donations were perceived to be much less successful means (Lord 2000). Another study finds that contributions to Political Action Committees (PACs) in the United States, channelling donations to political campaigns, are dwarfed by corporate lobbying expenses and charitable donations (Milyo et al. 2000).

Furthermore, when TNCs lobby for regulatory changes in developing countries, they often do so via international trade and investment agreements (Vander Stichele et al. 2006). The US government and the European Commission are the main channels of corporate political pressure to influence such agreements, as evidenced by the large numbers of professional lobbyists operating in Washington and Brussels.

The regulation of corporate lobbying

Very different approaches exist for ensuring that lobbying conforms to principles of good governance. The sections that follow look at different types of government regulation as well as the role of corporate self-regulation and voluntary initiatives, and reflect on their effectiveness.

Government regulation

Lobbying is a legitimate element of the democratic process and numerous types of policies are set by governments to regulate corporate lobbying. These include the registration of lobbyists, regulations on revolving door practices, and requirements for the disclosure of political donations, lobbying positions and payments to lobby firms.

Several members of the Organisation for Economic Co-operation and Development (OECD) have tried to regulate lobbying, with different levels of success. An increasing number of political systems have implemented lobbying regulations, notably the United States, Australia, Canada, Germany and the European Union (Chari et al. 2007). A comparative review of experiences in North America, Europe and Australia shows that lobby regulations have developed incrementally. Requirements in lobby regulation have ranged from registering interests appearing before legislative committees to requiring extensive disclosure of lobby activities. Regulatory schemes vary, depending on the cultural and constitutional background of each political system. The OECD argues that where transparency and integrity are the main goals of regulations, effectiveness is best achieved if definitions are broad and inclusive, and the 'theatre of lobby activities is also defined broadly and inclusively' (OECD 2008: 10). Moreover, the OECD states that compliance is best secured if definitions and exemptions are unambiguous and clearly understood by lobbyists and public officials, practical in application and robust enough to support legal challenges (OECD 2008).

An interesting recent example of lobby regulation is the register of interest representatives and the code of conduct linked to this register created by the European Commission in 2008. The commission also established a monitoring and enforcement mechanism for the code and the register whereby anyone is able to lodge a complaint with the commission when a breach of the code is suspected. In the event of such a complaint and before a formal process is launched, the commission requests that the concerned entity clarify the issue, and invites this entity to abide by the rules or correct any false or misleading information in the register (Commission of the European Communities 2008).

The United States has a relatively large number of disclosure laws in place. Political donations by corporations have been the subject of considerable scrutiny and reform there. In November 2002, the US Congress enacted legislation (the McCain-Feingold Act) that prohibits national political parties from soliciting and receiving 'soft money' contributions.

According to the framework developed by Chari et al. (2007), regulation schemes can be classified as highly, medium and lowly regulated systems. Germany and the European Parliament, for example, are considered to have lowly regulated lobbying systems. Those in place at the US and Canadian federal level are at the intermediate point. Only in the United States at state level are there examples of highly regulated systems with 25 of the 49 states having lobbying legislation falling into this category (Chari et al. 2007). Table 6.2 summarizes the characteristics of the different levels of lobbying regulation.

The effectiveness of government regulation

As we have seen above, several developed countries have attempted to regulate some aspects of corporate lobbying, by requiring registration of professional lobbyists, payments made to lobby firms, revolving door practices and political donations. If more governments adopt such regulation, this could enhance transparency and reduce some forms of undue influence. However, none of the legal structures created so far require companies to disclose their lobby positions, without which corporate accountability remains severely limited. Enforcement of laws that seek to regulate irresponsible forms of policy influence by companies is likely to be very complicated and burdensome. As direct lobbying is an important channel but largely an informal process, it is difficult to detect and prove any violations of government regulation on direct lobbying (MacGillivray et al. 2005).

Government regulation of corporate lobbying might also lead to a shift in lobbying practices rather than a decrease in corporate political influence. In the United States, for example, soft money donations to political parties were prohibited in 2002. As a result, independent organizations were created to receive financial resources intended for political parties. These organizations are often called '527 organizations', because 527 is the tax code section that regulates them. According to research undertaken by SustainAbility and the World Wide Fund for Nature (WWF) (2005),

> The 527s have become an important political force in the United States. [...] 527s may not directly advocate the election or defeat of any federal candidate, although they may support other political activities, including issue advocacy. As 527s are not election associations, they are not regulated by the Federal Elections Commission and only report income to the Internal Revenue Service, a much less detailed and rigorous procedure. Although they existed before 2002, more and more corporate money is now channelled in this way. (SustainAbility and WWF–UK 2005)

Table 6.2 Different types of regulation schemes

	Lowly regulated systems	**Medium regulated systems**	**Highly regulated systems**
Registration regulations	Rules on individual registration, but few details required	Rules on individual registration, more details required	Rules on individual registration are extremely rigorous
Spending disclosure	No rules on individual spending disclosure, or employer spending disclosure	Some regulations on individual spending disclosure; none on employer spending disclosure	Tight regulations on individual spending disclosure, and employer spending disclosure
Electronic filing	Weak online registration and paperwork required	Robust system for online registration, no paperwork necessary	Robust system for online registration, no paperwork necessary
Public access	List of lobbyists available, but not detailed or updated frequently	List of lobbyists available, detailed and updated frequently	List of lobbyists and their spending disclosures available, detailed and updated frequently
Enforcement	Little enforcement capabilities invested in state agency	In theory, state agency possesses enforcement capabilities, though infrequently used	State agency can, and does, conduct mandatory reviews/audits
Revolving door provision	No cooling off period before former legislators can register as lobbyists	There is a cooling off period before former legislators can register as lobbyists	There is a cooling off period before former legislators can register as lobbyists

Source: Adapted from Chari et al. (2007), 428.

Business approaches to responsible lobbying

Within the field of CSR, attention has recently turned to the issue of 'responsible lobbying', which can be defined in a variety of ways. From a practitioner perspective, a focus on operational aspects alone, such as transparency about lobbying positions, is considered insufficient. The reason is that the content of policy positions that companies seek to promote are important as well. If a company, for example, is transparent about how it is lobbying to narrowly further its own interests at the expense of marginalized communities and society at large, this would usually not be regarded as a responsible business practice. However, it may be impossible to define broadly accepted moral criteria to assess the content of lobbying positions because different groups in society have conflicting political priorities. As a consequence, it may be more useful to define responsible lobbying as lobbying that is consistent with the policies and commitments espoused by a company (MacGillivray et al. 2005). These include general business principles, codes of conduct, and endorsement of international norms and standards. This approach is laid out below.

In practice, several operational aspects are essential for the implementation of responsible lobbying by large TNCs. These provide additional criteria for the analysis of responsible lobbying. Apart from the alignment of lobbying positions with company strategies and commitments, the operational aspects include mapping who is lobbying on behalf of the company, adopting management systems to ensure that lobbying strategies are also implemented in practice, and being transparent about lobbying positions as well as practices (MacGillivray et al. 2005).

Approaching responsible lobbying from an investor's perspective, Lascelles (2005) identified several best practices which are sometimes more specific than those mentioned by MacGillivray et al. (2005). The most important of these is the fact that lobbying activities should be governed by a specific set of company policies and standards that are enforceable. While lobbying objectives and policy positions should be publicly stated, any political donations should be approved by shareholders, and reported and evaluated in annual reports. In addition, companies should disclose membership of industry associations and other interest groups and ensure that these groups apply similar standards for responsible lobbying. With regard to transparency, the reporting framework of the GRI, which is the main source of guidance for reporting on corporate responsibility used by TNCs, includes two indicators on lobbying. The first is the so-called core performance indicator S05 on 'Public policy positions and participation in public policy development and lobbying'. GRI core performance indicators are assumed to be material for most companies. According to this indicator, companies should list 'the significant issues that are the focus of the reporting organization's participation in public policy development and lobbying'. In addition, a company should disclose the 'core positions held on each of the reported issues ... and explain any significant differences between lobbying positions and stated policies, sustainability goals, or other public positions' (GRI 2006: 7). The second relevant GRI indicator is additional performance indicator S06, which suggests disclosure of the 'Total value of financial and in-kind contributions to political parties, politicians, and related institutions by country' (GRI 2006: 8), if relevant to the company. The GRI reporting framework provides some further technical guidance on these two indicators.

Company reporting

There seems to be a growing awareness in business of the need for well-grounded principles to guide political activity (Lascelles 2005; Blueprint et al. 2007). Reporting about certain forms of lobbying is probably the most developed aspect of current business approaches to responsible lobbying. According to research undertaken by SustainAbility and the WWF in 2005, about half of the world's largest companies provide at least some degree of transparency concerning their lobbying activities. Many of the world's largest companies are transparent about political donations, with some providing a great amount of detail, listing all individual recipients. However, no major company discloses the amount of money they pay to professional lobbyists (SustainAbility and WWF–UK 2005). Taking into account the relative importance of the different channels of policy influence discussed above, this means that thus far disclosure about lobbying activities is focused on one of the least important channels, thereby providing a partial picture at best.

Some TNCs also try to see to it that their lobbying practices are not in contradiction with their CSR policies. However, in 2005, SustainAbility found that none of the companies in their analyses had made an explicit link between corporate values and principles, corporate governance and other core business decision-making processes on the one hand, and the company's approach to public policy on the other (SustainAbility and WWF–UK 2005). Lascelles (2005) similarly concluded that very few companies have fully developed policies regarding lobbying. More recently, a few firms have adopted a more integrated approach to reporting about public affairs. Some leading companies are now disclosing their support, or opposition, to specific regulations that are material to their business. Yet only a few explain how these positions relate to their CSR policies or to broader and longer-term business objectives (Blueprint et al. 2007).

The cases of Volkswagen and Ford show how information about corporate lobbying in CSR reports can range from rather meaningless to relatively detailed statements. Both companies apply the GRI core indicator for reporting about corporate lobbying and their reports are externally certified as fully consistent with the GRI guidelines. *Volkswagen's Sustainability Report*

2007/2008 provides the following information about its corporate lobbying activities:

> As both a company and a part of society, the Volkswagen Group applies the pluralistic principles of that society to campaign for its corporate interests. [...] The Volkswagen Group recognises the applicable regulations and agreements entered into by the company ... and is committed to compliance with these regulations and agreements. (Volkswagen 2008: 35)

This basically states that the company is lobbying without violating the law, but not how or on which issues. In contrast, the following excerpt from *Ford's Sustainability Report 2006/7* is considerably more detailed:

> Ford supports the reduction of vehicle CO_2 emissions ... However, the entire automobile industry is united in opposition to the AB 1493 rules [of California] because they constitute state fuel economy standards.... State-by-state regulation of fuel economy is unworkable because it raises the prospect of an unmanageable patchwork of state standards. [...]
>
> In December 2004, the Alliance of Automobile Manufacturers filed an action in federal court in California seeking to overturn the AB 1493 regulations. [...] All members of the Alliance (BMW, DCX, Ford, GM, Mazda, Mitsubishi, Porsche, Toyota and Volkswagen) supported taking this action. (Ford Motor Company 2007: 20).

Thus, Ford does not just disclose its general values in relation to lobbying positions or the issues that it is lobbying on and the positions it takes on these issues. It also provides information on the company's involvement and position regarding collective lobbying practices at industry level. However, the company stops short of explicitly reporting on the link between its lobbying positions and CSR policies. Nevertheless, Ford's disclosure on lobbying positions and lobbying practices might be considered a best practice.

Case studies

Ultimately, any regulation of corporate lobbying, including self-regulation, would only work if it prevents the companies from achieving certain lobbying goals. This might explain why business approaches to corporate lobbying have generally been flawed (MacGillivray et al. 2005). The next section presents two more elaborate cases that highlight the challenges with regard to the alignment of corporate lobbying and CSR policies.

Individual and collective lobbying in the pharmaceutical industry

The lack of adequate policies regarding corporate lobbying can be illustrated with reference to the pharmaceutical industry. Lobbying by the pharmaceutical industry is of particular relevance to developing countries because of its influence on intellectual property rights, which directly affects the availability of cheap generic drugs in these countries. For example, over the past years, the United States has concluded various bilateral trade agreements with developing countries that require them to provide stronger intellectual property protection than that required by the WTO agreement on Trade-Related Aspects of Intellectual Property Rights (TRIPS). This is often referred to as 'TRIPS-plus' legislation. It extends market exclusivity for branded drug companies, many of which are US-based, but goes against the developing countries' public policy interests.

In late 2005 and early 2006, the Centre for Research on Multinational Corporations (SOMO) was commissioned by a consumers' organization to analyse the CSR policies and practices of 20 large pharmaceutical companies, including lobbying positions and corporate policies on lobbying conduct. Data were collected from company reports, company web sites, press databases and CSOs, as well as questionnaires, email correspondence and/or telephone interviews with a sample of companies. The analysis identified a number of controversial practices. The results show that many pharmaceutical companies have a policy on political donations and publish the amount of contributions. A small number of companies also list the industry associations to which they are affiliated. However, the relatively high transparency on these issues is in stark contrast with the general non-disclosure of the policy positions that companies actually advocate (Weyzig et al. 2006). These results are similar to the findings of the SustainAbility survey among the Standard & Poor's (S&P) Global 100 companies in 2005 (SustainAbility and WWF–UK 2005).

The SOMO report highlights how various companies had lobbied developing country governments to take actions that were inconsistent with their own corporate CSR policies on patent flexibility. Whereas several companies indicated where the responsibility for lobbying efforts lies within the company, only GlaxoSmithKline (GSK) stated that it also has a system in place to align lobbying activities with its access-to-medicines policy. This CSR policy of GSK, however, does not extend to lobbying undertaken on its behalf by pharmaceutical industry associations (Weyzig et al. 2006). That is an important limitation (Sustainability and WWF–UK 2005), because these associations are a main channel for the pharmaceutical industry to influence government policies in developing countries. Out of the 20 companies, only GSK and Novartis have stated that they were not lobbying developed country governments to press for so-called TRIPS-plus legislation in their bilateral negotiations with developing countries (Oxfam et al. 2002).

But even when pharmaceutical companies do have explicit CSR policies on lobbying positions, the value of such statements may be limited. GSK, for example, has questioned the concept of TRIPS-plus, while Novartis has been criticized for starting lawsuits in developing countries that reinforce patent protection and constrain the production of far cheaper generic drugs. In 2005, Novartis initiated a lawsuit to force Argentina to adopt TRIPS-plus legislation (Weyzig et al. 2006). The following year, the company initiated court proceedings in India to challenge both a provision in Indian patent law which, it claimed, stifled innovation, and a decision by the Indian patent office to reject a patent for its anti-cancer drug Glivec on the grounds of insufficient 'inventiveness' and additional efficacy. A High Court decision in 2007 dismissed the former aspect of the case, while, at the time of writing, the Intellectual Property Appelate Board is considering the decision to reject the patent. Novartis also petitioned the High Court for a new technical member to replace the Controller General of the Indian Patent Office who had originally rejected the patent.[6]

To summarize, some pharmaceutical companies have CSR policies on specific types or lobby conduct, notably political donations, and a few have made CSR statements about lobbying positions as well. However, it must be concluded that these policies are far from sufficient to ensure that all lobbying efforts are consistent with a company's own access to medicines position (if it exists). Addressing political influence via industry associations that is contradictory to the CSR commitments of individual companies remains a major challenge. Such contradictions and challenges persist despite the considerable criticism of the role of the pharmaceutical industry and strong intellectual property rights in developing countries that has emerged over several years.

Chinese labour law reform

The case study of the pharmaceutical industry demonstrated that companies may support lobbying positions through industry associations that are inconsistent with their own CSR policies. The lobby through the US and EU Chambers of Commerce on Chinese labour law reform provides another concrete example of this mismatch.

In early 2006, the Chinese government published a draft version of its proposed new labour law and invited comments through a broad consultation procedure. According to trade unions, one of the main improvements of the proposed labour law is that all employment relations shall be on the basis of contracts. In case no contract is signed, a default standard contract will automatically apply. This would offer protection for workers without a contract, which currently includes millions of migrant workers. Thus far, many court cases involving labour law violations have been rejected because such employment contracts did not exist.

Lobbying against improvement in labour rights clearly contravenes corporate CSR policy, yet several companies and business associations have actively lobbied against the law or for changes to the proposal. US-based companies have formed especially vocal lobbies, going far beyond contributing comments through the consultation procedure. Although some firms have directly addressed Chinese policy-makers, most lobbying was conducted at the collective level, in what appears to be a well-organized, concerted effort. The American Chamber of Commerce in Shanghai and US–China Business Council have been leading actors in the opposition to the new law (Global Labor Strategies 2007, 2006).

Whereas the EU Chamber of Commerce in China, in general, adopted a more moderate position, some perceived that it still opposed the new law. In its letter submitted in the public consultation procedure, for example, the chamber encouraged the Chinese government 'to focus its efforts on improving the implementation of existing regulations ... before passing additional laws'. Reportedly, the Chamber has also said that the new law will increase production costs in China and will 'force foreign companies to reconsider new investment or continuing with their activities in China' (Buckley 2006). Thus, the lobbying strategy involved threats about the withdrawal of investments as well.

The Dutch transnational Philips is a member of the EU Chamber of Commerce in China. However, in research conducted by SOMO, Philips and the EU Chamber of Commerce deny that they would have lobbied against the law or against improvement of Chinese labour conditions in general, such as mandatory contracts (Weyzig and Schipper 2007). This illustrates that a TNC may not wish to be engaged in policy influence inconsistent with its own CSR principles, including at the collective level, but may find it difficult to implement this in practice and fully prevent apparent inconsistencies.

Conclusions and policy propositions

It can be concluded that consistency between corporate lobbying practices and CSR principles is often lacking. Empirical findings from previous research, supplemented with several case studies, have demonstrated that powerful TNCs support lobbying efforts that are not in line with their own public policy statements or CSR policies. Moreover, most companies do not disclose public policy positions at all and lack a comprehensive system to align lobbying practices with CSR policies. The resulting inconsistencies can have important negative impacts for developing countries, including when the direct target of corporate lobbying is not the legislation in a developing country itself, but, for example, an international trade agreement.

Although lobbying has rarely been integrated into corporate CSR policies and management systems, some companies do provide transparency on specific aspects of lobbying. Disclosure of political donations seems to be the most advanced aspect of CSR practice with regard to lobbying. Unfortunately, the review of lobbying channels in this chapter shows that this is one of the least important channels of influencing public policy and that, as a result, current disclosure practices are insufficient to hold companies to account for their lobbying activities. Direct lobbying and constituency building by individual companies, as well as various collective strategies, tend to have a much larger influence and account for a far greater share of lobbying budgets. Direct lobbying by corporate executives and lobbying strategies at the collective level remain a black box, the former because the lobbying itself can remain completely hidden and the latter because the role and involvement of individual companies can be impossible to determine.

Governments in a few high-income countries have attempted to regulate some aspects of corporate lobbying, such as registration of professional lobbyists and payments to lobby firms, revolving door practices and political donations. Although policy influence can never be fully regulated through national legislation, the adoption of such regulation by more governments could greatly enhance transparency and reduce some forms of undue influence. However, the current legislation does not require TNCs to disclose their policy positions, thereby severely limiting corporate accountability on lobbying practices. Moreover, enforcement of lobbying regulations may be very difficult because violations can be difficult to detect due to the nature of lobbying practices.

Compliance with lobbying regulations may be best secured if definitions and exemptions are unambiguous and clearly understood by lobbyists and public officials, practical in application and robust enough to support legal challenges. However, where transparency and integrity are the main goals of regulations, effectiveness is likely to be best achieved if definitions are broad and inclusive, covering all relevant channels of policy influence.

Ultimately, self-regulation initiatives and individual company policies are critical to improving the consistency between CSR policies and lobbying practices. Disclosing lobbying positions, funding critical research by think tanks, CSOs and academics, and reassessing a company's input into its business associations are some possible actions that can be taken to bring the two into greater alignment. However, demonstrating whether such measures will effectively avoid the inconsistencies outlined in this chapter will require a great deal more work.

Notes

1. For a study on corporate lobbying success in Brazil, see Chapter 9 by Wagner Mancuso in this book.
2. Anastasiadis (2006); Boddewyn (2007); Bonini et al. (2006); Hillman and Hitt (1999); Hillman (2003); Coen (1998); Windsor (2007).
3. For an analysis of this strategy in the context of Peru, see Chapter 7 by Francisco Durand in this book. For a study of the extent of the 'revolving door' phenomenon in recent US government administrations, see Etzion and Davis (2008).
4. All references to $ are to US dollars.

5. See WHO (2000).
6. See Novartis (2007); Anderson (2007); Commons-Law Relay (2008).

References

Anastasiadis, S. (2006) 'Understanding Corporate Lobbying on Its Own Terms', ICCSR Research Paper Series, No. 42 (Nottingham: International Centre for Corporate Social Responsibility).

Anderson, Tatum (2007) *Ruling on Novartis Challenge to WTO Rules in India Could Come Early*, Intellectual Property Watch, 4 April, at: www.audace-ass.com/News_database/PI_innovation_interet_general/Ruling-on-Novartis-challenge-WTO-rules-India-Could-come-early_5April2007.pdf (accessed 25 January 2009).

Bird, G. and R. S. Rajan (2001) 'Banks, Financial Liberalisation and Financial Crises in Emerging Markets', *The World Economy* 24 (7), 889–910.

BLIHR (Business Leaders Initiative on Human Rights) (2003) *Business Leaders Initiative on Human Rights Report 1: Building Understanding* (London and Amsterdam: BLIHR).

——— (2004) *Leading International Businesses Detail Their Activities in 2004 BLIHR Report and Suggest a Unified Corporate Responsibility Framework*, Press Release, 9 December, at: www.bhrseminar.org/2004%20Documents/BLIHR%20Press%20Release.doc (accessed 25 January 2009).

Blowfield, M. (2004) 'CSR and Development: Is Business Appropriating Global Justice?', *Development*, 27 (3), 61–8.

——— (2005) 'Corporate Social Responsibility: Reinventing the Meaning of Development?', *International Affairs*, 81 (3), 515–24.

Blueprint, SustainAbility and WWF–UK (2007) *Coming in from the Cold: Public Affairs and Corporate Responsibility* (London: Blueprint/SustainAbility/WWF-UK).

Boddewyn, J. J. (2007) 'The Internationalization of the Public-Affairs Function in U.S. Multinational Enterprises: Organization and Management', *Business & Society*, 46 (2), 136–73.

Bonardi, J.-P. and G. D. Keim (2005) 'Corporate Political Strategies for Widely Salient Issues', *Academy of Management Review*, 30 (3), 555–76.

Bonini, Sheila M. J., Lenny T. Mendonca and Jeremy M. Oppenheim (2006) 'When Social Issues Become Strategic – Executives Ignore Sociopolitical Debates at Their Own Peril', *The McKinsey Quarterly*, No. 2, 20–32.

Brown, Doug, (2001) 'Meet the Wonk', *E-Week Enterprise News and Reviews*, 13 August.

Buckley, C. (2006) 'Foreign Investors May Quit If China Tightens up Labour Law', *Times Online*, 19 June, at: http://business.timesonline.co.uk/tol/business/markets/china/article676240.ece (accessed 1 March 2007).

Chari, Raj, Gary Murphy and John Hogan (2007) 'Examining and Assessing the Regulation of Lobbyists in Canada, the USA, the EU Institutions, and Germany: A Report for the Department of the Environment, Heritage and Local Government', *The Political Quarterly*, 78 (3), 422–38.

Cisco (2008) Cisco web site: About Cisco, Facts and Information, Government Affairs (2008), at: www.cisco.com/web/about/facts_info/index.html (accessed 1 July 2008).

Coen, D. (1998) 'The European Business Interest and the Nation State: Large-Firm Lobbying in the European Union and Member States', *Journal of Public Policy*, 18. (1), 75–100.

Commission of the European Communities (2006) *Green Paper: European Transparency Initiative (Presented by the Commission)*, COM 194 final (Brussels: Commission of the European Communities, 3 May), at: http://eur-lex.europa.eu/LexUriServ/LexUriServ.do?uri=COM:2006:0194:FIN:EN:PDF (accessed 12 March 2009).

——— (2008) *European Transparency Initiative. A Framework for Relations with Interest Representatives (Register and Code of Conduct)*, Communication of the Commission {SEC (2008) 1926} (Brussels: Commission of the European Communities, 27 May), at: http://ec.europa.eu/transparency/docs/323_en.pdf (accessed 12 March 2009).

Commons-Law Relay (2008) *[Commons-Law] Update on the Novartis Case before IPAB – 17 November 2008*, Chennai: at:. http://commonslaw.freeflux.net/blog/archive/2008/11/17/commons-law-update-on-the-novartis-case-before-ipab-17-november-2008.html (accessed 25 January 2009).

Cummings, J. (2007) *Pit Boss: Lobbying Firm Mines Calif. Connections' Politico*, 30 April, at: http://dyn.politico.com/members/forums/thread.cfm?catid=1&subcatid=3&threadid=4636 (accessed on 29 September 2007).

Dahl, Robert A. (1983) *Dilemmas of Pluralist Democracy: Autonomy vs. Control* (New Haven: Yale University Press).

Detragiache, E., T. Tressel and P. Gupta (2006) *Foreign Banks in Poor Countries: Theory and Evidence*, Working Paper No. 06/18 (Washington, DC: IMF).

Dharanajan, S. (2005) 'Managing Ethical Standards: When Rhetoric Meets Reality', *Development in Practice*, 15 (3–4), 529–38.

Eagleton, D. (2006) *Under the Influence: Exposing Undue Corporate Influence over Policy Making at the World Trade Organisation* (Johannesburg: ActionAid).

Etzion, Dror and Gerald F. Davis (2008) 'Revolving Doors? A Network Analysis of Corporate Officers and U.S. Government Officials', *Journal of Management Inquiry*, 17 (3), 157.

Ford Motor Company (2007) *For a More Sustainable Future: Connecting with Society. Ford Motor Company Sustainability Report 2006/7*, at: www.ford.com/aboutford/microsites/sustainability-report-2006-07/documents/2006_7_Sustainability.pdf (accessed 25 January 2009).

Getz, K. (1997) 'Research in Corporate Political Action: Integration and Assessment', *Business and Society*, 36 (1), 32–7.

Global Labor Strategies (2006) *Behind the Great Wall of China: U.S. Corporations Opposing New Rights for Chinese Workers*, at:. http://laborstrategies.blogs.com/global_labor_strategies/files/behind_the_great_wall_of_china.pdf (accessed 1 September 2007).

——— (2007) *Undue Influence: Corporations Gain Ground in Battle over China's New Labor Law*, at: http://laborstrategies.blogs.com/global_labor_strategies/files/undue_influence_global_labor_strategies.pdf (accessed 1 September 2007).

Global Policy Forum (2004) 'Shell Leads International Business Campaign against UN Human Rights Norms', at: www.globalpolicy.org/reform/business/2004/0315norms.htm (accessed 9 February 2009).

GRI (Global Reporting Initiative) (2006) *Sustainability Reporting Guidelines, Indicator Protocols Set: SO* (Amsterdam: GRI).

Henriques, Adrian (2007) *Corporate Truth: The Limits to Transparency* (London: Earthscan).

Hillman, A. J. (2003) 'Determinants of Political Strategies in U.S. Multinationals', *Business & Society*, 42 (4), 455–84.

Hillman, A. J., and M. A. Hitt (1999) 'Corporate Political Strategy Formulation: A Model of Approach, Participation, and Strategy Decisions', *Academy of Management Review*, 24 (4), 825–42.

Hillman, A. J., G. D. Keim and D. Schuler (2004) 'Corporate Political Activity: A Review and Research Agenda', *Journal of Management*, 30 (6), 837–57.

Holme, R. and P. Watts (2000) *Corporate Social Responsibility: Making Good Business Sense* (Geneva: World Business Council for Sustainable Development/WBCSD).

Kennedy, S. (2007) 'Transnational Political Alliances: An Exploration with Evidence from China', *Business and Society*, 46 (2), 174–200.

Kolk, A and J. Pinske (2007) 'Multinationals' Political Activities on Climate Change', *Business and Society*, 46 (2). 202–28.

Lascelles, D. (2005) *The Ethics of Influence: Political Donations and Lobbying* (London: Institute of Business Ethics).

Lindblom, Charles E. (1977) *Politics and Markets: The World's Political-Economic Systems* (New York: Basic Books).

Lord, M. D. (2000) 'Corporate Political Strategy and Legislative Decision Making', *Business and Society*, 39 (1), 76–93.

MacGillivray, A., P. Raynard and S. Zadek (2005) *Towards Responsible Lobbying: Leadership and Public Policy* (London: AccountAbility).

Mahoney, Christine (2007) 'Lobbying Success in the United States and the European Union', *Journal of Public Policy*, 27 (1), 35.

Milyo, J., D. Primo and T. Groseclose (2000) 'Corporate PAC Campaign Contributions In Perspective', *Business and Politics*, 2 (1), 75–88.

Novartis (2007) *Novartis Concerned Indian Court Ruling Will Discourage Investments in Innovation Needed to Bring Better Medicines to Patients*, Media Release, 6 August. at:. www.novartis.com/newsroom/media-releases/en/2007/1144199.shtml (accessed 25 January 2009).

OECD (Organisation for Economic Co-operation and Development) (2000) *Codes of Corporate Conduct – An Expanded Review of Their Contents*, TD/TC/WP(99)56/FINAL (Paris: OECD).

——— (2008) *Lobbyists, Governments and Public Trust: Building a Legislative Framework and Accountability in Lobbying*, GOV/PGC(2007)17/REV1 (Paris: OECD).

Olson, Mancur (1982) *The Rise and Decline of Nations: Economic Growth, Stagflation and Social Rigidities* (New York: Yale University Press).

Oxfam (2001) *Formula for Fairness: Patient Rights before Patent Rights* (Washington, DC: Oxfam).

Oxfam, VSO and Save the Children (2002) *Beyond Philanthropy: The Pharmaceutical Industry, Corporate Social Responsibility and the Developing World* (Washington, DC: Oxfam).

Public Citizen (2005) *Congressional Revolving Doors: The Journey from Congress to K Street* (Washington, DC: Public Citizen).

Richter, Judith (2004) *Public-Private Partnerships and International Health Policy-Making: How Can Public Interests Be Safeguarded?* (Helsinki: Ministry of Foreign Affairs of Finland).

Sandell, C. (2006) 'Senators to Exxon: Stop the Denial', *ABC News*, 27 October, at: http://abcnews.go.com/Technology/story?id=2612021&page=1 (accessed 1 July 2008).

SustainAbility and WWF–UK (2005) *Influencing Power: Reviewing the Conduct and Content of Corporate Lobbying* (London: SustainAbility/WWF-UK).

US Senate Office of Public Records (2007) *Office of Public Records Lobby Filing Disclosure Program, Cisco Filings*, at: http://sopr.senate.gov (accessed 29 September 2007).

Utting, Peter (2000) *Business Responsibility for Sustainable Development*, Occasional Paper No. 2 (Geneva: UNRISD).

——— (2007) 'CSR and Equality', *Third World Quarterly*, 28 (4), 697–713.

Vander Stichele, Myriam (2005) *Critical Issues in the Financial Industry* (Amsterdam: SOMO).

Vander Stichele, Myriam, Kim Bizzarri and Leonard Plank (2006) *Corporate Power over EU Trade Policy: Good for Business, Bad for the World* (Brussels: Seattle to Brussels Network).

Vidal, J. (2005) 'Revealed: How Oil Giant Influenced Bush', *The Guardian*, 8 June, at: www.guardian.co.uk/news/2005/jun/08/usnews.climatechange (accessed 15 June 2009).

Volkswagen (2008) *Sustainability Report 2007/2008* (2008), at: www.volkswagenag.com/vwag/vwcorp/info_center/en/publications/2007/09/sustainability_report.-bin.acq/qual-BinaryStorageItem.Single.File/sustainability_report_07-08_engl.pdf (accessed 3 July 2008).

Ward, Bob (2006) *Royal Society Letter to Exxon* (London: Royal Society), 4 September, at: www.exxposeexxon.com/newsroom/Royal-Society-Ltr-Sept-06.pdf (accessed 1 July 2008).

Webb, T. (2004) 'Human Rights Norms at the UN', *Ethical Corporation*, 24 October (2004).

Weyzig, Francis and Irene Schipper (2007) *Philips Electronics: Overview of Controversial Business Practices in 2006*, report commissioned by the Dutch Association of Investors for Sustainable Development (VBDO) (Amsterdam: SOMO).

Weyzig, Francis, Irene Schipper and Rieneke Slager (2006) *ICRT Pharma: Description of CSR Issues*, report commissioned by International Consumer Research and Testing (ICRT) (Amsterdam: SOMO).

WHO (World Health Organization) (2000) *Tobacco Company Strategies to Undermine Tobacco Control Activities at the World Health Organization: Report of the Committee of Experts on Tobacco Industry Documents* (Geneva: WHO).

Windsor, D. (2007) 'Toward a Global Theory of Cross-Border and Multilevel Corporate Political Activity', *Business & Society*, 46 (2), 253–78.

7
Corporate Rents and the Capture of the Peruvian State

Francisco Durand

In the 1980s and 1990s, when Latin America and Eastern Europe underwent an economic and political transition, analysts focused on the development of 'emerging markets' and 'democratic consolidation'. In the twenty-first century, as most of the developing world still struggles to contain authoritarian threats and corruption, the focus shifted to institutional weakness and democratic deconsolidation. In this context, the question of state capture has emerged and provoked a stimulating debate about the paradox of strong corporations operating with weak states in deconsolidated democracies.

The major source of concern in state capture studies is that politicians and policy-makers were seduced by empowered economic interests to generate rents in a predatory environment. Hence, the need to explain 'what went wrong', how the newly acquired economic and political power has been used, and how it affects resource allocation, policy quality, institutional development and the business climate.

The first studies of state capture focused on corruption in the former Soviet nations, in particular Russia and the 'oligarchs', were sponsored by international financial institutions (IFIs) and based on surveys. Given the institutional outreach of such organizations, the studies awakened a theoretical debate developed long ago by sociologists and political economists (Drazen 2000; Neuman 2005).

Two basic perspectives have emerged. The normative approach envisions state capture as a dangerous deviation from the right developmental path that is manifested when firms of all sizes 'purchase . . . laws and decrees' (Kaufmann et al. 2000: 5). In this perspective corrupt or 'bad networks' may control governments and can even obtain representation in international organizations. Corporations not involved in corrupt rent-seeking practices are perceived as 'good networks' (Moreno Ocampo 2007). Business is seen as practising influence over policy generation, that is, the 'firm capacity to have an impact on the formation of the basic rules of the game without necessarily recourse to private payments' (Hellman et al. 2000: 2). An underlying assumption is that nations can develop and thrive with strong market forces and minimalist states, yet they must fight corruption and be careful not to fall in the state capture trap.

An alternative approach provides a realist view of state capture and is more qualitative and abstract in nature. Rather than corruption, it focuses on how corporations, now the most powerful economic actors, obtain privileged access and undue influence over the most important branches of the state apparatus, relying on corruption and/or 'influence'. In this perspective, business empowerment creates state dependence on capital, a context where government officials 'bend to pressure', and defend the most powerful private interests at the expense of the public one.[1] Corporations are perceived as the main 'captor actors' (Omelyanchuk 2001: 5). Realists look at the interaction between the concentration of economic and political power, accountability and the institutional history of state bureaucracy to propose better regulation and a more balanced business–government relationship, yet few provide empirical evidence of state capture and its consequences.

This chapter analyses the Peruvian case from a realist and dynamic perspective, with a particular focus on analysing the specifics. It looks at a Latin American country that has suffered from extreme state capture since 1990, in a context of a weak state and a frail civil society, and when regimes and policies shifted in the direction of 'market democracies'. Interestingly enough, in this case, corporate actors, who initially operated in an authoritarian setting, found themselves in 2000 in a democratic environment that moderated but did not eliminate state capture. Democratization, a process accompanied by growing tensions inside the state, and an eruption of demands from civil society, made it more difficult, but not impossible, to defend rents and control conflicts of interest. Peru's analysis thus illustrates the conditions and dynamics of two state capture modes.

A dynamic study

This chapter specifies when and in what context business becomes empowered, how it goes about its 'conquest' of the state and what instruments it uses for that purpose. It seeks to explain state capture modes (extreme or moderate) by studying variations over time (1990–2008) and by looking at the two sides of the state capture equation: the supply (business) and the demand (state) sides.

The study of state capture modes rests on the following assumptions. First, state capture begins with the introduction of a neoliberal policy paradigm in 1990. Neoliberal forces strengthen the environment under which state capture emerges. It facilitates the growth of the private sector and within it the rise of domestic and transnational corporations (TNCs), while at the same time reducing state powers, opening decision-making agencies to private sector influence and disempowering civil society organizations (CSOs). In our view, state capture flourishes under neoliberalism and paves the way to extreme concentration of economic power, one of the key independent variables.

Second, the goal of the most powerful economic actors is to secure a direct and permanent presence in key governmental branches in order to generate policies, prevent changes, monitor implementation and defend 'acquired rights'. In contrast to some studies, this chapter is not limited to regulatory branches (Eisner 1993). Instead, it focuses on the true centres of the economic policy-making process in a given political system. Unlike the normative approach, it is neither limited to analysing corruption, that is, 'buying laws and decrees', nor to one phase of the policy-making process (policy generation).

Third, state capture implies more than access and influence. It becomes a reality due to the appointment of individuals from the business sector as top policy-makers, and the use of a 'revolving door' between the public and the private sector as a transmission belt for private sector influence.[2]

Fourth, political variables condition and codetermine state capture. The more authoritarian and the weaker the horizontal and vertical forms of accountability, the more extreme the state capture mode. Extreme concentration of political power contributes to the concentration of economic power, providing legal provisions and protections that facilitate or accelerate market trends. The more modern and relatively autonomous the branches and agencies of the state, the more likely one is to expect containment efforts to control state capture.

Fifth, state capture provokes tensions and conflict. Capture is easier when captor actors operate with weak, inefficient and corrupt, and psychologically subordinate bureaucracies, and thrive under authoritarian systems. Yet, empirical evidence shows that in the case of meritocratic branches, influence and control (particularly in the cases of rent) is harder and chances of horizontal accountability increase. A weak civil society is not capable of exercising vertical accountability but, when it demands freedoms and rights, it can make corporations and the state accountable. In this context, tensions develop and erupt, and conflicts eventually unfold when executive agencies and/or branches (Congress) attempt to defend the public interest by eliminating or controlling rents and corruption, and when civil society protests against undue business influence or policies approved under conditions of state capture. The outcomes of these struggles indicate who wins and who loses in the political game.

The study of the Peruvian case demonstrates the changing nature of state capture. The extreme mode, as Table 7.1 indicates, developed under the Fujimori administration (1990–2000). After the restoration of democracy in 2000, the political dynamics changed, opening avenues for higher accountability. In this relatively modified context, state capture is moderated after a brief interlude where control over the state was momentarily lost and then recovered, but operating under new conditions. In this mode the concentration of economic power continues while political power is less concentrated

Table 7.1 Modes of state capture in Peru, 1990–2006

Capture of the state	Concentration of economic power	Concentration of political power	Bureaucratic quality	Civil society
Extreme mode (1990–2000)	High	High	Low (no horizontal accountability)	Repressed (low vertical accountability)
Moderate mode (2001–6)	High	Low	Low (low/medium horizontal accountability)	Proactive (higher vertical accountability)

Source: Author's analysis.

and civil society awakened. Yet, captor actors manage to accommodate to shifting political circumstances by relying on networks.

This chapter relies on a process-tracing case methodology constructed from semi-structured interviews, congressional documentary analysis, tax court decisions, news reports and secondary studies. Tracing processes in this manner helps decode the nature of state capture and reconstruct the interaction of factors that generate the predatory environment under which it emerges.

This chapter also emphasizes an empirical dimension rarely addressed by realist or normative studies. It does so by looking at tax cases of rent and/or corruption, all fairly well documented in the case of Peru. In terms of legislation, it narrows the field to legal stability agreements (LSAs) signed with top corporations, tax exonerations for various economic activities, including the leading economic sectors, and tax assessments of corporations based on Tax Merger Law (DS 120-94-EF). Consequently, the chapter looks at agencies that play a critical decision-making role in economic and tax issues: the Ministerio de Economía y Finanzas (MEF/Ministry of Economy and Finance), the most powerful cabinet position, and the tax administration, Superintendencia Nacional de Administración Tributaria (SUNAT/National Superintendency of Tax Administration of Peru), the relatively autonomous internal revenue service.

Neoliberalism

Contemporary state capture is related to the introduction of a neoliberal policy regime. This contextual variable is critical because neoliberalism defines new rules of the game, marking the arena by specifying the policy areas where rents become more likely, and by provoking changes in the relative strength of powerful contenders within business and between business and government.

New policies were abruptly adopted in 1990 by the administration of Alberto Fujimori, a leader who added new elements to make state capture possible. He was the winner of fair and free elections, but quickly concentrated executive power at the expense of Congress and the courts, and also within the executive, the presidency, the MEF and the security apparatus.

Power concentration was seen as necessary to provide order in the midst of chaos, following a model of authoritarian modernization similar to that of Chile's Pinochet. In 1990, the country suffered its worst crisis of the century and feared a 'collapse of the state'; thus Peruvian neoliberalism was introduced in an increasingly authoritarian environment. The combined effects of a high concentration of political and economic power and weak institutions and civil society generated an extreme mode of state capture, one where all forms of accountability ceased to work.

The radical policy shift was in part triggered by the extreme financial needs of the state, low international reserves and active capital flight. Those factors made the Peruvian state more dependent on international capital than other countries. External financing was the only available source of credit and it was accessible only if policy changes intended to 'stabilize the economy' were introduced and monitored by the International Monetary Fund (IMF) and the World Bank. The inordinate amount of influence of neoliberal international institutions, a desperate domestic situation, and the corresponding concentration of political power to correct it led to the introduction of one of the most drastic and authoritarian forms of neoliberalism seen on the continent (Gonzales de Olarte 1998).

In these initial obliging circumstances, the executive adopted policy changes in a top-down process. A total of 923 executive decrees were issued between early 1991 and December 1992 (Boloña 1993: 55). MEF became the leading policy decision-maker, a position of power fully supported by Fujimori, the IFIs and the business sector. New policies were implemented in an elitist manner: without an open public debate but with extensive business participation channelled through the Confederación Nacional de Instituciones Empresariales Privadas (CONFIEP/National Confederation of Private Business Associations of Peru). Initially, the MEF operated with congressional authorization, but since the June 1992 presidential coup against Congress and the judiciary (an event that empowered the other two gravitational centres inside the executive, the presidency and the security apparatus), the MEF acted alone. During the subsequent years policy-makers at the MEF issued 745 decrees in a few months, representing 80 per cent of the total legislative *tsunami*. The shift was consolidated with the approval of the 1993 neoliberal constitution.[3] After returning to elections in 1995, subsequent reforms and rents were generated by the MEF, with full support from a subservient legislature (Arce 2006: 37–40).

Some shades of grey can be observed. The first wave of neoliberal reforms was more institutional in nature than rent-oriented because of the crisis and the fact that corporate power was not strong. Given the context and the nature of external influences, policies first aimed at generating general changes and modernizing administrative reforms. As in other countries, the crisis-ridden reform process was 'sound' in nature (Grindle and Thomas 1991: 155–6). However, it was also deeply elitist and authoritarian and far from devoid of interests. At this time, the Peruvian state experienced partial administrative reform, a condition that would make state capture more difficult because it would eventually trigger a defence of the public interest inside the government.

Given its financial and administrative autonomy from the MEF, SUNAT became the best example of an administrative reform, thanks to the quality of the policy team and the adoption of a rigorous merit-based recruitment system (Durand and Thorp 1998). In the early 1990s, the judicial system also experienced partial reform (creation of a Constitutional Tribunal), and regulatory agencies developed (appointed by the President with participation of interest groups, including business). In addition, the Banco Central de Reserva del Perú (BCRP/Central Reserve Bank of Peru) was also freed from political appointees and given strict but limited powers to regulate monetary matters and inflation.

SUNAT and the BCRP became the most bureaucratically advanced and technically powerful agencies within the executive, but operated as two relatively independent islands of modernity. In this context, the MEF fought hard in the post-crisis period (1992–2000) to influence or subordinate all superintendencies and regulatory agencies, and to limit or reduce their autonomy, thus facilitating rents. Coincidentally, the ministry would not experience any significant internal administrative reform, an outcome that may indicate that captor actors were not truly interested in reforming it.

The reason why some branches and agencies were modernized during the crisis is related to the systemic need to have better institutions in order to improve policy implementation. Yet, when the crisis dissipated, and corporate interests became structurally and politically empowered in the mid-1990s, the goal of institutional reforms waned. As politics became 'business-as-usual', the newly formed or reformed agencies clashed with captor actors when particularistic economic interest arose. Hence, a need to go in the opposite direction developed: control the centres of bureaucratic oversight to facilitate economic favours and pork-barrel spending.

In this context, the MEF was crowned as the uncontested economic decision-making centre, thus becoming the main target of captor actors. The MEF prepared and executed the budget, designed and/or suggested economic policies, approved public works, implemented policies and oversaw all regulatory agencies, with the exception of the Central Bank and SUNAT. Direct presence at the MEF gave enormous power and influence.

As the Fujimori administration concentrated powers and gave MEF a free hand, state capture was institutionalized. Once empowered, the MEF proceeded to eliminate checks and balances within the executive, subordinating SUNAT and isolating the BCRP, while Fujimori and the security apparatus controlled all venues of executive, congressional, judicial and civil society oversight. Vladimiro Montesinos and the intelligence services, an ally of business interests, intent on organizing corruption on a grand scale, did the rest, including a tight and almost complete control over the mass media (Dammert 2001).

The predatory context contributed to consolidate the extreme mode of state capture and led to the formation of an organized system of rents mixed with corruption, a situation where the 'good networks' (corporations, international organizations) interacted with the 'bad networks' (corrupt politicians and bureaucrats). It happened not only because many decisions required MEF authorization (for example, weapon purchases negotiated by Montesinos and his network), but also because they supported each other to the end. CONFIEP ended up being influenced by the MEF during the Camet era and backed Fujimori for 10 years, while independent business associations (the Lima Chamber of Commerce, the National Society of Industries) abandoned the confederation (Durand 2003).

Under neoliberalism, rent-seeking was confined to given policy areas, while being reduced or eliminated in others. Laws and regulations pertaining to taxation and privatization, in particular, triggered a more aggressive projection of business interests in politics. In order to stimulate supply and comply with the logic of rents, policy-makers insisted on placing a strong emphasis on legal protections to big investors, in particular, TNCs and tax giveaways. Lack of transparency and low or non-existent accountability facilitated the adoption of these policies. Decision-makers operated in an environment of secrecy. In policy areas related to demand stimulation, neoliberalism did the opposite by eliminating or reducing tariffs, credit and exchange rate rents and various subsidies (Boloña 1993).

A new power structure

The combined effect of externally induced, sudden and drastic, authoritarian and elitist policy changes created the conditions for the extraordinary rise of private sector power; TNCs in particular were the main beneficiaries of privatization, deregulation and economic liberalization. A wave of mergers and acquisitions after the economy turned around in 1994 (when inflation was controlled and Peru resumed growth after years of stagnation), economic globalization, and the normalization of international credit, further consolidated TNCs' structural power and political influence.

The private sector as a whole took the leading role in the economy after more than 150 state-owned enterprises were sold to the highest bidders for a total of $9.2 billion.[4] Out of the 16 largest enterprises, sold for $4.5 billion, only one was bought by local investors, while in others they participated as minority shareholders (COPRI 2001). In addition, the opening offered extraordinary business opportunities for new productive and financial investment protected by LSAs, a provision adopted in the 1993 constitution. Between 1991 and 2000, a total of 332 LSAs were signed by the MEF and the Ministry of Mining and Energy (286 with TNCs). The privatization process and the buyout of local companies generated a wave of more than 600 mergers (CIDEF 2001, 2002). In a few years, a handful of powerful TNCs and a few remaining domestic corporations ended up controlling the communications, banking and pension fund sectors, as well as the empowered import-export economy.

At the same time, the repressive powers of the state, justified as a need to fight terrorism, and the increasing control of the press by the intelligence services, continued to undermine civil society. In this repressive climate, grassroots organizations and non-governmental organizations (NGOs) retreated from the political arena. Not even the strongest labour federations were able to organize any effective form of resistance. In sum, Peru became socially silent during the 1990s, and gave the false impression of living a time of 'peace, prosperity and order'.

Appointing the right people

The capture of the state takes place when private sector interests determine the appointment process of key parts of the state apparatus, a process that is politically more relevant than the question of external private influences over the state and bribes taken by officials and given by private interests – variables emphasized by the normative approach. A realist view indicates that the main targets of captor actors linked to or representing big business are the decision-making centres that set the tone and the course of economic policy generation, implementation and evaluation. Business influence over presidents and parties in office before and during the appointment process triggers state capture because the decision-makers use their influence to limit the government's choice to a pool of candidates 'with the right credentials'. When elections take place, campaign financing creates the opportunity for state capture to be initiated or continued. Yet there are also systemic or structural forces at work as economic growth gravitates around a handful of powerful foreign and domestic conglomerates, whose structural power and influence is recognized by the political class.

Once it occurs, corporate forces monitor state capture inside and outside of government. Since corporate influence is not limited to the captured part of the apparatus, various defensive mechanisms (influence over the news media, collective action, lobbying) operate to guarantee state capture or restore it when lost. When legislation or decisions that clearly favour economic interests and affect the public interest are put into question, a captured agency pays little attention to people's opinions, and is generally unwilling to listen to the occasional press reports or demands from civil society that may emerge, thus weakening the overall accountability process.

It must be taken into account that state capture, however strong it may be, is neither uniform, permanent, nor devoid of problems. Since there are power struggles, and accommodation to shifting circumstances dictated by political needs, captor actors cannot fully control all agencies at all times. Even in a dictatorship it is not possible to avoid bureaucratic infighting or protest movements. However, greater uncertainty for captor actors is usually generated during political and economic crises, regime transitions and elections. Moderate modes of state capture are more likely in democratic regimes because there is a higher balance of power among governmental branches and more efficient forms of vertical and horizontal accountability.

In the case of Peru, since the MEF is the most important cabinet position, and SUNAT and the BCRP play an important role in economic policy-making, we must emphasize the appointment process and rotation in office in these key agencies. Control of the appointment process depends on factors such as norms, the bureaucratic tradition and quality of institutions, interagency relations and levels of bureaucratic autonomy.

The MEF is an old ministry with a heterogeneous body. It has experienced top administrators who earn high salaries, while the rest of the bureaucracy is undertrained and underpaid. The ministry never experienced administrative reforms, so officials are used to the coming and going of top administrators and offer little resistance to lobbying, corruption and state capture. They are all used to watching a parade of petitioners of all kinds, as well as ministers and advisers, intimately linked to the private sector that attempt to access and influence them, including law firms that introduce policy changes to favour their corporate clients.[5]

SUNAT, given its shorter history and higher degree of institutional quality, differs in many ways. Thanks to the 1991 reform effort, the tax administration became a financially autonomous and modernized institution. Given its role and expanded capabilities, and the concentration of rents and favours around taxation, the power struggle over SUNAT was quite intense (Estela 2001). Directors and technocrats consciously opposed and resisted capture, even after the government, the MEF or the President appointed a superintendent associated with business interests (Durand and Thorp 1998). Yet, despite this, SUNAT was eventually neutralized thanks to decisions taken by the presidency or the MEF, the only two power centres with enough leverage in the Peruvian bureaucratic universe to do so.

Due to a strongly rooted tradition of autonomy and high-quality personnel, the BCRP enjoyed more independence than SUNAT. The executive director and part of the directory is appointed by Congress, a decision that is public and needs a broad political consensus.

Under Fujimori, the new generation of energy, communications, pension fund and stock exchange regulatory bodies were led by boards of directors appointed by the President and picked from various institutions, including interest groups and consumer representatives. These bodies were both modern and semi-autonomous, but financially dependent on the MEF and subject to its pressure. According to Távara (2006: 217), who worked with the Public Defender overseeing regulatory agencies, and whose studies indicate state capture conditions in this area, 'little was done . . . with respect to transparency, participation and accountability'.

Basic questions on the specific dynamics of state capture (when, how, whom, for how long), are usually the most difficult to answer. Researchers face enormous problems in determining the specifics of the appointment process, identifying cases of tailored legislation, accurately estimating the cost of rents, or even understanding the decision-making rationale of top state officials. Nevertheless, important cases eventually emerged thanks to scandals and congressional investigations. Once identified and traced, the cases may indicate how key players act in the long run and help explain state capture and rent dynamics.

Appointment patterns, and the identification of a revolving door between the private and the public sector, a variable that stands out in business–government relation studies (Cohen 1986), shed light in the dark room of political decision-making. From 1990 to 2006, unlike previous administrations, the presidential choice of MEF ministers has been solely focused on business people. This pattern is a break from the past. During the García populist government (1985–90), all MEF ministers were either party members or independent economists affiliated with or loyal to the party. The criterion suddenly changed in favour of business leaders, an indication of the newly acquired weight of neoliberal forces and the private sector. From July 1990 to November 2000, the president appointed business people at the MEF (Juan Hurtado, Jorge Camet, Víctor Joy Way and Efraín Goldenberg), or economists working for corporations or think tanks intimately associated with big business (Carlos Boloña and Jorge Baca).[6]

Interestingly enough, after the Fujimori regime collapsed, the pattern temporarily changed (November 2000 and July 2001): the provisional Paniagua government appointed by Congress was not influenced by business interests. Javier Silva Ruete, an economist with formal training at the BCRP and with strong links to domestic corporations, and who had instructions to control state capture and eliminate rents and corruption, became MEF minister.[7] Yet, from July 2001 to July 2006, the Toledo government, strongly influenced by business interests, first appointed Pedro Pablo Kuczinsky, a global corporate manager, but then replaced him with Silva Ruete when social movements against privatization forced Kuczinsky's resignation. Kuczinsky came back from 2003 until 2005, when he was replaced by Fernando Zavala (an economist from Apoyo, a corporate think tank) at Kuczinsky's suggestion, while Kuczinsky switched positions and became the premier. The García government – elected in 2006 – followed the same pattern by appointing Luis Carranza, an economist from Banco Bilbao Viszcaya Argentaria, who was briefly MEF vice-minister in 1998. In sum, in more than 17 years, and unlike past populist administrations, with the exception of Silva Ruete no independent economist coming from universities or the government served as MEF minister.

From 1991 to 2009, the government selected SUNAT superintendents either by presidential decision (Manuel Estela, Sandro Fuentes, Adrián Revilla and Enrique Díaz) or by ministerial decision, that is, the MEF (Jorge Baca, before he became MEF minister; Jaime Iberico, who replaced him once at the MEF; Rosario Almenara, Luis Arias, Beatriz Merino, Nahil Hirsch, Laura Calderón and Manuel Velarde). Those selected had more diverse backgrounds since, out of the 11, six were economists or lawyers with training in the government, mostly the BCRP (Estela, Arias, Diaz, Revilla, Calderón) and the MEF (Hirsh, Velarde), one a private lawyer who was SUNAT's advisor (Fuentes), two who were corporate economists or accountants (Baca and Iberico, both working for Grupo La Fabril), and one a former corporate manager and independent lawyer (Merino). Note that the large number of appointees indicates struggles to control it. Given its technical nature, the criterion used was to select professional administrators or experts in fields related to the art of taxation. Of all the superintendents, the only ones who enjoyed substantial autonomy were the first two appointees of the Fujimori administration (Estela and Fuentes, from February 1991 to May 1994), Diaz (for only two months, beginning in July 2000 until he was abruptly removed by Boloña when Diaz fired a pro-MEF board of directors), and Arias (appointed by the provisional Paniagua administration in November 2000 and demoted by Toledo in July 2001). All were part of the original reform team that modernized and cleaned up SUNAT in the early 1990s. The rest came from other quarters; they were all subject to strong pressure from the MEF, or directly appointed by MEF in order to guarantee SUNAT's capture. The loss of SUNAT's autonomy became evident when Baca was appointed in May 1994 (Estela 2001; Taliercio 2001).

SUNAT's autonomy was short-lived, an outcome to be expected under state capture conditions. When Baca became superintendent, and with the exception of Arias who worked for the Paniagua government, SUNAT was fully or partially subordinated to the MEF and subject to the dynamics of state capture (Estela 2002).

Extreme mode (1990–2000)

State capture in Peru began in the midst of policy transition, when President Fujimori decided to appoint as MEF ministers only persons intimately connected with or belonging to the private sector. The process later consolidated with the 1992 coup and the approval of the 1993 pro-business constitution. The two factors empowered the executive and big business, while at the same time weakening labour unions and creating more difficult conditions for NGOs to support civil society, particularly in the area of labour demands and human rights. State capture became evident when Camet, at that time minister of industry and a former leader of CONFIEP, replaced Boloña at the MEF. Camet remained in power for five years and six months (9 January 1993 to 6 June 1998), becoming the longest serving MEF minister in history. Once in power, he and his inner circle of external and internal advisers quickly extended his influence over SUNAT and other regulatory agencies, while limiting the role of the BCRP to monetary matters. State capture in the post-Camet era was indeed facilitated by extreme concentration of economic and political power. This situation continued under other MEF ministers in a more complicated political scenario, because the 1998 financial crisis forced the government to suspend some tax exonerations despite business opposition, and also because Fujimori muddied the waters when he attempted another re-election in 2000.

Political decisions taken by the presidency, the MEF and the intelligence apparatus – the three great power centres of the 1990s – helped shut off governmental control mechanisms. All operated with a subservient Congress and used the mass media to organize misinformation campaigns. The latter in large part became part of the 'bad networks' and the subject of intense bribery (Dammert 2001: Section V). Also, the regime weakened all popular organizations with repressive measures, using the war against terrorism as an excuse to neutralize civil society (Schonwalder 2002). By the end of the 1990s, there was neither horizontal nor vertical accountability. By 2000, a political crisis eventually provoked changes in state capture mode, thanks to the sudden activation of civil society and the opposition parties. Before the regime crisis, few media outlets and CSOs escaped this oppressive trend, and even fewer dared to challenge the regime. The more extreme form of concentration of political power opened the gates to abuse, rents and corruption, benefiting collectively the corporate sector, and individually a small circle of well-connected firms.

In order to secure access and expand influence, a revolving door mechanism became visible when captor actors used it as a transmission belt between the private and the public sector. The process came about when Roberto Abusada, the MEF's top adviser, left his position in the government to participate in a privatization venture in early 1993 (Dammert 2001). Abusada, one of the nation's top economic policy experts, managed to return to power soon afterwards when he formed Instituto Peruano de Economía (IPE/Peruvian Institute of Economy) in 1994. IPE used the revolving door mechanism in the most sophisticated manner.

IPE was conceived as a 'private policy institute', funded by the MEF, the World Bank, CONFIEP, and top multinational and domestic corporations, the de facto powers of the neoliberal era. For this purpose the MEF even signed a contract to fund IPE in exchange for 'policy advice' on tax and commercial matters, a mechanism that blurred the distinction between private and public interests. This transmission belt was depicted by some top analysts as a privatization of public policies that enabled rentism on a large scale (Estela 2002; Arce 2006).[8] IPE's formal goal was to 'attract private sector participation in public policy debates' (IPE 1994: 6), but it went so far beyond this that well-informed sources suggested in interviews that it dictated policy.

The IPE transmission belt remained secret for many years, becoming public thanks to the congressional investigations that followed Fujimori's fall. The 2000 political crisis, and the accountability efforts it triggered, became the main lightning rod that illuminated the dark room of extreme state capture mode.

During the 1994–8 period, the revolving door between IPE and the government was used by the following persons, a pattern that provides insight on the top players involved in the game of state capture:

- Alfonso Bustamante, former minister of industry and premier (1991–3), and later appointed chief executive officer (CEO) of Telefónica del Perú, the nation's largest and politically best-connected company, became IPE president from 1994 to 1997. He left Telefónica in 2003 and became director of Banco Interamericano, a foreign-owned bank.
- Arturo Woodman, a top manager of Grupo Romero, the most powerful domestic conglomerate, held various positions in the Fujimori administration before and after becoming CONFIEP president. He acted first as IPE's secretary (1994–6) and later as its vice-president (1996–8). Woodman served in all administrations from 1990 to 2008.
- Francisco Moreyra, a corporate lawyer, was MEF minister Jorge Camet's legal advisor, serving at the same time as an adviser to companies who bought government debt bonds at bargain prices and later used them to buy state-owned enterprises. Moreyra was an IPE board member between 1994 and 1998.
- Fritz Dubois was the leading advisor at the MEF from 1991 to 1998, despite the fact he did not even have a bachelor's degree. He became part of IPE's directory when he left the MEF in 1998, soon after joining the board of directors of Banco Interamericano.
- Jorge Baca, already mentioned, was IPE's manager before becoming SUNAT superintendent in 1997 and, later, minister when he replaced Camet at the MEF in 1998. He became an IMF consultant right afterwards and was prosecuted on corruption charges in 2001 and imprisoned in 2007.
- Camet himself joined IPE's directory after he left MEF, a move that indicated the intimate connections in place. He also joined the board of directors of Banco de Crédito, Peru's most powerful bank, controlled by the Romero group (Durand 2003: 419). He was prosecuted and placed under house arrest in 2002.

These captor actors, given their decision-making power and intimate connections, generated rents mostly in the form of tax exonerations that benefited two circles: first, whole business sectors (particularly mining, oil, gas and banking), and second, the politically connected corporations, in particular those engaged in state capture.

Privatization programmes and acquisitions, according to congressional investigative committees, were two other extraordinary forms of rents. State-owned corporations, including Aeroperú, were sold to the highest bidders in a context of increased corruption and discretionality. These bureaucratic deviations indicated a more extensive form of rent and corruption – in all cases the MEF was directly involved since it played a key role, including the approval of tens of secret, unnumbered executive decrees (Dammert 2001; CIDEF 2001; Ugarteche 2005). The cases thus indicate that in economic policy-making the line that separates 'good' and 'bad' networks is blurred.

Two tax policy areas with a direct impact on the profitability of business constitute the first type of rent to be analysed in detail. The Tax Merger Law made possible tax-free mergers and the subsequent revaluation of assets for buyers who enjoyed the possibility of increased depreciation through asset revaluation. Under existing rules, the assets were revalued freely, based on company estimates and without state supervision, an indication of low policy quality. In principle, the Tax Merger Law aimed at business consolidation in order to have more powerful and efficient firms. Two facts make this law a near perfect case of tailored legislation: 1) it was issued in secret by the minister and his private advisors, despite the opposition of the MEF's legal experts and of SUNAT (as congressional investigative committees discovered when Fujimori fell); and 2) though it was initially valid only for a few months (September to December 1994), its application was extended every year until 1998 with congressional authorization at a time when the administration and business interests controlled Congress (Arias 2003). In the end, the Tax Merger Law generated an environment conducive to rents and corruption that had little to do with increased business efficiency. The fact that the law helped to revalue assets to lower taxation twisted the stated objectives. To business, profits at all costs became more important than business consolidation. After all, state capture generated legal rents and ample room for legal interpretation, even if the practices were questionable and against the public interest.

The law was approved in September 1994 and validated until 1998 as a provisional norm. In more than four years, about 1,500 companies used it to consolidate assets for a total of 62 billion Peruvian nuevos soles (S/.) (Campodónico 2006: 181). The numbers are so high because, as time passed, more companies learned about the tax benefits and engaged in real or phoney mergers and acquisitions. Several of the companies that used the Tax Merger Law, as illustrated in Figure 7.1, also signed LSAs. In some extreme cases, five major corporations decided to interpret the law in such a way that the provisional benefit, as demonstrated by the fact it was extended every year by Congress, was arbitrarily made permanent. These clusters considered

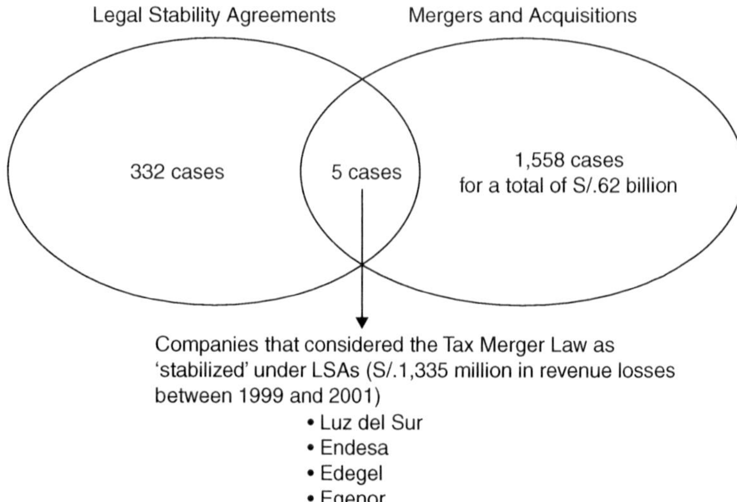

Figure 7.1 Tax Merger Law, legal stability agreements, and mergers and acquisitions, 1990–2001
Sources: Arias (2003); Campodónico (2006); CIDEF (2002).

that the benefits could be incorporated into their LSAs and should last until the expiration of agreements. As a result of this extreme form of behaviour and, given the fact that state capture provided a safety net, the benefits of these five companies were extended beyond the limit established by law. Wrongful or questionable business behaviour became evident as small companies owned or created by the same shareholders bought giant ones in order to revalue their assets. Many companies also revalued assets above market value, thus further lowering tax contributions.

Electric companies such as Edelnor (owned by Endesa, a Spanish TNC), Luz del Sur (United States) and Edegel (Panama), and the mining company Barrick Misquichilca (Canada) generated revenue losses between 1999 and 2001 estimated at S/.1,335 million (Campodónico 2006: 183). The most extreme case was Edelnor, which paid zero income taxes for five consecutive years! This particular finding corroborates the hypotheses of state capture studies that, 'once a country has fallen into the trap of state capture economy, foreign direct investment can magnify the problem' (Hellman and Kaufmann 2001: 6).

Various tax benefits and exoneration policies that generated serious fiscal losses over the years were also issued during the Camet era at a time when the IPE 'good network' became the main policy advisor in matters related to taxation and trade. It must be noted that there is no hard evidence that all, or some, of these provisions were generated or influenced by IPE (the black box prevents verification), yet it is important to point out that opinion leaders consulted by the author unanimously considered that the policy institute had both privileged access and enormous influence.

This influence eventually extended to SUNAT when its autonomy was lost.[9] In this sense, World Bank expert Taliercio (2001: 7) correctly argues that: 'From 1991 to 1998 SUNAT's autonomy was assaulted along several dimensions. Different ministers of finance had tried to retake control of the agency.' Estela, the superintendent who initiated the 1991 reform, the most respected professional voice in tax matters, is even more emphatic when he states: 'IPE became the instrument to demolish SUNAT's autonomy' (2003: 21).

At first, in May 1995, when Revilla became superintendent (and right after Fuentes, a member of the SUNAT team, manifested his opposition to DS 120-94-EF), MEF minister Camet succeeded in extending his influence over SUNAT by constantly pressuring the superintendent. Subsequently, the MEF achieved full control, when in February 1997, IPE manager Baca, Camet's protégé, was appointed superintendent. This situation continued when, after a privatization scandal, Camet resigned in June 1998, and the revolving door was used to make Baca minister, who, in turn, appointed his trusted advisor, Iberico, as head of SUNAT.

It must be emphasized that rents generated by 'good networks' and corruption generated by 'bad networks' became intertwined at this point. During Baca's tenure, SUNAT covered up a scandal involving Montesinos, Fujimori's security advisor, failing to audit his case, and later went even further by creating a list of companies that could be audited only with Baca's authorization (CIDEF 2002). Characters such as Montesinos, Joy Way and Camet used the mechanism to shield their companies. At this point, all the pieces of the puzzle had fallen in the right place for captor actors. Rentism and corruption exploded, thanks to extreme concentration of economic and political power and the lack of any working corrective mechanism outside or inside the state.

Another important case is related to sectoral tax exonerations granted by the MEF to lower or eliminate payments on sales and income taxes (the two most important sources of state revenue). Exonerations blossomed during the 'business as usual' Camet era. According to official studies, the exonerations generated an estimated fiscal cost in 2000 of $815 million a year in mining, $577 million in agriculture, $171 million in gas and oil, $549 million in the case of the Amazon region (the leading oil companies being the main beneficiaries), $42 million in tourism, $100 million in construction (the sector where Minister Camet's family firm operated with success, according to congressional investigative committees and press reports), and $105 million in the service sector. All these exonerations became known in the late 1990s only when an IMF study leaked to the press raised the alarm. The report estimated total losses at $2.36 billion, about 1.34 per cent of gross domestic product (GDP). These revelations occurred at a time when the economy was slowing down and the fiscal deficit was increasing. SUNAT, the MEF and Congress subsequently initiated investigations.

In reality, the situation was even more serious since the study did not include tax breaks for the financial sector on savings and stock exchange operations (Campodónico 2006). Bavaria corporation, for example, bought the Backus beer corporation under this provision in 2002, and the Polar company, which sold part of its Backus shares to Bavaria, did not pay taxes estimated at $78 million (Campodónico 2006: 196). By 2005, despite various unsuccessful attempts during the Paniagua period and the Toledo congress to reduce exonerations generated by the Fujimori administration, revenue losses on sales tax alone were estimated at $1.2 billion.

The Camet era thus generated a legacy that continued over the years thanks to state capture and despite mode variations (Campodónico 2006). The fiscal cost estimates demonstrate the extent of the revenue losses. The changes in the power structure, brought about by the introduction of neo-liberalism, resulted in neither the government nor the news media nor civil society being capable of discussing and controlling private influence over policy and of attempting to stop or reduce the losses. Changes only came in the form of anti-corruption efforts and higher vertical and horizontal accountability when Peru returned to democracy. Symptomatically, in 2001, during the provisional government, and at a time when SUNAT regained its autonomy briefly, a study showed that for the 1995–2000 period the 60 largest taxpayers were the only ones who reduced their fiscal contribution (from $714 million in 1997 to $350 million in 2000), while the rest actually increased their contribution. For the same period income tax collection as a percentage of GDP declined from 2.66 per cent to 1.78 per cent (Campodónico 2006: 184).

During the Camet era, tax minimisation, evasion and fraud became common, and tax breaks increased by leaps and bounds. The pattern was so generalized that corporate lawyers coined the term 'non-taxable profits'. Thanks to ongoing state capture and the effects of the Tax Merger Law, this situation continued after Fujimori. Income tax collection for companies reached a high point in 1997, representing 2.66 per cent of GDP, declined to 1.78 per cent in 2000 and registered a modest increase to 1.87 per cent in 2002 (Campodónico 2006: 184).

It is interesting to note that during the 1998 crisis, despite business protest, the government terminated the Tax Merger Law and attempted to diminish some rents for the mining sector – a rare event, but understandable because political elites faced a difficult fiscal situation. However, thanks to organized business opposition and corporate lobbying, many tax exonerations remained in place, an indication of what was about to come. Once empowered, the corporate sector considered the rents as 'acquired rights' and developed the will and the means to defend them.[10] In the same period (1998–2000) SUNAT was paralysed, and failed to initiate auditing operations, even if the superintendent, worried about declining revenues and fully informed by the IMF about the fiscal cost of exonerations, asked the MEF for permission to deal with the most striking cases of tax evasion. Permission was denied.

Moderate mode (2001–9)

The crisis of the Fujimori regime led to higher accountability, thanks to a greater separation of powers and a proactive civil society that helped moderate but not alter the essence of state capture. The concentration of political power indeed diminished, yet economic power concentration, as well as the institutional quality of the state, remained constant. In this context, business interests accommodated themselves to a more open and uncertain environment while still concentrating their hold on executive power. To prove the point, as suggested above, the provisional Paniagua government acted as a natural control variable because it was devoid of business influence.

The fact that Paniagua suddenly became President made it impossible for business interests and state captors to influence his administration. In addition, Paniagua's emphasis on ethics and higher accountability at all levels further limited spaces for lobbying tactics.[11] Given the lack of control of the appointment process, MEF and SUNAT acted in a more independent manner. Under presidential guidance, SUNAT became willing to use its powers to oversee corporate behaviour to correct the wrongs of the 1990s, triggering a clash of interests and making clear the asymmetries of power.

SUNAT, now led by a BCRP economist, Luis Alberto Arias, enjoyed full support from the MEF and the presidency. Arias proceeded to remove officials linked to Montesinos and private consulting firms, thus neutralizing the influence of 'good' and 'bad' networks. Once 'liberated', SUNAT investigated the causes of declining revenues and decided to audit and later assess powerful corporations that included Telefónica del Perú, a Spanish TNC, and the five companies mentioned above, all of whom, despite making profits, paid no or very little income taxes in the late 1990s (Arias 2003).

The assessment went on despite pressures that came from inside the MEF, orchestrated by officials identified with the Camet era, and from the outside by the companies and the trade associations representing the electric and mining companies being audited. Interestingly enough, CONFIEP remained silent because the conflict touched only individual interests, not collective ones. The arguments of business critics was that SUNAT 'had sharp teeth' and needed to be 'defanged'; that sectoral exonerations and the benefits of the Tax Merger Law incorporated into LSAs should be considered as rights; and that any initiative to assess the companies, or to change 'the rules of the game', would generate economic uncertainty.

SUNAT's actions triggered private sector initiatives, particularly by the corporations being assessed, which attempted first to lobby president Paniagua and, when this failed, penetrated the Toledo campaign and his inner circle. Interestingly enough, during the campaign Toledo echoed business interests and attacked 'damned SUNAT'.[12] Once elected and the cabinet nominated, both the President and key cabinet members, including Kuczyinski, the new MEF minister, bitterly criticized SUNAT. Their vision was simple: the state, not big business, was abusing its powers in a political attempt to derail the era of order and progress initiated by Fujimori.

Once this 'upside down' perspective was adopted, captor actors tried to stop SUNAT. Days before inauguration, two future ministers, Raul Diez Canseco and Kuczynski, called Arias and strongly demanded that the electric companies not be assessed. Arias rejected this attempt as arbitrary interference. SUNAT then sought and obtained presidential and cabinet support and, with their blessing, proceeded to assess electric companies for unpaid taxes. Later he disclosed the interference attempt to a congressional oversight committee and the press reported on it, initiating a public debate Not surprisingly, as the public was unaware of the internal conflict, Arias was immediately demoted and replaced by Beatriz Merino, a conservative lawyer and former Procter & Gamble executive. Merino moderated SUNAT's approach and concentrated only in continuing with the cases initiated by Arias, thus limiting the scope of the investigations. The MEF announced in parallel that the five companies had the right to arbitrate the conflicts, supporting the questionable claim that the LSAs were violated (temporary exonerations cannot be included in the agreements because the benefits were phased out), and appointed members of an arbitration commission filled with pro-corporate lawyers.

This was the moment when, thanks to campaign contributions, influences over the appointment process, and the effective use of the revolving door, state capture was reinstated. Captor actors managed to influence the MEF, and to some extent SUNAT and other regulatory agencies. But Congress, now more responsive to civil society and the public interest, proved more difficult to influence. Investigative committees started to study white collar crimes, and the information on tax privileges and abuses became known through press releases and comments made by independent journalists.

In this new climate, captor actors managed to obtain some victories and eventually managed to influence Congress, whose zeal for oversight waned as time passed, but lost credibility as they became the subject of more intense congressional and public scrutiny. In 2002 the arbitration commission ruled in favour of the five companies assessed by SUNAT, arguing that the LSAs were violated. However, when SUNAT took the case to the Tax Tribunal, at a time when Silva Ruete was at the MEF, it ruled that SUNAT could continue its investigations using other instruments. Since it seemed companies deliberately attempted to diminish tax collections by forming small companies with the purpose of buying the big ones, a questionable legal decision under Article VIII of the Tax Code, SUNAT proceeded with other assessments.

Yet Merino's SUNAT deliberately limited the investigations to the five cases instead of expanding its scope, as Congress and tax experts demanded, thus moving into line with the vision of Minister Kuczynski. This was a clear indication of SUNAT bending to collective corporate pressure and political influence coming from the MEF. It strongly suggested business influence, since the congressional investigative committees revealed that more than 1,500 companies merged and used the Tax Merger Law with a fiscal loss of S/.14 billion; they asked SUNAT for a report. SUNAT and the MEF (this time under Kuczynski) deliberately issued the report based on samples instead of conducting a general study, and kept it secret for a long time to slow down the public and congressional debate. By doing so, the extent of tax evasion by big business remained unknown. Symptomatically, the MEF later took the initiative to prevent SUNAT from sanctioning the five companies, using its regulatory powers in reverse. For that purpose Kuczynski (back in the ministry since July 2003) created a Taxpayer Defender, an initiative that in principle supported accountability by the private sector. Firms now could appeal SUNAT's sanctions to the MEF, thus limiting SUNAT's powers (Campodónico 2006: 359–66). Not surprisingly, when the five companies appealed, the Taxpayer Defender (appointed by the MEF) ruled in favour of their demands and blocked any further action.[13]

In this pro-business climate, exonerations continued and tax audits stopped. Neither Congress nor the MEF, when it had authorization to issue executive decrees in tax matters, was capable of eliminating or even reducing the exonerations. Kuczynski maintained them all and, in 2006, under the García administration, the MEF again lacked the will to introduce major changes. Only the Amazonian region lost subsidies (a decision that provoked violent regional movements), while economic sectors and corporations that benefited from the status quo were untouched and continued to enjoy the rents. The new MEF minister, Carranza, continued with the tradition of state capture, indicating the ongoing nature of the phenomena. These decisions had political implications since, despite continued business victories, the nation witnessed a lively debate about economic policies and taxation, one of the first times that the neoliberal policy regime was discussed.

The most important contribution came from congressional investigative committees, independent academics and journalists specializing in economic matters. The news media played a limited role, reporting only when the cases became public and doing so with a clear pro-business bias. The vertical accountability system was not fully activated because state capture continued. In this context, where the state seemed weak civil society stepped in. Social movements became intense, particularly in the cases of mining regions, where income depended on tax revenues that had been artificially diminished by rents. Barrick became known as one of the most extreme examples of areas where firms reduced taxable profits under the Tax Merger Law. Resources in these regions arrived late and in a limited manner because diminished income tax contributions reduced resource allocations (Campodónico 2006: 323–63). Since 2000, towns and grassroots organizations supported by NGOs (Oxfam-Peru and others) mobilized to demand resources for the regional governments and municipalities, and marched against water and land contamination. Almost all major mining centres witnessed waves of protest and political violence (Yanacocha, Tintaya, Tambo Grande, Majaz, Cerro Verde and Barrick) (DESCO 2004). Between 2007 and the first half of 2009, waves of national protests erupted in reaction against government corruption, red tape, privatization, free trade and corporate privileges.

In this context, corporate reputation and, more generally, business legitimacy suffered. The sign of the times became evident in the 2006 election, when radical political leaders demanded the elimination of tax rents, the revision of LSAs and, in the case of centre and leftist parties, opposition to a trade agreement with the United States. All top candidates asked for economic policy changes due to lack of social progress, yet none of these changes took place. With the appointment of Carranza to the MEF, and Laura Calderón to SUNAT (a former member of the Baca team demoted by Arias in 2001, a decision that demoralized the institution), moderate state capture continued unchanged under President García.

Conclusions

The strongest impact of state capture is the blurring of the differences between private and public interest to the benefit of the former. This condition, as the Peruvian study indicates, can translate into fiscal losses, generate tensions and conflict within the state and between the state and civil society, and prevent business collective action.

When economic elites participate in a ruling coalition under authoritarian conditions, the quality of policies and the strength of democratic, civil and governmental institutions tend to diminish. In this context of extreme state capture mode, as the Peruvian case demonstrates, 'good' and 'bad' networks support each other and, at times, overlap. Democracy helps control 'bad networks', and brings back a balance of political power and higher accountability that can help control abuses and privileges by 'good networks', especially after kleptocratic episodes, yet it is quite vulnerable to empowered economic interests.

In the two modes discussed in this chapter, government quality is not likely to improve because captor actors tend to prevent institutional reforms in order to defend rents. To prove the point, the Paniagua government acted effectively against state capture and in favour of private interests. This rare event happened because it was neither influenced by economic interests and captor actors nor willing to consider private interests as more or equally important than public ones.

Under conditions of state capture, government, business and society pay a high price. First, decreasing tax collection from highly profitable firms in the form of particular or sectoral rents creates unnecessary privileges for the privileged. Second, diminished corporate tax contributions reduce social policy funding, particularly in regional and municipal governments that depend on profit-sharing programmes. Third, state capture degrades vertical and horizontal accountability, particularly, but not only, in the extreme mode. Fourth, despite material gains, business suffers too.

This point merits further elaboration because it links the discussion with the question of risk. When economic elites are perceived as privileged, the political environment is more likely to be confrontational. In the long run, tensions and conflicts associated with state capture fuel sociopolitical instability and, given the leading role of TNCs, economic nationalism. In addition, negative perceptions of business are likely to appear, a trend that neutralizes the positive business effects of higher efficiency, job creation and corporate 'social responsibility' programmes. Within the business class, state capture weakens or prevents collective action because a network of established interests is unwilling to change the pattern of business–government relations that already runs along private lines and networks.

To correct these interrelated trends, action is needed at several levels to control state capture, enhance accountability, improve the quality of policies and resource allocation, and avoid political risks. Through independent NGOs and universities, civil society can discuss the nature and consequences of state capture. Congress should aim at legislation to eliminate rents, regulate lobbying and conflict of interest, and upgrade sanctions on corruption and white collar crimes. Complementarily, political leaders and institutions should exert a tighter control over the appointment process, close the revolving door, and strengthen the relative autonomy, powers and quality of the revenue service and regulatory agencies. Finally, if good governments provide the right incentives, business participation in policy debates could rest less on large firms and more on peak associations, thereby making policy debates more transparent and engaging because small-sized firms can participate.

Notes

1. See Bruszt (1991); Campbell (2001); Eisner (1993); Távara (2006).
2. State capture is irrelevant if limited to marginal agencies.
3. Pro-market and anti-labour policies, and the notion that the state plays a 'subsidiary role' in the economy, were introduced in the 1993 constitution.
4. All references to $ are to US dollars.
5. According to a former MEF official, the ministry has always been subject to private influence, particularly corporate law firms that 'write decrees' (private conversation, Lima, May 2001).
6. Appointments in other ministries (Industry, Energy, Transportation and Communications, and Fishing) followed the same pattern.

7. As we will discuss later, SUNAT followed the same trend.
8. See World Bank (1994).
9. Based on private conversations with top officials from SUNAT, the MEF and the BCRP, business leaders, Congress, and the Diez Canseco (2001–2) and Herrera investigative committees (2003–4). Autonomy is always relative.
10. Numerous articles were published, arguing that policy changes, such as the exonerations and the termination of the Tax Merger Law, would scare investors (*Expreso* 1998; *El Comercio* 1998).
11. The author held several private conversations with the president and Alberto Adrianzén, his closest advisor, during and after the Paniagua administration.
12. On Toledo's criticism on SUNAT, see *Caretas,* section 'Nos escriben y contestamos' (26 May 2000), www.caretas.com.pe (accessed 28 May 2000).
13. It must be noted that, in doing so, the MEF ignored a congressional vote taken on 10 July 2001, arguing that the Tax Merger Law was unconstitutional.

References

Arce, Moisés (2006) *The Difference That Neoliberalism Makes: The Societal Consequences of Market Reforms in Peru* (University Park: Pennsylvania State University Press).

Arias, Luis Alberto (2003) 'La controversia tributaria derivada de la reorganización de las empresas eléctricas privadas', *Análisis Tributario,* March, 5–6.

Boloña, Carlos (1993) *Cambio de Rumbo,* third edition (Lima: Instituto de Economía de Libre Mercado).

Bruszt, László (1991) 'Market Making as State Making: Social Cost and Social Peace in East Central Europe', *East European Politics,* 6 (1), 55–72.

Campbell, John L. (2001) 'Institutional Analysis and the Role of Ideas in Political Economy', *Theory and Society,* 27 (3), 377–409.

Campodónico, Humberto (2006) *Cristal de Mira: 2002–2006* (Lima: Universidad Nacional Mayor de San Marcos).

CIDEF (Comisión Investigadora de Delito Económico Financiero) (2001) *Balance de la Inversión Privada y Privatización* (Lima: Fondo Editorial del Congreso).

——— (2002) *Informe Final de la Comisión,* versión digital (Lima: Congreso de la República).

Cohen, Jeffrey E. (1986) 'The Dynamics of the 'Revolving Door' on the FCC', *American Journal of Political Science,* 30 (4), 689–708.

COPRI (Comisión de Promoción de la Inversión Privada) (2001) *Información General de Administración,* Mayo (Lima, COPRI).

Dammert, Manuel (2001) *El Estado Mafioso* (Lima: Editorial El Virrey).

DESCO (Centro de Estudios y Promoción del Desarrollo) (2004) *Los Mil Días de Toledo,* Serie Perú Hoy (Lima: DESCO).

Drazen, Allan (2000) *Political Economy in Macroeconomics* (Princeton: Princeton University Press).

Durand, Francisco (2003) *Riqueza Económica y Pobreza Política* (Lima: Fondo Editorial de la Pontificia Universidad Católica del Perú).

Durand, Francisco and Rosemary Thorp (1998) 'Reforming the State: A Study of the Peruvian Tax Reform', *Oxford Development Studies,* 26 (2), 133–51.

Eisner, Marc Allen (1993) *Regulatory Politics in Transition* (Baltimore: Johns Hopkins University Press).

El Comercio (1998) '¿Y la estabilidad para los inversionistas?', 28 December, 2.

Estela, Manuel (2001) *Perú: Ocho Apuntes para el Crecimiento con Bienestar* (Lima: Fondo Editorial del Banco Central de Reserva del Perú).

——— (2002) *El Perú y la Tributación*, Serie Aportes, Cuaderno No. 4 (Lima: SUNAT).

——— (2003) *La Política Económica y el Subdesarrollo Peruano: La Historia Reciente y la Lejana* (Lima: mimeo).

Expreso (1998) 'Crédito se encarecerá por eliminación a fusiones empresariales', 25 December, 11.

Gonzales de Olarte, Efraín (1998) *Neoliberalismo a la Peruana* (Lima: Instituto de Estudios Peruanos).

Grindle, Merileee S. and John W. Thomas (1991) *Public Choices and Policy Changes*, (Baltimore: Johns Hopkins University Press).

Hellman, Joel S., Geraint Jones and Daniel Kaufmann (2000) *Seize the State, Seize the Day: State Capture, Corruption and Influence in Transition*, Policy Research Working Paper No. 2444 (Washington, DC: World Bank), September.

Hellman, Joel S. and Daniel Kaufmann (2001) 'Confronting the Challenge of State Capture in Transition Economies (Oligarchic Corruption and Economic Reform)', *Finance & Development*, 38 (3), 1 September, 31.

IPE (Instituto Peruano de Economía) (1994) *A Private Technical Assistance Institute* (Lima: IPE), April.

Kaufmann, Daniel, Joel S. Hellman, Geraint Jones and Mark A. Schankerman (2000) 'Measuring Governance Corruption, and State Capture: How Firms and Bureaucrats Shape the Business Environment in Transition Economies', Policy Research Working Paper No. 2312 (Washington, DC: World Bank).

Moreno Ocampo, Luis (2007) 'State Capture: Who Represents the Poor?', *Development Outreach*, January.

Neuman, W. Lawrence, (2005) *Power, State and Society* (New York: McGraw-Hill).

Omelyanchuk, Olesky (2001) *Explaining State Capture and State Capture Modes: The Cases of Russia and Ukraine* (Budapest: Central European University).

Schonwalder, Gerd (2002) *Linking Civil Society and the State* (University Park: Pennsylvania State University Press).

Taliercio, Robert (2001) *Unsustainably Autonomous? Challenges to the Revenue Authority Reform Model in Latin America*, paper presented at the Annual Meeting of the American Political Science Association, Chicago, 30 August–2 September..

Távara, José (2006) 'The Regulation of Market Power in a Democratic Transition', in John Crabtree (ed.), *Making Institutions Work in Peru: Democracy, Development and Inequality since 1980* (London: Institute for the Study of the Americas).

Ugarteche, Oscar (2005) *Vicios Públicos: Poder y Corrupción* (Lima: Sur).

World Bank (1994) *World Bank Memorandum 'IDF Grant no. 20044'*, 9 September (Washington, DC: World Bank)

8

The Ascent of Business Associations in Russia: From Capture to Partnership?

David W. O'Brien

Introduction

In the exit from state socialism across the former Soviet Union, the emergence of, participation rates in, and the influence of business associations varies considerably. Perhaps nowhere have these patterns been of more concern for progressive collective action and policy formation than in Russia. While there are conflicting views on whether Russian business associations have captured the state (Hellman et al. 2000) or vice versa (Hanson and Teague 2005), there is little dispute that public welfare has borne the cost of state–business interaction (Hoffman 2003). This prevailing view is consistent with Olson's (1982) thesis that when business associations emerge, they tend to advance their interests (Pyle 2006; Recanatini and Ryterman 2001) to the neglect or detriment of the public's.

This chapter traces these trends across the former Soviet Union and in Russia in particular. The rise of business associations and their interaction with the state over the first 15 years of Russia's exit from socialism (1989–2004) does suggest that they are capable of generating returns for their members but that they have done little to develop a social agenda or market conditions benefiting the wider society.

I turn to the empirical record to document these developments and offer an institutionalist interpretation of why this might be the case. There are three parts to this analysis. In the second section, I identify explanations for 1) why business associations emerge, and 2) what impacts they can have on members and society (Doner and Schneider 2000). I suggest that institutional approaches, which seek to understand the informal and formal rules that shape actors choices and institutional arrangements, are useful for understanding these two questions (North 1990).

The third section explains how institutions shaped during the demise of Russia's command economy influenced the emergence and orientation of business associations. I then draw on cross-national data to illustrate the unequal growth in business associations across the former Soviet Union, the disproportionate voice of big business associations within countries, and business association members' perceptions of their influence on development agendas. This section employs the European Bank for Reconstruction and Development/EBRD–World Bank Business Environment and Enterprise Performance Survey data to highlight the evolution and influence of business associations in a comparative setting (BEEPS 1999/2002/2005).

In the fourth section, I examine a Russian initiative that had unintended outcomes. It involves the rise of nascent business associations formed by graduates of a federal management training programme for young entrepreneurs. The composition, actions and contributions of these associations at the local level are small-scale, but nevertheless represent an encouraging development. Of particular interest is the emergence of constructive business–state relations suggesting that government action may have contributed to the creation of the conditions for the collective organization of Russia's future leaders. This section is based on field research and surveys (O'Brien 2006: 78–9),[1] investigating the structure of emergent business associations, their objectives, operations and influence from the vantage point of both the executive leadership and regular members.[2]

Understanding the emergence and influence of business associations

There are various explanations for why and when actors organize themselves to represent their interests. Micro-analytic accounts influenced by rational choice logic argue that the principal determinant explaining collective action lies in the financial calculations made by actors weighing the opportunity cost of participating in business associations. In this vein, Recanatini and Ryterman (2001: 2) posit that the emergence of business associations in Russia is best explained as the strategic response by firms to boost firm growth by collectively addressing missing markets and poor information. In their view, those that do not join are not necessarily irrational but have alternative preferences. Institutionalists, by contrast, suggest that there is more to the emergence of business associations than the work of like-minded individuals advancing their financial interests. To explain new organizational arrangements in the market, government or society, institutionalists draw attention to laws, customs, historical precedents and political constellations which have an independent effect on the way actors interpret their environment and are able to shape it (March and Olsen 1984). There is also greater use of behavioural assumptions that accept non-economic motives for investing time in business associations. Stemming from this, the literature investigates the social determinants and socializing effects of membership organizations. It is this combination of individual motives, social learning and structure that makes for the potentially transformational nature of business associations (Lin 2002: 194).

Informed by institutionalist thinking, the *constructability thesis* advanced by Evans (1996) suggests that actors in government and society can transform their relations and co-construct alternative development pathways. In Evans's assessment of numerous case studies, he observes that 'creative action by government organizations can foster social capital; linking mobilized citizens to public agencies can enhance the efficacy of government' (Evans 1996: 1130).[3] For Evans, as civil society organizations grow in number and diversity, they both demand and support better government.[4] This observation about organized civil society also applies to the emergence and performance of business associations.

The creative action that Evans refers to between government and society is not a hallmark of contemporary Russia. For decades, the central tendency of the Russian state has been to direct rather than to enable change (Gorbachev 1987). With the demise of central planning, the prospects for dialogue with business became a possibility but the platforms for state–business interaction were virtually non-existent.[5] Moreover, the prevalence of short-term business strategies, an incentive structure that rewarded informal lobbying and influence ties, and a weak and unsupportive state that has not invited broad-based participation in public policy, all had distorting affects on the emergence and conduct of business associations. Institutionalists would argue that unless these conditions were altered in some way, one should not expect business associations to make a progressive contribution to economic and social policy.

In contrast to the Olsonian-informed literature that is sceptical of business associations making a progressive societal contribution, the abovementioned civil society and social capital literatures tend to be more optimistic about the transformative potential of social organization in the market and society. According to Doner and Schneider (2000), the public good potential of business associations is realized when associations organize market-supporting actions. Market-supporting actions influence who participates in policy formation and implementation, and its substance. This notion is contrasted with market-complementing actions, which seek to promote business development among and for members, and are more aptly described as club goods.

Table 8.1 categorizes each function through specific examples.

In Russia, all of these market-supporting and complementing activities had been the formal responsibility of the state. Market-supporting actions now tend to involve private sector coordination with government, and seek to change the institutional environment. As such, the benefits resulting from market-supporting actions are not solely captured by those who initiate change, whereas market-complementing actions are.

Table 8.1 Examples of market-supporting and market-complementing actions

Function	Examples
Market-supporting actions (~ public good)	Creating norms and processes for political participation in public policy Contributing, advising or critiquing existing or proposed legislation/regulation Defending or upholding property rights Enhancing social or business infrastructure (for example, corporate social responsibility/CSR) Supporting more effective administration/state capacity
Market-complementing actions (~ club good)	Standard-setting across industry Coordinating horizontal/vertical production chains Lowering information costs to business Skill-upgrading/training Incubating business/market innovations

Source: Adapted from Doner and Schneider (2000).

Regional patterns and business associations in Russia

The emergence of business associations

This section highlights the institutional influences on the evolution of state–business interaction. From the early to mid-1990s, President Yeltsin introduced a slate of stabilization and structural reforms seeking to extract the state from the market. When commercial restrictions were lifted, Russians exhibited a Smithian propensity to truck, barter and trade, despite the seven-decade-strong legacy of central planning (Gaidar 2002). The proliferation of kiosks and street-level trading across Russia, however, masked fundamental problems. The exit from socialism resulted in a sharp and protracted decline in economic output and social conditions, as well as market dislocation (Blanchard and Kremer 1997; Tchernina 1996; World Bank 2002). Market dislocation refers to the weakening or disappearance of personal relationships and coordinating bodies that enable senior managers to exchange business information, and build reputations and trust. It is in this vacuum that business associations could assist in the rebuilding of market relations.

President Yeltsin acknowledged that after years of overhauling Soviet legislation and implementing structural reforms, the transition was stuck somewhere between a socialist and capitalist order (Åslund 2000), and all the while social conditions continued to decline. Writing a decade after the onset of Yeltsin's reforms, Broadman remarked:

> There is little question that Russia has made significant progress in dismantling the central planning system. But, to date, the development

> of . . . basic market institutions to take the place of central planning remains nascent – especially in regional markets, where day-to-day business transactions are conducted. (Broadman 2002: 1)

Between the state and dominant industries, who were the actors and organizations supporting and complementing markets? Who pressures government to enforce commercial legislation, regulate financial markets or provide options for judicial recourse when desired? Or who builds industry standards, monitors professional conduct or promotes skills and learning? A regional economic planner might identify a trade union or regional chamber of commerce and responses would vary across regions, but the absence of candidates would be striking.[6]

There is an institutional explanation for this.[7] When Gorbachev introduced *perestroika* in the late 1980s, he envisioned a mixed economy in a socialist society. Actors in industry and in public life were to be stakeholders in development and have greater voice in policy arenas (Gorbachev 1987: 102–5). Measures designed to relax economic planning did increase entrepreneurial activity but over time it had a distorting influence on public dialogue between the private and public sectors, and on the agendas of emerging business associations.

In allowing nascent forms of private sector activity, *perestroika* created a new entrepreneurial class. Many of the early entrepreneurs thrived by exploiting the contradictions of nascent private enterprise in a crumbling socialist economy. In finding solutions, successful entrepreneurs created what Yurchak refers to as a coexisting hybrid state wherein entrepreneurs selectively interacted with an 'officialized public sphere' and a 'personalized public sphere':

> These two public spheres corresponded to two distinct ways of understanding and shaping public practices and relations in everyday life. The practices of the former [officialized public sphere] were regulated by the written laws and rules of the state that were represented in the official Party and state texts and documents, and could be compared to 'statute law.' Unwritten cultural understanding and nonofficial agreements that could be compared to 'customary law' regulated the practices in the latter sphere [personalized public sphere] (Yurchak 2002: 287).

These distinct ways of engaging state actors played an instrumental role in the emergence of entrepreneurial activity in the mid-1980s, and on the character of business organizations in the 1990s. In the early 1980s, Communist Party factions debated the introduction of market-based incentives to create a 'valve' that would help equilibrate the supply and demand for goods. Under pressure, Gorbachev's government piloted pro-market experiments during the 1986–8 period. One of these, the Law of Cooperatives, allowed private enterprises to be registered under legislation.

It was hoped this law would create small enterprises specializing in services that the state had failed to provide, and were in high demand. Food production and retail, construction and car repair were services the authorities hoped the 'cooperators' would supply. The law's unrestrictive character even allowed cooperatives to establish banks, which became the source of tremendous private wealth and political influence for many who founded them. From small islands of free enterprise within a socialist state, cooperators developed a parallel economy that supplied the official economy and consumers with a range of goods and services that the command economy had rationed.

What relevance did these developments have in terms of understanding institutional arrangements and informal rules by which entrepreneurs operated? Part of the answer lies in explaining how entrepreneurs interacted with the officialized and personalized state. In the late Yeltsin period, those who had profited from privatization and privileged relations with the state used their new economic power in the personalized public sphere to exert their political influence. This trend undermined the hope that democratic, pluralist traditions could yet be cultivated in Yeltsin's growing illiberal democracy (Weigel 2000).

With time the state itself became 'entrepreneurial' through the arbitrary practice of charging for public services, or the enforcement of ambiguous laws and regulations and seeking payment for leniency. When President Putin replaced Yeltsin, he was determined to stop big business interference in the business of Russia's lawmakers as well as bureaucratic practices, which, in Putin's language, created a 'market for legalized corruption'.[8]

The legacy of business promoting the personalized public sphere and avoiding the officialized public sphere chipped away at the public space that civil society has historically relied on to create formal organizations through which it has engaged government. Contrary to liberal expectations, this independent space was slow to emerge during Russia's exit from socialism. The outcome, as Rose suggests, is a 'missing middle' in Russia.[9]

Table 8.2 identifies the growth of business associations, a component of this missing middle. It presents participation rates in business associations by regime type, suggesting that political conditions matter. Competitive political regimes (liberal democracies), as a general rule, have laws and practices that protect freedom of association and promote representation and contestation in political life. Concentrated regimes may have similar political, economic and social rights but public debate and freedom of association is restricted by state practices. Moreover, the party system provides a weak avenue for citizens to participate in the political process.[10] In non-competitive or authoritarian political systems, actors are even more restricted in exercising freedom of association.[11]

According to BEEPS (1999) data, there is a significant relationship between regime type and participation in business associations. According to the classification method employed, Russia is a concentrated regime. As illustrated

Table 8.2 CEO participation in business associations by regime type, 1999 (per cent)

Regime type	Business association member	Non-member	N=
Competitive	39	61	1,077
Concentrated	19	81	1,590
Non-competitive	16	84	405

Note: Chi-square, significant at the 1 per cent level.
Source: BEEPS (1999).

Table 8.3 Firm representation in business associations, by size and select countries (per cent)

	Small (2–49 employees)		Medium (50–249)		Large (250+)	
	1999	2005	1999	2005	1999	2005
Poland (competitive)	17	23	37	49	26	59
Hungary (competitive)	74	47	75	65	88	86
Ukraine (concentrated)	10	16	17	41	25	57
Russia (concentrated)	14	13	13	29	26	38
Belarus (non-competitive)	16	13	6	28	17	46
Kazakhstan (non-competitive)	11	15	13	29	29	42

Sources: BEEPS (1999, 2005).

above, private sector entrepreneurs in competitive regimes demonstrate much higher participation rates in business associations (39 per cent) than their counterparts in concentrated (19 per cent) or non-competitive regimes (16 per cent).

Characteristics of Russian business associations

Representation by firm size

Table 8.3 samples two countries from each of the different political systems to illustrate the composition of business associations by firm size.

For Poland, 17 per cent of small firms were represented by business associations in 1999, which increased to 23 per cent by 2005. Small business participation rates are higher in these countries with competitive political systems than in concentrated (Russia and Ukraine) and non-competitive political systems (Belarus and Kazakhstan). A common feature across these countries and groupings is that larger companies are better represented in business associations. Larger firms have the resources to dedicate to collective organization but we should not assume they share similar views on ways to improve the business environment. In other words, the impacts of the political, economic and social reforms in Russia were not disproportionately borne by big business, triggering an excessive organizational response by them. What is disproportionate is the representation of large enterprises in setting the agenda of Russian business associations.

Geographical and demographic representation

Owing to the concentration of economic power and political life in Moscow, the headquarters of prominent business and professional associations are located there. Some of these organizations, like the Chamber of Commerce and Industry (CCI) are federated organizations with regional chapters. Other powerful associations, such as the Russian Union of Industrialists and Entrepreneurs (RUIE), are apex bodies that unite regional associations, prominent firms and individuals.[12] Sector-wide associations and international chapters of professional associations also emerged in Moscow. While data on regionally based associations has not been systematically collected, participation rates in and the number of associations declines as one moves away from Moscow.[13]

Another feature is the generational composition of business associations. The Recanatini and Ryterman (2001: 30) survey of business association membership suggests that the majority of key organizers were former ministry officials, while a minority were employed by an industrial enterprise. While future survey data may contradict the demographic profile reported in this small study (n = 58), the dominant presence of ex-party officials and minority representation of new entrepreneurs is a very plausible generalization (Gerber 2000). The generation entering the workforce during the Gorbachev and Yeltsin period showed only marginal interest in civil society organizations that engaged directly or indirectly with the state (Titarenko 1999).

Returning to Broadman's concern about market development, economic planners in regional governments did not benefit from the range of insights business associations can bring to economic policy formation to the extent their counterparts did in Central Europe where business associations are more prevalent (World Bank 2002). When business associations did intervene, their demographic profile and the recycling of party officials into leadership positions raises questions as to whether the more liberal leanings of younger business leaders were represented.

Services

The BEEPS data set, designed to better understand business leaders' perceptions of the business environment and government, did not solicit information on the social services or advocacy positions of business associations. Asking these questions might have yielded some interesting findings about the social orientation of business associations. However, given the state of economic disorganization, the focus on how business associations sought to influence their environment (narrowly defined) is understandable.

In a fixed list of services provided by Russian business associations, the top three most valuable were: 1) information and/or contacts on domestic product and input markets; 2) accrediting standards on quality of products and reputational benefits; and 3) information on government regulations. Considered less valuable by business association members were the roles played by their associations in facilitating international commercial contacts, dispute resolution, and lobbying government (BEEPS 2002).

Perhaps not surprising, the top four services with direct impact on a firm's bottom line relate to relationship building with business/commercial partners and services to reduce transaction costs. Most of these services are market-complementing actions. Lobbying government, likely to be the only market-supporting action listed, was not considered to have the immediate returns to a firm's performance of the other services.

Channels

A promise of business associations is that they mobilize firms, aggregate their preferences and institutionalize relations (among members and with other organizations). On the first promise, Table 8.4 assesses whether Russian business association members are more likely to pursue active strategies to affect their environment compared to non-members. In the first row, 38 per cent of business association members reported they acted in the previous year to affect a national-level law or regulation that impacted them. By contrast, only 11 per cent of firms that did not belong to a business association made a similar effort. The data for 2005 identifies similar differences between members and non-members but there is a sharp decline in active strategies apparent by 2005. This apparent retreat of business association activism likely reflects Putin's signals to the business community that political interference in state business would not be tolerated (Hanson and Teague 2005: 663–4).

When motivated to influence policy, what is the preferred route to government? A past president of the Chamber of Commerce and Industry argues that firms and associations tend to lobby the state through personalized channels: '[Russia] does not have a recognized civilized democratic procedure

Table 8.4 Russian firms engaging government, 2002 and 2005

Firm acted to affect laws and regulations last year that had a substantial effect on respondent's firm (per cent, yes)	**Business association member**	**Non-member**	
2002 national level	38	11	*
2005 national level	17	5	*
2005 local or regional level	18	7	*

Note: Chi-square, * significant at 1 per cent level.
Sources: BEEPS (2002, 2005).

Table 8.5 Preferred route to affect government laws, 1999

	Business association members	
	In competitive regimes (%)	**In concentrated regimes (%)**
Use trade association or lobby group	73	60
Use firm's direct ties to public officials/other	27	40
Total	100	100

Note: Chi-square, significant at 1 per cent level.
Source: BEEPS (1999).

whereby the business community participates in the drafting, evaluation, discussion and amendment of laws. . . .' Where industry has wielded influence, Stanislav Smirnov concludes, it 'is exerted not through the front entrance, but through the back door, so to speak' (Smirnov 1997).

Table 8.5 reveals the preferred route that business association members typically rely on to influence government. Business association members were asked to select whether they would likely work through the front door or use their direct ties to influence public officials through the back door. The table's columns group responses by firms located in competitive and concentrated political systems.

Table 8.5 illustrates that in politically competitive environments, business members are more inclined to work through their business associations than lobby government on a private basis. In other words, three out of four members favour the collective route. The ratio is less favourable for public debate and openness in concentrated regimes.[14] The data indicate that members of business associations in concentrated regimes are less inclined than their counterparts in competitive political systems to utilize their business associations as conduits for change.

Among the individual and organized voices vying for political attention and influence, data collected through the BEEPS survey indicates a consensus view held by chief executive officers (CEOs) in Russia that business associations are not the most influential force in shaping national legislation. Both CEOs belonging and not belonging to business associations concur that dominant firms, regional government and the business elite with close government ties have greater influence at the national level than the business associations they know of or belong to (BEEPS 2002). Again pointing to a trend is the view that two of the top three means of influencing government are dominant firms acting independently and individuals exploiting their personal ties. The same group did maintain, however, that business associations were more influential than their own firms or labour unions.

Advancing a social agenda?

In terms of the agendas advanced by business associations, their contribution as agents for social development is certainly under-researched. Even if research did investigate the role of business associations in the social sphere during the 1990s, there were likely few significant initiatives to document.[15] However, signs of a changing orientation occurred early in Putin's government.

The 2002–4 period marked a turning point for the inclusion of social concerns in the agendas of apex business associations. President Putin made it clear to the business community that their interference in the political domain would not be tolerated, that they needed to be better corporate citizens, and that his government would engage with civil society organizations in an open and public manner. A first response to these new terms of engagement was the Togliatti Dialogue, a series of consultations and public meetings between the civil society organizations (including business associations) and the state. One of the interesting openings this dialogue created was a 'Society and Business' platform that brought together a wide spectrum of social and business associations (UNDP 2003: Chapter 8). Organizations such as the RUIE, the CCI and human rights organizations reached an agreement through the Togliatti Dialogue to promote and protect social and economic rights together. This joint platform included pension reform, regulation of civil society organizations and proposals to institutionalize public scrutiny on bills affecting the social sphere (for example, housing and environmental codes).

While this was an endogenous expression of business associations taking leadership on socioeconomic conditions, the other development was catalysed by the spread of corporate social responsibility and awareness-raising through the Global Compact. In 2004, the CCI and RUIE, together with other business associations, media and NGOs, launched what is seen as the first concrete effort to promote CSR norms in Russia (UNDP 2007: 4). That year the RUIE drafted the Social Charter of Russian Business and began to promote its ideals and adherence to it through its membership. The Charter, and the Global Compact, were 'used as benchmarks for aligning corporate policies and conduct with the principles and objectives of sustainable development' (UNDP 2007: 6). These two initiatives depart from the central tendency of Russian business associations to confront the state on economic policy. As President Putin closed off informal channels for the business elite and major business associations to lobby for their interests, such developments could be explained as efforts by organized business to improve their tarnished image in the eyes of the public and the Kremlin.

To conclude, this section has identified the following trends:

1. Dominant enterprises translated their economic weight into political influence, primarily through informal networks. This influence channel was more prevalent in concentrated regimes than in competitive regimes, and characteristic of Yeltsin's presidency.

2. Across the former Soviet Union participation in business associations is lower in concentrated than in competitive political systems, suggesting a relationship between the institutional environment and incentives to participate in business associations.
3. Small and medium-sized enterprises are poorly represented in business associations with ensuing implications for whose agenda is being articulated through business associations.
4. The younger generation entering leadership positions in business during the 1990s has eschewed political engagement with the state, and has not assumed a noticeable presence in business associations.
5. With little voice and ensuing influence, small and medium-sized enterprises (SMEs) and the first generation of young entrepreneurs coming into corporate leadership positions were under-represented in business associations.
6. On balance, the market-complementing actions of business associations are more prevalent (or possibly more researched) than market-supporting outcomes.
7. Business associations in Russia did not pay explicit attention to a social agenda during the 1990s and were only guided in this direction following signals from President Putin.

With these trends serving as a backdrop, the following sections describe an experiment that resulted in a different dynamic in the emergence of business associations and their interaction with the state.

Case study

In light of the trends noted above, this section introduces a case study that points to an alternative trajectory in state–business relations. The example is of interest for two reasons. First, it illustrates the potential of creative public policy and government actors to induce and scale up the collective organization of businesses. Second, the case highlights both the market-supporting and market-complementing actions of emergent business organizations led by the younger strata of the business elite.

The departure point is the President's Management Training Programme (PMTP).[16] This was a high profile, prestigious, nation-wide programme that sought to invigorate economic growth through training 5,000 young managers (25–40 years) per year with the new skills needed to restructure privatized enterprises and to lead the new private sector. Nation-wide advertisements invited company executives to nominate promising young managers to apply. Those selected from the highly competitive selection process committed to a year-long training programme, which was equivalent to an executive Master of Business Administration (MBA) programme.

The PMTP was conceived of and designed by a group of liberal reformers based in several federal departments. Implementation and funding relied on a tripartite structure that joined industry, higher education institutions and federal and regional government administrations. The expectation was that introducing a new business education model throughout Russia and training a critical mass of talented managers would reap short- and long-term benefits.

An unanticipated direction in the design of the programme was the gradual introduction of a post-training component that encouraged alumni and stakeholders to apply their insights in support of local economic development agendas. Towards this end, the programme began sponsoring thematic training workshops and structured dialogues on business development topics.

This addition to the core curriculum responded to and supported those alumni who began to organize informal networks among themselves in several regions to maintain friendships, make sense of their rapidly changing environment and pursue joint business opportunities. As the number of graduates grew through annual intakes, these networks became larger and more formalized. Some regional administrations coordinating the PMTP programme locally identified the instrumental value of working with these alumni networks to assist them in promoting and improving the PMTP's recruitment and trainee-selection processes, and in refining the training course. Typically, this overture by regional administrations was positively received by the alumni networks.[17] For many graduates, the training programme accelerated their career path or catalyzed new business ventures, and they were willing to give back to the programme in this way.

At the federal level, these experiments in alumni–regional government cooperation were profiled at national conferences, which, in turn, stimulated new thinking regarding how PMTP alumni and their networks could contribute to the multiple challenges regional administrations were grappling with, recognizing that they often lacked the capacity and the insights of the private sector. This federal-level attention prompted other regional administrations to explore what they might offer and gain from alumni. This led, for example, to regional officials referring alumni to government offices with the authority to solve business licensing and other regulatory requirements that stifled firm growth and new business start-ups. Other regional governments requested alumni to provide advisory services to restructure municipal-owned enterprises. Jointly sponsoring business development events, such as trade fairs, was another form of cooperation. These were novel developments that broke from past traditions of government and business working in isolation, or where one unduly influenced the other. This emerging dynamic supports Schneider's (2004: 24) thesis that state actors can create favourable incentives for businesses to organize and form business associations.

Within five years of the PMTP's creation, informal networks had evolved into alumni business associations (ABAs) in half of the 80 regions where the PMTP was operating.[18] The hope of the federal and some regional administrations was that these associations would unite graduates, generate business opportunities for them, and create an enduring platform for social learning and collective action.[19]

The following discussion highlights the initial contribution of these emergent business associations in collaborating with government to diagnose and develop policies or projects to ameliorate the social and economic costs of enterprise restructuring, and in supporting members through peer mentoring, referrals and the flow of other social resources. This approach illuminates the emergence, composition and influence of these emergent business associations.

Building network ties through ABAs

This section highlights the contribution of ABAs to expanding members' social networks and the opportunities that inhere in them.[20] Specifically, the following questions are addressed: 1) whether graduates consider ABAs an effective pathway to establish important external ties over other available means; 2) whether ABAs were proactive in creating contacts with business, government and social actors; and 3) whether the contacts established through ABAs were reciprocal.

Network development and the relative importance of ABAs

The following two tables highlight the importance of ABAs relative to other mechanisms available to graduates for establishing 'important contacts' with business development and civil society organizations, and with different levels of government.

A two-step question informs these tables. The first step asked members to identify whether they had established an 'important contact' recently in each of the indicated areas (column headings). If respondents felt that contacts were unimportant or were not established, they had the option of selecting 'no contact established'. If respondents could identify an important contact, in the second step they identified the means through which the contact was made (first column).

Table 8.6 illustrates the importance of ABAs as a pathway to establishing government contacts. It shows that ABAs are the single most important vehicle for facilitating contacts with government officials. Table 8.7 illustrates that where contacts are established with organizations in the economic and cultural sector, ABAs are also the most important pathway. The only exception in this table relates to financial institutions where firm and individual means were more important.

As illustrated, ABAs were clearly an important mechanism in developing government connections but were less important relative to other means in creating relations with financial organizations. These latter relations were cultivated through pre-existing personal and business relations.

It is interesting to note the frequency with which members turn to their associations rather than to friends and colleagues. This finding is even more

Table 8.6 The relative importance of ABAs in attaining important government contacts

Attained important contacts with	**Local government (N = 276)**	**Regional government (N = 277)**
Means of making contact (select one)	%	%
Through family member or friend	2	5
Through colleague at work and business associate	16	16
Through ABA member	*34*	*28*
Through member of another organization	3	3
Through other means	14	16
Through yourself (no one assisted in making contact)	16	16
No contact established	15	17
Total	100	100

Source: MQ – Based on author's surveys and data, 2003.

surprising given that Russian society has tended to privilege informal, family-based networks over other means to obtain goods, services and favours (Ledeneva 1998). The fact that members were turning to their associations for referrals suggests that ABAs were making an important contribution to extending their members' external networks. This was an important function as the structural reforms had torn apart the social relations and structures on which market activity depend, and which was only beginning to be rewoven at the time these ABAs were emerging (Stiglitz 1999).

Policy domains and reciprocity

Business associations need to be placed in a dynamic environment to appreciate the networked structure through which they acquire information and influence. Given that ABAs were new organizations, one would expect to see them proactively engaging the government and the business sector. If these associations have a presence in their region, one would also expect to see external organizations engaging ABAs, though to a lesser extent. The former expectation indicates whether these associations are actively setting their own agenda. The latter expectation indicates whether external organizations recognize ABAs, and the degree of reciprocity between them.

The tables that follow are based on responses from an executive council member of separate ABAs. They were asked whether they involve local authorities and vice versa in policy discussions across seven policy domains. In Table 8.8, for example, the columns under the heading of private sector development policy show that approximately half (52 per cent) of the ABA leaders felt that local authorities never or rarely involved them in discussions, whereas a quarter of the ABAs surveyed (25 per cent) responded that they do not engage local authorities on the issue.

Table 8.7 The relative importance of ABAs in attaining important contacts

Attained important contacts with	Professional or business associations (N = 273)	Financial organizations (N = 275)	Mass media (N = 280)	Cultural organizations (N = 278)
Means of making contact (select one)	%	%	%	%
Through family member or friend	2	6	4	5
Through colleague at work and business associate	19	23	16	14
Through ABA member	*25*	*13*	*21*	*17*
Through member of another organization	6	3	1	1
Through other means	12	17	21	15
Through yourself (no one assisted in making contact)	14	17	17	14
No contact established	22	21	20	34
Total	100	100	100	100

Source: MQ – Based on author's surveys and data, 2003.

Table 8.8 Government and ABAs interaction (1)

	Private sector development policy	
	Government involves ABAs (N = 23)	ABA involves government (N = 24)
Level of involvement	%	%
Never or rarely	52	25
Sometimes	18	25
Often or always	30	50
Total	100	100

Source: LQ – Based on author's surveys and data, 2003.

The above pattern of ABAs promoting interaction with government to a greater extent than government engaging ABAs is consistent across all the remaining policy areas.

Tables 8.8 to 8.11 also indicate what issue areas that merit deliberation with local authorities are of primary concern to the ABAs. The main priority area is private sector development, but the responses also show these associations actively engaging with government on access to information, social policy and training/education policy. Less emphasis is paid to the environment, infrastructure and trade policy (which is mainly a regional and federal government responsibility).

Table 8.9 Government and ABAs interaction (2)

	Access to information		**Social policy**	
	Government involves ABAs (N = 22)	**ABA involves government** (N = 23)	**Government involves ABAs** (N = 23)	**ABA involves government** (N = 23)
Level of involvement	%	%	%	%
Never or rarely	50	35	52	26
Sometimes	36	30	30	44
Often or always	14	35	18	30
Total	100	100	100	100

Source: LQ – Based on author's surveys and data, 2003.

Table 8.10 Government and ABAs interaction (3)

	Education/training policy		**Trade development**	
	Government involves ABAs (N = 20)	**ABA involves government** (N = 21)	**Government involves ABAs** (N = 22)	**ABA involves government** (N = 22)
Level of involvement	%	%	%	%
Never or rarely	45	33	64	59
Sometimes	45	33	23	18
Often or always	10	33	13	23
Total	100	100	100	100

Source: LQ – Based on author's surveys and data, 2003.

Table 8.11 Government and ABAs interaction (4)

	Infrastructure		**Environmental issues**	
	Government involves ABAs (N = 23)	**ABA involves government (N = 23)**	**Government involves ABAs (N = 21)**	**ABA involves government (N = 22)**
Level of involvement	%	%	%	%
Never or rarely	52	44	62	59
Sometimes	30	30	24	18
Often or always	18	26	14	23
Total	100	100	100	100

Source: LQ – Based on author's surveys and data, 2003.

Table 8.12 Contribution of the ABAs to regional/policy development objectives

	Increased access to government decision makers (N = 292)	**Worked through ABAs to affect change in government policy (N = 286)**	**Worked through ABAs to improve business environment (N = 292)**
	%	%	%
Significant contribution	55	34	55
Modest contribution	23	27	24
Minor contribution	13	27	14
No expectation	9	13	6
Total	100	100	100

Source: MQ – Based on author's surveys and data, 2003.

Influence

Above, ABA leaders reported that their associations were proactive in engaging government in economic and social policy domains. However, what did members perceive the results to be?

Table 8.12 reveals members' expectations and their assessment of the contribution of their ABAs. First, members were asked whether they expected their participation in ABAs to result in any of the outcomes listed by column. Second, they were asked to assess whether ABAs made a significant to minor contribution to fulfilling their expectations.

In the second to last row of Table 8.12, only a small percentage of members did not expect their ABA to work toward these objectives ('no expectation').

Table 8.13 Likelihood of policy engagement and preferred pathway to affect change

Policy domains	Likelihood of engagement (%)	Preferred pathway to affect change (top choice)
Trade development (local and abroad) (N = 270)	89	ABA
Taxation policy (N = 280)	86	Firm connections
Access to government information (N = 279)	84	ABA
Investment (N = 280)	84	ABA
Business/private sector development policy (N = 281)	77	ABA
Social policy (N = 282)	76	ABA
Education/training policy development (N = 278)	74	ABA
Public infrastructure development (N = 279)	63	ABA
Environment (N = 283)	59	ABA

Source: MQ – Based on author's surveys and data, 2003.

Where expectations existed, the plurality of members considered their ABA to have made a significant contribution. In particular, members felt ABAs played a major role in increasing access to decision-makers in government and in promoting cooperation among members to improve the business environment.

The organizational basis of business associations establishes a mechanism for entrepreneurs to mobilize and articulate their preferences in the public sphere over time. Table 8.13 reports on whether members would likely use the ABA channel over other means should a new policy direction negatively affect their firm. For those who responded affirmatively, they were asked what influence channel they would utilize. The pathway choices were to work through 1) existing firm channels, 2) other membership organizations they or their company belong to (that is, trade/business associations) or 3) their ABAs.

Overall, members reported a high degree of likely engagement. Trade development, tax policy, access to information and investment policy elicited strong responses with over 80 per cent of members indicating they would likely get involved. The potential for mobilization was lower when the policy domain concerned infrastructure and environmental issues.

The third column of Table 8.13 illustrates that members would likely turn to their ABAs over firm and other membership organizations as channels to influence change in eight out of nine policy domains. The only exception was tax policy where firm-based channels were considered more effective (or appropriate).

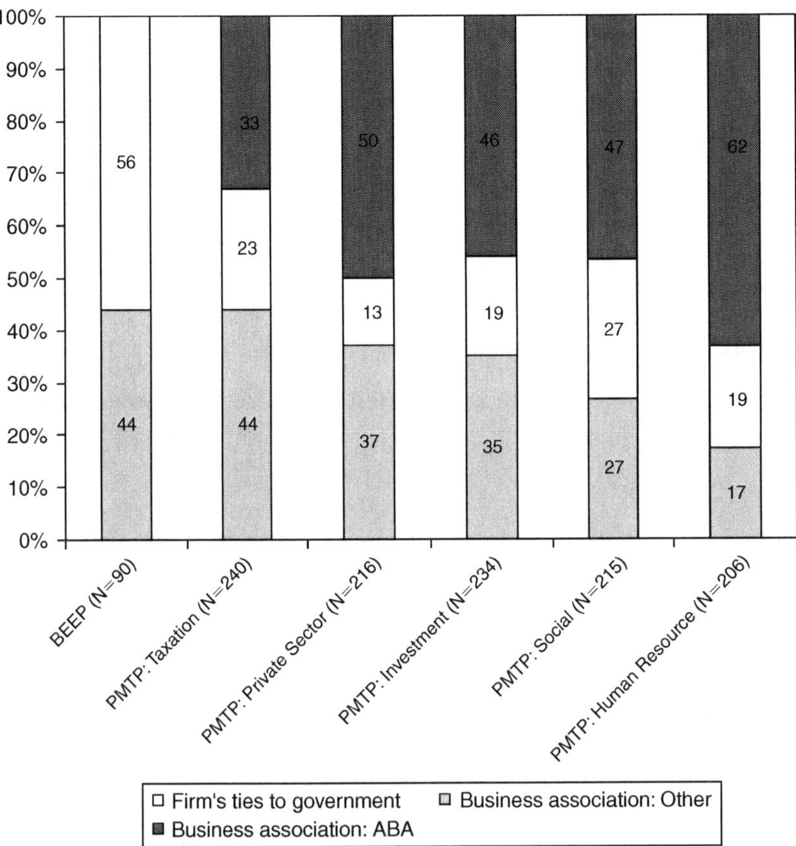

Figure 8.1 Pathway choice to affect change in policy arenas
Sources: BEEPS (1999); MQ – Based on author's surveys and data, 2003.

The question asked above on members' likely engagement on policy issues replicates a question asked in the BEEPS 1999 Russia survey.[21] Figure 8.1 compares responses to this question from the BEEPS Russia sample and the MQ using firm-based and association-based pathway options.

The first column represents the BEEPS comparison group. For the BEEPS Russia survey, 90 of 552 CEOs sampled belonged to a business or lobby association. Within this group, 44 per cent reported they would likely use firm-based connections and 56 per cent stated they would use association-based channels to respond to policies negatively impacting their company.

The five columns to the right indicate the pathway choice of ABA members in response to specific policy issues. To the right of the BEEPS column, ABA members report what channel they would use to affect change in tax policy. The divide between firm-based and association-based responses is identical to the BEEPS data. Similarly, 44 per cent of PMTP graduates belonging to an ABA would lobby government through their firms. The remaining respondents stated that their preference for association-based means to affect change. The breakdown of this 56 per cent provides an insight into the relative importance of ABAs over other like organizations. As illustrated, the greater proportion (33 per cent) of ABA members would use their ABAs over other business associations they or their companies have access to (23 per cent). As a policy area becomes less sensitive (tax policy being a very sensitive issue owing to the arbitrary application of rates and enforcement) the figure shows that the use of association-based channels to affect a policy outcome increases over the BEEPS comparison group.

Illustrative examples of market-complementing and market-supporting actions

Annexes 8.2 and 8.3 highlight examples of market-supporting and complementing actions undertaken by ABAs during the 2000–2 period. The intent of these annexes is to document the range of activities, rather than their frequency, across numerous ABAs. Data for these tables are derived from interviews, presentations given by ABA members and newsletters.

Doner and Schneider (2000) suggest that market-supporting actions are a higher-order contribution to economic development than market-complementing actions. In their formulation, market-supporting actions have a public goods character to the extent that associations create public dialogue and information on the way governments formulate and implement policy. In Annex 8.2, ABAs were involved in the range of activities. As mentioned earlier, almost all ABAs supported regional government capacity through supporting PMTP implementation. For example, ABA members nominated high-potential managers to apply to the entry competition, participated in the interview process, provided feedback on programme implementation and facilitated exchange of information among the training institutions, businesses and government. These and other examples are noteworthy for their interaction across the private–public divide.

The core market-complementing actions of ABAs shown in Annex 8.3, on the other hand, tend to see the flow of benefits returning to members. Typical of business associations, the services they provide increase access to information and build understanding of the market environment and how to operate effectively in it. Programming in this area typically involved workshops, and organizing trade fairs and related business development events. For these events, the ABAs acted independently or in concert with government and the business community. These were common functions that all ABAs undertook in one form or another. Somewhat less common were business innovation services such as creating business incubators, or expert databases for referrals and advisory services. Completely missing were activities in the area of standard-setting, and vertical and horizontal coordination for production. This gap is not surprising as these actions tend to be pursued by industry-wide associations that have an ability to regulate standards or coordinate production in a given sector. In contrast, the multi-sector composition of ABAs steered members toward activities that had an information-dissemination or skills-improvement dimension.

Conclusions

Assessing the progressive or regressive influence of Russian business associations depends on the scale of analysis. At the firm and individual level, studies have demonstrated the benefits of membership (Pyle 2006; Recanatini and Ryterman 2001). At the macro level, the verdict is contingent on whether business associations are seen as capturing the state or vice versa. Perspectives are not static either, as the balance of power between associations and the state has shifted over time. It is clear that Putin's government closed down much of the privileged access that big business had on government policy formation under Yeltsin. Putin's administration also played a role in redirecting private sector organizing away from political interference and promoted a 'patriotic' dialogue on how the private and not-for-profit sector could enhance social conditions in Russia.

Aside from this recent departure, the weight of evidence suggests that the interaction between Russian business associations and the state has not advanced a progressive development agenda in the economic or social sphere.

I introduced an institutional explanation as to why the outcome of state–business interaction has been regressive. To summarize, the argument was as follows:

1. The hybrid state created two channels for businesses to interact with it. The early incentives steered businesses toward the privatized public sphere.
2. When channels to government are informal, there is little incentive for businesses to organize collectively.
3. Dealing with the state informally had a corrupting influence over time. When firms manipulated the rules and regulatory processes, it engrained the view that that was how firms prospered in Russian capitalism.
4. With the early concentration of wealth from privatization, dominant firms became politically powerful and crowded out the voices of small and medium-sized businesses.
5. The reticence of the state to listen to the range of business perspectives in public fora postponed opportunities for dialogue and bred suspicion between government and business.

The case example pointed to a different experience involving the next generation of Russia's business elite. In the third section, I charted the emergence and development of business associations, and outlined some concrete examples of the market-supporting and market-complementing actions they have undertaken. These actions were more transformational in a symbolic sense than in instrumental terms, given the early stage of ABA development. They were symbolically important because ABAs created a collective pathway that enabled a younger generation of entrepreneurs to engage with municipal and regional governments on matters of social and economic policy in the officialized public sphere.

Evans asks whether the development of mutually beneficial relations between state and society is limited by initial conditions or can be constructed. If social organization depends on the prior existence of social and cultural patterns historically rooted in society, then encouraging business organization may well be immune to external influence, even in the presence of economic incentives to collectively organize. A 'constructability' perspective is more optimistic. It frames social organization as a latent possibility, waiting to be created by institution builders (Evans 1996: 1124).

The PMTP case example brings this potential into focus. I will conclude by highlighting three facilitative roles that are particular to the case example but may have applications in other jurisdictions where the state seeks a new dynamic with business leaders:

1. In the early years of the programme, officials took deliberate and public steps to promote the programme and its graduates. The PMTP cultivated an identity around new managers that emphasized their leadership role. In post-training surveys, there was an almost unanimous perception that the programme had elevated their self-esteem. This enhanced self-confidence coupled with the desire of many to make a difference and shape the environments they would have to conduct business in created favourable conditions for experimenting with new forms of collective organization.
2. Efforts were taken to learn and share results among managers and organizers of the programme. Repeated discussions nationally and regionally created opportunities for managers to share innovative ideas and cultivate networks among them. Emergent associations were recognized by government and they, in turn, served as role models for others who were interested in their results and the opportunities they created.
3. Programme implementation created direct opportunities for the business community and the state to learn from each other. While there exists a cautious attitude toward officials, graduates who positively evaluated the government's approach to post-training activities tended to get involved in building new associations. In some regions, the constructive interest of government elicited a positive response from the private sector to continue a dialogue. Without this dynamic, it is reasonable to assume that collective organization among graduates, and the range of actions pursued, would not have occurred.

The PMTP did not set out to create business associations but the fact they emerged in the context of a government-sponsored management programme suggests that government facilitation played a role.

In an effort to further the continuation of social learning and support among graduates, foster dialogue and focus graduate and stakeholder attention on the wider economic reform objectives, the PMTP developed a post-training component. In contrast to the supply character of the training programme, the post-training component was iterative, with an emphasis on promoting beneficial connections and dialogue. Thus, in what may be called a social capital approach to management training, the post-training component promoted relationship-building among public, private and civil society organizations. When graduates in several regions began to self-organize and form business networks, the designers of the PMTP programme supported the strengthening and replication of these efforts. It was hoped that ABAs would generate business opportunities, and create an enduring platform for social learning and collective action.

The post-programme component was distinctive in at least two respects. First, it was a government-sponsored programme that extended the definition of management training to include business leadership in the public sphere, and promoted the status and involvement of a new generation of entrepreneurs in dialogues that were previously the exclusive domain of government. Second, it concentrated on managerial changes both within firms, and between business managers and government agencies and civil society organizations. In these ways, the PMTP contributed to the building of both human and social capital. The facilitative role of government actors in nurturing interactions across the public–private divide was an instrument for fostering network coordination, a coordination mechanism that, in contrast to hierarchy and market, is only slowly beginning to be recognized in Russia.

Annex 8.1: Survey characteristics

BEEPS

The BEEPS data sets were collected in three rounds, in 1999, 2002 and 2005. The survey solicits views from a representative sample of firms from Central and Eastern European countries on the ways government develops and implements public policy. The following common features of each round help describe their design.

- Countries and cases: 1999 – 25 countries, 4,104 cases; 2002 – 27 countries, 6,667 cases; 2005 – 27 countries, 9,655 cases.
- Size: At least 10 per cent of the sample was to be in the small (2–49 employees) and 10 per cent in the large (250–9,999 employees) categories.
- Sectoral representation: The samples are chosen in a uniform way in each country, with sector composition divided according to contribution to gross domestic product (GDP).
- Location: At least 10 per cent of firms were to be in the category 'small city/countryside' (that is, population under 50,000).
- Age: Enterprises which began operations in the three years prior to the survey were excluded.

PMTP Leadership and Membership Questionnaires

The Leadership Questionnaire (LQ) concentrated on ABAs' organizational structure and external networks. The Membership Questionnaire (MQ) sought responses on members' interests, participation and the perceptions of members on the contribution of ABAs to the range of expected PMTP outcomes.

	Leadership Questionnaire (LQ)	**Membership Questionnaire (MQ)**
Target population	Executive members of all ABAs	A representative sample of members in each ABA
Population	~40 ABAs	not known
Surveys administered: Responses	~40: 26	n/a : 299
Response rate	65%	n/a
Date administered	December 2001	April 2002
Geographic representation	26 of 80 regions	20 regions (high response rate from Tomsk, Penza, Kirov, Vologda)
Delivery method	By hand	Mail

Source: Based on the author's surveys and data, 2003.

Annex 8.2: Selected examples of market-supporting actions (2000–02)

Potential actions	Location of ABA and corresponding activity
Participation in public policy	Chuvash: Signed framework agreement with Ministry of Economic Development and Trade establishing a platform for consultations on the social and economic development of the region. Sverdlovsk: Held working-level meetings with Ministry of Trade regarding international trade opportunities and constraints. Kirov: Members participated in, and consulted by, the governor's Economic Council on wide range of topics concerning enterprise restructuring and business development. Saratov: Collaborated with management training centres and governor's office to review bankruptcy legislation and impact on regional businesses. Voronezh: Cooperation agreement signed between of the City of Voronezh, Territorial Management of the Ministry of Property and Central Black Earth branch of the Savings Bank of Russia to coordinate investment and identify priority social and economic investment in the city.
Contributing, advising or critiquing existing or proposed legislation/regulation	Mary-El: Series of consultations held with governor and administrative bodies to revamp human resource development policy. Komi: Participated as external advisors to the development of Komi Republic's skills development and learning policy framework. Vologda: Prepared submission to Department of Human Resources on options to strengthen the region's human resource development strategy. Penza: Advised on the drafting of the 'Law of Investment'.
Defending or upholding property rights	Krasnodar: ABA wins governor's competition for most socially significant project (2004) for organizing a workshop series for young entrepreneurs and business executives on civil law protection, administrative law and business rights, and investment and tax law.
Enhancing social or business infrastructure	Chuvash: Signed agreement with State Committee on Youth Affairs to run a regional competition to sponsor and mentor young entrepreneurs and their innovative business plans; consulted with authorities on access and adequacy of social service provision for youth. Voronezh: Created a regional charitable lottery 'Family and Children' to raise funds for community projects.

(*Continued*)

Potential actions	Location of ABA and corresponding activity
	Saratov: Established pilot project with local businesses and correctional services to provide skill-development training for incarcerated young offenders. Kursk: Established partnership with Rotary Club to raise public awareness and fundraise for disabled children. Tomsk: Created partnership with Department of International Relations to host European trade fair in Tomsk bringing together wide spectrum of industries in the region.
Supporting effective administration/state capacity	* A majority of ABAs are involved with the PMTP to help with the selection and mentoring of PMTP trainees and graduates. Ivanovsk: Created database on PMTP alumni management expertise; database access provided to officials involved in restructuring municipal and state-owned enterprises and government management systems. Ryazan/Krasnodar/Sverlovsk/Kemerovo: Launched standing offer agreement with regional governments to provide restructuring advice to state and large enterprises facing bankruptcy. Saratov: Revamped Trade and Industry's web site on foreign investment opportunities to make the information accessible and relevant to foreign investors. Voronezh/Penza: Established language centre to support the PMTP foreign-language training component and upgrading of ABA members' language skills.

Source: O'Brien (2006).

Annex 8.3: Selected examples of market-complementing actions

Potential actions	Location of ABA and corresponding actions
Standard-setting across industry	None identified
Horizontal coordination for production	None identified
Vertical coordination for production	None identified
Lowering information costs	* A majority of ABAs have developed databases on members and their firms for information, career and business development purposes. Several prominent ABAs spearhead the establishment of the 'Inter-regional Council for Information and Coordination' to 'improve the infrastructure and management procedures within the Russian economy through stimulation of business contacts between the [ABAs] in various regions' (mission statement). Forty-eight ABAs sign on to the Council's Charter. Kaliningrad/St Petersburg: Analysed and published newsletters on business climate and trends in respective regions. Nizhny-Novgorod: Compiled case studies on effective restructuring projects and established a databank on investment projects in the region.
Skill-upgrading/training	* A majority of ABAs organize professional development workshops, seminars and training for members. Japan Association: Coordinate regular professional development seminars by local and international speakers in several regions. Sverdlovsk: Established partnership with local businesses to host an annual international workshop for managers and executives on issues of total quality management and other business topics. Voronezh: Ran annual business seminar series. Tomsk: Regular seminars on management, marketing and financial analysis. Perm/Penza: Organized programme for foreign language training for members and non-members. Kostroma: Workshops and programme development for executives of regional enterprises interested in presenting investment opportunities to national and international clients.

(Continued)

Potential actions	Location of ABA and corresponding actions
Business or market innovation	Swedish Association: Developed bilateral exchange programme for managers and executives between Russian/Swedish companies to facilitate understanding and trade opportunities. Vologda: Market research project on foreign investment opportunities in the oblast. Krasnodar/Stavropol/Astrakhan: Hosted and organized an international trade show with German and European companies. Tver/Kaluga/Moscow: Established business advisory centres for members. Actions include peer-review of business plans, identification of potential investors and clients. Kostroma: Developed and operated the interregional marketing centre 'Kostroma-Moscow' to facilitate trade and business development between regional oblasts.

Source: O'Brien (2006).

Notes

1. See Annex 8.1 for a description of these data sets. This study benefited from the involvement and guidance of Li Zong, Galina Gradoselskaya, Harley Dickinson and Niels Röling. Support from the Higher School of Economics (Moscow) and the Canadian International Development Agency is gratefully acknowledged.
2. In the ensuing discussion, the survey instrument for executive members is referred to as the Leadership Questionnaire (LQ), and for regular members as the Membership Questionnaire (MQ).
3. Of course, state interventions seeking to facilitate new social relations can go terribly wrong, as Scott (1998) describes in Russia and elsewhere.
4. Woolcock (1998: 179–82) provides a useful literature review of both top-down and bottom-up dilemmas of social organizations influencing development agendas. He discusses the literature consistent with Evans' view as well as the critics.
5. See Fortescue (1997) for a discussion on the presence and performance of coordinating bodies and mechanisms in Soviet industry, which all but disappeared with the onset of the radical market liberation in the early 1990s.
6. For an in-depth analysis of the composition of the regional elite in the late Yeltsin and early Putin period, consult Chirikova and Lapina (2001). Their investigation into who holds influence in Russia's regions is remarkable for the lack of actors not associated with political parties, the state or major industries.
7. There is a fairly developed empirical literature on the legal, cultural and political reasons why independent civil society has been slow to emerge in the former Soviet Union (Howard 2000; Stuart 2002; USAID 1995, 1997; Weigel 2000). I highlight here one dimension that supports the argument that business associations emerge in a dynamic relationship to the state (Schneider 2004: 20–56).
8. Vladimir Putin, cited in the *Moscow Times* (2001). This was not a fleeting concern for Putin. A year later, in his Presidential Address, he indicated that removing the administrative barriers remained a priority: 'The higher the barrier, the larger the bribe and the number of bureaucrats who take them. [It's] extremely difficult to conduct civilized business in Russia' (cited in *Russian Regional Report*, 7 (15), 2002).
9. Rose's (1998) statement is overstated. Numerous studies document the growth of civil society organizations in Russia (for example, Weigel 2000) but, when comparing Russian to European levels, Rose's metaphor does have descriptive value.
10. One business reporter offered this observation on municipal politics in St Petersburg: 'since there are no stable political parties or deputy factions in the city legislature, businesses have difficulty organizing effective representation of their interests here. Each deputy has his own connections to the business community working as an individual. Most likely, the deputies receive some money from business for specific services that they provide' (*Russian Regional Report* 2002).
11. Regime classification is based on an index of political rights and civil liberties for the years 1990–9 (World Bank 2002: 97–101). *Competitive regimes*: Czech Republic, Slovenia, Hungary, Poland, Lithuania, Estonia, Latvia. *Concentrated regimes*: Slovak Republic, Bulgaria, Romania, Ukraine, Russia, Croatia, Moldova, Kyrgyz Republic. *Non-Competitive regimes*: Belarus, Kazakhstan, Uzbekistan, Turkmenistan.
12. The RUIE and the CCI are the largest business associations in Russia. The RUIE was created just prior to the collapse of the Soviet Union. Today, it has a diversified

membership base and represents companies that control more than half of Russia's gross domestic product. RUIE maintains it has 330,000 members, representative offices in each of regions, and formal arrangements with a number of national and international business associations. In the late 1990s, the so-called oligarchs increasingly coordinated their lobbying efforts through the RUIE. See Hanson and Teague (2005) for a recent discussion of the RUIE's changing political orientation and membership. The CCI, by contrast, has it origins in the pre-revolution period. Today, it has a more diverse regional representation and broader-based representation across industry sectors and firm sizes than the RUIE. Like the RUIE, it seeks to represent its members' interests in legislative debates, but it has a more complete range of services than the RUIE, which range from analytical services to standard-setting and commercial arbitration.

13. Numerous examples of new business associations emerging in Russia's regions have been reported in the *Russian Regional Report*, but coverage tends to suggest that new organizations fill a void, whereas this is not the case in Moscow and other major centres.
14. Data for Russia, reported in Figure 8.1, are below the average for concentrated regimes.
15. This missing agenda stands at odds with the historic role socialist firms played in providing a range of social services for employees. Housing, sports and recreation, continuing education and skill development were all part of the social contract that firms provided. In the 1990s, state funding for these services ended and social provision became delinked from the employment contract. The ensuing deterioration of social conditions was deeply troubling for workers and presumably firms interested in a stable and productive workforce. However, there is little reporting of business associations taking on these concerns.
16. The PMTP began in 1997 under Yeltsin and received continued political and financial support throughout Putin's presidency (2000–8).
17. In O'Brien (2006: 138–44), the positive perception of the regional government's role in programme implementation was a significant variable for why alumni participated in ABAs. This was more important than individual characteristics or firm/employment-related variables. This finding departs from Dolgopyatova's (2000) finding that established business association members react negatively to Russian government interest in their organizations.
18. The main structural difference in ABAs was membership size which ranged from over 200 members in some regions to fewer than 50 in others. Differences were often explained by the number of graduates trained in each of the 80 regions, but concentration of graduates in major regional cities also facilitated networking and interaction.
19. The design of this programme and a fuller description of the associations are described by O'Brien (2006: 19–47).
20. Mark Granovetter (1973) inspired a body of literature in economic sociology that investigates how actors are embedded in social networks and the consequences of this for social mobility and firm performance, among other applications. This analysis is grounded in that literature. For a review of ensuing debates, see Granovetter (1985), and Yakubovich and Kozina (2000) for an application to Russia.
21. The question reads: 'When a new law, rule, regulation, or decree is proposed that would have a substantial impact on your firm, which channel would you typically rely on to affect the outcome?' (BEEPS 1999).

References

Åslund, Anders (1999) 'Why Has Russia's Economic Transformation Been So Arduous?', Paper presented at the Annual World Bank Conference on Development Economics, Washington, DC, 28–30 April 1999 (Washington, DC: Carnegie Endowment for International Peace).

BEEPS (1999/2002/2005) *EBRD – World Bank Business Environment and Enterprise Performance Survey*, for the years 1999, 2002 and 2005, at: www.ebrd.com/country/sector/econo/surveys/beeps.htm (accessed 5 July 2007).

Blanchard, Olivier and Michael Kremer (1997) 'Disorganization', *The Quarterly Journal of Economics*, 112 (4), 1091–126.

Broadman, Harry (2002) *Unleashing Russia's Business Potential*, World Bank Discussion Paper No. 434 (Washington, DC: World Bank).

Chirikova, Alla and Natalia Lapina (2001) 'A Quiet Revolution on a Russian Scale', Regionalization of Russian Foreign and Security Policy Working Paper No. 4 (Zurich: Center for Security Studies and Conflict Research).

Dolgopyatova, Tat'yana (2000) 'The Evolution of New Institutions in the Small Business Sector', in Stephanie Harter and Gerald Easter (eds), *Shaping the Economic Space* (Farnham: Ashgate Publishing Limited).

Doner, Richard and Ben Ross Schneider (2000) 'Business Associations and Economic Development: Why Some Associations Contribute More than Others', *Business and Politics*, 2 (3), 261–88.

Evans, Peter (1996) 'Government Action, Social Capital and Development: Reviewing the Evidence on Synergy', *World Development*, 24 (6), 1119–32.

Fortescue, Stephen (1997) *Policy-Making for Russian Industry* (New York: St Martin's Press).

Gaidar, Yegor (2002) Interview, 10 May 2000, in *Commanding Heights: The Battle for the World Economy*, William Cran and Daniel Yergin (producers) (Boston: Public Broadcast Service/PBS, Boston), at: www.pbs.org/wgbh/commandingheights/lo/people/pe_name.html.

Gerber, Theodore (2000) 'Membership Benefits of Selection Effects? Why Former Communist Party Members Do Better in Post-Soviet Russia', *Social Science Research*, 29 (1), 25–50.

Gorbachev, Mikhail (1987) *Perestroika* (New York: Harper & Row).

Granovetter, Mark (1973) 'The Strength of Weak Ties', *American Journal of Sociology*, 78 (6), 1360–80.

——— (1985) 'Economic Action and Social Structure: The Problem of Embeddedness', *American Journal of Sociology*, 91 (3), 481–510.

Hanson, Phillip and Elizabeth Teague (2005) 'Big Business and the State in Russia', *Europe-Asia Studies*, 57 (5), 657–80.

Hellman, Joel, Geraint Jones and Daniel Kaufmann (2000) *Seize the State, Seize the Day: State Capture, Corruption, and Influence in Transition Economies*, World Bank Policy Research Working Paper No. 2444 (Washington, DC: World Bank).

Hoffman, David (2003) *The Oligarchs: Wealth and Power in the New Russia* (New York: Public Affairs).

Howard, Marc Morjé (2000) *Free Not to Participate: The Weakness of Civil Society in Post-Communist Europe*, Studies in Public Policy No. 325 (Glasgow: University of Strathclyde, 2000).

Ledeneva, Alena (1998) *Russia's Economy of Favours: Blat, Networking and Informal Exchange* (Cambridge: Cambridge University Press).

Lin, Nan (2002) *Social Capital: A Theory of Social Structure and Action* (Cambridge: Cambridge University Press).

March, James and Johan Olsen (1984) 'The New Institutionalism: Organizational Factors in Political Life', *The American Political Science Review*, 78 (3), 734–49.

Moscow Times (2001) 'Putin: Graft Killing Small Businesses', 5 December.

North, Douglass C. (1990) *Institutions, Institutional Change and Economic Performance* (New York: Cambridge University Press).

O'Brien, David W. (2006) *Das Social Kapital: Institutions and Entrepreneurial Networks in Russia's Exit from Socialism*, PhD thesis, Wageningen University, at: http://library.wur.nl/wda/dissertations/dis4018.pdf.

Olson, Mancur (1982) *The Rise and Decline of Nations* (New Haven: Yale University Press).

Pyle, William (2006) 'Collective Action and Post-Communist Enterprise: The Economic Logic of Russia's Business Associations', *Europe-Asia Studies*, 58 (4), 491–521.

Recanatini, Francesca and Randi Ryterman (2001) 'Disorganization or Self-Organization: The Emergence of Business Associations in a Transition Economy', Policy Research Working Paper No. 2539 (Washington, DC: World Bank).

Rose, Richard (1998) 'Getting Things Done in an Anti-Modern Society', Social Capital Initiative Working Paper No. 6 (Washington, DC: World Bank).

Russian Regional Report (2002) 'Business and Politics in St Petersburg', 7 (24) (New York: EastWest Institute).

Schneider, Ben Ross (2004) *Business Politics and the State in Twentieth-Century Latin America* (New York: Cambridge University Press).

Scott, James C. (1998) *Seeing Like a State: How Certain Schemes to Improve the Human Condition Have Failed* (New Haven: Yale University Press).

Smirnov, Stanislav (1997) 'Back Door Entry to Economy Is Wrong', *Russia*, 2, 16.

Stiglitz, Joseph (1999) *Whither Reform? Ten Years of the Transition*, keynote address at the World Bank's Annual Bank Conference on Development Economics, Washington, DC, 28–30 April.

Stuart, Jennifer (ed.) (2002) *The 2002 NGO Sustainability Index for Central and Eastern Europe and Eurasia* (Washington, DC: United States Agency for International Development/USAID).

Tchernina, Natalia (1996) *Economic Transition and Social Exclusion in Russia* (Geneva: International Institute for Labour Studies, ILO).

Titarenko, Larissa G. (1999) 'Post-Soviet Youth: Engagement in Civil Society – Belarus and Beyond', *Demokratizatsiya*, 7 (3), 413–36.

UNDP (United Nations Development Programme) (2003) *Human Development Report Russian Federation 2002–3: The Role of the State in Economic Growth and Socio-Economic Reform* (Moscow: UNDP).

——— (2007) *Russian Business and the UN Global Compact*. at:. www.undp.ru/publications/GC_3_en.pdf (accessed 5 August 2007).

USAID (United States Agency for International Development) (1995) *Public Organization Attitudes and Awareness Study: Report on Results of a Quantitative Research in Omsk, Krasnodar and Stavropol*, Civic Initiatives Programme (Moscow: USAID).

——— (1997) *Public Organization Attitudes and Awareness Study: Follow up Quantitative Research in Omsk, Krasnodar and Stavropol*, Civic Initiatives Programme (Moscow: USAID).

Weigel, Marcia (2000) *Russia's Liberal Project: State–Society Relations in the Transition from Communism* (University Park: Pennsylvania State University Press).

Woolcock, Michael (1988) 'Social Capital and Economic Development: Toward a Theoretical Synthesis and Policy Framework', *Theory and Society*, 27 (2), 151–208.

World Bank (2002) *Transition: The First Ten Years* (Washington, DC: World Bank).

Yakubovich, Valery and Irina Kozina (2000) 'The Changing Significance of Ties', *International Sociology*, 15 (3), 479–500.

Yurchak, Alexei (2002) 'Entrepreneurial Governmentality in Postsocialist Russia: A Cultural Investigation of Business Practices', in Victoria E. Bonnell and Thomas B. Gold (eds), *The New Entrepreneurs of Europe and Asia: Patterns of Business Development in Russia, Eastern Europe, and China* (New York: M.E. Sharpe).

9

Lobbying to Reduce the 'Brazil Cost': The Political Strategies of Brazilian Entrepreneurs

Wagner Pralon Mancuso

This chapter examines the political strategies adopted by industrial entrepreneurs in their campaign for reducing the so-called 'Brazil cost' (*custo Brasil*) – which refers to factors and conditions that are perceived as hindering competitiveness – and the outcomes achieved through this campaign. It covers a period of 12 years that embraces President Cardoso's two terms in office (1995–2002) and President Lula's first term (2003–6).

The chapter is divided into three sections. The first presents how the reduction of the Brazil cost became a 'flag' under which members of the business community congregated. Two factors are of importance here. One is of an economic nature – the process of organization and mobilization against the Brazil cost was unleashed by the processes of market liberalization carried out during the 1990s (starting with Collor in 1990, and sustained by Franco and Cardoso), and reinforced by the prospect of even greater opening, via hemispheric integration through the Free Trade Area of the Americas (FTAA). In this scenario, the challenge of international competition elevated *competitiveness* to the level of a top-priority goal to be pursued by Brazilian companies. However, this economic factor should be considered a necessary, albeit not sufficient, cause of the campaign for reducing the Brazil cost. It is also necessary to emphasize the intentional political action that paved the way for the campaign. Therefore, the second factor is of a political nature. The Confederação Nacional da Indústria (CNI/National Confederation of Industry) played an important role of 'political entrepreneurship' in the organization and mobilization of the business community. The CNI is the peak association of the corporatist system of representation of industrial interests in Brazil. Located at the apex of this system, and backed by a stable source of financial resources, the CNI was able to act as a 'political entrepreneur', internalizing the costs involved in organizing the movement for reducing the Brazil cost. This initiative had the direct effect of reducing the costs that other business organizations would incur to take part in collective action. The reduction in participation costs made the involvement option much more attractive to those entities.

The second section presents how these organized business interests attempt to shape the policy process related to the Brazil cost through lobbying. Industrial entrepreneurs have been working together since the mid-1990s to identify, keep track of and promote their demands on legislative proposals – the approval, rejection or alteration of which have a direct impact on the Brazil cost. These demands are communicated in the *Agenda Legislativa da Indústria* (*Legislative Agenda of Industry*, hereafter referred to as *Legislative Agenda*), an annual publication prepared by a network of dozens of industrial associations, and organized and published by the CNI. In order to promote the demands that they have announced, entrepreneurs and their associations – both from the corporatist and extra-corporatist systems – perform lobbying activities throughout the various stages of each proposal's legislative cycle. This kind of ad hoc political action, intended to exercise pressure along several independent decision-making processes, was once seen as typical of pluralist systems, but is becoming more and more common in Brazil, where corporatist associations (unions, federations and confederations) still form the largest part of the system of representation of business interests. This development is of great interest, particularly given the complete absence of any regulation of lobbying activities in Brazil.

The third section measures the degree of political success that industrial entrepreneurs have achieved under the Cardoso and Lula governments, regarding 'Brazil cost'-related proposals formulated either by the executive or legislative branches. I develop a method which compares business demands and results of congressional decisions. The method allows the classification of business political successes into two categories: gain (when a business-supported proposal becomes a norm and effectively reduces the Brazil cost) and relief (when a proposal opposed by business is rejected, withdrawn, or shelved, thus avoiding the rise of the Brazil cost). The method also allows the classification of business/political failures into two categories: loss (when a proposal opposed by business becomes a norm and effectively raises the Brazil cost) and frustration (when a business-supported proposal is rejected, withdrawn or shelved, thus avoiding the reduction of the Brazil cost). In general, the results show that industrial entrepreneurs operating in Brazil have achieved a high degree of political success.

Economic and political underpinnings of collective action

The 1990s brought a profound change in the environment in which the business community operated in Brazil. The fundamental cause of this change was the liberal inflection in the country's economic stabilization policy, the implementation of which dates back to the start of the Collor government (1990). Liberalization was intended to deal with the crisis that devastated Brazil from the beginning of the 1980s up to the first half of the 1990s, a crisis which had uncontrolled inflation as its most conspicuous symptom.

The opening of the Brazilian economy to international commerce was a process that involved two simultaneous movements.[1] The first was an 'inward'-opening movement, which resulted in substantial expansion of competition in the domestic market, on account of the growth of the volume of imported products. Such growth was favoured by the fall of tariff and non-tariff barriers to imports, and by the overvaluation of the Brazilian real. The other movement was an 'outward' opening, characterized by the goal of winning over new international markets. The expression 'export or die' indicates the level of priority that the government and the business community started to attribute to Brazil's competitive integration with the global economy.[2]

The 1990s were also marked by Brazil's involvement in various international negotiation processes, particularly the FTAA. Hemispheric integration would mean a second commercial liberalization blow to national business activities, the impact of which can hardly be underestimated. Naturally, the effect of hemispheric integration would be heterogeneous – for internationally competitive business segments, the expansion of opening in the sphere of the FTAA would produce opportunities for gains, such as access to new markets, expansion of production scales and others. However, the situation would be inverted for segments with serious competitive deficiencies, for which the increase in commercial opening and imports signified a risk of significant losses.

From the outset, Brazil's process of economic opening exerted a significant impact on business activities throughout the country. Numerous firms were forced to close down (Birchal 2002), particularly in industrial branches, such as auto parts, textile products and footwear (Oliveira 2002). The decade was also marked by a major increase in merger and acquisition activity, spearheaded by national and foreign entrepreneurs interested in controlling firms less qualified to deal with the new situation (Bonelli 2000; Miranda 2001). Overall, most companies had to undergo an intense adjustment process.[3] Firms adjusted in various ways. There were cases in which the adjustment called for concentration on activities of greater competence, which resulted in the contraction of work developed inside the firm ('deverticalization') and in outsourcing. In other cases, the adjustment was characterized by the rationalization of productive processes and by the reduction of hierarchical levels in companies. The implementation of time- and material-saving techniques, as well as the deployment of programmes for control and optimization of the quality of products, was also widespread. In brief, bankruptcies, mergers, disposals and adjustments were the immediate 'microeconomic' responses offered by companies that were unable to remain immune to the new scenario of expanded competition that prevailed from the 1990s onward.

These events contributed significantly to the large-scale process of organization and political mobilization of the business community. With the onset of economic liberalization, the search for competitiveness and the means by which to achieve it became the highest priority for companies. The reduction of the Brazil cost became the 'flag' around which members of the business community rallied. Brazil cost is an expression that is used to refer to the set of national factors or conditions that the Brazilian business community believes hinder competitiveness. By reducing the Brazil cost, national companies would be able to face foreign competition under conditions of greater equality. In the conception utilized in this article, six factors comprise the Brazil cost: excessive and poor quality regulation of economic activity; inadequate labour legislation; a tax system that overburdens production; a high cost of financing of productive activity; insufficient material infrastructure; and deficient social infrastructure (CNI 1996a, 1998).

However, the enhanced organization and mobilization of the Brazilian business community in the 1990s cannot be interpreted as a spontaneous outcome. Economic liberalization and the need for greater competitiveness should be considered a necessary, albeit insufficient, cause for the aforesaid change of attitude of the business community towards collective action. A proper account requires emphasizing the intentional political action that paved the way for substantive advances in terms of organizational capacity and mobilization.

The CNI played an important role of political leadership in the organization and mobilization of the business community that took place in the 1990s. In May 1995, it organized a seminar titled 'Brazil Cost: Dialogue with National Congress', an event that, for the first time, brought entrepreneurs and members of parliament from different political parties face to face to discuss the decisions that could be made in the sphere of the federal legislative branch to boost business competitiveness in the country. Following this seminar, the CNI decided to invest resources in a permanent undertaking that consisted of identifying and keeping track of legislative proposals, the approval, rejection or alteration of which would have a relevant impact on the Brazil cost. The CNI's decision gave rise to the *Legislative Agenda*, which has been published continuously since 1996 (CNI 1996a–2006) and which still represents the most consistent, enduring and important initiative of the country's industrial sector to combat the Brazil cost throughout the federal legislative production process.

The *Legislative Agenda* highlights those legislative proposals running in National Congress which are believed to have the capacity to increase or reduce the systemic competitiveness of Brazilian companies. Besides highlighting the principal legislative proposals related to the Brazil cost, the *Legislative Agenda* also presents the following information: 1) the industrial sector's point of view regarding each of the components and subcomponents of the Brazil cost to which the legislative proposals are related; 2) the summary of the content of each legislative proposal; 3) the consensual position of industry in relation to each legislative proposal, which can be classified as convergent; convergent with caveats; divergent with caveats; or divergent; 4) the justification that supports industry's standpoint in relation to the legislative proposal; and 5) the stage of the procedure of each legislative proposal. The proposals focused on by the *Legislative Agenda* can be found at any stage of consideration at the Chamber of Deputies or the Federal Senate.

From the publication of the first *Legislative Agenda* in 1996 up to the publication of the eleventh *Agenda* in 2006, the preparation of the document involved a growing number of organizations that represent the interests of companies from an increasingly diverse number of industrial sectors. Only in 1996 was the preparation of the *Legislative Agenda* conducted exclusively by the CNI. From 1997 on, each of the 26 State Federations of Industry, and the Federation of Industry of the Federal District, participated in the formulation of the *Legislative Agendas*. As of 2001, a large number of sectoral organizations of national scope began to collaborate in the preparation of the document: 28 sectoral organizations in 2001, 31 in 2002, 33 in 2003, 42 in 2004, 50 in 2005 and 46 in 2006. In all, 53 different national sectoral organizations have at some point participated in the preparation of the *Legislative Agenda*. In 2004, União da Agroindústria Canavieira de São Paulo (UNICA/Union of the Sugar Cane Agribusiness of São Paulo) became the first sectoral association at the state level to take part in the preparation of a *Legislative Agenda*.

Accordingly, it is possible to conclude that the preparation of the *Legislative Agenda* is a major collective effort – one that is still gradually expanding. The struggle for the reduction of the Brazil cost requires the peak association of the industrial sector, the federations of industries and many other organizations that represent specific sectors in the national and state sphere to work side by side. Analytically, the formation of the common agenda related to the reduction of the Brazil cost can be interpreted as the solution to a problem of collective action, a subject that has received extensive attention from contemporary political scientists.

In fact, the reduction of the Brazil cost is an outcome that clearly possesses the two essential requirements to qualify as a 'collective benefit' (Samuelson 1954; Hardin 1982: 17; Sandler 1992: 5). First, the reduction of the Brazil cost is marked by 'non-excludability': as of the moment when a legislative proposal that reduces the Brazil cost is transformed into a legal norm, the enjoyment of the beneficial effects of that political decision cannot be refused to any company.[4] Second, the reduction of the Brazil cost is characterized by 'non-rivalness': the enjoyment by a company of the effects of a legal norm that reduces the Brazil cost in no way decreases the beneficial opportunities available to other companies.

The provision of benefits, such as the reduction of the Brazil cost, typically implies collective action problems (Olson 1965). The most common manifestation of the collective action problem is the free-riding phenomenon. To this effect, the term 'free-riding' designates the attitude of individuals who, while considering the securing of a collective benefit desirable, are not willing to collaborate towards it, as they expect other individuals to do so. Free-riders prefer that other individuals sustain the burden of obtaining the collective benefit, so that they can enjoy the resulting benefits without having to expend their own resources. The presence of such collective action problems frequently renders the actual provision of the benefit unfeasible, or causes the provision of the benefit to occur at a suboptimum level.

Therefore, in light of the theory of collective action, the non-involvement of business organizations in an extensive movement to reduce the Brazil cost would not be a surprising outcome, even if organizations were to desire the advantages that the reduction of the Brazil cost would produce for the represented companies, and to admit that their active involvement in the movement could make it stronger and more representative. Thus the observation that the movement was not only formed but also strengthened requires an explanation of how the potential collective action problem was overcome.

The principal impulse for the resolution of the collective action problem came, as mentioned before, from the CNI, which played the role of 'political entrepreneur'. In this context, the term 'entrepreneur' does not allude to the figure of the businessperson who performs duties related to the production or distribution of goods and services. Some political science literature uses the expression 'political entrepreneur' to refer actors who decide, on their own account, to assume the cost necessary to start off and organize collective action, with a view to the provision of the benefit sought by all (Hardin 1982: 34–7; Moe 1988: 33).

The CNI occupies a particularly favourable position for performing the aforementioned role of political entrepreneur, as it is the association occupying the highest level inside the corporatist system of representation of industrial interests. The exclusive condition of peak association determines that the CNI shall dedicate its time to promoting the collective interests of its sector in the national sphere, thus offering a counterpoint to the performance of the other organizations geared towards the defence of particular interests of specific branches of industrial activity, or of specific business communities located in a given area of the country.

The CNI has the resources necessary for this action. Its maintenance as an association is assured by the rules of the corporatist system. The financial mainstay of the corporatist system is the union contribution. Every legally organized industrial company is obliged to contribute to the union that represents it, a sum that varies according to the capital owned by the company. The union contribution is the main source of funds that guarantees the survival of the CNI, as it receives 5 per cent of the levy obtained by all the industrial business unions of the country. The CNI has used these resources to coordinate Brazilian business efforts in favour of systemic competitiveness.[5] More specifically, the CNI has invested significant resources in the maintenance of a Legislative Affairs Unit, which has a staff consisting of lawyers, economists and political scientists, and has focused exclusively on federal legislative branch activities. This unit works almost year-round on the preparation of the *Legislative Agendas*. Moreover, the CNI also invests resources in the publication and disclosure of the *Legislative Agenda* itself, distributing copies to all the members of the National Congress (deputies and senators), members of the federal executive branch, the press, entrepreneurs and other stakeholders. The other business organizations also disseminate copies to their target audiences.

In summary, the CNI, located at the apex of the system of representation of industrial interests, and backed by a stable source of financial resources, acts as a political entrepreneur, internalizing the costs involved in organizing the movement for reducing the Brazil cost. This initiative has had the direct effect of reducing the costs that other business organizations would need to incur to take part in collective action. The reduction of participation costs has made involvement more attractive to those entities.

The dynamics of lobbying

Economic activity is exposed to the impact of countless decisions made on a day-to-day basis by individuals occupying positions of authority in the different branches – executive, legislative and judiciary – of the municipal, state and federal spheres. The perception that government decisions have the power of interfering in the activities of companies leads many entrepreneurs – directly or by means of representatives – to develop activities of interest articulation.

In this chapter, I focus exclusively on the articulation of interests of the industrial business community during the federal legislative production process. In this manner, I follow in the footsteps of authors who first pointed out that Brazil's redemocratization during the mid-1980s resulted in the increase of prerogatives and the political relevance of the National Congress, attracting to this forum the participation of social sectors – including industrial entrepreneurs – the attention of which was concentrated primarily on the internal decision-making processes of the executive branch (de Aragão 1994, 1996, 2000; Diniz and Boschi 1997, 2000).

It is not feasible to reconstitute in detail the entire process of articulation of the interests of industrial entrepreneurs during the legislative process. The main source of information about the political activity of industry that I utilize in this chapter is LEGISDATA, an electronic database that the CNI maintains and updates daily.[6] It is composed of information referring to the industrial sector's lobbying activities in the face of thousands of legislative propositions that are of interest to the sector and that ran, or are still running, in the Chamber of Deputies, the Federal Senate or the National Congress. Among all the propositions that form LEGISDATA, I concentrate my attention on a specific subgroup: those that are presented in the *Legislative Agenda*. It is not possible to affirm that LEGISDATA contains the complete and all-encompassing description of the articulation of interests of industrial entrepreneurs while these propositions are running. However, the analysis represents an effort to explore this rich source of information.

Industry engages in intense political action during the running of proposals that appear in the *Legislative Agenda*. The activities carried out by industry can be classified into five categories: monitoring, analysis, position-taking, orientation and pressure. *Monitoring* the evolution of projects entails keeping track of each step of the process in the federal legislative houses, from the initial stage of presentation of propositions up to the conclusive stage, in which the decision that ends the progress of proposals is taken.

The second activity, *analysis,* requires examining each of the legislative propositions in detail. The analysis process is ongoing, that is, the subjects of analysis are not only the original propositions. Every time an alteration is introduced during the running of the bill in question – which occurs when amendments or substitute bills are presented in committees or in a plenary sitting – industry prepares a new analysis, emphasizing the meaning of the alteration introduced in light of the interests of the sector. Technical experts who focus on the propositions according to their area of specialization draw up analyses. Several technical experts with different specialities frequently analyse the same bill. These analyses are often accompanied by alternative proposals in the form of amendments or completely new bills.

The third activity of *taking a position* on each bill is based on this technical analysis. The position taken in relation to each proposal is one of the following: opposed, opposed with restrictions, neutral, favourable with restrictions or favourable. The position that industry takes on a bill can be altered for several reasons. The change of position can be related to the adoption of a substitute bill, the introduction of amendments in the original bill or the appearance of new bills attached to the original bill. Industry may be totally opposed to a bill at a given time (or have specific reservations in relation to it), but then change its position to being in favour of it if it perceives that worse alternatives could be adopted. Similarly, industry may change its mind on a bill that it favours, ceasing to support it if it recognizes the possibility of a better alternative. The change of position in any possible direction can also be associated with the appearance of new information or reports.

The fourth activity, *orientation,* mainly targets the entities that represent the industrial sector. The idea is to disseminate the result of the technical analyses of legislative propositions, providing information on what is at stake, justifying the standpoint adopted and shaping a homogeneous evaluation of the propositions. Orientation is important to ensure that industrial organizations do not act in a dispersed or contradictory manner, but rather in an integrated fashion, presenting a united front, thus bolstering the demands presented by the sector.

The last activity, the application of *political pressure,* corresponds directly to the articulation of interests, that is, to the presentation of demands to decision-makers (Almond and Powell Jr 1972: 52). Of all the actions performed by industry, political pressure is the one that achieves by far the most visibility. For this reason, I will analyse this activity in greater depth.

Political pressure does not have a predetermined nature. Rather, the meaning and the intensity of pressure vary according to the nature of the bill under analysis. In some cases, pressure is of a defensive nature – this happens when the goal is to avoid the damage that certain legislative propositions may pose to manufacturing companies. Under these circumstances, pressure is oriented towards ending the progress of the proposal, or suspending it, or at modifying the proposal, making it more acceptable. In other cases, pressure is of a more offensive nature – when the idea is to propose or support bills that are considered capable of promoting the competitiveness of companies in the country.

Whatever the case, political pressure is exercised by several different types of agents, from isolated individuals through to various types of collectivity. These include entrepreneurs (or contracted representatives) that may act on their own account, or on behalf of their companies or groupings of companies, or business entities that envisage common interests. Companies and business entities can constitute ad hoc temporary coalitions (cases in which a specific issue provokes a phase of intense mobilization, followed by a phase of demobilization) through to permanent groups with a high level of formal organization, simultaneously focused on numerous issues (for example, organizations from the corporatist and extra-corporatist systems).

All the stages that form the federal legislative production process are permeable to the exercise of political pressure. The articulation of industrial interests begins when the proposition is being formulated. The participation of industry in this early stage of legislative production takes place in several ways. There are cases in which entities from the industrial sector officially take part in the preparation of the draft bills, which will subsequently be submitted by members of parliament or by the executive branch. There are also cases in which the author, aware of the potential impact of a proposal on industry, takes the initiative of listening to the opinion of the segment before defining the final content of the proposal. Members of parliament presenting the bills may also share industrial entities' interests and/or concerns, and opt to adopt bills prepared by the technical staff of those entities. In all these cases, the interests of the sector are furthered even before the legislative process begins.

Intense political pressure also occurs in the stages of discussion of and voting on legislative propositions, both in the sphere of committees and in the sphere of plenary sittings. In fact, a significant part of the legislative work is carried out in the committees of the Chamber of Deputies, of the Federal Senate and in mixed committees. As a result, a significant amount of political pressure is targeted at these forums. The defence of industrial interests also frequently takes place at events such as public hearings, seminars and work meetings, which are convened to provide representatives of the sector with an opportunity to come face to face with decision-makers, debate the legislative proposition under analysis with them and express their demands.

Nevertheless, the pressure from industry at the level of committees is not restricted to events of an official nature. In countless situations, the initial contact is not undertaken by members of parliament, but by the actual representatives of the trade segment. The bill's rapporteur typically becomes the target of political action until the report is concluded. The idea is to ensure in advance that the content of his report mirrors the interests of the sector. Depending on the situation, industry presses the rapporteur to totally or partially reject or approve the main bill, any attached bills or amendments. After the presentation of the report, the focal point of pressure shifts to the members of the committee to approve, reject or modify the report of the rapporteur, in keeping with the interests defended.

The work of political pressure continues when propositions run in the plenary sitting of the Chamber or of the Senate. Here, government and political party leaders become important targets of industry lobbying for the bill in question to be rejected, altered or approved.

The legislative powers conferred by the Brazilian Constitution to the executive branch of government enable it to play a crucial role in the country's legislative production, as the author of most propositions effectively transformed into law (Figueiredo and Limongi 2001). Accordingly, there is a strong stimulus for the industrial sector to exert political pressure on the executive branch over the course of the legislative process. In fact, industry pressure transcends cases in which the executive is the author of the proposition under analysis. Pressure on the executive branch also occurs during the negotiation of bills of members of parliament in which the government gets involved as a stakeholder or as an arbitrator of conflicts between and among different interests.

In the many cases where the industrial sector applies pressure on the executive branch, the pressure can occur at the time the proposition is being written, during the negotiation process of the bill in parliament or when the President is supposed to decide whether to sanction or veto (in full or in part) a proposition approved by the legislative branch. In case of dissatisfaction with vetoes imposed by the President of the republic, pressing members of parliament for the suppression of vetoes remains an alternative.

Hence this chapter confirms an issue to which other Brazilian political scientists have already drawn attention: the pattern of political activity of business entities, *including entities from the corporatist system*, is becoming more and more similar to lobbying – understood as a specific and scattered activity aimed at the exercise of pressure throughout countless singular decision-making processes – a phenomenon generally associated with pluralist systems and considered atypical in systems of state corporatism such as Brazil (Vianna 1994, 1998; Diniz and Boschi 1997).

Measuring political success and failure

This section presents the method formulated to evaluate the extent to which the results of the legislative process effectively correspond to the interests of industry. The cases under analysis are the bills that appear in the *Legislative Agenda* published between 1996 and 2006.

Table 9.1 exhibits the criteria adopted to classify the various types of decision as successes or failures for industry. There are five kinds of decision that put an end to the progress of a legislative proposition. A proposition can be: 1) *transformed into law*; 2) *filed* (the proposition in question is *prejudicada*, that is, it loses its opportunity due to a decision being made referring to another proposition); 3) *rejected* (in committees with concluding power or in the plenary sitting of the Chamber of Deputies, of the Federal Senate or of the National Congress); 4) *removed by the author*; or 5) *shelved at the end of the legislature session.*

When a legislative proposition is transformed into law and the opinion of industry in relation to the final version of the bill is favourable, with or without restrictions, then we consider this decision an example of success. On the other hand, if industry is opposed, with or without restrictions, to the proposition transformed into law, then the decision is considered a failure.

Table 9.1 Criteria utilized to classify decisions as successes or failures of industry

Decision	Position of industry on final decision	Result
New rule of law	Favourable	Success
New rule of law	Favourable, with restrictions	Success
New rule of law	Opposed, with restrictions	Failure
New rule of law	Opposed	Failure
Filed	Favourable	Success
Filed	Favourable, with restrictions	Success
Filed	Opposed, with restrictions	Failure
Filed	Opposed	Failure
Rejected	Opposed	Success
Rejected	Opposed, with restrictions	Success
Rejected	Favourable, with restrictions	Failure
Rejected	Favourable	Failure
Removed by the author	Opposed	Success
Removed by the author	Opposed, with restrictions	Success
Removed by the author	Favourable, with restrictions	Failure
Removed by the author	Favourable	Failure
Shelved	Opposed	Success
Shelved	Opposed, with restrictions	Success
Shelved	Favourable, with restrictions	Failure
Shelved	Favourable	Failure

Source: Author's analysis.

Table 9.2 Impact of cases of success on the 'Brazil cost'

Decision	Impact on the 'Brazil cost'
New rule of law	Reduces the 'Brazil cost'
Filed	Reduces the 'Brazil cost'
Rejected	Prevents the increase of the 'Brazil cost'
Removed by the author	Prevents the increase of the 'Brazil cost'
Shelved	Prevents the increase of the 'Brazil cost'

Source: Author's analysis.

The very same criterion also applies to the case of propositions that were filed due to the approval of other proposals. If industry is in favour of the bill that was actually approved, with or without restrictions, then the decision is considered a case of success. If industry is opposed to the bill, with or without restrictions, then the decision is considered a case of failure. When the approval of a bill simultaneously files two or more propositions, the decision is only classified once, to avoid the multiple counting of the same event.

The opposite occurs in the other three cases. If the opinion of industry is in favour of a bill, with or without restrictions, and it is rejected, removed by the author or shelved at the end of the legislature session, then the decision should be understood as a failure for industry. On the other hand, if the opinion of industry is opposed to the bill, with or without restrictions, and the bill is rejected, removed or shelved, then the decision should be conceived as a political success for industry.

Table 9.2 shows that the political successes of industry can be divided into two groups. The first group comprises the successes that effectively *reduce the Brazil cost*. This is what happens, for example, when a bill supported by industry becomes law. The same thing happens when a bill is filed due to the approval of another bill that industry supports. Both cases involve a concrete *gain*, that is, a change of the status quo for the better, according to the point of view of industrial entrepreneurs. Successes that form the second group have a different meaning. These successes *impede the increase of the Brazil cost*. This type of success occurs when industry is opposed to a proposition and it is rejected, removed or shelved. All cases involve *relief* for industry, inasmuch as despite a real risk of a worsening of the status quo, it was successfully maintained.

Table 9.3 illustrates that the political failures of industry can also be divided into two groups. The first consists of propositions that *increase the Brazil cost*. This type of failure occurs when a proposition opposed by industry becomes law. It also occurs when a bill is filed due to the approval of another bill that industry rejects. From the perspective of industrial entrepreneurs, in both cases there was a *loss*, because the status quo changed for the worse. In the other three cases, something different takes place. Failures

Table 9.3 Impact of cases of failure on the 'Brazil cost'

Decisions	Impact on the 'Brazil cost'
New rule of law	Increases the 'Brazil cost'
Filed	Increases the 'Brazil cost'
Rejected	Prevents the reduction of the 'Brazil cost'
Removed by the author	Prevents the reduction of the 'Brazil cost'
Shelved	Prevents the reduction of the 'Brazil cost'

Source: Author's analysis.

that constitute the second group *prevent the reduction of the Brazil cost*. They occur when entrepreneurs from the industrial sector favour propositions that are rejected, removed or shelved. In these cases, despite an opportunity for improvement of the status quo this opportunity was not grasped. The result for industry is *frustration*, since the status quo was maintained instead of improved.

Before moving on to the discussion of results, it is necessary to recognize a limit inherent to the method adopted, which can be summed up as follows: verifying the occurrence of a success does not correspond to saying that the success occurred *on account of* the political influence of industry. The concept of influence has a *causal* connotation. Saying that player *A* influences player *B* as regards decision *x* is to say that the behaviour of *B* in the case of decision *x* alters in the respect desired by *A*. The desire of *A* is the cause, while the behaviour of *B* is the effect (Dahl 1988: 26–7). The basis of every causal argument is counterfactual reasoning (King et al. 1994: 76–82). In this manner, declaring that the influence of a player is the cause of an observed decision involves declaring that said decision did not stem from other factors and that, therefore, it would not have happened – or would be different – if the player had not exercised its influence.

We will take as an example the five types of decision that permanently end the progress of a legislative proposition: *shelving* at the end of the legislature session; *removal* by the author; *rejection*; the approval of another proposition that *files* it; or *transformation into law*. In the first three types of decision, attributing cases of success to the influence of industry would be tantamount to saying that, instead of any other factor, it was lobbying in opposition to the legislative propositions that determined the shelving, the removal or the rejection of proposals. In the remaining two types of decision, attributing cases of success to the influence of industry would consist of affirming that, instead of any other factor, it was the lobbying in favour of effectively approved legislative propositions that provoked the approval of those propositions. However, under no circumstances does the information produced by the application of the method support the counterfactual reasoning that political successes of industry would not have taken place if industry had not performed its lobbying, whether defensive or offensive. Consequently, the

Table 9.4 Decisions classified as successes or failures of industry

Decisions	Total (%)
New rules of law	77 (30.9)
Propositions rejected	50 (20.1)
Propositions removed by the author	29 (11.6)
Propositions shelved at the end of the legislature session	93 (37.3)
Total	249 (100.0)

Sources: Brazilian Federal State (n.d.); CNI (n.d.).

Table 9.5 Result of the decision, by type of decision

	Rules of law	Rejected	Removed	Shelved	Total
Success	62 (80.5)	32 (64.0)	13 (44.8)	57 (61.3)	164 (65.9)
	3.3	–0.3	–2.5	–1.2	
Failure	15 (19.5)	18 (36.0)	16 (55.2)	36 (38.7)	85 (34.1)
	–3.3	0.3	2.5	1.2	
Total	77 (100.0)	50 (100.0)	29 (100.0)	93 (100.0)	249 (100.0)

Note: χ^2 = 14,006 (0.003).
Sources: CNI (n.d.); CNI, *Legislative Agendas of Industry* (1996–2006).

information generated by the method does not permit the attribution of the result of the legislative process to the influence of industry.

Table 9.4 contains decisions classified as successes or failures for industry. Out of a total of 249 cases, 77 decisions (30.9 per cent) became law; 50 bills (20.1 per cent) were rejected through decisions made in committees or in the plenary sitting of the Chamber, the Senate or National Congress; 29 propositions (11.6 per cent) were removed at the initiative of the actual author; and 93 proposals (37.3 per cent) were filed in the Chamber or in the Senate at the end of the legislature session.

Table 9.5 presents the results obtained with the employment of the method outlined earlier for identifying the successes and failures for industry.

The last column of Table 9.5 shows that, irrespective of the type of final decision made, industry obtains success in no fewer than 65.9 per cent of the cases considered (164 successes for a total group of 249 decisions). Thus, in general, approximately two cases of success occur for each case of failure experienced by the sector.[7] Among new laws, there are significantly more cases of success for industry (80.5 per cent against 19.5 per cent). Among the propositions rejected and the propositions shelved at the end of the legislature session, the percentage of successes is much higher than the percentage of failures (respectively, 64 per cent as opposed to 36 per cent and 61.3 per cent as opposed to 38.7 per cent), but is slightly lower than what occurs in general. Only among

Table 9.6 Result of the decision by impact on the status quo

	Changes the status quo	Maintains the status quo	Total
Success	62 (37.8)	102 (62.2)	164 (100.0)
Failure	15 (17.6)	70 (82.4)	85 (100.0)
Total	77 (30.6)	172 (69.4)	249 (100.0)

Notes: χ^2 = 10,650 (0.001) ϕ = 0.207 (0.001).
Sources: CNI (n.d.); CNI, *Legislative Agendas of Industry* (1996–2006).

the propositions removed by its author is it possible to observe a prevalence of failures over successes (55.2 per cent against 44.8 per cent).[8]

Table 9.6 rearranges the information offered by Table 9.5 to emphasize the impact that cases of success or failure of industry exercise on the Brazil cost.[9] The first row of the table shows that 37.8 per cent of political successes for industry (62 successes) are obtained with the approval of new legislation that reduces the Brazil cost. This therefore represents a concrete gain for the sector, as it changes the status quo for the better as perceived by industry. The first row also shows that 62.2 per cent of the political successes of industry (102 successes) are of a different nature. They do not represent direct gains for the sector, but produce relief by means of the rejection, removal or shelving of bills that, if approved, would increase the Brazil cost and change the status quo for the worse.

The second row indicates failures. Of these, 17.6 per cent (15 failures) represent real losses for industry, given the approval of legislation of which the sector disapproves. The said failures worsen the status quo and increase the Brazil cost. However, 82.4 per cent of the failures (70 failures) are of a different kind and consist of wasted opportunities that *frustrate* industry. These are bills that would reduce the Brazil cost if they were approved, but that in fact were rejected, removed or shelved at the end of the legislature session, thus preserving the status quo instead of improving it. Although the frequency of successes that reduce the Brazil cost is lower than the frequency of successes that prevent its increase, it is possible to affirm that there are significantly more cases of success that change the status quo – and significantly fewer cases of success that maintain the status quo – than expected. It is also possible to affirm that there are significantly more cases of failures that maintain the status quo – and significantly fewer cases of failures that change the status quo, bringing real losses – than expected.[10]

The elevated degree of political success of industry in relation to decisions that change the status quo can be explained, to a large extent, by the alignment of the sector's interests with the final version of the propositions drawn up by the executive branch, which is predominant in national legislative production. Recent studies have demonstrated that the executive branch dominates federal legislative production in Brazil (Figueiredo and Limongi 2000, 2001). In accordance with this work, the capacity of

Brazilian presidents to dictate the agenda of the parliament derives from two factors.

The first factor is the ample legislative powers that the constitution of 1988 granted to the executive branch of the government. The President can issue provisional decrees (*medidas provisórias*) that take effect as of their publication, provoking immediate alteration of the status quo; can request that his bills be treated as urgent, thus unilaterally forcing the examination of propositions that he presents within a given timeframe; and can partially or totally veto the propositions that the parliament sends for his sanctioning. In addition, the President has the exclusive prerogative of initiating legislation relating to federal administration and of formulating the annual budget bill, which members of parliament can amend, but that has a limit to expenditures that cannot be raised.

Second, the capacity derives from the use of political resources to build majority coalitions of support in parliament. In this aspect, the role of political party leaders is crucial. Presidents negotiate with the leaders of the political parties that will form their basis of support and offer control over public offices and political influence in the government in return for support from these parties. The possession of these resources enables leaders to reward loyal members of parliament and punish those disloyal to the party orientation. Hence the leaders can fulfill, by means of party discipline, their part of the agreement: to guarantee the support of their parties to the proposals of the executive. Having far-reaching legislative powers and with the discipline of a majority allied base, the President can, to a large extent, determine the propositions that will be considered by the federal legislative branch of the government, and when they will be considered.

In this scenario, where the executive branch intervenes heavily in the promotion of legislation, in general it is reasonable to assume that the same predominance will appear in the subgroup of laws that interest industry the most. Hence the fortune of industry as regards political decisions that change the status quo will depend, to a large extent, on congruence between its opinion and the texts resulting from bills of the executive branch. Successes that produce tangible gains will occur frequently if the level of congruence is high; failures that entail losses will be frequent if the level of congruence is reduced.

The general trend in legislative production is also evident among the propositions considered the most important to industrial entrepreneurs, as shown in Table 9.7.[11] Among the decisions that result in new law and therefore change the status quo – whether these are classified as successes or failures for industry – decisions referring to bills of the executive branch are clearly predominant over those referring to bills of the legislative branch. In the particular case of successes, the proportion of decisions relating to bills of the executive attains 80.6 per cent (50 of 62), while in the case of failures the proportion corresponds to 73.3 per cent (11 of 15).[12] As such, the crucial

Table 9.7 Origin of bills by result of the decision and impact on the status quo

	Success		**Failure**		
	Changes the status quo	**Maintains the status quo**	**Changes the status quo**	**Maintains the status quo**	**Total**
Executive	50 (80.6) 9.2	8 (7.8) –7.0	11 (73.3) 3.4	13 (18.6) –3.0	82 (32.9)
Legislative	12 (19.4) –9.2	94 (92.2) 7.0	4 (26.7) –3.4	57 (81.4) 3.0	167 (67.1)
Total	62 (100.0)	102 (100.0)	15 (100.0)	70 (100.0)	249 (100.0)

Note: χ^2 = 110,596 (0.000).
Sources: CNI (n.d.); CNI, *Legislative Agendas of Industry* (1996–2006).

advantage to industry is that its position tends to converge with laws resulting from bills of the executive branch. The first column of Table 9.7 shows that convergence occurs in 50 cases, while the third column shows that divergence occurs in only 11 cases. That is, for a total of 61 laws originating from bills of the executive branch, the success/failure ratio is approximately 4.5 to 1. In other words, for two episodes of failure for industry, in which the status quo is perceived by industry to change for the worse and the Brazil cost increases, there are more than nine episodes of political success, in which the status quo changes for the better and the Brazil cost decreases.[13]

The trend in favour of the approval of bills from the executive branch coexists with the trend opposed to the approval of bills from the legislative branch. This statement is correct in general and, in particular, for the subgroup of bills that are most relevant to industry. Table 9.7 reveals that, among the decisions that maintain the status quo, decisions relating to bills of the legislative branch clearly surpass those relating to bills of the executive branch – regardless of the qualification of these decisions as successes or failures for industry. In the case of successes, the proportion of decisions relating to bills of the legislative branch attains the extremely high mark of 92.2 per cent (94 of 102), while in the case of failures the proportion is 81.4 per cent (57 of 70).[14] In this manner, when bills from the legislative branch fail to be approved, the decision to maintain the status quo instead of modifying it represents relief for industry and not frustration. The second column of the table shows that there are 94 episodes in which the decision made corresponded to relief (62.2 per cent of the unapproved bills from members of parliament) and the fourth column shows that there are 57 frustration events (37.8 per cent of the bills not approved). That is, for a total of 151 decisions referring to bills from the legislative branch that were not approved, the number of successes is approximately 65 per cent higher than the number of failures.

To summarize, Table 9.7 indicates that successes for industry prevail over failures in the two most common situations: when bills of the executive branch are transformed into law and when the bills of the legislative branch fail to be approved. In other words, industry is simultaneously benefited by the two predominant trends in the Brazilian legislative production process: on the one hand, there is the trend in favour of the approval of bills from the executive branch, and this trend works in favour of industry, given the high degree of affinity of the sector with government proposals; on the other hand, there is the trend opposed to the approval of bills of the legislative branch, and this trend also works in favour of the segment, as the majority of proposals from members of parliament are interpreted as threats and not as opportunities. Successes are also more frequent than failures in a less common situation: when the bills of the legislative branch are transformed into law. In the 16 cases where this occurs, there are 12 successes (75 per cent) and four failures (25 per cent), which corresponds to three political successes for industry for every failure. Finally, a predominance of failures over successes is only verified in one circumstance: when the bills from the executive fail to be approved. In this uncommon circumstance, the aforementioned affinity of industry's agenda with the agenda of the executive explains why episodes of frustration (13 observations) surpass episodes of relief (eight observations).

The data from Table 9.8 allow us to verify that successes predominate over failures in all the items that comprise the Brazil cost. Of these, the highest percentage of successes can be found among social infrastructure propositions (education, health and social welfare). In this component, the level of success attains the high mark of 78.9 per cent of cases. The level of success is also higher than the general level (65.9 per cent) in two other components of the Brazil cost: among labour legislation propositions (76.1 per cent) and among those relating to material infrastructure (69.6 per cent). The degree of success is lower than the general level among the propositions relating to financing costs (62.5 per cent), to the regulation of economic activity (60.5 per cent) and to the tax system (54.3 per cent).[15]

What can be said when the successes and failures for industry in each component of the Brazil cost are evaluated in terms of the impact they produce on the status quo? In each component, what is the proportion of successes that effectively changes the status quo by bringing about tangible gains for industrial entrepreneurs? What is the proportion of successes that brings relief to the sector, preventing the worsening of the status quo? Component by component, is the proportion of successes of each type always similar to the proportion observed in general, as shown in Table 9.6? Or are there relevant variations? Concerning failures, what is the proportion of decisions that causes real loss in each component? What is the proportion of decisions that frustrates the hopes of industry? Does the proportion of failures of each type, in each component, closely

Table 9.8 Result of the decision, by component of the decision

	Regulation of the economy	Labour legislation	Financing cost	Material infrastructure	Tax system	Social infrastructure	Total
Success	52	51	5	16	25	15	164
	(60.5)	(76.1)	(62.5)	(69.6)	(54.3)	(78.9)	(65.9)
	–1.3	2.1	–0.2	0.4	–1.8	1.3	
Failure	34	16	3	7	21	4	85
	(39.5)	(23.9)	(37.5)	(30.4)	(45.7)	(21.1)	(34.1)
	1.3	–2.1	0.2	–0.4	1.8	–1.3	
Total	86	67	8	23	46	19	249
	(100.0)	(100.0)	(100.0)	(100.0)	(100.0)	(100.0)	(100.0)

Note: $\chi^2 = 8,589$ (0.127).
Sources: CNI (n.d.); CNI, *Legislative Agendas of Industry* (1996–2006).

Table 9.9 Result of the decision, by impact of the decision on the status quo, controlled by component of the decision

Component	**Result**	**Changes the status quo**	**Maintains the status quo**	**Total**
Regulation of the economy	Success	32 (61.5)	20 (38.5)	52 (100.0)
	Failure	5 (14.7)	29 (85.3)	34 (100.0)
	Total	37 (43.0)	49 (57.0)	86 (100.0)
Labour legislation	Success	5 (09.8)	46 (90.2)	51 (100.0)
	Failure	1 (06.3)	15 (93.8)	16 (100.0)
	Total	6 (09.5)	61 (90.5)	63 (100.0)
Financing cost	Success	3 (60.0)	2 (40.0)	5 (100.0)
	Failure	–	3 (100.0)	3 (100.0)
	Total	3 (37.5)	5 (62.5)	8 (100.0)
Material infrastructure	Success	10 (62.5)	6 (37.5)	16 (100.0)
	Failure	–	7 (100.0)	7 (100.0)
	Total	10 (43.5)	13 (56.5)	23 (100.0)
Tax system	Success	4 (16.0)	21 (84.0)	25 (100.0)
	Failure	7 (33.3)	14 (66.7)	21 (100.0)
	Total	11 (23.9)	35 (76.1)	46 (100.0)
Social infrastructure	Success	8 (53.3)	7 (46.7)	15 (100.0)
	Failure	2 (50.0)	2 (50.0)	4 (100.0)
	Total	10 (52.6)	9 (47.4)	19 (100.0)
	Total	77 (30.9)	172 (69.1)	249 (100.0)

Regulation of the economy	**Labour legislation**	**Financing cost**	**Material infrastructure**	**Tax system**	**Social infrastructure**
$\chi^2 = 18.39$ (0.000)	Fisher = (1,000)	Fisher = (0.196)	Fisher = (0.007)	Fisher = (0.298)	Fisher = (1.000)
$\varphi = 0.462$ (0.000)	$\varphi = 0.053$ (0.664)	$\varphi = 0.600$ (0.090)	$\varphi = 0.580$ (0.005)	$\varphi = 0.202$ (0.170)	$\varphi = 0.027$ (0.906)

Sources: CNI (n.d.); CNI, *Legislative Agendas of Industry* (1996–2006).

follow the proportion observed in Table 9.6? Table 9.9 provides the answers to these questions.

The data from Table 9.9 supplement the information from Table 9.8. Successes predominate over failures in all the components that comprise the Brazil cost, but the prevalent type of success in each component is not always the same.

There are two components in which a significant predominance of political successes that give rise to tangible gains for industry can be noticed: regulation of the economy and material infrastructure.[16] Successes that alter the status quo for the better are also a majority among decisions relating to financing costs and to social infrastructure, but in this case the superiority is not statistically

Table 9.10 Successes: Origin of the bills, by impact of the decision on the status quo, controlled by component

Component	Origin	Changes the status quo	Maintains the status quo	Total
Regulation of the economy	Executive	26 (100.0)	–	26 (100.0)
	Legislative	6 (23.1)	20 (76.9)	26 (100.0)
	Total	32 (61.5)	20 (38.5)	52 (100.0)
Labour legislation	Executive	5 (41.7)	7 (58.3)	12 (100.0)
	Legislative	–	39 (100.0)	39 (100.0)
	Total	5 (09.8)	46 (90.2)	51 (100.0)
Financing cost	Executive	2 (100.0)	–	2 (100.0)
	Legislative	1 (33.3)	2 (66.7)	3 (100.0)
	Total	3 (60.0)	2 (40.0)	5 (100.0)
Material infrastructure	Executive	8 (100.0)	–	8 (100.0)
	Legislative	2 (25.0)	6 (75.0)	8 (100.0)
	Total	10 (62.5)	6 (37.5)	16 (100.0)
Tax system	Executive	4 (100.0)	–	4 (100.0)
	Legislative	–	21 (100.0)	21 (100.0)
	Total	4 (16.0)	21 (84.0)	25 (100.0)
Social infrastructure	Executive	5 (83.3)	1 (16.7)	6 (100.0)
	Legislative	3 (33.3)	6 (66.7)	9 (100.0)
	Total	8 (53.3)	7 (45.7)	15 (100.0)
Total		62 (37.8)	102 (62.2)	164 (100.0)

Regulation of the economy	Labour legislation	Financing cost	Material infrastructure	Tax system	Social infrastructure
$\chi^2 = 32.50$ (0.000)	Fisher = (0.000)	Fisher = (0.400)	Fisher = (0.007)	Fisher = (0.000)	Fisher = (0.119)
$\varphi = 0.791$ (0.000)	$\varphi = 0.594$ (0.000)	$\varphi = 0.667$ (0.136)	$\varphi = 0.775$ (0.002)	$\varphi = 1$ (0.000)	$\varphi = 0.491$ (0.057)

Sources: CNI (n.d.); CNI, *Legislative Agendas of Industry* (1996–2006).

significant. Hence it can be observed that for these specific components of the Brazil cost, the predominant type of success is different from the type that prevails for the general set of decisions, as shown in Table 9.6. In another two components – labour legislation and tax system – what predominate are precisely defensive political successes, which provide relief to industry through rejection, removal or shelving of bills, the approval of which would increase the Brazil cost. In these cases, however, the frequency of defensive successes observed is not significantly higher than the expected frequency.

Table 9.10 helps us to understand why, in some components of the Brazil cost, successes that confer gains to industrial entrepreneurs stand out, while in other components successes that cause relief form the majority.

The difference among the components of the Brazil cost as regards the prevailing type of success is mainly explained by the origin of bills. The executive branch wrote most of the bills for regulation of the economy and material infrastructure that resulted in successes for industry. In both cases, the trend in favour of the approval of bills from the executive operated at full power: all the bills of the executive were transformed into law.[17] The percentage of this type of success was increased a bit more in the two components due to the approval of some bills originating from the legislative branch. In the case of bills relating to financing costs, two from the executive branch were also approved, but individually they would be insufficient to guarantee the prevalence of successes that reduce the Brazil cost. This prevalence occurred because a bill of the legislative branch obtained approval. Something similar occurred in the case of bills relating to social infrastructure: five bills of the executive branch (83.3 per cent) were approved, but alone they would not guarantee the prevalence of successes that reduce the Brazil cost. The prevalence occurred because three bills from the legislative branch were approved.

On the other hand, members of parliament wrote most of the bills relating to labour legislation and to the tax system. The trend opposing the approval of bills of the legislative branch was fully active for these two components, as all the bills of deputies and senators were rejected, removed or shelved, which determined the predominance of relief for industry.[18]

The consistent inferiority of failures in relation to successes, irrespective of the Brazil cost component, is not the only fact that attracts attention. It should also be emphasized that in no component of the Brazil cost can the preponderance of more dangerous political failures for industry, those that impose effective losses on the sector, be verified. In almost all the components of the *Legislative Agenda*, the vast majority of failures consist of decisions that disappoint industry, through the rejection, removal or shelving of bills that it supports – precisely the same type of failure that prevails in the general set of decisions (Table 9.6). The exception consists of social infrastructure propositions, in which the frequency of the two types of failures is the same.

The origin of bills also helps to understand why the frustration of opportunities is the most frequent type of failure in almost all the components of the Brazil cost – as indicated in Table 9.11.

Except in the case of social infrastructure bills, the legislative branch was the origin of most bills that resulted in failures for industry. The trend of opposing the approval of bills from members of parliament was apparent in practically all the components of the Brazil cost. Accordingly, the defeats of industry consisted predominantly of frustration arising from the impossibility of realizing the potential benefits promised by proposals from members of parliament.

Table 9.11 Failures: Origin of bills, by impact of the decision on the status quo, controlled by component

Component	Origin	Changes the status quo	Maintains the status quo	Total
Regulation of the income	Executive	3 (30.0)	7 (70.0)	10 (100.0)
	Legislative	2 (08.3)	22 (91.7)	24 (100.0)
	Total	5 (14.7)	29 (85.3)	34 (100.0)
Labour legislation	Executive	1 (50.0)	1 (50.0)	2 (100.0)
	Legislative	–	14 (100.0)	14 (100.0)
	Total	1 (06.3)	15 (93.7)	16 (100.0)
Financing cost	Executive	–	–	–
	Legislative	–	3 (100.0)	3 (100.0)
	Total	–	3 (100.0)	3 (100.0)
Material infrastructure	Executive	–	2 (100.0)	2 (100.0)
	Legislative	–	5 (100.0)	5 (100.0)
	Total	–	6 (100.0)	7 (100.0)
Tax system	Executive	6 (75.0)	2 (25.0)	8 (100.0)
	Legislative	1 (07.7)	12 (92.3)	13 (100.0)
	Total	5 (33.3)	11 (66.7)	16 (100.0)
Social infrastructure	Executive	1 (50.0)	1 (50.0)	2 (100.0)
	Legislative	1 (50.0)	1 (50.0)	2 (100.0)
	Total	2 (50.0)	2 (50.0)	4 (100.0)
Total		12 (16.7)	60 (83.3)	72 (100.0)

Regulation of the economy	Labour legislation	Financing cost	Material infrastructure	Tax system	Social infrastructure
Fisher = (0.138)	Fisher = (0.125)	Fisher = –	Fisher = –	Fisher = (0.003)	Fisher = (1)
$\varphi = 0.279$ (0.104)	$\varphi = 0.683$ (0.006)	$\varphi =$ –	$\varphi =$ –	$\varphi = 0.693$ (0.001)	$\varphi = 0.000$ (1)

Sources: CNI (n.d.); CNI, *Legislative Agendas of Industry* (1996–2006).

Conclusions

The industrial business community has emerged as a political player strongly interested in the reduction of the Brazil cost, that is, in the implementation of public policies that the sector deems necessary to improve the competitiveness of companies based in Brazil in relation to companies located in other countries.

With this purpose, industrial entrepreneurs have undertaken extensive collective work to identify, among the bills running in National Congress, those with a greater potential impact on the Brazil cost; to define a unified opinion about the most relevant bills; and to disseminate their opinion during the decision-making process. This joint work has been coordinated by the CNI, primarily via the *Legislative Agenda*, a publication that has synthesized and expressed the standpoint of the country's industrial segment annually since 1996.

Brazilian industry has not only been capable of identifying bills referring to the Brazil cost and of defining and defending its viewpoint in relation to them, but has also obtained a high rate of lobbying success – a conclusion supported by the systematic comparison of positions adopted by industry and the content of the final decision about bills from the *Legislative Agenda*. Successes prevail over failures, both among decisions that change the status quo – that is, there are more gains than losses – and among decisions that maintain the status quo – that is, there is more relief than frustration. Successes that maintain the status quo are more frequent than successes that alter it; yet the chance of success of industry in relation to decisions that change the status quo – and, therefore, have greater practical consequences – is greater than the chance of success in relation to decisions that preserve it. The most frequent type of political failure is precisely the most inoffensive – the type that provokes frustration of expectations, but does not cause real loss.

This situation, which is extremely positive for industrial entrepreneurs, exists mainly because the two principal trends of the Brazilian legislative process operate in favour of the segment: on the one hand, because of the high degree of affinity of the sector with legislation originating from propositions of the federal government, the trend of the approval of bills by the executive branch generally benefits industry; on the other hand, the trend of non-approval of bills of the legislative branch benefits rather than handicaps industry, as it assesses the majority of proposals presented by representatives and senators as a threat to its interests.

Successes predominate over failures in all the components of the Brazil cost and, in spite of variations in the degree of success from one component to another, the observed incidence of success is not significantly lower than the expected incidence in any of them.

The two main trends of the federal legislative process also help to explain the predominant type of success and of failure in each component of the Brazil cost. In some components – especially regulation of the economy and material infrastructure – there is a clear superiority of successes that change the status quo for the better, generating gains for industry, over the successes that maintain the status quo, causing relief. Hence for these cases, the usual type of political success is the opposite of the most frequent type in general. To a large extent, this result occurs because the executive branch proposes the majority of bills that give rise to successes for industry. The trend in favour of the approval of bills from the executive, associated with industry's affinity with legislation originating from bills of the executive, explains the high frequency of gains in both cases. In other components of the Brazil cost – labour legislation and tax system – what can be seen is a clear preponderance of successes that offer relief. The result is mainly explained by the fact that most of the bills that produce such successes derive from bills from members of parliament that represent a risk to the interests of industry, but that are subject to the trend of non-approval of bills originating from the legislative branch. In practically all the components of the Brazil cost – except social infrastructure – what prevails is the same type of failure that prevails in general: the less prejudicial failure that produces frustration instead of loss. This occurs, to a large extent, because in almost all the components the noteworthy majority of decisions classified as failures refer to bills from members of parliament, which corresponded to the interests of industry, but were not approved.

The degree of success obtained by the industrial sector appears significant. Yet it should be acknowledged that there is insufficient evidence to affirm that political successes occurred *because of the lobbying* performed throughout the legislative process by the industrial entrepreneurs and/or representatives of their interests. It should also be acknowledged that the impressive rate of political success attained by industry refers to a precise historical period, from the mid-1990s to the mid-2000s. The fact that the National Congress recovered its political prerogatives in full as a result of the redemocratization that began in the mid-1980s suggests the need to consider whether the business community has always maintained such a high level of success in the federal legislative process. An investigation of broader historical scope could possibly ascertain that the preponderance of successes in the period analysed is an exception to the rule. Going forward, there is nothing to guarantee that the current situation favouring the business community will continue, and nothing to prevent the situation from taking a change for the worse. In politics victories are often fleeting, and the dynamic nature of the political process makes the majority of successes obtained by a social player in the present subject to reversal in the future.

Notes

1. In addition to commercial opening, the liberal inflection also involved other measures that were (and continue to be) introduced in the country with a varied pace and depth, such as privatizations, the concessions of utilities to private enterprise, the greater opening to direct foreign investment, financial liberalization, the deregulation of economic activity, fiscal discipline, administrative reform, tax reform and the review of priorities for public expenditures. The content of the liberal inflection implemented in Brazil corresponds largely to what Williamson (1993) designated the 'Washington consensus', a set of policies towards which several countries from Latin America, Eastern Europe and other parts of the world converged with varied intensity from the 1980s.
2. Speech by President Fernando Henrique Cardoso on 23 August 2001, at the ceremony of investiture of Sérgio Amaral as minister of development, industry and foreign trade.
3. See Saboia and Carvalho (1997); Ferraz et al. (1997); Bonelli and Gonçalves (1998); Haguenauer et al. (2001); Miranda (2001).

4. Naturally, this does not mean that all the political decisions that reduce the Brazil cost benefit all companies. For example, a law that offers more assurance to electronic commerce directly benefits companies that make regular use of this mechanism, in proportion to the frequency of use. In this case the 'non-excludability' consists of extending the benefit of the law to all the companies that utilize electronic commerce either in the present or in the future.
5. The Brazilian system of representation of industrial interests has a 'dual' structure (Diniz and Boschi 1979). On the one hand, industrial companies are free to form as many associations as they wish. On the other hand, they are obliged to pay a financial contribution (the 'union contribution', also known as the 'union tax') to the official system of interest representation – the 'corporatist' system. The corporatist system has three levels, and it is the same for every sector of the Brazilian economy (that is, industry, agriculture, commerce, financial services and so on). The first level is formed by *unions*. The Brazilian Constitution establishes the 'union unicity', which consists in attributing to only one union the right of officially representing all companies of a same economic category that are located in its region. Companies are obliged to pay the 'union contribution' for the union that officially represents them, in a sum that varies according to the capital owned by the company. Sixty per cent of the money remains with the unions. The second level is formed by *federations*, which encompass unions from diverse economic categories. In the case of industry, there is one Federation of Industry for each of the 26 states, and there is one Federation for the Federal District. Fifteen per cent of the money goes to this level. The third level is formed by *confederations*. In the case of industry, there is only one confederation: the Confederação Nacional da Indústria (CNI/National Confederation of Industry). Five per cent of the money remains at this level. The remaining 20 per cent goes to the Ministry of Labour and Employment.
6. CNI's Legislative Affairs Unit (COAL) kindly granted the researcher access to LEGISDATA, in an infrequent and praiseworthy example of transparency.
7. There is solid evidence against the hypothesis that there is no association between the type of final decision and the result attained by industry. Indeed, the *chi-square* test indicates a very low risk of error (0.003) in sustaining the alternative hypothesis, that is, that the type of final decision and the result obtained by industrial entrepreneurs are associated. In this chapter, the hypothesis of dissociation will not be rejected when 'type I' risk of error (to reject the null hypothesis when it is true) is higher than 0.05.
8. The adjusted residual is calculated for each cell of a contingency table (see Agresti 1996: 31–2). For each cell, it indicates if there are significantly more – or significantly fewer – cases than would be expected if the variables were not associated. The adjusted residual indicates that there are significantly more cases than expected when it is higher than 1.96. On the other hand, it indicates that there are significantly fewer cases than expected when it is lower than –1.96. When it is situated between –1.96 and 1.96, it indicates that there is no significant difference between expected and observed numbers of cases. The statistical package used rounds the values of adjusted residuals to the nearest first decimal place. Therefore, adjusted residuals will be considered statistically significant when its value is equal or higher than 2.0.
9. The *chi-square* test suggests that the risk of error is very small (0.001) in rejecting the hypothesis of disassociation between the variables and in accepting the opposite hypothesis that the result obtained by industry and the effect of the political decision on the status quo are associated.

10. These affirmations are based on the result of the *phi* test (φ). When the result of the *phi* test is positive and statistically significant, it indicates that there are significantly more cases on the main diagonal of the table than to be expected if the variables were not associated. When it is negative and statistically significant, it indicates that there are significantly more cases on the opposite diagonal than to be expected if the variables were dissociated. In this article, I consider that the result of the *phi* test is statistically significant if the *p-value* is equal to or less than 0.05.
11. There is solid evidence of association between the authorship of bills and the impact of final decisions on the status quo, as the *chi-square* test suggests that the risk of error involved in affirming that said association exists is remote (0.000).
12. The analysis of adjusted residuals indicates that, *in both cases*, there are significantly more decisions relating to bills of the executive than to be expected if the origin of the bills and the impact of final decisions on the status quo were not associated. The magnitude of adjusted residuals indicates that the difference between the quantity of cases observed and expected is much more ample among successes than among failures.
13. Of the 61 laws, 44 (72.1 per cent of the total) came from bills presented by the Cardoso government. Of these, 36 are classified as successes (81.8 per cent), while the other eight are classified as failures (18.2 per cent). Successes also surpass failures among the three norms (5 per cent of the total) that came from bills of the Collor government (two successes and one failure); among the five norms (8.2 per cent of the total) originating from bills from the Franco government (five successes) and among the nine norms (14.7 per cent of the total) originating from bills of the Lula government (seven successes – 77.8 per cent; and two failures – 22.2 per cent).
14. The analysis of adjusted residuals indicates that, *in both cases*, there are significantly more decisions referring to bills of the legislative than to be expected in the case of independence between the origin of bills and the impact of final decisions on the status quo. The magnitude of adjusted residuals indicates that the difference between the quantity of cases observed and expected is much higher among successes than among failures.
15. The *chi-square* test does not offer evidence against the hypothesis that there is no association between the components of propositions and the result attained by industry. In fact, the risk of error in rejecting the null hypothesis is very high (0.127).
16. The risk of error in affirming that the result of the decision and the effect of the decision on the status quo are associated is remote for the two components (respectively, 0.000 and 0.007). For the two components, the *phi* test indicates that there are more cases of success that change the status quo and of failures that preserve it than is to be expected in the absence of association. The *chi-square* test of independence of variables is not suitable for 2×2 tables in which the number of cases expected in any cell is lower than 5. For these tables, I examined the hypothesis of independence with *Fisher's exact test*.
17. The tests reveal that the risk of error in rejecting the hypotheses of independence between the origin of the bill and the type of success in case of regulation of the economy (0.000) and material infrastructure (0.007) is small. In both cases the *phi* test indicates that the main diagonal of the table concentrates more observations than would be expected if the variables were independent.
18. The tests present solid evidence against the hypothesis of independence in the case of labour legislation and tax system bills – in both, the risk of type I error is

equal to 0.000. Also, in these two cases the *phi* test indicates that the main diagonal of the table concentrates more observations than would be expected by the hypothesis of independence of variables.

References

Agresti, Alan (1996) *An Introduction to Categorical Data Analysis* (New York: John Wiley & Sons).

Almond, Gabriel and G. B. Powell Jr (1972) *Uma Teoria de Política Comparada* (Rio de Janeiro: Zahar Editores).

de Aragão, Murillo (1994) *Grupos de Pressão no Congresso Nacional: Como a Sociedade Pode Defender Licitamente Seus Direitos no Poder Legislativo* (São Paulo: Maltese).

——— (1996) 'A ação dos grupos de pressão nos processos constitucionais recentes no Brasil', *Revista de Sociologia e Política*, 6/7 (1996), 149–65.

——— (2000) *Brasil e Argentina: Abordagem Comparada sobre Grupos de Pressão no Poder Legislativo*, PhD thesis (Brasília, DF: Centro de Pesquisa e Pós-Graduação sobre a América Latina e Caribe, Universidade de Brasília, DF).

Birchal, Sérgio (2002) 'Globalização e desnacionalização das empresas brasileiras: 1990 a 1999', in Ana Maria Kirschner, Eduardo R. Gomes and Paola Cappellin (eds), *Empresa, Empresários e Globalização* (Rio de Janeiro: Relume Dumará/FAPERJ).

Bonelli, Regis (2000) *Fusões e Aquisições no Mercosul*, Discussion paper No. 718 (Brasília, DF: IPEA).

Bonelli, Regis and Robson R. Gonçalves (1998) *Para Onde Vai a Estrutura Industrial Brasileira?*, Discussion paper No. 540 (Brasília, DF: IPEA).

Brazilian Federal State (n.d.) *SICON-SF, Sistema de Informações do Congresso Nacional* (database) (Brasília, DF: Federal State), at: www6.senado.gov.br/sicon/PreparaPesquisa.action (accessed July 2003).

CNI (Confederação Nacional da Indústria) (1996a–2006) *Agenda Legislativa da Indústria* (Brasília, DF: CNI, annual publications for the years 1996, 1997, 1998, 1999, 2000, 2001, 2002, 2003, 2004, 2005, 2006).

——— (1996b) *Custo Brasil: Agenda no Congresso Nacional* (Brasília, DF: CNI).

——— (1998) *Custo Brasil: O Que Foi Feito, o Que Ainda Precisa ser Feito* (Brasília, DF: CNI).

——— (n.d.) *LEGISDATA* (database) (Brasília, DF: CNI), at: www.legisdata.cni.org.br (accessed July 2003).

Dahl, Robert (1988) *Análise Política Moderna* (Brasília, DF: Editora da Universidade de Brasília).

Diniz, Eli and Renato Boschi (1979) 'Autonomia e dependência na representação dos interesses industriais', *Revista Dados*, 22, 25–48.

——— (1997) *O Legislativo como Arena de Interesses Organizados: A Atuação dos Lobbies Empresariais*, mimeo.

——— (2000) 'Globalização, herança corporativa e a representação dos interesses empresariais: Novas configurações no cenário pós-reformas', in Renato Boschi (ed.), *Elites Políticas e Econômicas no Brasil Contemporâneo: A Desconstrução da Ordem Corporativa e o Papel do legislativo no Cenário Pós-Reformas* (São Paulo: Fundação Konrad Adenauer).

Ferraz, João Carlos, David Kupfer and Lia Haguenauer (1997) *Made in Brazil: Desafios Competitivos para a Indústria* (Rio de Janeiro: Editora Campus).

Figueiredo, Argelina and Fernando Limongi (2000) 'Presidential Power, Legislative Organization and Party Behavior in Brazil', *Comparative Politics*, 32 (2), 151–70.

Figueiredo, Argelina and Fernando Limongi (2001) *Executivo e Legislativo na Nova Ordem Constitucional* (São Paulo: Editora FGV-FAPESP).

Haguenauer, Lia, Luiz Dias Bahia, Paulo Furtado de Castro and Márcio Bruno Ribeiro (2001) *Evolução das Cadeias Produtivas Brasileiras na Década de 90*, Discussion paper No. 786 (Brasília, DF: IPEA).

Hardin, Russell (1982) *Collective Action* (Baltimore: Johns Hopkins University Press).

King, Gary, Robert Keohane and Sidney Verba (1994) *Designing Social Inquiry* (Princeton: Princeton University Press).

Miranda, José Carlos (2001) *Abertura Comercial, Reestruturação Industrial e Exportações Brasileiras na Década de 1990*, Discussion paper No. 829 (Brasília, DF: IPEA).

Moe, Terry (1988) *The Organization of Interests* (Chicago: University of Chicago Press).

Oliveira, Ribamar (2002) 'Emprego', in Bolívar Lamounier and Rubens Figueiredo (eds), *A Era FHC: Um Balanço* (São Paulo: Cultura Editores Associados).

Olson, Mancur (1965) *The Logic of Collective Action: Public Goods and the Theory of Groups* (Cambridge, MA: Harvard University Press).

Sabóia, João and Paulo M. de Gonzaga Carvalho (1997) *Produtividade na Indústria Brasileira: Questões Metodológicas e Análise Empírica*, Discussion Paper No. 504 (Brasília, DF: IPEA).

Samuelson, Paul (1954) 'The Pure Theory of Public Expenditure', *Review of Economics and Statistics*, 36 (4), 387–9.

Sandler, Todd (1992) *Collective Action* (Ann Arbor: University of Michigan Press).

Vianna, Maria Lucia T. W. (1994) *Lobismo: Um Novo Conceito para Analisar a Articulação de Interesses no Brasil*, Texto para Discussão No. 25 (Rio de Janeiro: Centro de Estudos de Políticas Públicas/CEPP).

——— (1998) *A Americanização (Perversa) da Seguridade Social no Brasil: Estratégias de Bem-Estar e Políticas Públicas* (Rio de Janeiro: IUPERJ-UCAM/Editora Revan).

Williamson, John (1993) 'Democracy and the "Washington Consensus"', *World Development*, 21 (8), 1329–36.

10
Government–Industry Partnership in South Africa: Social Bias in the Automotive Industry

Martin Kaggwa

Introduction

Addressing economic and social disparities created by the legacy of apartheid was one of the priorities of the new democratic government in South Africa (Bruggemans 2004: 67). A key socioeconomic objective of the government was to create a better life for the poor, the vulnerable and the excluded in society through economic empowerment. As such, post-apartheid national development strategies were designed in a way that would serve this objective. While the role of the corporate sector in achieving socioeconomic objectives was clearly recognized, the space provided for the sector to participate in and influence the national policy process varied greatly.

The government provided homes, running water, health services and electricity to previously neglected communities (Visser 2004: 7). The direct involvement of government in efforts to meet the socioeconomic aspirations of the majority of South Africans, however, had limitations in as far as job creation was concerned. Although gainful employment was key, the number of people the public sector could employ was limited. Much of the potential for job creation resided in industrial activities that remained firmly under the control of the corporate sector, as was the case during the apartheid regime (Chabane et al. 2006: 549). The main challenge government faced concerned coming up with creative ways to partner with the private sector to stimulate the level of economic activity in a way that generated significant employment opportunities.

The corporate sector was wary of what it perceived to be the 'interventionist-developmental' state model pursued by the new government. Business groups argued that such an approach would be detrimental to national economic growth, as it would lead to a rise in national debt, inflationary pressures and escalation of taxes and the national trade deficit (Kotze 2000: 84). The South Africa Foundation (SAF) spearheaded the campaign to clearly communicate this macroeconomic point of view (Handley 2005: 215). With membership comprising 50 of South Africa's largest firms, its opinion could not be ignored by the new government. Recognition of the critical role of the corporate sector in meeting the socioeconomic objectives of the new government, on the one hand, and the strong scepticism of how the sector could be partnered with in this regard, on the other, had a bearing on the structuring of national development strategies implemented following the 1994 democratic transition in South Africa. The ensuing partnership between government, labour and the corporate sector opened up opportunities for the corporate sector to influence post-apartheid policy at national and industry levels in South Africa.

This chapter looks at the impact of this government–labour–industry partnership upon the country's automotive industry policy and its implication for the industry's socioeconomic objectives. The chapter is organized as follows. The first section explores broadly how post-apartheid government–labour–industry dynamics have influenced national policy as it relates to social and labour market issues. In this regard, the changing role of the private sector, organized labour and government under the Reconstruction and Development Programme (RDP) and the Growth, Employment and Redistribution (GEAR) programme is reviewed. The second section reviews the advent and factors leading to government adoption of the Motor Industry Development Programme (MIDP), one of the first industry policy frameworks formulated through a consultative process between government, organized labour and industry. The third section focuses on automotive industry performance under the MIDP, examining both economic and social outcomes of the government–industry–labour partnership. The fourth section analyses the extent to which industry has progressed towards becoming globally competitive, as an indicator of sustainability of benefits from the consensus-based automotive policy. The final section reflects on how the government–industry–labour partnership can serve national social aspirations in a 'quasi'-liberalized economy based on the South African automotive experience.

Changing role of the corporate sector on South Africa's policy space under RDP and GEAR

The government–labour–industry partnership and its impact on automotive industry policy can be better understood in the context of the changing role of the corporate sector in the country's national policy space. The broad national policy framework adopted by the post-apartheid government in South Africa included the Reconstruction and Development Programme of 1994 and the Growth, Employment and Redistribution of 1996. The institutional forums linked to these programmes provided the spaces within which government–business–labour dynamics played out in influencing national policy direction. Two challenges were at the heart of devising and formulating the national development frameworks: 1) growing the economy in a liberalized international environment by taking advantage of global markets that the country had access to after the lifting of trade embargos; and 2) ensuring that nationals equitably shared benefits from the growing economy. There was a general acknowledgement that the domestic market could not support the higher economic growth needed to meet the country's socioeconomic aspirations. Domestic market limitations and the need to enter international markets necessitated liberalization of the national economy. Hence, the 1994 political transition in South Africa was also closely followed by the phased liberalization of the national economy. Economic liberalization, however, limited the South African government's control of domestic industry and interfered with intentions to influence domestic economic activities in a manner that supported national socioeconomic priorities.

An outright embrace of economic liberalization was prevented, in part, by organized labour, which had forged an alliance with the new government. Intensive lobbying by organized labour under the Congress of South African Trade Unions (COSATU) led to the country's adoption of COSATU's RDP. A redistributive and socially inclined development strategy, RDP was posited as the best means of tackling poverty in South Africa (Kotze 2000: 92). The programme's six basic principles were: 1) an integrated and sustainable programme; 2) a people-driven process; 3) peace and security for all; 4) nation-building; 5) linking reconstruction and development; and 6) democratization of South Africa (ANC 2007: 1). The RDP also included an explicit commitment to increase participation of black people in national economic activities through Black Economic Empowerment (BEE).

Despite the explicit recognition of the need for the corporate sector to participate in its implementation, RDP's prioritization of social concerns relegated the influence of the corporate sector on national policy. The programme put far more emphasis on achieving social objectives than on the needs or role of the corporate sector in the national development effort. This could be attributed to the untested relationship between the new government and the corporate sector. To further encourage national dialogue, the National Economic Development and Labour Advisory Council (NEDLAC) was formed in 1995 to bring together the state, organized business, labour and community groupings to discuss and try to reach consensus on issues pertaining to national social and economic policy (Knight 2006: 7). Although corporate sector participation was encouraged, little flexibility was granted at the NEDLAC forum and, as a result, the private sector's influence upon the national policy direction was minimal. This was unsurprising, given that the RDP was a politically driven policy framework – having been presented as part of the African National Congress (ANC) manifesto during the 1994 campaigns, it was considered a binding agreement between government and the people that elected it to power. Therefore, the corporate sector was expected to participate in mapping out how to implement the RDP, but not to influence the direction or objectives of the national framework.

Despite the high priority placed on achieving national socioeconomic objectives and political consensus under which the RDP was constituted, the programme was replaced by GEAR after only two years of implementation. The termination of RDP was motivated, partly, by the realization that the programme's objectives were too ambiguously defined to be achievable. Terreblanche (2003: 109) and Meyer (2000: 2) contend that the RDP was too broadly formulated and ended up as a wish list for many people. Moreover, the economic growth trend realized in the first two years of the programme was less than what had been anticipated. The new government had hoped for economic growth rates of 4 to 6 per cent per annum but actual growth was only slightly above the natural population growth rate of 2.5 per cent (Midgley 2001: 270). Underperformance on the economic front sounded a warning bell for potential failure to realize social objectives in the medium and long term. The intertwined nature of social and economic objectives and the fact that government could not consider success on one without the other became evident (Gray 2006: S53). The clear need to enrol the corporate sector, combined with its lukewarm attitude to the RDP, motivated government technocrats to devise a new programme that the corporate sector would support without strong reservations.

Under GEAR, the government redefined its role in the national development process as that of creating a conducive environment for private investment. Social and labour market issues ceased being the central focus of government intervention. Instead, GEAR placed a strong emphasis on economic development driven by the private sector and elevated the role of business in national development policy. Unlike RDP, GEAR strategy was not cross-sector consensus-based but, rather, drafted by technocrats who were more inclined to a neoliberal approach to economic development. Implicit in the GEAR framework was the relegation of social priorities and the strong focus on economic growth. The economy had to realize high economic growth in order to serve national social aspirations. Fiscal discipline, inflation control through inflation targeting and interest rate management became the major preoccupation of government technocrats. The neoliberal school of thought underpinning GEAR proposes that the relation between economic and social objectives is a causal one, from economic to social aspiration. People's welfare is market-driven and, as a result, market-dependent (Gray 2006: S57). In the long term, benefits of economic growth spill over down to the masses. Hence, priority had to be given to economic growth even if it meant sacrificing social objectives in the short term under GEAR.

Although government–labour–business consultative forums like NEDLAC and BEE efforts were maintained under GEAR, the people-oriented development policy under RDP was shelved. Under GEAR, the corporate sector was given far more space to participate in national policy formulation and review. Endorsement of government policy by the corporate sector became a standard procedure in national and sector policy implementation. Moreover, since technocrats strongly inclined to liberal economic policies spearheaded GEAR, the corporate sector had a clearly defined and friendly constituency to lobby. To a large extent, government influence on national policy direction was compromised during the GEAR era.

South Africa's Motor Industry Development Programme (MIDP)

At industry level, the 1994 reintegration of South Africa into the global economy after many decades of economic isolation created a new challenge in sustaining domestic industrial production. Previously, domestic industries had been protected from external competition; as such, they could afford to produce at suboptimal levels. One of the industries that had thrived under the protection curtain was the automotive industry. Despite producing many models at uncompetitively low levels, the high vehicle prices in the domestic market ensured its continued profitable existence. A significant employer, with direct employment of more than 100,000 people, the automotive industry supported a number of locally based component manufacturers. With the opening up of the domestic automotive market, vehicles produced at cheap locations in the world could be imported in the country with minimum restrictions. In line with the 'tariff-jumping' theory, there was a possibility that some of the locally based vehicle manufacturers could opt to shift production to cheaper locations in light of dismantled barriers to the South African market. Market liberalization had a potential to reduce industry investment, domestic production, and subsequent upstream and downstream benefits derivable therefrom. In recognition of this, government took the initiative to invite labour and industry to jointly map out the future of the industry, given the economic and social problems that could result if the industry were to collapse under international competitive pressures.

Consultations between government, labour and industry on how to sustain domestic automotive industry growth under the new market conditions culminated in the state's adoption of the MIDP in 1995. Under the programme, government undertook to offer the automobile industry duty-free allowances and import rebates based on the levels of local content exported, pricing of vehicles being produced, and on the value of investment in productive assets, including research and development.

The overarching objective of the MIDP was to support the industry in becoming competitive in the long term. The programme also had specific stated social and economic objectives:

- Vehicle affordability to domestic buyers: In this regard, a small vehicle incentive in the form of an additional duty-free allowance was to be granted to domestically based vehicle manufacturers in respect of motor vehicles below a net ex-factory selling price of 40,000 rand (R). The incentive was to be phased out over a period of three years.

- Employment: The focus was to create permanent employment opportunities that would provide employees with current income but also offer medical and retirement benefits. It was anticipated that direct employment in the industry would have a downstream employment multiplier effect in sectors like the motor retail and after markets, vehicle insurance and vehicle financing. Due to the influence of the industry in the MIDP formulation process and despite the importance attached to job creation by the new government in South Africa, the employment objective under the MIDP was toned down to read that the programme objective, in this regard, was to stabilize rather than create employment.
- Local supplier development: Since South Africa did not have its own vehicle brand, the intention for the government was to motivate and facilitate increased vehicle assembly in the country in a way that allowed sourcing of local components from domestic manufacturers. It was envisaged that by facilitating business relationships between domestic component manufacturers and global vehicle manufacturers, the domestic industry would be enabled to participate in the global automotive value chain to which the country had been denied due to economic embargos under apartheid.
- Improvement of industry trade balance: This would mean that the industry would earn more money from the international markets than it would spend there, with resultant positive spin-offs going to the nationals (Thedti 1994: 68).

In implementing the MIDP, government opted for a public–private partnership (PPP) model. It set up a Motor Industry Development Council (MIDC) to be a forum for joint deliberation on the future of the domestic automotive industry. Representation at the MIDC included the government's Department of Trade and Industry, vehicle assemblers, automotive component manufacturers' associations and organized labour.

Government committed itself not to change policy relating to the industry without carrying out consultations with the industry stakeholders participating in the MIDC. In return, industry sectors had to provide their respective performance data for review at the MIDC. This allowed government and organized labour to monitor performance of the MIDP against its objectives, with a view of taking remedial measures in case of significant deviations. Representatives at the MIDC, including organized labour, could table for discussion any issue of concern pertaining to the MIDP. To create joint ownership of the industry policy, some form of consensus had to be reached at the MIDC before government could take forward the forum's recommendations.

Although no explicit dispute resolution mechanism was agreed upon in the implementation of the MIDP, provision was made for the MIDC to commission independent studies on contentious issues raised at the forum to support its recommendations. Organized labour, for example, requested the MIDC to commission a study to explore the retention and creation of employment in the automotive sector during 2005. This was done against the background of industry performance data showing that job creation in the industry lagged behind investment. As a result, organized labour became increasingly convinced that the MIDP was under-delivering on its employment objective while industry was adamant that this was not the case. Recommendations from this study were submitted to the MIDP review process, which at the time of writing was still ongoing.

Industry performance under the MIDP

After the inception of the MIDP, industry performance was vital in influencing dynamics between government, labour and industry in taking forward the country's automotive policy. As noted previously, the intention of the MIDP was to support and facilitate continued growth of the industry in the light of new domestic market conditions and global influences. The emerging trend of key industry performance variables was informative as to the extent to which socioeconomic objectives were being met. The performance provided the basis for continuation or alteration of the consensus-based MIDP policy framework.

Investment

Increased and sustained investment in the automotive industry, though not an explicit objective of the MIDP, was critical in the realization of the programme's success. High investment levels would permit increased productive activities and as a result were likely to increase industry demand for labour. Further still, external investment is known to be a potential conduit for new technology and specialized skills to a recipient country through the introduction of new machinery and offering relevant training to local employees to operate the machines (UNCTAD 2005: 15). Hence, there was expectation that industry investment would also be accompanied by acquisition of specialized and marketable skills by the local labour force.

Economic theory is unfortunately ambiguous on the relationship between liberalization and investment. Depending on market conditions, the opening up of a previously protected market may or may not increase investment. In the case of South Africa's automotive industry and in accordance with the tariff-jumping argument, there was a possibility that trade liberalization measures could result in a reduction in the cost of trade and would provide disincentives for inward investment on the part of manufacturers (UNCTAD 2003: 13). At the commencement of the MIDP in 1995, despite the protected regime under which the industry had been operating, seven global vehicle manufacturers – BMW, Daimler Chrysler, Volkswagen, Toyota, Fiat, Ford and Nissan – had invested and were operating in the country. General Motors and Peugeot had previously withdrawn production due to political pressure related to the apartheid regime. The highly protected South African automotive industry had been successful in attracting major global automotive companies prior to 1995, and it was therefore a widely accepted view that the liberalization of the industry should not lead to less investment. The fear however, was that domestic vehicle manufacturers would switch production to cheaper locations overseas and simply import products into South Africa under the relaxed trade regime. If this were to happen, it would jeopardize the objective of building a competitive economy that could sustain higher levels of labour absorption. Investment in the industry was, therefore, an important variable to keep track of as the industry opened up.

The MIDP seemed to reverse the falling investment levels. Vehicle manufacturers' investment jumped from R492 million in 1994 to R1,171 million in 1996, an increase of 138 per cent. By 1999, investment by the manufacturers had reached R1,511 million. Overall, between 1996 and 2005, the average annual growth rate of investment by original equipment manufacturers (OEMs) was 17.5 per cent. At the end of the first 10 years of the programme, the MIDP seemed to have been an effective policy in stimulating industry investment (see Figure 10.1).

However, since increase in industry investment was not desired for its own sake, it was prudent to consider how the increased investment had made gainful employment available to those previously excluded from participating in national economic activities. McAlinden et al. (2003: 7), using the case of the United States (US), argued that the automotive industry was, and could be, a significant employer and an important contributor to the economy. The expectation was that an increase in industry investment would be accompanied by increased employment. This, however, did not occur. Vehicle manufacturers' headcount decreased from 38,600 to 32,300 between 1995 and 2000. Despite the high industry investment realized during the MIDP period, vehicle manufacturers' headcount in 2005 was less than at the inception of the programme (Figure 10.1). To the extent that direct employment accruing to a particular investment was a proxy for socioeconomic benefits derivable therefrom, increased vehicle manufacturers' investment under the MIDP did not result in commensurate socioeconomic benefits to the populace in the period under consideration.

It should be acknowledged that people who happened to be employed by the industry benefited from specialized training offered by industry to enable them operate new machinery and equipment imported to manufacture vehicles in the country. Nonetheless, there was little evidence to support the assertion that a significant skills transfer, greater technology expertise and higher-paying jobs resulted from increased investment levels.

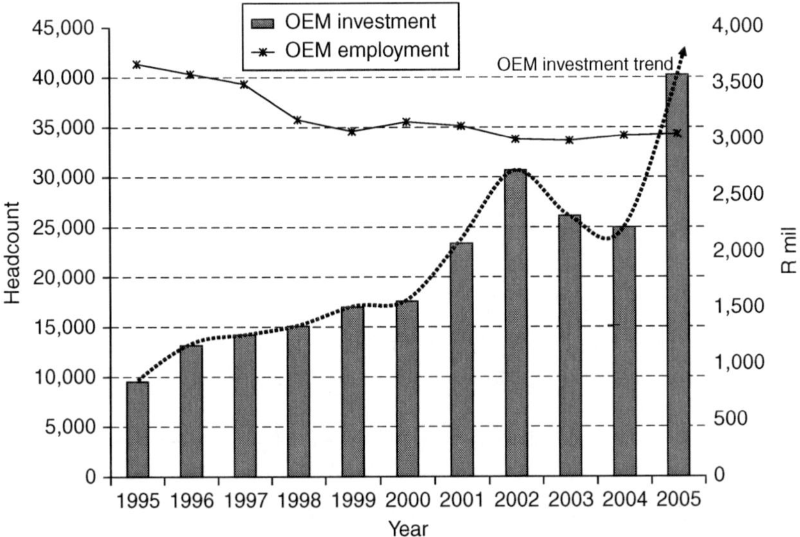

Figure 10.1 South Africa's OEM investment and employment, 1995–2005
Source: Adapted from NAAMSA (2007), 16–17.

Production and exports

Although investment was to be the driving factor for industry growth, it had to do so through increased production levels. The logic was that investment would increase production capacity and subsequently industry output, and increased production would lower average costs through the realization of economies of scale. Low average costs would contribute towards industry competitiveness and consequently to a larger market share in both domestic and international markets. The industry would be put on a high growth trajectory. Demand for factor inputs would increase, more people would be employed and sourcing of local components would be on the rise.

On average, production (units of vehicles produced) decreased by 1.4 per cent per year between 1995 and 2000. After 2000, production grew by an average of some 6 per cent. The MIDP exhibited limited ability to stimulate domestic production to high levels. This was a paradox that MIDP policy-makers had to contend with; the programme was delivering on desired investment but the effects of increased investment were not being realized in terms of increased production levels. This was not only limiting employment but also meant that the envisaged domestic component-sourcing levels would not be realized. If productivity was not decreasing, which was less likely because increased investment is often associated with improved technology, the production trend presented an anomaly that required further investigation.

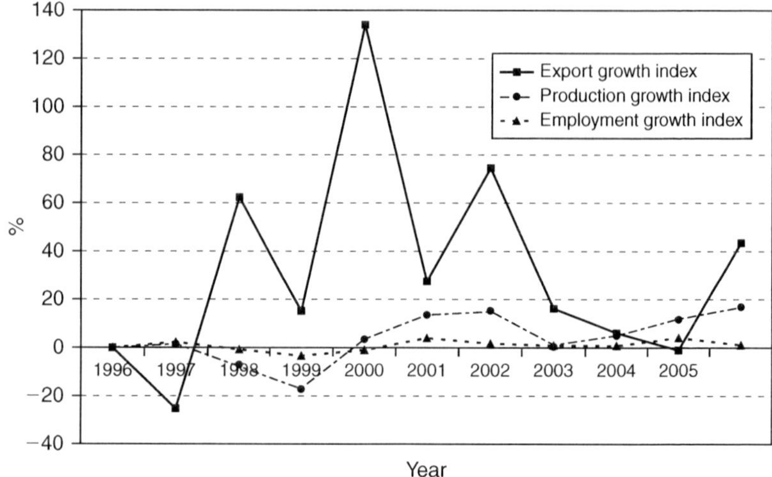

Figure 10.2 South Africa's automotive production, export and total-industry employment growth indices
Source: Adapted from NAAMSA (2007), 16, 22.

In as far as supply to international markets was concerned, the MIDP was successful in increasing automotive exports. Apart from an export reduction in 1996, average annual increase in automotive exports was above 20 per cent throughout the MIDP period. High export levels provided an opportunity for external income for the economy in general assuming that local content of exported products was substantial.

In terms of enabled employment creation, the total employment index growth remained static and below the production and export growth index (see Figure 10.2) – an indication, again, that the MIDP may have been under-delivering on its socioeconomic objectives in this respect.

Supplier development

The MIDP was intended to facilitate the integration of domestic component manufacturers into the global automotive value chain. It was envisaged that by supporting local vehicle manufacturers in supplying international markets, taking advantage of supply contracts negotiated and facilitated by their parent companies, domestic automotive component suppliers would be afforded an opportunity to participate in the global automotive business. Interactions between domestic component suppliers and domestic subsidiaries of global vehicle manufacturers would also have positive spin-offs in terms of technology transfer and process efficiency. The low pre-1995 production levels of local manufacturers were insufficient to support a vibrant, locally based automotive component sector. Yet, in the automotive industry, the component sector often has a bigger potential to create jobs and to stimulate domestic technological capabilities through spill-over effects (Humphrey and Memedovic 2003: 19). Supplier development, therefore, had to be part of the overall industry development strategy.

The extent to which local supplier development had taken place under the MIDP was an elusive aspect to evaluate as no explicit data was available from industry or government on this aspect. Assessment of local supplier development could only be done using proxies, such as local content use and component exports. Although supplier development could also be evaluated using other proxies, like the level of training that component manufacturers had received and the level of other positive externalities emanating from component manufacturers' interaction with vehicle manufacturers, relevant data was not obtainable and, where available, it was unreliable. As a result, local content use and domestic component sourcing remained the main indicators used to judge the extent to which domestic suppliers were enabled to participate in the global value chain of the automotive business. The extent to which subsidiaries of transnational OEMs sourced from domestic suppliers, as well as local content utilization in domestically produced completely built-up units (CBUs), were taken to be indicative of supplier development.

Bell and Madula (2003: 28) mention that the share of locally sourced components used in domestic vehicle assembly under the MIDP was on a downward trend. There was a substantial reduction in the share of locally sourced components as a proportion of total component usage, from 40.1 per cent in 1996 to 33.8 per cent in 2000. By implication, local component manufacturers were proportionally benefiting less from vehicle production by the domestic manufacturers. If the proportion of local components per each manufactured CBU were to continue on the same declining trend of 1996, it would mean that the MIDP was becoming less and less effective in supporting local component manufacturers despite industry growth that had started to pick up in 2000. The declining trend of local content use and of domestic component sourcing by vehicle manufacturers was expected to worsen as duties on imports decreased. It was anticipated that cheaper imports would find their way to the domestic market and would put more pressure on domestically produced components. At a qualitative level, sourcing of components from the local manufacturers was constrained by the 'follow-sourcing' phenomenon in the industry, a situation where international subsidiaries operating in a foreign location invite international suppliers to set up operations close to their main established customers worldwide, leading to a condition where the indigenous suppliers face difficulties in establishing business relationships with the subsidiaries (Ivarsson and Alvstam 2004: 27). As a result of follow-sourcing, local suppliers lose out on the opportunity to leverage on the relationship with international subsidiaries to increase their business operations, technological capabilities and process efficiency. Overall, supplier development was yet another deliverable on which the MIDP yielded disappointing results – the support and development of a vibrant local component-manufacturing sector did not play out as envisaged.

Vehicle prices

The gradual opening up of the domestic automotive market had a potential to benefit domestic consumers of automotive products by way of access to such products at lower prices. Prior to 1995, the automotive industry in South Africa had been producing too many models at a low and inefficient scale. The cost of inefficiency was passed on to domestic consumers by way of high prices. The opening up of the industry was expected to lead to competition between domestically produced and imported automotive products and would subsequently mitigate high domestic vehicle prices.

Failure to make vehicles affordable in the domestic market has important social consequences. Flatters and Netshitomboni (2006: 12) contend that the negative impact of vehicle prices on low-income groups is aggravated by the urban configuration legacies from the past that led to wide separation between work and accommodation. Apart from separation of people according to race, the apartheid regime concentrated most economic activities outside the residence areas of the majority of black people. Thirteen years after the introduction of the new democratic regime, the situation has changed little. In order to be gainfully employed or access quality services in education and health, previously disadvantaged people have to commute long distances from their home locations to urban areas. Access to affordable transport has a bearing on the likelihood that a previously disadvantaged person obtains gainful employment and improves his or her quality of life. For many of the employed people staying in the black townships, the cost of transport is an unavoidable expense that crowds out some of the income that would have otherwise served their social needs.

From 1995 to 1998, new vehicle price increases remained well below the domestic inflation rate measured in terms of consumer price index. The years in question were characterized by relative exchange rate stability, significant reductions in levels of protection and increased competition through the arrival of new importers and distributors in the local automotive industry (NAAMSA 2006: 7). The trend could not, however, be sustained – from 1999 to 2003 car price increases in the country were above domestic inflation according to the national inflation rate and vehicle price indexes (see Table 10.1). Although 2004 and 2005 saw the increase in vehicle prices return to below national inflation levels, previous increases in vehicle prices had already placed vehicles out of reach of average South Africans.

The failure of the MIDP to make vehicles affordable to domestic consumers has since become a point of contention between the trade unions and

Table 10.1 Inflation and vehicle price indexes in South Africa

Year	Inflation (% change in consumer price index for metropolitan areas)	% in vehicle price index for metropolitan areas
1995	8.7	
1996	7.3	2.7
1997	8.8	6.3
1998	6.7	4.3
1999	5.2	6.0
2000	5.4	7.2
2001	5.7	5.4
2002	9.1	9.4
2003	5.9	3.8
2004	1.4	−1.2
2005	3.4	−1.5

Source: Adapted from NAAMSA (2007), 7.

industry. The former contend that the MIDP has had skewed benefits in favour of locally based vehicle manufacturing subsidiaries, with little benefit to workers and the public. The industry was receiving a large subsidy from government by way of import rebates but this had not translated into lower vehicle prices for local consumers. The trade unions' position is supported by some academics who argue that MIDP incentives have been costly policy errors and that the attention given to the sector exceeds its contribution to the general welfare of the populace (Flatters 2002: 2).

One limitation to judging whether the MIDP was succeeding in reducing domestic vehicle prices was the fact that vehicle prices could also be dependent on other factors such as interest rates, financing options and packages, and insurance premiums. Vehicle financing institutions, vehicle dealers and the insurance industry had an impact on the pricing and accessibility of vehicles in the country. Despite the fact that vehicle prices could not be controlled within the confines of the MIDP policy framework, there was general understanding and agreement at the inception of the MIDP that a key objective of the programme included making vehicles affordable to the people. Therefore, a case can be made for the fact that because the MIDP was clearly expected to strive to find ways of making vehicles cheaper and affordable to domestic consumers, the programme could not be exonerated from the general failure to do so. By failing to reduce the cost of transport via vehicle affordability, the MIDP fell short of supporting the new government efforts to create more opportunities for previously disadvantaged South Africans to improve their quality of life.

Black Economic Empowerment in the automotive industry

Difficulties also arose in relation to industry compliance with the government's flagship initiative, Black Economic Empowerment (BEE). BEE is a national development initiative undertaken by the South African government to fast-track integration of previously disadvantaged black people into mainstream economic activities. The aim of BEE is to substantially increase the number of black people who have ownership and control of existing and new enterprises in strategic sectors of the economy (Knight 2006: 8). BEE is an explicit and proactive approach through which government seeks to expedite redress of socioeconomic imbalances in an economic environment dominated by previously advantaged sections of the population. The BEE strategy was part of the RDP initiative but has been carried forward under GEAR. Theoretically, the weakness of the MIDP model in delivering its socioeconomic objectives could be compensated for, partly, by success of the BEE initiative within the automotive industry. This, however, has also not been the case. Due to the complexities that surrounded BEE implementation and its potential negative effect on industry competitiveness, government opted for a flexible approach in implementing BEE at an industry level. Different sectors were allowed space to determine the nature and form of implementing BEE, given their specific circumstances. Sectors like mining and banking have since come up with their sector-specific BEE charters. The expectation was that the automotive industry would follow, but this has not happened.

The automotive industry agreed in principle to support the BEE initiative and even proposed that it would prefer to have a separate automotive BEE charter. However, the industry dragged its feet when it came to implementation. It argued that because all domestic vehicle manufacturers were subsidiaries of international companies, local managers lacked the mandate to make decisions on issues pertaining to BEE, particularly on ownership. In 2003, government came up with a refinement of the BEE initiative by issuing codes of good practice for Broad-Based Black Economic Empowerment (BBBEE). These included elements of human resource development, employment equity, enterprise development and preferential procurement as well as investment, ownership and control of enterprise and economic assets (Knight 2006: 8). Under the BBBEE, the automotive industry was provided with other elements, apart from ownership, on which it could deliver in terms of BEE.

Both the vehicle and component-manufacturing sectors have put in place taskforces to explore how BEE can be implemented in the industry, but still there is no automotive industry BEE charter after more than a decade since the commencement of the government BEE initiative.

Industry progress to competitiveness

Meeting socioeconomic objectives of the post-apartheid government in South Africa and sustaining economic growth benefits to the populace requires that government-supported growth initiatives are sustainable. Specific to gainful employment in the automotive industry, it was important that productive activities supported under the MIDP be sustained in the new competitive environment in which the country was operating. Attaining industry competitiveness was thus a necessary, though not sufficient, condition for sustaining socioeconomic benefits from the automotive industry. The MIDP was a well-intentioned programme intended to usher a previously protected industry into a competitive global environment in order to take advantage of new opportunities without losing achievements made thus far. The offer of incentives under the programme created a business case for continued production of vehicles and automotive components in South Africa as it offset costs related to the country's location disadvantage relative to major global markets.

Competitiveness refers to the ability of a firm or industry to increase in size, market share and profitability. Quoting the US Presidential Commission on Industrial Competitiveness, Clark and Guy (1998: 364) define competitiveness as 'the degree to which it (a nation) can, under free and fair market conditions, produce goods and services that meet the test of international markets while simultaneously maintaining and expanding the real income of its citizens'. The definition takes cognizance of the welfare effects of increased productive activities as a country captures bigger market shares. Some other authors have linked the definition of competitiveness with an increase in per capita income and employment (Oughton 1997: 1486). They argue that competitiveness is a product of increased productivity. To achieve competitiveness, output per each factor of production, including labour, has to increase, with other factors held constant. Assuming perfect market conditions or at least market conditions that support a positive correlation between reward for factor inputs and productivity, wage rates payable will increase with productivity. Competitiveness will therefore lead to an increase in gross domestic product (GDP) per capita and overall improvement in national welfare.

According to the *European Competitiveness Report 2004* (European Commission 2004), industry competitiveness can be assessed based on the extent to which an industry has defended, and/or gained, market share in open markets relying on price and/or quality of its goods. Common indicators for assessing industry competitiveness include growth rate or increase in domestic market share of locally produced vehicles and export growth rate (Narayanan 1998: 219). Competitiveness indicators for South Africa's automotive industry in the period 1995 to 2005 showed mixed results. The domestic market share of locally produced vehicles decreased from 93.2 per cent in 1995 to 71.6 per cent in 2004. From 2004 to 2005 sales of locally produced vehicles increased by 11.6 per cent, while that of imported vehicles increased by 70.2 per cent (NAAMSA 2006).

On the other hand, industry achieved high growth rates in vehicle exports between 1997 and 2001, indicating that more automotive products from

South Africa were being put on the global market. Favourable trade agreements and concessions that South Africa signed with trading partners contributed to making it profitable to carry out manufacturing in South Africa and then export to international markets. In particular the African Growth and Opportunity Act (AGOA) provided duty-free access for South African exports into the United States in respect of a broad range of products, including vehicles and automotive components. A vehicle model manufactured in South Africa would enter the US market without paying duties but if the same vehicle model were to be manufactured in Europe it would be subjected to import duties. AGOA resulted in many European companies delegating their South African subsidiaries to take over production for export contracts to the United States. The South African market continued to be of importance to vehicle assemblers but it was generally accepted that the market was not growing fast enough to sustain high and efficient vehicle and automotive component production.

In the context of the automotive industry in South Africa, however, export growth rates can be a weak proxy for international competitiveness. The offer of export-based import rebates, as an incentive under the MIDP, cushions domestic vehicle manufacturers from competitive pressure. Although increase in exports is a desirable effect of the MIDP, one has to take into account the government support received on exports before a statement on industry competitiveness based on increased exports can be made.

Still, if one was to consider the industry trade balance, as another proxy of industry competitiveness, it was unambiguous that the industry has a long way to go before it can be considered competitive. Oughton (1997: 486) points out that deteriorating trade balance and reducing world exports are indicative of declining competitiveness. South Africa's automotive industry trade balance has been deteriorating since the inception of the MIDP and the status quo was not helped by the introduction of the Productive Asset Allowance (PAA) incentive in 2000 which provided additional import rebates to industry. Continued deterioration in the industry trade balance puts into question the sustainability of industry growth and the achievement of the competitiveness objective. Yet competitiveness is critically important to determining the continued contribution of the automotive industry to the socioeconomic aspirations of the populace.

Social policy insights

Although the tripartite government–labour–industry partnership has been successful in guiding the integration of South Africa's automotive industry into the global automotive value chain in general, the increased role of industry in policy formulation has led to the relegation of the programme's social objectives and, as a consequence, to industry policy instability. The success of the industry under the MIDP has frequently been alluded to without considering the social outcomes of the programme. The increased influence of industry in policy formulation led to structuring of the programme in a way that put emphasis on industry performance outcomes without explicit reference to wider social outcomes. Investments, production, level of exports and industry profitability have received prominence in adjudicating industry success under the MIDP. Employment, community empowerment and corporate social responsibilities are hardly mentioned in the industry performance appraisal.

During the programme's implementation process, government and labour realized that the industry development model was under-delivering on wider social aspirations. As a result, government has been compelled to review the MIDP policy framework twice during the last 10 years. However, in each of the reviews, done by independent consultants, industry has actively participated and strongly lobbied for its interests (in particular business profitability) not to be compromised. Business associations spearheaded the lobbying within and outside the MIDC forum. At the MIDC forum, the associations argued strongly for why the MIDP incentive dispensation should not be changed. Outside the MIDC forum, the associations arranged meetings between industry corporate executives and senior government officials to reinforce the point that continued growth of the domestic industry was dependent on keeping MIDP in place (Le Roux 2007). In particular, they emphasized that the large geographic distance separating South Africa from its major markets dictated that the incentives be left in place to offset the logistics disadvantage (Venter 2007). In the end, without a strong basis to counteract industry proposals, government conceded to industry's demands, making only cosmetic changes to the initial MIDP model and agreeing to postpone a more fundamental review of the industry support model.

Recently, government and labour have clearly understood the extent to which their lack of analytical capacity and resources devoted to industry policy formulation (in comparison to industry) has disadvantaged them and contributed to inadequate outcomes. This realization has compelled them to begin carrying out rigorous policy effect inquiry prior to negotiations with industry. Government and organized labour have always been clear on how the MIDP should contribute towards the social welfare of the populace – increase permanent employment, acquire specialized skills and make automotive products affordable for the local population. Their proposals, however, have often lacked concrete suggestions on how the programme should be structured to deliver on the intended deliverables. Industry, on the other hand, has consistently engaged services of private experts to advise it on alternative support models under the MIDP dispensation and potential benefits therefrom, giving it advantage in the negotiation process.

Keeping the intended socioeconomic aspirations on the MIDP agenda and their subsequent realization will depend on the extent to which government and organized labour will match private business preparedness at the negotiation table, among other factors. Without a deeper understanding of the industry development model being promoted by the corporate sector, the government may end up buying in and even sponsoring a socially sub-optimal development initiative, for a long period of time, before questioning its effectiveness in delivering on social objectives.

Government and labour need to develop capacity to rigorously interrogate sector development models proposed by the corporate sector during negotiations and be in a position to suggest alternatives if required. Ensuring responsible lobbying processes and attaining general consensus on what the corporate-initiated development model should achieve is insufficient for the achievement of socioeconomic outcomes. The corporate sector can always find reasons to justify why the model is not delivering on the aspirations of its partners in a particular period. There will always be a possibility for the corporate sector to take advantage of the blanket endorsement of a particular development model by its development partners to further its own interests. In this regard, a capacity to understand, evaluate and assess development models has to be enhanced to match the competency and resources invested by the corporate sector. Model performance under different scenarios vis-à-vis its key objectives should be articulated. Implicit assumptions should be brought into light and questioned. One-to-one mapping between inputs to support the model and intended outcomes should be avoided. Factors that operate between the model input and model output space need to be considered because these are critical to understanding unintended outcomes of any development model. The state agency concerned should have the instruments and capabilities required to question, negotiate, monitor and, if warranted, suspend the benefits extended to the development model, both pre- and post-implementation.

Without this rigorous approach to policy engagement with the corporate sector, there is a high likelihood that the social aspirations of a national government will be sacrificed or diluted during the execution process of the development model. Moreover, there will be a tendency towards periodic agitation for policy change as government and labour realize that the model they supported is not meeting its expectations in terms of social deliverables. Potential changes cause policy uncertainty within an industry or sector and at the extreme may lead to less productive activity being planned due to the increased risk of doing business in the affected industry. The result, in this extreme case, is that all parties lose out. Government and labour fail to realize their socioeconomic aspirations on the one hand, and the corporate sector must contend with increased business risk and potential profitability declines in the long term on the other.

It is imperative that the negotiations concerning such particular development models be based on national economic and social objectives. Expectations should be realistically set, outcomes monitored and contingent remedial measures agreed upon in case of significant deviations from the intended outcomes of the intervention. Such measures will contribute to minimizing the policy discontinuity and negative social consequences characterizing South Africa's automotive industry. This does not, however exonerate government and labour from the duty to develop capacity and capability to articulate, interrogate or even develop alternative development models other than those suggested at the negotiating table by the corporate sector. This will require acquiring specialized skills in policy analysis and the identification of external expertise to support model articulation and analysis processes. Strengthening research units within government departments and labour organizations to carry out proactive research on topical social and economic issues in the country is of critical importance. Personnel within these research units should be trained and equipped with research skills comparable to those of the private sector consultants. In cases of internal human-skill constraints, government and labour should form partnerships with specialized research and academic institutions to carry out these research functions on their behalf. The ultimate aim is for government and labour to match the expertise and preparation of the industry at the negotiating table for carrying forward the domestic automotive industry. These proactive research initiatives have to be driven by senior managers in both government departments and organized labour organizations.

Conclusion

On balance, although the MIDP enabled the industry to participate in the automotive global value chain, the programme under-delivered on its socio-economic objectives. As a result, the previous consensus among government, labour and industry that the programme was an effective tool to support future economic vibrancy of the industry has been weakening.

The partnership between government, labour and industry has played a crucial role in guiding South Africa's automotive industry transition to a less protected market environment. All stakeholders, however, have not equitably enjoyed the benefits of this successful transition. Two major lessons can be learned from this case: 1) an industry level government–labour–business partnership can play an important role in supporting domestic industry growth in the globalization era if certain conditions are met; 2) domestic industry growth may, however, result in skewed benefits and may at times be achieved at a cost to the social aspirations of a country.

The MIDP's policy design, implementation and monitoring processes were transparent but were strongly characterized by information asymmetries. Government and labour were disadvantaged in terms of access to knowledge of and insight into internal industry workings. The capacity to assess proposed development models and, if needed, devise and articulate alternatives is critical to developing government–labour–industry partnerships that successfully address economic and social objectives. Otherwise, broad national social goals risk being sacrificed for the economic benefit of a few.

References

ANC (African National Congress) (2007) *The RDP of the Soul*, at: www.anc.org.za/ancdocs/policy/2007/discussion/rdp.html (accessed 28 May 2009).

Bell, Trevor and Nkosi Madula (2003) *South African Motor Industry Policy in a Cloud of Uncertainty*, paper commissioned by the National Union of Metalworkers of South Africa (NUMSA) (Johannesburg: National Institute for Economic Policy/NIEP).

Bruggemans, Cees (2004) 'Economic Policy and Democracy in South Africa', *Politeia*, 23 (3), 60–83.

Chabane, Neo, Andrea Goldstein and Simon Roberts (2006) 'The Changing Face and Strategies of Big Business in South Africa: More than a Decade of Political Democracy', *Industrial and Corporate Change*, 15 (2), 549–77.

Clark, John and Ken Guy (1988) 'Innovation and Competitiveness: A Review', *Technology Analysis & Strategic Management*, 10 (3), 363–95.

European Commission (2004) *European Competitiveness Report 2004*: at: http://ec.europa.eu/enterprise/enterprise_policy/competitiveness/doc/comprep_2004_en.pdf (2004) (accessed 28 May 2009).

Flatters, Frank (2002) *From Import Substitution to Export Promotion: Driving the South African Motor Industry*, at: http://qed.econ.queensu.ca/faculty/flatters/writings/ff_driving_the_motor_industry.pdf (accessed 28 May 2009).

Flatters, Frank and Nnzeni Netshitomboni (2006) *Trade and Poverty in South Africa: Motor Industry Case Study*, University of Cape Town's Southern Africa Labour & Development Unit (SALDRU) Trade and Poverty Project, at: www.tips.org.za/files/trade_flattersnetshitomboni.pdf (accessed 28 May 2009).

Gray, Mel (2006) 'The Progress of Social Development in South Africa', *International Journal of Social Welfare*, 25 (1), S53–S64.

Handley, Antoinette (2005) 'Business, Government and Economic Policymaking in the New South Africa, 1990–2000', *Journal of Modern African Studies*, 43 (2), 211–39.

Humphrey, John and Olga Memedovic (2003) *The Global Automotive Industry Value Chain: What Prospects for Upgrading by Developing Countries* (Geneva: United Nations Industrial Development Organization/UNIDO).

Ivarsson, Inge and Claes Göran Alvstam (2004) 'International Technology Transfer to Local Suppliers by Volvo Trucks in India', *Tijdschrift voor Economische en Sociale Geografie (Journal of Economic and Social Geography)*, 95 (1), 27–43.

Knight, Richard (2006) *South Africa 2006: Challenges for the Future*, South Africa Delegation Briefing Paper (New York: Shared Interest), November, at: http://richardknight.homestead.com/files/SouthAfrica2006-ChallengesfortheFuture.pdf (accessed 28 May 2009).

Kotze, Hendrik Jakobus (2000) 'The State and Social Change in South Africa', *International Social Science Journal*, 52 (163), 79–94.

Le Roux, Mathabo (2007) 'Costly MIDP Might Have Outlived Its Usefulness', *Business Day*, 30 July.

McAlinden, Sean H., Kim Hill and Bernard Swiecki (2003) *Economic Contribution of the Automotive Industry to the U.S. Economy – An Update*, a study prepared for the Alliance of Automobile Manufacturers (Ann Arbor: Economics and Business Group, Center for Automotive Research/CAR), at: www.cargroup.org/pdfs/Alliance-Final.pdf (accessed 28 May 2009).

Meyer, Michael J. (2007) *Globalisation: An Issue of Contestation and Struggle in South Africa* (2000), at: http://motspluriels.arts.uwa.edu.au/MP1300mm.html (accessed 20 September 2007).

Midgley, James (2001) 'South Africa: The Challenge of Social Development', *International Journal of Social Welfare*, 10 (4), 267–75.

NAAMSA (National Association of Automobile Manufacturers of South Africa) (2006) *National Association of Automobile Manufacturers of South Africa: Annual Report* (Cowies Hill, Durban: Balgair Publications).

——— (2007) *National Association of Automobile Manufacturers of South Africa: Annual Report* (Cowies Hill, Durban: Balgair Publications).

Narayanan, Kumar (1998) 'Technology Acquisition, De-Regulation and Competitiveness: A Study of the Indian Automotive Industry', *Research Policy*, 27 (2), 215–28.

Oughton, Christine (1997) 'Competitiveness Policy in the 1990s', *The Economic Journal*, 107 (444), 1486–1503.

Terreblanche, Sampie (2003) *A History of Inequality in South Africa, 1652–2002* (Pietermaritzberg: University of Natal Press).

Thedti (The Department of Trade and Industry of South Africa) (1994) *Board of Tariffs and Trade: Notice 1345 of 1994, Motor Industry Development Programme, Revised Proposals* (Pretoria: Thedti).

UNCTAD (United Nations Conference on Trade and Development) (2003) *World Investment Report. FDI Policies for Development: National and International Perspectives* (New York: UNCTAD).

——— (2005) *Economic Development in Africa: Rethinking the Role of Foreign Direct Investment* (New York: UNCTAD).

Venter, Irma (2007) 'Auto Policy Key to SA's Continued Competitiveness', *Engineering News*, 21 September.

Visser, Wessel (2004) '"Shifting RDP into GEAR". The ANC Government's Dilemma in Providing an Equitable System of Social Security for the "New" South Africa', paper presented at the 40th ITH Linzer Conference, Stellenbosch, 17 September, at: http://academic.sun.ac.za/history/downloads/visser/rdp_into_gear.pdf (accessed 28 May 2009).

11

New Standards and Partnerships in Latin America: Implications for Small Producers and State Policy

Paola Perez-Aleman

Introduction

This chapter brings together two issues that until now have been discussed separately: the rise of new standards in global supply chains and development policy. It presents these issues in order to develop a perspective that argues for the promotion of policies and strategies that combine competitiveness with both inclusion and social equity by improving the productive capacities and wellbeing of small producers in Mexico and Central America. As these countries move away from the previous focus on the 'Washington consensus' strategy, the recent rise of supply chain standards and transnational corporation–non-governmental organization (TNC–NGO) partnerships can provide some lessons for thinking about how to advance social development policies.

New standards that address social and environmental practices, focused on process and production conditions, are prominent today. This is a result of two factors: 1) visible and persuasive social movements and 2) the rise of environmental and health and safety regulations in the context of increasing trade integration. Especially since the 1990s, NGOs have organized activities and been part of social movement campaigns that aim to influence business practice on issues such as human rights, labour standards, environmental sustainability and poverty reduction (Bartley 2003; Spar and LaMure 2003). In many industries, such actions have led to new standards, codes of conduct and certification programmes that represent norms and practices that define expectations for more socially and environmentally sustainable production processes.[1] These new and wide ranging corporate codes of conduct and sustainability standards are tied up with an increasing number of associations, partnerships, collaboration or alliances made up of TNCs and NGOs.[2]

At the same time, globalization has widened the expansion of international trade under a regime of liberalization concurrent with a rise of health, safety and environmental regulations in Europe, North America and Japan (Vogel 1995). Trade agreements between nations leading to economic integration processes, as well as NGO mobilization, have influenced the rise of new public regulations, particularly in the European Union and North America. These international agreements, in turn, are having an important influence on national policies related to social and environmental issues in developing countries. For example, a recent study shows that the Central America Free Trade Agreement (CAFTA) has compelled the member countries' governments to enforce labour regulations (Schrank and Piore 2007).

Parallel to the above shifts in global (public and private) regulation, the national policies of Mexico and Central American countries have been tied until recently to the Washington consensus, focused on market liberalization and macroeconomic reforms, pursuing a narrow notion of competitiveness. For the past two decades, there has been a dichotomous development strategy as these countries approached competitiveness and poverty alleviation as two largely separate and unrelated agendas. On the one hand, competitiveness policy focused on creating a national business climate free of government intervention. On the other, social investment funds to compensate for macroeconomic reforms were at the centre of poverty-reduction efforts. Both of these neglected the development of the productive capacity of local producers, particularly smallholders and rural areas.

Existing research indicates that negative social consequences have resulted from the exclusion of small producers and small firms from both the definition and implementation of new regulations (standards) in the global economy and national-level competitiveness policies. Given widespread poverty in developing countries, this segment has a large presence and a substantial economic role, but often operates under arrangements that constrain their ability to survive and compete. Standards, especially when cumulative, can represent significant barriers to entry for poorer producers, small farms and enterprises.[3] They can lead to the concentration of production in the hands of large companies and estates, as poorer producers are excluded from markets because they are unable to meet the changes required by the new standards.[4]

The current debate on the new standards has centred on the private-versus-public nature of the regulations, with an ongoing tension between the voluntary and legal approaches to making improvements in the targeted social and environmental areas. A second line of research has focused on monitoring and compliance mechanisms. Many researchers have analysed the effectiveness of monitoring and auditing systems, the independence of monitors, and the variety of ways to evaluate corporate compliance.[5] However, research has not addressed the challenges in implementing these at the level of poorer producers and small suppliers, when attempting to comply with these standards. The developmental concerns, the impact on the poorer producers (small-scale farmers, small and micro-enterprises) and their ability to make improvements along the new standards have been marginal to most of the existing discussion (Clay 2005; Utting 2007).

Similarly, policy discussions of competitiveness have excluded the poorer groups. The national policy focus on 'business climate' has targeted macroeconomic reforms since the early 1990s, which brought macroeconomic stability and openness to foreign trade and investment. Competitiveness Committees created in each country and the National Competitiveness Agendas have included only the largest business groups and the wealthiest entrepreneurs (OECD 2006). Rural producers and small and medium firms have not participated in these policy circles. Little support for their productive activities meant a lack of technical services, infrastructure and credit to improve the productivity of their assets.

The efforts to foster competitiveness have focused on large enterprises. The poor who live in rural areas and those in the urban informal sector have remained largely disconnected from the competitiveness plans of the region (OECD 2006). Yet they are actively involved in sectors of the economy that hold great potential for growth but, because they are neglected, are in a state of economic depression. For example, coffee production is in the hands of small producers in regions lacking roads, potable water, electricity, laboratories for testing quality, and production infrastructure such as roasters (Mendoza 2000). Moreover, existing state policies have not connected the new environmental and social standards to efforts to improve the ability of small producers to access markets, a strategy that would require investment.

As Mexico and Central American constituencies are challenging the Washington consensus, there is an opening for policies that move beyond the previous trend described above. We can gain insights by examining how the implementation of new standards works when small producers are included. This chapter looks at TNC–NGO partnerships to see what lessons they might provide for social policy-making. How do sustainability standards, intertwined with the growth of TNC–NGO partnerships, successfully support the inclusion of small producers? What do they tell us about governance for development? Such an examination of TNC–NGO partnerships that include poorer groups could improve our understanding of the process of upgrading of social and environmental standards and inclusive development potential in developing economies.

The following sections discuss a global supply chain where small-scale producers in Mexico and Central America have an important presence. Using the case of the specialty coffee chain, and specifically the Starbucks and Conservation International (CI) alliance, I examine the evolution from standard-setting to implementation, and the conditions which foster the inclusion of poorer producers.

I suggest that this recent experience in elaborating and implementing new standards through TNC–NGO partnerships reveals possible routes for fostering inclusive development strategies. Though a private regulatory form, it can provide insights for thinking about the state's role in a post-Washington consensus era, and for strategies that combine poverty alleviation and competitiveness. In particular, TNC–NGO partnerships that follow an active assistance approach at the small-scale producer level show ways to build the capacities of small producers to meet the standards and create supporting conditions for development. The state, a broadly representative private sector, and NGOs have the potential to create policies that link social and economic development.

Standards, TNC–NGO partnerships, business and small producers

Little attention has been given to the dynamics of actually implementing the new codes and standards in developing economies, particularly from the perspective of small producers, who as suppliers carry out many of the activities that are the focus of social and environmental sustainability norms. Understanding this aspect is important because current studies reveal the implications of the new standards, which can threaten exclusion of the small producers and the further marginalization of the poor in developing countries. Increasing quality requirements as well as social and environmental norms limit the access of small businesses and poor producers to high-standard supply chains, and facilitate the extraction of rents by TNCs and developing-country elites.[6] For example, in Pakistan's soccer ball industry, the new norm set by global brands to remove child labour brought about loss of income and exclusion of the poorest, particularly women (Khan et al. 2007). Other studies highlight that small farmers in Africa and Latin America are excluded from export supply chains due to new norms, resulting in a shift in production to large industrial estate farms (Dolan and Humphrey 2000; Humphrey 2005). Another literature indicates the challenges developing-country firms face when attempting to shift their existing practices and adopt international quality standards that differ significantly from their traditional local ones.[7]

The challenges posed by the new standards have particular relevance for those concerned with poverty alleviation in developing economies. Existing literature suggests the need for more bottom-up and South-centred approaches in the standard-making process, which has been mainly discussed as 'corporate social responsibility' (CSR) (UNRISD 2003). But more research is needed that examines the design and implementation of global standards from the perspective of developing-country producers' conditions. How is the perspective of small-scale producers included or excluded in standard-setting and implementation? How can standards be made to work for poorer producers, and what are the mechanisms underlying when and how they work to benefit the poor? How do TNC–NGO partnerships work successfully to improve conditions for the poor and for their inclusion in global supply chains? What approaches to standard-making and implementation in developing economies work both for local producers and communities and for reaching sustainability goals?

These questions offer a window from which to address the challenges faced by poorer producers, who are often in isolated communities, where they lack services, infrastructure and ties with channels for export markets. As the rural sector remains a large reservoir of poverty, any effort to reduce it has to pay particular attention to rural areas. Compared to the rest of Latin America, poverty in Mexico and Central America remains primarily rural. The incidence of rural to urban poverty remains high in all countries; only Costa Rica and Panama register relatively lower rural poverty (ECLAC 2002). The share of the rural sector in total poverty is greater than 50 per cent in all countries except Mexico, where it is 33 per cent. In all countries, the share of extreme poverty that is rural is even higher, and above 50 per cent of total extreme poverty (De Janvry and Sadoulet 2001). Studies indicate that rural poverty decline has been mainly a result of out-migration to urban areas. Therefore, for rural and urban poverty reduction, the growth of new economic activities in rural regions is essential. Whether and how the small-scale producers are included or excluded from global markets has important social implications. This is why linking the discussions on standards and on development strategy can offer insights for future avenues.

The links between new standards and improvements of small producers have also been marginal to another process that has occurred parallel to the rise of the new forms of global regulation. The local policy agenda has centred on business competitiveness and integration. The most recent example of this is CAFTA, which entailed a set of reforms. Much political action by business groups in Central America in the period preceding CAFTA focused on creating a 'business climate' for competitiveness. The largest Central American enterprises and business groups have organized in Competitiveness Committees or Councils, from which many policy proposals originated. For example, measures to improve the 'business climate' included macroeconomic reforms, trade liberalization, customs regulations, ports and road infrastructure. Environmental and social dimensions have not been at the centre of the agenda of the large businesses and organizations represented in these committees. Nevertheless, international pressure from the United States (US) and labour and human rights organizations led the governments involved in regional trade agreements to reform their labour codes (Schrank and Piore 2007). However, local policy-making focused on competitiveness has been disconnected from policies for poverty alleviation.

Is there a way to connect the processes of global standard-creation and social and economic development? What lessons can TNC–NGO partnerships provide for thinking about policy strategies that include poorer groups? What insights do these partnerships provide concerning ways to connect state and society to further development goals?

Case study: the Starbucks and Conservation International partnership

The following discussion is based on the case of the partnership between the Starbucks Coffee Company and the NGO Conservation International (CI) that targeted small coffee producers in Mexico and Central American countries in an effort to foster sustainable production in the coffee value chain. An at least decade-long experience allows the study of how the TNC–NGO partnership evolved over time and of the nature of its activities.[8]

Small-scale family farms constitute an important sector in the global supply chain, producing over 70 per cent of the world's coffee in 85 Latin American, Asian and African countries (Bacon 2005). An estimated 85 per cent of Central America's coffee farmers are micro and small-scale producers (Bacon 2005). Starbucks is part of the global coffee supply chain, which includes small farms, large growers, processors, roasters and retailers (Ponte 2002). Coffee farms range in size from very small farms (under one hectare), to cooperatives, to large plantations. Whereas large plantations often process and export their own produce, the smaller producers, organized in cooperatives or independent family farms, typically sell their 'green beans' to processors or agents, who in turn sell to exporters.

Starbucks and the CI established a partnership, starting with a pilot phase in Chiapas, Mexico, expanding to other phases when Starbucks developed its own code of conduct for coffee purchasing in locations in Mexico, Nicaragua and Costa Rica. The CI is an international NGO that focuses on the conservation of global biodiversity. It is one of the 'big three' global conservation NGOs, along with the World Wildlife Fund and The Nature Conservancy. Starbucks is a specialty roaster and retailer, purchasing about 2 per cent of the global coffee supply, making it the largest purchaser of specialty coffee in the world (Starbucks Coffee Company 2005). The company buys green unroasted coffee from exporters, farmers and cooperatives, and sells it in retail stores and to foodservice accounts.

The partnership is representative of a growing number of alliances involved with sustainability standards (Linton 2005). NGOs have actively mobilized to create a more sustainable supply chain in the coffee trade. Starbucks faced several periods of NGO activism. First in 1994, when the Chicago-based, US/Guatemalan Labor Education Project (US/GLEP), launched a leaflet campaign at their retail outlets; then, in 1999 and 2000, when the Global Exchange NGO pressured Starbucks to begin purchasing Fairtrade coffee. Soon after, Starbucks signed a licensing agreement with TransFair to buy Fairtrade coffee for use in its retail outlets.

NGO pressure on Starbucks occurred simultaneously with a major coffee production crisis, due to a dramatic fall in world coffee prices in 1998–2002.[9] Small-scale farmers in Latin America, who live in relatively isolated higher-altitude areas, experienced increasing poverty in the face of the drop in coffee prices. Many small farmers pursued two survival strategies. First, tens of thousands left the coffee-growing regions of Mexico and Central America to migrate to urban areas and to the North (United States) (Murray et al. 2006). Others started switching to alternative agricultural activities, such as corn-growing and cattle-raising, which require more intensive land use and clearing of forest land (Lewis and Runsten 2007).

The threat of forest loss and the potential risk for continued coffee supply from the desired highland regions to support the growing specialty market nurtured the relationship between the CI and Starbucks. The CI had identified a link between their main goal (conservation) and the cultivation of coffee, which is grown in many of the 'conservation hotspots' that the CI was attempting to protect.[10] Farmers living on the edge of the conservation biospheres faced a dramatic decline in coffee prices, which exacerbated bad practices, including cutting more trees, introducing livestock, polluting water sources and resettling inside the biosphere reserves, as farmers tried desperately to earn a living (Millard 2005). Shade-grown coffee cultivation was the next best thing to conserving forest and could potentially provide farmers around the protected zone with a viable way of life. For its part, Starbucks' goal was to secure stable long-term access to high-altitude coffee sources.

In 1996–7, the CI's *Conservation Coffee Project* (CCP) was born in Chiapas, Mexico, with the goal of assisting farmers in shifting to shade-grown coffee cultivation (Millard 2005; Zettelmeyer and Maddison 2004). The project aimed to define and promote a set of land management practices to conserve biodiversity in the area adjacent to the El Triunfo Biosphere Reserve in Chiapas, by demonstrating that farmers could gain social and economic benefits. The pilot project started with six cooperatives comprising 1,000 small-scale coffee farmers in the buffer zone, together with initial funding from the Ford Foundation and the United States Agency for International Development (USAID) (Zettelmeyer and Maddison, 2004: 14). The CI approached Starbucks in 1997, attempting to secure a market for coffee that was grown using the best conservation practices. It hoped to create a market-based incentive system to improve the environmental and social impacts of coffee farming, processing and trading. If Starbucks, as a key buyer, could purchase their coffee supply from the *Conservation Project*, resulting in increased earnings for farmers, then they would gain a stable long-term supply of high-quality coffee while promoting the conservation of biodiversity (Zettelmeyer and Maddison 2004).

In 1998, the CI and Starbucks formally initiated their partnership with the purpose of collaborating on the *Conservation Coffee Project* in Chiapas. While the CI worked to convince local producers to adopt new production practices, Starbucks would agree to buy *Conservation Coffee*. In the initial stage, Starbucks provided a $150,000[11] grant but did not formally commit to purchase coffee. By 1999, Starbucks had established a new coffee brand, *Organic Shade Grown Mexico*, which was the product emerging from the CI's *Conservation Project*. In 2000, Starbucks and the CI renewed and expanded their partnership. In addition to the project in Chiapas, the two partners would collaborate to expand to new locations and to develop a permanent product line of Starbucks sustainable coffee, with standards and coffee-sourcing guidelines, and seek to engage other leaders in the coffee business to articulate industry-wide practices.[12] In October 2003, Starbucks announced a $2.5 million direct loan to the CI for the newly launched Verde Ventures Fund to provide loans to small producers (Starbucks Coffee Company 2003). The partnership continued to expand both in scope and scale, and in 2004 Starbucks and the CI announced yet another renewal of the alliance for three more years.

Creating standards: experimental projects and local participation

A central focus of the Starbucks–CI partnership was the creation of a new model of sustainable coffee production through the elaboration of new norms. Starbucks had no experience in this area, while the CI had been active in developing sustainable production practices for other commodities grown in ecological conservation hotspots. The CI's efforts were part of a broader movement among a group of international NGOs, such as the Rainforest Alliance and the World Wildlife Fund, to develop standards for sustainable agriculture and certification systems to stop tropical deforestation.

A key aspect of the CI project in Chiapas was the development of what constitutes 'best practices for coffee production'. This goal was tied to the development of *Conservation Principles for Coffee Production*, which were eventually published in 2001 by a group of NGOs, including the CI, the Rainforest Alliance, and the Smithsonian Migratory Bird Center, with input and endorsement from Starbucks (Conservation International et al. 2001). To develop these norms, the CI collaborated and built partnerships with local Mexican organizations, including academic institutions such as El Colegio de la Frontera Sur (ECOSUR)[13] and the Universidad Autónoma de Chiapas (UNACH), the government agency Comisión Nacional de Áreas Naturales Protegidas (CONANP)[14] and the Banco Nacional de México (BANAMEX)[15] to define and refine the practices specifically for the Chiapas context (Zettelmeyer and Maddison 2004).

The goals of the *Conservation Principles for Coffee Production* include: aligning coffee production with biodiversity conservation; creating tools and incentives that promote and reward good stewardship in the coffee industry; strengthening collaboration and facilitating local standards development; informing planning and monitoring; and influencing public policy and financing (Conservation International et al. 2001). The *Principles* also include general guidelines on what constitutes conservation-friendly coffee production (wildlife, soil, water, energy and ecosystem conservation, waterway protection, and pest, disease and waste management) and sustainable livelihoods for coffee producers. They are a framework for the development of local conservation standards and codes of conduct in public and private spheres.

Awareness of poverty among the small-scale coffee producers and NGO environmental advocacy contributed to a notion of a sustainable supply chain for coffee in which current and future economic, social and environmental needs are met for actors at all levels of the value chain. Efforts to introduce this concept into practice include the rise of 'sustainable' certifications, such as *Fair Trade, Organic,* and *Shade Grown* coffees, which are officially administered by NGOs, farmer associations and for-profit organizations.

Based on the experience in Chiapas, Starbucks built on the NGOs' *Conservation Principles for Coffee Production* to develop its company-wide coffee purchasing code. In November 2001, Starbucks began the Pilot Phase of its *Preferred Supplier Program* (PSP) in collaboration with the CI's Center for Environmental Leadership in Business (CELB). The criteria in the PSP derived directly from the *Conservation Principles,* developed through the interaction between the CI, other environmental NGOs, and local Mexican producers and organizations (Millard 2005; Starbucks Coffee Company 2001b). Starbucks defines 'sustainability' as 'an economically viable model that addresses the social and environmental needs of the participants in the coffee supply chain from producer to consumer' (Starbucks Coffee Company 2001b). The company's compliance with NGO demands for sustainability was integrated into Starbucks' long-term coffee procurement strategy. The two-year PSP pilot phase ended in 2003.

In February 2004, Starbucks held a Stakeholder Feedback Session in Seattle to gather feedback on the PSP guidelines and elaborate the next steps. Attendees included multiple stakeholders and advocates in the sustainable coffee world (academics, international NGOs, unions, Mexican producer-cooperative representatives, Oxfam, the International Labour Organization/ILO), as well as critics of Starbucks and experts in other kinds of 'sustainable coffee' certifications. Workshops were held on different issues (economic, environmental and social) related to the PSP. Importantly, Starbucks' PSP received two criticisms. First, the social dimensions were underdeveloped, while the environmental areas were quite rigorous (Lee 2004). This was a reflection of the environmental emphasis and expertise of the CI. Second, the standards were judged inappropriate for small-scale farmers and cooperatives.

In particular, the standards were found to be inappropriate for smaller, family-run farms; for example, the rules about labour organization and wages are not easily applicable to family members. Also, since small farms do not sell to Starbucks directly, but rather through a consolidating vendor, the standards needed to be adaptable to different supply chain configurations (such as vendors, plantations and cooperatives). Finally, stakeholders were concerned that the incentives for upgrading to the standards were not enough to offset the cost of compliance, and that the standards might in fact hurt or exclude smallholders (Lee 2004). Recent studies also note that while Starbucks has engaged in extensive consultation with local producers and international NGOs, this has not included farm workers and their organizations (Macdonald 2007).

Some of the concerns raised at the 2003 and 2004 feedback sessions were addressed in the next phase of the programme. In 2004, the new *Coffee and Farmer Equity (C.A.F.E.) Practices* made transparency on payments a prerequisite for participation in Starbucks' supply chain. Participants (be they cooperatives, processors or exporters) must be able to provide paperwork to trace the coffee and the price paid to each producer all the way from the farm. In addition, the C.A.F.E. phase included two major developments: the introduction of Scientific Certification Systems (SCS) as the coordinator of an independent verification process and validation of the various verifiers (primarily local government agencies, farmer organizations and NGOs); and the development of a smallholder supplement, designed to adapt the standards to the specific circumstances of small-scale farmers and their respective supply chains. In 2006, Starbucks more than doubled its previous year's C.A.F.E.- certified coffee purchases (representing 53 per cent of its total green coffee purchases) (Starbucks Coffee Company 2006).

The evaluation grid of the *C.A.F.E. Practices* has five categories with 28 indicators that constitute scoreable points: Product Quality, Economic Accountability, Social Responsibility, Environmental Leadership (Coffee Growing) and Environmental Leadership (Coffee Processing) (Starbucks Coffee Company 2004a). For example, 'Economic Accountability' refers to demonstration of transparency and the equity and financial viability of their supply network (that is, to ensure that farmers are receiving an equitable share of the income). The 'Social Responsibility' category outlines requirements for hiring, employment and working conditions. The 'Environmental Leadership' for both Growing and Processing categories outlines the environmental standards (water use, soil, biodiversity conservation, waste management and energy use) for each respective stage of production.

The influence of these standards went in several directions. Starbucks' *C.A.F.E. Practices* were influenced by and evolved from their long-term relationship with the CI's *Conservation Coffee* projects. Moreover, the *C.A.F.E. Practices* set the bar for other regions, as both partners started new *Conservation Coffee* sites in Colombia, Peru and Costa Rica (Linton 2005). The C.A.F.E. standards also influenced other countries where Starbucks buys coffee, such as Nicaragua and Costa Rica. The Costa Rican government, for example, created a national sustainability seal for local coffee producers based on the C.A.F.E. model (SCAA 2006). Furthermore, the standards that evolved from the CI partnership influenced those in the broader industry through Starbucks' active involvement in the National Coffee Association and the Specialty Coffee Association of America (SCAA) (Macdonald 2007).

The SCAA, for instance, adopted an organizational mission that integrated a broad notion of quality: quality of coffee, quality of life of producers and environmental quality.

While standard-making for sustainability has expanded global supply chain actors' efforts to improve social and environmental performance in developing countries, their implementation faces important challenges that have been given less attention. Some of them relate to the specific conditions of small rural producers (Perez-Aleman and Sandilands 2008), while others have to do with the lack of coordination between supply chain initiatives and state actors, which have limited their translation into broader government policy action (Macdonald 2007).

Beyond compliance: complementary support infrastructure to assist upgrading of small-scale producers

Adopting sustainability standards (such as *Conservation Coffee Best Practices* and the *C.A.F.E. Practices*) entails many challenges for the rural poor in the coffee-growing regions of Mexico and Central America. First, due to extremely low coffee prices and lack of access to affordable credit, poorer farmers can rarely afford to make investments in purchasing equipment, hiring more workers and paying higher wages (Muradian and Pelupessy 2005). In addition, there is a lack of financial-service providers to make such investment possible (Oxfam International 2004). Moreover, small-scale farmers generally lack the technical information to evaluate and improve their product quality to address the quality and sustainability components that the specialty coffee industry requires (Bacon 2005). Furthermore, geographical isolation is a major factor in limiting small-scale farmers' markets. Often there are only a few choices, and these might not give the farmers optimal price for their coffee. The farmers living in geographically isolated areas also tend to suffer from lack of rural infrastructure such as good roads (Oxfam International 2004).

In addition, small-scale farmers face an information gap when making decisions about whether or not to strive for certification (Kilian et al. 2006). They lack production-cost information and reliable market-price data. They often cannot afford the cost of certification or re-certification, given a bad year or two. This is exacerbated by the notorious lack of transparency in the coffee value chain; intermediaries cut farmers off from contact with roasters and vice versa. Farmers do not know where their coffee goes, or what price is paid for it further up the chain. They send it off in bags to the processor and, although they can be penalized for low quality, they are not rewarded for high-quality product. The benefits of switching to certified sustainable production (namely a price premium, access to a differentiated market, and possibly better buyer relations) are offset by the costs (switching production methods, more input, possible reductions in yields, and the initial and ongoing certification price) (Giovannucci and Ponte 2005; Humphrey

2005). These costs can represent a significant barrier to entry for smallholders. Finally, small-scale farmers who are not members of a cooperative are often shut out of the lucrative certified markets because certifiers and global buyers do not want to bother with contracts for small amounts.

Looking at the CI–Starbucks partnership experience in Chiapas reveals that a major focus of their efforts and activities addressed the above challenges that small-scale producers confront in the complex adoption and implementation of sustainability standards. From the beginning, the Chiapas project focused on small producer upgrading to meet the demands of this new market; fostering horizontal cooperation and coordination to achieve scale; and facilitating the emergence of supporting markets for financial services and technical assistance.

The Chiapas project offered technical assistance for growing and quality improvement techniques, and organizational assistance to cooperatives to help them market their coffee more effectively and efficiently. The CI provided technical assistance for farmers to adopt the agroforestry Conservation Best Practice, and it acted as a broker between the cooperatives and buyers in order to secure a market for the coffee and provide the all-important economic incentive to farmers. Starbucks had a role in technical assistance for quality control in the *Conservation Coffee Project* while CI's team visited every farm and monitored progress.[16] The CI provided training courses in villages on quality control, organic farming methods, tree planting and pulping, and business management. The CI also supported the creation of a training centre and nursery to provide coffee plants and organic fertilizer, sold at a reduced price. The CI provided farmers with technical assistance to improve agricultural techniques, thereby increasing crop yields and reducing reliance on fertilizers and pesticides.

Later, Starbucks directly supported the provision of technical assistance to farmers both for quality and environmental upgrades. To help small producers meet the new PSP standards, in January 2004 Starbucks opened the Costa Rica Agronomy Company (or Farmer Support Center – experts in soil management and field-crop production), and established the SCS as the administrator of the verification process (Starbucks Coffee Company 2004b). Starbucks employees, through the centre, administer the PSP and work directly with farmers in Mexico and Central America, providing services to them. Although the centre is clearly a key sourcing strategy for Starbucks' supply needs, it also has a strong mandate to work on 'sustainability issues' with farmers and local governments and oversee social programmes. As such, the centre administers the entire C.A.F.E. programme and is a resource for technical assistance to farmers (Starbucks Coffee Company 2005). The establishment of the Farmer Support Center represents yet another example of an active-assistance approach in the process of achieving sustainability in the coffee supply chain.

Equally important, 'financial assistance' through affordable credit to farmers has been central to upgrading. The Mexican government, international donors and Starbucks provide financial support and backing to several microcredit organizations, including EcoLogic Finance and Verde Ventures. These non-profit financial organizations provide small loans to farmers to supplement their income between coffee harvests (pre- and post-harvest loans). In addition to providing income stability, these loans are often used by the farmers to purchase capital equipment or make other investments in the farm in the effort to improve quality and/or comply with environmental standards. Quality upgrades lead to better coffee prices from Starbucks, and environmental upgrades lead to certification premiums or advantages under the C.A.F.E. programme. Supporting affordable credit programmes is a key part of the implementation of Starbucks' 'sustainability goals' in general and *C.A.F.E. Practices* in particular. Cooperatives that commit to purchasing agreements with final buyers, such as Starbucks and Green Mountain Coffee Roasters, have access to Verde Ventures and EcoLogic Finance funds for the coming production cycle or to make longer-term investments in capital equipment and sustainable farming techniques (USAID 2006).

While it is not easy to find extensive studies of the socioeconomic impact of the *Conservation Coffee* programme on the livelihoods of participating farmers, some evaluations commissioned by the CI report that, in the case of Mexico, producers have benefited from higher productivity, profitability and price received for coffee, and have performed better on various measures of living conditions such as income, meat consumption and housing quality (Millard 2005). There is also some evidence that in the Central American region the CI–Starbucks programme has had impacts similar to those of Fair Trade (Murray et al. 2003; Bacon 2005). In addition to the tangible benefits to participants' livelihoods, the programme had a positive impact on the environmental sustainability of the biosphere reserve. At the farm level, there is evidence of environmental improvements related to waste-water treatment from wet mills and systems for managing, storing and using chemicals (Macdonald 2007). Of course, the results of the programme are difficult to capture in resource-limited short-term impact studies, and many direct and indirect impacts will only be visible after several years.

From the business organization angle, there are several ways in which to analyse the pattern observed in this case. At one level, the business–NGO interaction has led to new governance at the supply chain level as new standards and codes have multiplied in the coffee industry. The CI–Starbucks experiment has guided and influenced norms that were later adopted by the SCAA, the largest coffee industry business organization.

Equally important, at the level of small producers, the process has contributed to strengthening their organizations. The partnership has developed in a context where small coffee producers are organized into cooperatives, which occurred prior to the CI–Starbucks project. The sustainability initiatives, however, support the collective organizing through joint access to export markets as well as through capacity-building as NGOs and companies work with cooperatives to improve their managerial and organizational capabilities. In addition, organizational strengthening has enabled producers to establish links with many NGOs and with the government to gain access to resources, such as additional credit, road and electricity infrastructure, and health and educational facilities. In Mexico, for example, the government banks engaged in the provision of rural credit. Undoubtedly, further improvements in their social and economic conditions depend on strengthening the small producers' multiple levels of organization, beyond the TNC–NGO initiatives. While these partnerships can catalyse the growth of cooperation among producers and can assist in the creation of networks that expand across cooperatives and internationally, ultimately the collective organizing goes beyond the initial goals of the TNC–NGO partnership. However, the partnership highlights the importance of building an organizational infrastructure that assists both the representation and participation of small producers in national, local and supply chain decisions.

Furthermore, there is evidence that more extensive changes required to improve access to health and education for farm workers, as well as to enact other social and environmental improvements at the farm level, present substantive challenges for small producers that highlight the need for coordination between supply chain actions and government policy (Macdonald 2007). In the case of Nicaragua, Macdonald (2007) shows that schooling or medical care, which C.A.F.E. standards evaluate, are seen in the verification stage as the responsibility of the individual farmer, without any interaction between verifiers, corporate buyers, local suppliers and the local and national government. This example reveals the need to expand the connections between sustainability-standard processes in supply chains with state actors and government policy-making.

Conclusion

As the governments of Latin America devise policies to address poverty and foster development, they must go beyond the dichotomous strategy of previous decades, and toward one that combines social inclusion with competitiveness. Such a strategy would simultaneously raise social and environmental standards, along with the productive capacities of the diverse private sector, including poorer producers. The Starbucks–CI partnership suggests there are complementarities: small-scale producers improve their assets, income and quality of life; firms and raw material suppliers achieve better product quality; the conditions of those in rural areas improve.

The TNC–NGO partnership experience with the new standards suggests new forms of strategic collaboration. Obviously, this example is far from achieving many social development goals. However, the actions at the global and local production levels, combined with a renewed interest in building state capacity in a post-Washington consensus period, provide an opportunity for implementing some lessons from existing TNC–NGO partnerships and new standards. What lessons can one take from the Starbucks–CI case? What would development policy look like?

First, developing and implementing sustainability standards requires a focus on process, not outcomes. This process involves space to experiment and discover what works in practice in the local context of developing countries. The social and environmental standards evolve experimentally, through concrete pilot projects in the local setting of small-scale producers. Standards must be grounded in the local reality and local conditions, and then they are built upward. This is different than a standard-making process that is imposed from the top, or from an advanced-country context. Using field 'tests' to develop standards allows their modification as lessons are learned, and a design that adapts to local circumstances. Global standards must have flexibility in their design to account for the wide variety of conditions and starting points among local developing-country producers.

Second, the standard-making process has as a crucial component: the involvement of small-scale suppliers, workers and local communities in the dialogue to generate the standards. The close connection with local groups and producers is essential for such grounding. Far from being only a set of techniques or norms to be complied with, standards evolve from and constitute a discussion that includes not only international NGOs and the TNC, but also local producers and local organizations (governmental and non-governmental). The issue of who participates in creating standards is central; the process has to ensure access, representation and involvement of those at the 'bottom' who are at the heart of the targeted activities.

A third lesson from this analysis is that active assistance accompanies the efforts to implement and achieve the adoption of the sustainability standards. An important aspect of the partnership is the joint action to assist small-scale producers in the supply chain so that they can achieve the standards in the face of multiple difficulties and challenges to meet them – financial, informational, technical, managerial and administrative, as well as expanded labour requirements. These supportive activities are very different from setting regulation (private or public) and monitoring compliance, which have been the focus of academic and practitioner discussions. Providing financial resources and technical support to enable small-scale producers to make the necessary adjustments to meet new standards becomes a central focus of partnerships that can include government, firms and NGOs.

A crucial condition for small-scale producers' inclusion is to move beyond certification towards the active implementation approach by supporting the upgrading and participation of small-scale producers. Governments and private companies play a role in creating supporting conditions for the inclusion of those at the bottom in developing countries. With resources and actions aimed at fostering upgrading and inclusion of small-scale farmers and firms, strategic collaborations and standards can act as conduits for social and economic development. These collaborations require the involvement of new actors: local governments, NGOs, small-producer organizations, among others. Traditionally, state policy-making has been managed by central governments, through national committees that include representatives from large individual firms or important business groups. A future development agenda that combines social and economic development needs to bring in a broad representation, including poorer producers.

While there is an extensive literature pointing to the limits of TNC–NGO partnerships in effecting change in trade relations and in global production systems, these collaborations support an approach to development strategies that combine competitiveness and equity. First, they highlight a notion of sustainability that can be integrated into efforts to improve competitiveness by improving the assets of the poor through environmental, social and quality upgrading. Second, given the active role of NGOs in partnerships promoting sustainability in production, there is a new way to think about development and state–society relations. While NGOs have targeted mainly the building of links with private firms, there is the potential for building more and closer ties between the state and private actors (NGOs and firms) to create private–public networks that support sustainable development through complementary activities. The combination of the state, private firms, organized smallholders and NGOs can be a powerful tool for social and economic development. Governments alone have not produced development in the past. Governments cannot be effective without the participation of societal actors. NGOs also cannot on their own bring about the widespread changes necessary to improve a critical mass of rural producers. Moreover, private firms should not be seen always as the enemy, as many are willing to engage in efforts that enhance rural producers' welfare. The state, NGOs, firms and organized rural producers, among others, can associate and collaborate to devise a public–private institutional infrastructure that supports strategies for improving social welfare and economic growth. The implication of this discussion is that the design of social and economic policy can operate across a wide collaboration of public and private organizations, rather than being seen as centralized in the hands of the state, or as privatized under TNC–NGO partnerships.

Notes

1. Conroy (2007); Frenkel and Scott (2002); Fung et al. (2001); Jenkins (2001).
2. Argenti (2004); Austin (2000); Bartley (2003); Berger et al. (2004); Doh and Teegen (2003); Spar and LaMure 2003.
3. Khan et al. (2007); UNRISD (2003); Utting (2007); Raynolds (2004).
4. Clay (2005); Raynolds (2004); Reardon et al. (2001).

5. Fung et al. (2001); O'Rourke (2003); Seidman (2003).
6. Dolan and Humphrey (2000); Farina (2002); Raynolds (2004); Reardon et al. (2001).
7. Amsden (1989); Dussel Peters et al. (2002); Hausmann and Rodrik (2003); Henson and Loader (2001); Nadvi (1999); Perez-Aleman (2005).
8. Parts of this section draw from a more extensive discussion of the case presented in Perez-Aleman and Sandilands (2008). The research is based on primary and secondary sources, and field interviews and observations. Archival material on the partnership activities includes company and NGO reports, memos, web pages, project evaluation studies from international organizations, supplemented by interviews with small-scale producers in Central America and certifying organizations.
9. Osorio (2004); Oxfam International (2004); Ponte (2004).
10. Of the 25 biodiversity hotspots worldwide, 19 are major coffee-growing regions (Linton 2005; Zettelmeyer and Maddison 2004).
11. All references to $ are to US dollars.
12. Austin and Reavis (2004); Starbucks Coffee Company (2001a); Zettelmeyer and Maddison (2004).
13. www.ecosur.mx.
14. www.conanp.gob.mx.
15. The Bank of Mexico offered credits through two programmes: Fondo Acción and Fideicomisos Instituidos en Relación con la Agricultura (FIRA).
16. Austin and Reavis (2004); Conservation International (2001); Starbucks Coffee Company (2002).

References

Amsden, A. H. (1989) *Asia's Next Giant: South Korea and Late Industrialization* (New York: Oxford University Press).

Argenti, P. A. (2004) 'Collaborating with Activists: How Starbucks Works with NGOs', *California Management Review*, 47 (1), 91–116.

Austin, J. E. (2000) 'Strategic Collaboration between Nonprofits and Businesses', *Nonprofit and Voluntary Sector Quarterly*, 29 (1), 69–97.

Austin, J. E. and C. Reavis (2004) *Starbucks and Conservation International*, Harvard Business School Case 9-303-055, rev., 1 May (Boston: Harvard Business Publishing).

Bacon, C. (2005) 'Confronting the Coffee Crisis: Can Fair Trade, Organic, and Specialty Coffees Reduce Small-Scale Farmer Vulnerability in Northern Nicaragua?', *World Development*, 33 (3), 497–511.

Bartley, T. (2003) 'Certifying Forests and Factories: States, Social Movements, and the Rise of Private Regulation in the Apparel and Forest Products Fields', *Politics & Society*, 31 (3), 433–64.

Berger, I., P. Cunningham and M. Drumwright (2004) 'Social Alliances: Company/Nonprofit Collaboration', *California Management Review*, 47 (1), 58–90.

Clay, J. (2005) *Exploring the Links between International Business and Poverty Reduction: A Case Study of Unilever in Indonesia* (Oxford: Oxfam GB, Novib Oxfam Netherlands and Unilever).

Conroy, M. E. (2007) *Branded! How the Certification Revolution Is Transforming Global Corporations* (Gabriola Island: New Society Publishers).

Conservation International (2001) *CI Facts: Conservation Coffee*, at: www.conservation.org/sites/celb/Documents/ConservationCoffeeFactsheet5-22.pdf (accessed on 27 July 2009).

Conservation International, the Consumer's Choice Council, Rainforest Alliance, the Smithsonian Migratory Bird Center and the Summit Foundation (2001) *Conservation Principles for Coffee Production*, at: www.conservation.org/sites/celb/Documents/Cons_Principles.pdf (accessed on 14 July 2009).

De Janvry, A. and E. Sadoulet (2001) 'Concepts for an Approach to Rural Development in Mexico and Central America: Regional Development and Economic Inclusion', paper presented at IADB regional workshop, Developing the Rural Economy from Puebla to Panama, Guatemala City, 5–7 March.

Doh, J. P. and H. Teegen (2003) *Globalization and NGOs: Transforming Business, Government, and Society* (Westport: Praeger).

Dolan, C. and J. Humphrey, 'Governance and Trade in Fresh Vegetables: The Impact of UK Supermarkets on the African Horticulture Industry', *Journal of Development Studies*, 37 (2), 147–76.

Dussel Peters, E., C. Ruiz Durán and M. J. Piore (2002) 'Learning and the Limits of Foreign Partners as Teachers', in Gary Gereffi, David Spener and Jennifer Bair (eds), *Free Trade and Uneven Development: The North American Apparel Industry after NAFTA* (Philadelphia: Temple University Press).

ECLAC (Economic Commission for Latin America and the Caribbean) (2002) *Panorama Social De América Latina (Social Panorama of Latin America)* (Santiago: ECLAC).

Farina, E. (2002) 'Consolidation, Multinationalisation, and Competition in Brazil: Impacts in Horticulture and Dairy Products Systems', *Development Policy Review*, 20 (4), 441–57.

Frenkel, S. J. and D. Scott (2002) 'Compliance, Collaboration, and Codes of Labor Practice: The Adidas Connection', *California Management Review*, 45 (1), 29–49.

Fung, A., D. O'Rourke and C. Sabel (2001) *Can We Put an End to Sweatshops?* (Boston: Beacon Press).

Giovannucci, D. and S. Ponte (2005) 'Standards as a New Form of Social Contract? Sustainability Initiatives in the Coffee Industry', *Food Policy*, 30 (3), 284–301.

Hausmann, R. and D. Rodrik (2003) 'Economic Development as Self-discovery', *Journal of Development Economics*, 72 (2), 603–33.

Henson, S. and R. Loader (2001) 'Barriers to Agricultural Exports from Developing Countries: The Role of Sanitary and Phytosanitary Requirements', *World Development*, 29 (1), 85–102.

Humphrey, J. (2005) *Shaping Value Chains for Development: Global Value Chains in Agribusiness* (Eschborn: Deutsche Gesellschaft fur Technische Zusammenarbeit/GTZ and Federal Ministry for Economic Cooperation and Development).

Jenkins, R. (2001) *Corporate Codes of Conduct: Self-Regulation in a Global Economy*, Programme on Technology, Business and Society, Paper No. 2 (Geneva: UNRISD).

Khan, F., K. Munir, and H. Willmott (2007) 'A Dark Side of Institutional Entrepreneurship: Soccer Balls, Child Labor and Postcolonial Impoverishment', *Organisation Studies*, 28 (7), 1055–77.

Kilian, B., C. Jones, L. Pratt and A. Villalobos (2006) 'Is Sustainable Agriculture a Viable Strategy to Improve Farm Income in Central America? A Case Study on Coffee', *Journal of Business Research*, 59 (3), 322–30.

Lee, M. (2004) *Starbucks Stakeholder Engagement Event: Summary of Feedback on the Preferred Supplier Program* (London: SustainAbility).

Lewis, J. and D. Runsten (2007) 'Coffee, Migration and Environment in Southern Mexico: Preliminary Observations from a Study of 15 Communities in Oaxaca and Chiapas', paper presented at Latin American Studies Association, Montreal, 5–8 September.

Linton, A. (2005) 'Partnering for Sustainability: Business–NGO Alliances in the Coffee Industry', *Development in Practice*, 15 (3/4), 600–14.

Macdonald, K. (2007) 'Globalising Justice within Coffee Supply Chains? Fair Trade, Starbucks and the Transformation of Supply Chain Governance', *Third World Quarterly*, 28 (4), 793–812.

Mendoza, R. (2000) 'The Hierarchical Legacy in Coffee Commodity Chains', in R. Ruben and J. Bastiaensen (eds), *Rural Development in Central America: Markets, Livelihoods and Local Governance* (Basingstoke: Palgrave Macmillan; New York: St Martin's Press).

Millard, E. (2005) *Sustainable Coffee: Increasing Income of Small-Scale Coffee Farmers in Mexico through Upgrading and Improved Transparency in the Value Chain*, Accelerated Microenterprise Advancement Project (AMAP) microREPORT #45 (Washington, DC: USAID).

Muradian, R. and W. Pelupessy (2005) 'Governing the Coffee Chain: The Role of Voluntary Regulatory Systems', *World Development*, 33 (12), 2029–44.

Murray, D. L., L. T. Raynolds and P. L. Taylor (2003) *One Cup at a Time: Poverty Alleviation and Fair Trade Coffee in Latin America* (Fort Collins: Colorado State University, Fair Trade Research Group).

——— (2006) 'The Future of Fair Trade Coffee: Dilemmas Facing Latin America's Small-Scale Producers', *Development in Practice*, 16 (2), 179.

Nadvi, K. (1999) 'Collective Efficiency and Collective Failure: The Response of the Sialkot Surgical Instrument Cluster to Global Quality Pressures', *World Development*, 27 (9), 1605–26.

OECD (Organisation for Economic Co-operation and Development) (2006) *The Mesoamerican Region: Southeastern Mexico and Central America* (Paris: OECD).

O'Rourke, D. (2003) 'Outsourcing Regulation: Analyzing Nongovernmental Systems of Labor Standards and Monitoring', *Policy Studies Journal*, 31 (1), 1–29.

Osorio, N. (2004) 'Lessons from the World Coffee Crisis: A Serious Problem for Sustainable Development', paper presented at UNCTAD XI, Sao Paulo, June.

Oxfam International (2004) *Mugged: Poverty in Your Cup* (Washington, DC: Oxfam International).

Perez-Aleman, P. (2005) 'Cluster Formation, Institutions and Learning: The Emergence of Clusters and Development in Chile', *Industrial & Corporate Change*, 14 (4), 651–77.

Perez-Aleman, P. and M. Sandilands (2008) 'Building Value at the Top and the Bottom of the Global Supply Chains: Multinational-NGO Partnerships', *California Management Review*, 51 (1), 24–49.

Ponte, S. (2002) 'The "Latte Revolution"? Regulation, Markets and Consumption in the Global Coffee Chain', *World Development*, 30 (7), 1099–122.

——— (2004) *Standards and Sustainability in the Coffee Sector: A Global Value Chain Approach* (Winnipeg: International Institute for Sustainable Development/IISD).

Raynolds, L. T. (2004) 'The Globalization of Organic Agro-Food Networks', *World Development*, 32 (5), 725–43.

Reardon, T., J.-M. Codron, L. Busch, J. Bingen and C. Harris (2001) 'Global Change in Agrifood Grades and Standards: Agribusiness Strategic Responses in Developing Countries', *International Food and Agribusiness Management Review*, 2 (3/4), 421–35.

SCAA (Specialty Coffee Association of America) (2006) *Second Annual SCAA Sustainability Award: Nomination for Starbucks Coffee Company: C.A.F.E. Practices* (Long Beach: SCAA).

Schrank, A. and M. Piore (2007) *Norms, Regulations and Labor Standards in Central America* (Mexico, DF: ECLAC).

Seidman, G. (2003) 'Monitoring Multinationals: Lessons from the Anti-Apartheid Era', *Politics and Society*, 31 (3), 381–406.

Spar, D. and L. LaMure (2003) 'The Power of Activism: Assessing the Impact of NGOs on Global Business', *California Management Review*, 45 (3), 78–97.

Starbucks Coffee Company (2001a) *Corporate Social Responsibility Annual Report Fiscal 2001* (Seattle: Starbucks Coffee Company), at: www.starbucks.com/aboutus/gr.asp (accessed 28 April 2006).

——— (2001b) *Starbucks Green Coffee Purchasing Program Pilot Program for Preferred Suppliers* (Seattle: Starbucks Coffee Company), at: www.celb.org/xp/CELB/downloads/guidelines.pdf (accessed 12 July 2006).

——— (2002) *Corporate Social Responsibility Annual Report Fiscal 2002* (Seattle: Starbucks Coffee Company) at: www.starbucks.com/aboutus/gr.asp (accessed 28 April 2006).

——— (2003) *Corporate Social Responsibility Fiscal 2003 Annual Report* (Seattle: Starbucks Coffee Company), at: www.starbucks.com/aboutus/gr.asp (accessed 28 April 2006).

——— (2004a) *C.A.F.E. Practices Generic Evaluation Guidelines* (2004a), at: www.scscertified.com/csrpurchasing/docs/CAFEPracticesEvaluationGuidelines110904English.pdf (accessed 28 April 2006).

——— (2004b) *Starbucks Coffee Agronomy Company Opens in Costa Rica to Help Farmers Improve Their Coffee Quality*, 28 January, at: www.starbucks.com/aboutus/pressdesc.asp?id=381 (accessed 28 April 2006).

——— (2005) *Starbucks Corporate Social Responsibility Fiscal 2005 Annual Report* (Seattle: Starbucks Coffee Company), at: www.starbucks.com/aboutus/gr.asp (accessed 28 April 2006).

——— (2006) *Starbucks Corporate Social Responsibility/Fiscal 2006 Annual Report* (Seattle: Starbucks Coffee Company), at: www.starbucks.com/aboutus/gr.asp (accessed 27 July 2009).

UNRISD (United Nations Research Institute for Social Development) (2004) *Corporate Social Responsibility and Development: Towards a New Agenda?*, Geneva, 17–18 November 2003, Conference News No. 13 (Geneva: UNRISD).

USAID (United States Agency for International Development) (2006) *The Global Development Alliance: Public–Private Alliances for Transformational Development* (Washington, DC: USAID).

Utting, P. (2007) 'CSR and Equality', *Third World Quarterly*, 28 (4), 697–712.

Vogel, D. (1995) *Trading Up: Consumer and Environmental Regulation in a Global Economy* (Cambridge, MA: Harvard University Press).

Zettelmeyer, W. and A. Maddison (2004) *Agroforestry-Based Enterprise Development as a Biodiversity Conservation Intervention in Mexico and Ghana: Usaid/Pvc Matching Grant Program Final Evaluation Report* (Malaga, Spain and Hereford, UK: USAID), at: http://pdf.usaid.gov/pdf_docs/PDABZ650.pdf (accessed 15 July 2009).

Index

Bold page numbers indicate tables and figures

527 organizations 171

Abusada, Roberto 195
active assistance 306
activism 24, 34, 45, 154, 216, 297
African Growth and Opportunity Act (AGOA) 286
African National Congress (ANC) 273
agency power 65
Ahluwalia, M. S. 98
Almond, Gabriel 250
alter-globalization, blind spots 5–6
alumni business associations (ABAs)
  attaining contacts **223**
  development of 220–1
  influence 225–9
  interactions with government **223–5**
  market-complementing actions 228–9, 235–6
  market-supporting actions 228–9, 233–4
  network development 221–2
  pathways to change **227**
  policy domains and reciprocity 222–5
  policy engagement and change **226**
Amador, Mario 134, 144
American system of manufacturing 32
Amnesty International 83–4
Amsden, Alice 8, 9, 38, 42, 45
analysis 249
Anant, T. C. A. 91, 99, 106
Anastasiadis, S. 161
Andersen, Soren Kaj 41
ANITEC 146
Anti-CAFTA movement 148
Arce, Moisés 196
Arias, Luis Alberto 201–2
Artigas, Alvaro 114, 139
Arusha initiative 71
Asia, structural power 47
Asian Development Bank (ADB) 46
Asian Miracle 45
Åslund, Anders 211
Associated Chambers of Commerce and Industry of India (ASSOCHAM) 94, 95
asymmetrical power relations 15, 151
Atack, Jeremy 33
authoritarian modernization 188
authoritarianism 44–5
Aylwin, Patricio 116, 118

baby milk formula 84
Baca, Jorge 196, 199
Baccaro, Lucio 41, 46
Bacon, C. 297, 302, 304
BAE Systems 84
Bakan, J. 82
balance of forces 51
Barrios, Violeta 140
Bartley, T. 292
Bell, Trevor 281
Bernstein, Marver H. 34
Beyer, Jurgen 41
Bhattacharjea, A. 91
Bhavani, T. A. 101
Bhopal 84
BIAC (Business and Industry Advisory Committee to the OECD) 71
Biersteker, Thomas J. 114
Birchal, Sérgio 244
Bird, G. 163
Blanchard, Olivier 211
Blowfield, M. 160
Blueprint 160, 174
Blyde, J. Juan 115
Boloña, Carlos 188
Bonardi, J.-P. 166
Bonelli, Regis 244
Bonnet, K. 65
Borchgrevink, A. 142
Borrás, Susana 125
Boschi, Renato 248, 251

Boyer, Robert 9, 36
Brazil 16–17
benefits to industry of legislative process 259
classification of decisions 255–6
classifying decisions as political success or failure 252–3
Confederação Nacional da Indústria (CNI) 242, 245, 247–8
dynamics of lobbying 248–51
economic and political underpinnings of collective action 243–8
Free Trade Area of the Americas (FTAA) 244
industry participation in legislation 250–1
Legislative Agenda 243, 245–6, 248, 263
legislative powers of executive 257–8
lobbying 243, 265
measuring political success and failure 252–64
opening of economy 243–4
political role of business community 263
Brazil cost 242–3, 245, 256–9, 262–3
impact of cases of failure 253–4
impact of cases of success 253, 261
reduction as collective benefit 246–8
success and failure 264–6
Bremner, Robert Hamlett 34
briefcase politics 94, 97
Broadman, Harry 211–12, 215
Brown, Doug 164
Bruggemans, Cees 271
Buckley, C. 178
Bull, Benedicte 14, 110, 122, 139, 141
Bush, George W. 164
business
and civil society 140–2
and developmental welfare state 41–2
divisions 67
elites 4
and European welfare state 38–41
measuring political success and failure 252–64
political influence 161, 191–4
political pressure 249–51
power and influence 1, 19–20
pursuit of own interests 34–5
role in post-developmentalist welfare state 45–6
and social policy 6–12, 63, 70, 73–8
strategy and social concerns 51
support for progressive social policies 46–52
business associations
channels and influence 216–17
'encompassing' 13, 22
firm size 214–15
geographical and demographic representation 215
influence in Russia 229–31
public good 210–11
and regime type 213–14
services 215–16
social agenda 218–19
business climate 294
business constituencies 138–9
Business Environment and Enterprise Performance Survey (BEEPS) 209, 213, 215–17, 227–8
Business Leaders Initiative for Human Rights (BLIHR) 163
business needs, social and economic context 77
business power
in development context 65–8
forms of 1–2
implications for social policy 85
and public policy 3
realization of 67
rise in 1
theories of 64–5
business preferences 13, 51–2
Business Roundtable 37, 49
business-social policy nexus 68–73, 85, 128
Bustamante, Alfonso 196

Cáceres, S. 144, 145
California effect 112–13
Camet, Jorge 195, 196, 198–9, 200
Campero, Guillermo 110, 115
Campodónico, Humberto 200, 203, 204
Campos, José Edgardo 45
Canada, negotiations with Chile 119–21

CANISLAC 145, 147
capital mobility 66
Carrión, Gloria 15
cartels 35
Catholicism 39
causal relationships 254
Central America 17–18 *see also* Starbucks and Conservation International (CI) alliance
  business integration 141
  competitiveness 294, 296
  development dichotomy 293
  global business 140–1
  rural economies 296
  transnational capital 141
Central America Free Trade Agreement (CAFTA) 296
Centre for Research on Multinational Corporations (SOMO) 176, 178
Chandler, Alfred D. 32
Chang, Ha-Joon 43
change, resistance to 5
Chari, Raj 170, 171
Chatterjee, P. 104
Chile 14
  Acuerdos de Producción Limpia (APL) 126
  agreement with Mexico 119
  business and development 127–8
  business associations 117
  business preferences 111–15, 125–6
  business-social policy nexus 128
  business strategies 126
  CONOMA (Comisión Nacional del Medio Ambiente) 118–19
  corporate social responsibility (CSR) 126
  environmental regulation 118–19
  export orientation 117
  free trade strategy 110–11
  labour regulation 118
  labour rights 111
  mining 120
  negotiations with Canada 119–21
  negotiations with EU 124–5
  negotiations with United States 121–4
  neoliberalism 117
  SOFOFA (Sociedad de Fomento Fabril) 117–18, 120
  spillover effects from trade negotiations 126–7
  trade agreements **116**
  trade liberalization 115
  trade negotiations 110–11, 115–19
China 78, 80, 169, 177–8
CIDEF 197
Cisco, lobbying 164
civil society 5, 24, 140–2
civil society actors, (DR–CAFTA) negotiations 148–50
Clapp, Jennifer 114
Clark, John 285
class 7–10, 12, 31, 38, 45, 48, 54, 70, 212
Clay, J. 293
cleavages 67
Clinton, Bill 121
Cloward, R. A. 67
coalition politics, India 91, 104
Coates, D. 67
Coca-Cola 83–4
Coffee and Farmer Equity (C.A.F.E.) Practices 301
coffee, small-scale production 297–8
Cohen, Jeffrey E. 193
collaborative institutions 13, 49–51
collective action 2, 7, 10, 12, 14, 18, 31, 33, 38, 47, 49–50, 52, 90, 95, 135, 191, 204–5, 208–9, 221, 231, 242
collective bargaining 40
collective benefit 246
collective business action 20–2, 164–5, 243–8
Colombia 83–4
Commission of the European Communities 161
Companies Act, India 98
competitiveness 14, 18–19, 296
Confederação Nacional da Indústria (CNI), 16–17, 245
Confederation of Indian Industry (CII) 94, 95, 96, 102
conflict mediation 50
Congress of South African Trade Unions (COSATU) 273
consensus 50–1
Conservation Coffee Project (CCP) 298–9

Conservation International 297 *see also* Starbucks and Conservation International (CI) alliance
Conservation Principles for Coffee Production 299
constituency building 166
constructability thesis 210, 230
Contract Labour Act (India) 100
convergence hypothesis 138–9
coordinated market economies (CMEs) 9–11
COPRI 190
corporate accountability movement 21
Corporate Governance and American Competitiveness 37
corporate lobbying *see also* lobbying
- approach to political strategy 163–5
- case studies 175–8
- company reporting 174–5
- and corporate social responsibility 174
- disclosure practices 178–9
- effectiveness of government regulation 171–2
- ethics 160
- financial incentives 165
- financial services liberalization 163
- framework for analysis 167–9
- government regulation 170–2, 179
- Hillman and Hitt model 163
- integration into corporate social responsibility (CSR) policies 178–9
- international trade and investment agreements 169
- orientation of political strategies 166–7
- participation level 164–5
- regulation 170–2
- related to corporate social responsibility (CSR) 162
- responsible lobbying 173–5
- self-regulation 179
- strategies and channels of influence 163–7
- successful strategies 169
- targets 161–3
- type of political strategy 165–6
- understanding 161
- use of information 166–7

corporate philanthropy 37
corporate political activities, United States 35
corporate political influence *see* corporate lobbying
corporate social responsibility (CSR) 23, 31, 37–8, 41, 49, 54–5, 82, 84, 126, 160, 162–3, 166, 173–9, 211, 218, 295
- agenda 4, 5, 37
- business case for 37–8
- Chile 126
- and corporate lobbying 15, 174
- developing economies 295–6
- discourse 37
- downsizing in US 37
- links between developed and developing economies 84–5
- as response to social risk 49
- responsible lobbying 173–5
- Russia 218
- self-regulation 166
- transnational corporations (TNCs) 160

corporate social welfare 33, 34, 49, 51–2
corporatist policy making, East Asia 44–5
corruption 8, 12, 16, 20, 46, 55, 84, 98, 101, 184–7, 190, 192–3, 195–7, 199–200, 204–5, 213 *see also* state capture
Cox, R. 65
Crouch, Colin 2, 21, 38
CST-JBE (Central Sandinista de Trabajadores – José Benito Escobar) 148–9
Cummings, J. 164
Cutler, A. Claire 114
Czech Republic 78, 80, 81
CzechInvest 81

Dahl, Robert A. 67, 161, 254
Dammert, Manuel 190, 195, 197
Davis, Gerald F. 34, 37
Davos 95–6
de Aragão, Murillo 248
De Janvry, A. 296
de Tocqueville, Alexis 31
Debroy, B. 99, 106

decentralization, East Asia 43
decommodification 7
deep integration, business motives for 139
Delamonica, E. T. 72–3
deliberation councils 8, 45
Denmark, flexicurity 41
Depression 34
deskilling 32
Detragiache, E. T. 163
developing and transition countries, individuality 22
developing economies
  business and social policy 73–8
  corporate social responsibility (CSR) 295–6
  standards 294–5
developing states, pressure from IGOs 66
development
  and business power 65–8
  socially inclusive 53
  transformative patterns 5
development agencies, as knowledge agencies 142
development theory, mainstream 22
developmental state approach (DSA) 8–9, 10–12, 23
developmental welfare state 41–4
Dharanajan, S. 160
Diniz, Eli 248, 251
Djelic, Marie Laure 113
Dolan, C. 295
Domhoff, G. William 35
Dominican Republic–Central American Free Trade Agreement (DR–CAFTA) 15, 134–5
  impact 152
  influence of non-state actors 150
  labour and environmental issues 152
  limits of civil society actors 148–50
  negotiations 143–5
  Nicaraguan business 141–2
  Nicaraguan government campaign for 148
  Nicaragua's complementary agenda 148–50
  proposals and outcomes 145–7
Doner, Richard 8, 208, 210, 228
Drazen, Allan 184
dual transitions 2
Dubois, Fritz 196
Dugger, C. 141
Durand, Francisco 16, 189, 190
Durkheim, Emile 39

Eagleton, D. 165
East Asia
  corporatist policy making 44–5
  developmental welfare state 41–3
  erosion of mutual dependence 46
  industrialization 42–3
  political settlements 43–4
  role of business in post-developmentalist welfare state 45–6
  social legitimacy 45
  social policy 44
  structural power 48
East Asian Miracle 8
ECLAC 296
economic development
  and technological innovation 42
  and welfare provision 70
economic development models, of welfare growth 69
economic factors, in social policy 71–2, 74
economies of scale, effects in US 32–3
education 70, 80–2
Eisner, Marc Allen 186
Embassy of the Federal Republic of Nigeria 78
Employees' State Insurance (ESI) Act (India) 101–2
employment, terms and conditions 83
entrepreneurs 247
environmental damage 84
epistemic communities 4, 12, 138
Equipo Envío 140
ERT 82
Esping-Andersen, Gøsta 7, 32, 34, 39, 68
Estela, Manuel 196
Estevez-Abe, Margarita 10, 51, 70
ethical brands 84–5
ethics, of corporate lobbying 160
Europe
  business and welfare 38–41
  health care 39

industrialization of craft tradition 38–9
neocorporatist governance 39–40
post-neocorporatism 40–1
socialism and social democracy 39
structural power 47–8
welfare 39
European Commission, lobby regulation 170
European Competitiveness Report 285
European Union, negotiations with Chile 124–5
Eurosclerosis 40
Evans, Peter 8, 45, 210, 230
Evans, Rob 84
exploitation, of workers 83
ExxonMobil, funding to think tanks and research 166–7

Farnsworth, Kevin 13, 70, 71, 82
Fazio, Hugo 117
Federation of Indian Chambers of Commerce and Industry (FICCI) 94, 95
Fernández Jilberto, Alex E. 117
Fernández, Wilmer 145
feudalism 38
Ffrench-Davis, Ricardo 115
Figueirado, Argelina 251
Financial Leaders Group (FLG) 163, 164–5
financial resources, availability of 145
financial services, liberalization 163
firm-centred approaches 9–10
firm size 214–15
Flatters, Frank 282, 283
flexicurity 41
Fonseca-López, R. 148
Ford, *Sustainability Report* 175
foreign direct investment (FDI) 1, 3, 4, 20, 23, 77, 79, 141, 148, 151, 154, 198
Fordism 52
Foucault, Michel 137–8
Foxley, Alejandro 115
Frank, Volker 118
free-riding 246
Free Trade Area of the Americas (FTAA) 244
Freeman, Edward R. 37
Freeman, Richard 33
Frei, Eduardo 116, 118
Friedman, Lawrence Jacob 34, 49
Fuchs, Doris A. 1
Fujimori, Alberto 187–8, 194–5

Gaidar, Yegor 211
Gandhi, Indira 92
Gandhi, Rajiv 92–3, 94–5, 98
García, Alan 193
General Agreement on Trade in Services (GATS) 163
General System of Preferences (GSP) 120
Gerber, Theodore 215
Getz, K. 166
Giddens, Anthony 31
Giovannucci, D. 302
Giugni, M. 138
GlaxoSmithKline (GSK) 176–7
Global Compact 218
global governance, and empowerment 135
global, importance of 65–6
Global Labor Strategies 178
global organizations 66
Global Policy Forum 162
Global Reporting Initiative (GRI) 160, 173–4
global supply chain, small-scale producers 294–5
global value chains, and local communities 1, 4, 23
globalization
effects on business attitudes 84–5
effects on welfare 40–1, 292
Gomez, Edmund Terence 8, 44, 45
Gonzales de Olarte, Efraín 188
good governance agenda, failings 4–5
Gorbachev, Mikhail 210, 212
Gordon, Colin 33, 34, 35, 36
Gough, I. 68, 69, 70
governance, forms of 138
Gramsci, Antonio 137
Gray, Mel 274
Great Depression 34, 47–8
Green, Duncan 5
Grindle, Merilee S. 188
guilds 38, 48

Gulf War 93
Guy, Ken 285

Haas, Peter M. 12, 138
Hacker, Jacob S. 33, 34, 47
Haggard, S. S. 93
Hall, Bruce 114
Hall, Peter 9, 37, 49, 68, 73
Handley, Antoinette 271
Hanson, Phillip 208, 216
Hardin, Russell 246, 247
Hart, David M. 35, 36
Harvey, David 39
Haufler, V. 139
Hayek, F. 35
healthcare 39, 81–2
Hegel, Georg 39
hegemons 137
Hellman, Joel S. 184, 208
Henriques, Adrian 162
'high road' model 38
Hikino, Takashi 38, 42
Hillman, A. J. 161, 163–5, 167
Hirst, P. 66
Hitt, M. A. 163–5, 167
Hockin, Thomas A. 121
Hoffman, David 208
Hollingsworth, J. Rogers 9, 32, 35, 36, 39, 41
Holme, R. 160
Höpner, Martin 41
Huber, Evelyne 41
Humphrey, John 281, 295, 302
Hyman, Richard 41

ICC 82
ideological power 65
in-kind food aid, lobbying 165
inclusion, small firms and producers 306–7
inclusive development, prospects 22–4
income distribution, East Asia 43
India 14
  affirmative action in private sector 102–3
  attracting investors 78, 79
  business–government relations and labour policy 98–103
  business preferences and influence on labour policy 100–3
  coalition politics 91, 104
  collective business action 90–1, 94, 95–6
  economic performance 92–3
  effects of economic liberalization 90
  evolution of business–government relations 93–8
  federal dimension of business–government relations 98
  individual business lobbying 94, 96–7, 103
  information exchange 95, 97
  labour laws 99, 100
  labour markets 80, 99, 100–1
  liberalization 14
  limits to business influence 103–5
  market reforms 90
  1947 to 1991 93–4
  organized labour 99
  patterns of access 97
  policy implications 105–6
  political funding 97
  politics 91
  politics of opposition 104
  private investment 90
  public–private partnerships (PPPs) 96
  reforms and business-government relations 92–3
  skills development 102
  social security provisions 101–2
  transformation of the role of business in public policy 94–6
'India Everywhere' 95
industrial conflict, avoiding 33
Industrial Disputes Act (IDA) (India) 100
industrial social relations 32
industrialization 8, 38–9, 52, 96
inequality 37, 46
infant industry theories 8
information exchange, India 95, 97
information, use in corporate lobbying 166–7
Iniciativa CID 148, 149
Initiative for the Americas 119–21
institutional capture 4–5, 17, 19, 22
  see also state capture
institutional embeddedness 49
institutional innovation, drivers 52–3
institutions 49–51, 68

Intal-ITD-STA 110
integration, deep, business motives for 139
intellectual property rights (IPR) 143, 176
interest accommodation 41
intergovernmental organizations (IGOs) 63, 66, 71
International Business Interest Associations (IBIAs) 71
international financial institutions (IFIs), East Asia 46, 55
International Monetary Fund (IMF) 66
international negotiations, and domestic politics 136
international NGOs (INGOs) 68
international trade regimes, non-state actors 138–40
investment
  benefit and harm 82–3
  climate for 72
  competition for 85
  in corrupt/undemocratic states 83
  and liberalization 277–8
  relocation 66
  state control 74, 77
Investment Commission of India (ICI) 79
investment regimes 78
investment regimes and social policies **75–6**
inward investment 63–4, 74, 77

Jacobsson, Kerstin 125
Jacoby, Sanford M. 34, 36, 48
Jansen, Hans 152
Japan 42–3, 45, 48
Jayasuriya, Kanishka 113
Jenkins, R. 91, 97, 105
Johnson, Chalmers 8, 42, 43, 45
Jomo, Kwame Sundaram 8, 43, 45
Jordan, G. 65

Kaggwa, Martin 17
Katz, Lawrence F. 33
Kaufmann, Daniel 184
Kay, Cristóbal 43
Keeley, J. 136
Keim, G. D. 166
Kennedy, S. 169
Kenworthy, Lane 35, 39, 40
Kenya 78, 79, 81
Khan, A. U. 99
Khan, F. K. 295
Khan, Mushtaq H. 8, 43, 45
Kilian, B. 302
King, Gary 254
Kitschelt, Herbert 41
Knight, Richard 273, 284
knowledge networks 4
Kochanek, S. 92, 94, 97, 106
Kohli, A. 90, 92, 93, 98, 103, 104
Kolk, A. 165
Korea 42, 45–6
Korpi, Walter 7, 67, 68
Kotze, Hendrik Jakobus 271
Kramer, Mark R. 37–8
Kremer, Michael 211
Kwon, Huck-ju 43, 44, 45, 46

Labor-Management Relations Act 36
labour market flexibility, India 100–1
labour markets 80–2
labour movement 67–8
labour policy 12, 14, 90–1, 98–100, 103–5
labour unions, effects of globalization 12
Lagos, Ricardo 116–17, 118, 121
Lagos Weber, Ricardo 120
Lamoreaux, Naomi R. 32
LaMure, L. 292
Lanuza, Magda 147
Lascelles, D. 160, 173, 174
learning by doing 42
Ledeneva, Alena 222
Lee, M. 300
Lee, Pei-Shan 46
legal stability agreements (LSAs) 190
LEGISDATA 248–9
legislation, industry participation 250–1
legislative propositions, types of decision taken 254–5
Leigh, David 84
Lengyel, M. 135, 137, 138
Level I 136–7
Level II 136–7
Levy, David L. 6, 137, 139
Lewis, J. 298

liberal capitalism, pervasive model of 1
liberal ideology, classical 32
liberal market economies (LMEs) 9
liberalism 4, 35
liberalization
  India 14
  and investment 277–8
licence-permit raj 92, 94, 96
Lim, Sang-Hoon 46
Limongi, Fernando 251
Lin, Nan 210
Lindblom, C. E. 64, 65, 161
Linton, A. 297, 301
literature
  on business and social policy 6–12
  regime analysis 68
lobbying 15 *see also* corporate lobbying
  Brazil 243, 265
  definition 161
  dynamics of 248–51
  of IGOs by governments 66
  India 94, 96–7, 103
  transparency in 174
  United States 35
local communities, and global value chains 4
Lord, M. D. 166, 169

MacDonald, K. 301, 302, 304, 305
MacGillivray, A. P. 171, 173, 175
Maddison, A. 298, 299
Madula, Nkosi 281
Mahalingam, S. 98
Mahoney, Christine 161
Mailand, Mikkel 41
mainstream development theory 22
Mancuso, Wagner Pralon 16–17
Mandelson, Peter 125
Mann, M. 67
manufacturing, decline in US 33
March, James 209
Mares, Isabela 9
Marín, Alfredo 147
market dislocation 211
markets, context of 138
Marques, José Carlos 2, 13, 26, 41
Martin, Cathie Jo 36
Marxist theory 65
McAlinden, Sean H. 278
McCain-Feingold Act 171
McCarty, Nolan 37
McCraw, Thomas K. 32
McGarvie, Mark Douglas 34, 49
McQuaid, Kim 32, 35
Mehrotra, S. 73
Memedovic, Olga 281
Mendoza, R. 294
Mesquita Moreira, Mauricio 115
Mexico 17–18 *see also* Starbucks and Conservation International (CI) alliance
  agreement with Chile 119
  attracting investors 78
  competitiveness 294, 296
  Conservation Coffee Project (CCP) 298–9
  development dichotomy 293
  labour markets 80–1
  rural economies 296
Meyer, Michael 274
microcredit 304
Midgley, James 274
Miliband, R. 67
Millard, E. 298, 300, 304
Milyo, J. D. 169
Miranda, José Carlos 244
Mkandawire, Thandika 9, 25, 43–4
modernization, authoritarian 188
Moe, Terry 247
Moen, E. 66
monitoring 249
Montero, Cecilia 127
Montesinos, Vladimiro 190
Moreno Ocampo, Luis 184
Moreyra, Francisco 196
Motor Industry Development Programme (MIDP) 272, 275–7
  Black Economic Empowerment (BEE) 284
  competitiveness 284–6
  industry performance 277–86
  investment 277
  objectives 275–6
  overview and evaluation 289–90
  production and exports 279–80
  public–private partnerships (PPPs) 276
  social policy 286–9
  supplier development 280–2
  vehicle prices 282–3

Muradian, R. 302
Murali, Kanta 14
Muralidharan, S. 98
Murillo, Maria Victoria 118
Murray, D. L. 304
mutual dependence 45, 46

NAAMSA 279–80, 282–3, 285
Nagaraj, R. 91
Narayanan, Kumar 285
National Association of Software and Services Companies (NASSCOM) 95, 96, 102
national buffers 39
National Industrial Recovery Act (NIRA) 35
nationalism, economic 42
National Recovery Administration (NRA) 35
negotiating space 134
neo-Marxism 69
neocorporatism/neocorporatist 8–9, 11, 25, 31, 35, 40, 46, 50, 53–5
neocorporatist governance, Europe 39–40
neoliberalism 1, 2
  and state capture 185–6, 187–90
Nestlé 84
Netshitomboni, Nnzeni 282
Neuman, W. Lawrence 184
New Deal 34, 47
Newell, Peter 5, 114
Nicaragua 14–15, 305
  asymmetrical power relations 15
  beef 147
  business and civil society 140–2
  business influence 143–5
  civil society actors 142
  complementary agenda 148–50
  concepts and debates 136–40
  dairy producers 144–5, 147
  foreign direct investment (FDI) 141
  nongovernmental organizations (NGOs) 142–3
  privatization 140
  resources for negotiation 144
  social movements 143
  sugar 146–7
Nigeria 78, 80
Nixon, Richard 35
non-state actors, international trade regimes 138–40
nongovernmental organizations (NGOs) 67, 292
North American Free Trade Agreement (NAFTA) 112
North, Douglas C. 208
Northern Europe, structural power 47
Novartis 176–7
Nuñez, Orlando 145

O'Brien, David 16
O'Connor, Julia S. 7, 69
Odell, John 113–14
OECD 6, 160
OECD, attempts to regulate lobbying 170
Offe, C. 64
Oliveira, Ribamar 244
Olsen, Gregg M. 7
Olson, Johan 209
Olson, Mancur 36, 40, 161, 208, 246–7
Omelyanchuk, Olesky 185
Onis, Ziya 42, 43, 44
OpenSecrets.org 35
organizational strength 50
orientation 249
O'Sullivan, Mary 37
Oughton, Christine 286
Oxfam 164, 176, 302

Pakistan 295
Panagariya, A. 92
Paniagua, Valentín 193, 201
Parmalat 147
participatory councils 113–14
partnership(s) 3, 8, 17–18, 38, 41, 46, 234–5, 272, 286, 289, 292, 294, 295–9, 301, 303–8
paternalism 33
Pelupessy, W. 302
Peng, Ito 45
pensions 8–9, 37
perestroika 212
Perez-Aleman, Paola 17–18, 302
Perez, Sofia A. 41
Peru 15–16
  audit 201
  BCRP 192
  civil society 203

Peru – *continued*
effects of state capture 204–5
extreme mode of state capture 194–201
Fujimori administration 188–90, 192–3
García administration 193–4
Instituto Peruano de Economía (IPE) 195–6
key agencies 192
legal stability agreements (LSAs) 190
Ministerio de Economía y Finanzas (MEF) 187, 188–90, 192, 193–4, 195, 201–3
moderate mode of state capture 201–4
modes of state capture 186–7
neoliberalism and state capture 187–90
nongovernmental organizations (NGOs) 204
Paniagua administration 193, 201–2
power concentration 188
private sector influence on political appointments 191–4
privatization programmes 197
reforms 188–9
rent-seeking 190
research methodology 187
rise of private sector 190–1
sectoral tax exonerations 199–201
SUNAT 192, 194, 199, 201–3
tax breaks 200
Tax Merger Law 197–9, 200
Taxpayer Defender 203
Toledo administration 193
transnational corporations (TNCs) 190–1
Phelps, Edmund S. 40
philanthropy 34, 48–9, 82
Phongpaichit, Pasuk 46
Pierson, Chris 44
Pierson, Paul 33, 34, 41, 47
Pinochet, Augusto 115
Pinske, J. 165
Piore, M. 296
Piven, F. F. 67
Pizzorno, Alessandro 8, 39
pluralism, United States 34–6
Polanyi, Karl 39, 138
policy integration 50
policy making, bipartite and tripartite systems 50
policy networks 139
political corruption 15–16
political donations 165, 178
political exchange 7, 39
political funding, India 97
political pressure 249, 250–1
political settlements, developmental welfare state 43–4
political strategies 166–7
politics
corporate influence 191–4
India 91
Ponte, S. 297, 302
Pontusson, Jonas 41
Porras, José Ignacio 110, 116, 121
Porta, Alvaro 143
Porter, Michael E. 37–8
post-developmentalist welfare state, role of business 45–6
post-neocorporatism, Europe 40–1
post-Washington consensus 4
post-welfare capitalism, United States 36–8
poverty 3, 296, 300
Poverty Reduction Strategy Paper (PRSP) 66
Powell Jr, G. B. 250
power balance 5, 10, 12, 63, 192, 229
power balance, competing interests 63
power, discursive 1, 23–4
power, instrumental 20, 24, 34, 91
power relations, imbalances 1, 4–5, 24, 137, 169
power resources approach (PRA) 7, 10–11, 12, 23, 68–9
power resources theory (PRT) 7, 68
power structures, in trade negotiations 137–8
Prakash, A. 137, 139
pre-Depression, social policy 33
preferences, prioritizing 63
President's Management Training Programme 219–20
private sector, engagement in development agenda 30
privatization 84, 140
Pro México 80–1

process-tracing case methodology 187
profits, pursuit of 69–70
progressive social policies, business support for 46–52
Przeworski, A. 64
Public Citizen 164
public health, lobbying 167
public interest movement (PIM), United States 36, 49
public policies, influences in neoliberalism 2
public–private cooperation 8
public–private partnerships (PPPs) 4, 12, 17, 23, 96, 162, 276
Putin, Vladimir 213
Putnam, Robert D. 110, 134, 136
Pyle, William 208, 229

Quintana, Mario 149

Rajan, R. S. 163
Rao, Narasimha 93
rationalization cartels 43
Recanatini, Francesca 208, 209, 215
reform agendas, blind spots 3, 4–5
regional trade regimes 136
regulation 5, 112–13, 293
regulatory regimes 68
relations
  industrial social 32
  state–business–society 2
rent-seeking 190
resources 65
revolving doors 14, 16, 20, 163–4, 186, 195, 196
Riain, O. 138
Richter, Judith 84, 167
Ricker, T. 147
rigidities 22
risk, mitigation of social 48–9
risk reduction 40
rival interests 67
Roberts, Dan 37
Rodrik, Dani 4, 51, 90, 92
Ronge, V. 64
room next door 116–17, 143–5
Roosevelt, Franklin D. 35
Rudolph, L. 106
Rudolph, S. H. 106
Ruggie, John Gerard 4, 34, 39
Runsten, D. 298
rural economies 296
Russia 16
  alumni business associations (ABAs) *see* separate heading
  case study 219–21
  channels and influence 210–11, 216–17
  characteristics of business associations 214–17
  corporate social responsibility (CSR) 218
  emergence of business associations 209–10, 211–14
  entrepreneurs 212
  influence of business associations 229–31
  Law of Cooperatives 212–13
  market-complementing actions 235–6
  market-supporting actions 233–4
  'missing middle' 213
  parallel economy 213
  President's Management Training Programme 219–20, 230–1
  Putin administration 213, 218, 229
  social agenda 218–19
  state capture 184
  structural reforms 211
  survey characteristics 232
  trends in business influence 218
  Yeltsin administration 211–12
Ryterman, Randi 208, 209, 215

Sachs, Jeffery 3
Sadoulet, E. 296
Sáez, Sebastian 110
Sahlin-Anderson, Kerstin 113
Salisbury, Robert H. 35, 36
Samuelson, Paul 246
Sandell, C. 167
Sandilands, M. 302
Sandler, Todd 246
Schmitter, Philippe 40
Schneider, Ben Ross 8, 70, 208, 210, 220, 228
Schonwalder, Gerd 195
Schrank, Andrew 118, 296
Schurman, Rachel 118
Scoones, I. 136
second-best position 50, 51

Second World War 32, 47–8
Segovia, A. 141
self-regulation 166
Sell, Susan 2, 138, 139
Shadlen, K. 135
Shafer, Michael 45
shareholder market capitalism 37
Shell, corporate lobbying 162–3
Sherman Anti-Trust Act 32
Shin, Myung-Soon 43
Silva, Eduardo 110, 118
Silva, Patricio 115
Silva, Verónica 110
Singh, J. 137
Singh, Manmohan 93, 102
Sinha, A. 95, 98
skills, portability 9–10
Sklair, L. 66
Skocpol, Theda 33, 67
Slob, Bart 15
small and medium-sized enterprises (SMEs) 19, 22, 55, 117, 148, 219
small firms and producers
  exclusion from regulatory standards 293
  inclusion 306–7
  information gap 302
  standards 294–5
  support infrastructure 302–5
Smirnov, Stanislav 216
social concerns, and business strategy 51
social democracy, Europe 39
social dialogue 41
social groups, Europe 39
social housing 70
social legitimacy 45, 50
social movements, Nicaragua 143
social pacts 41
    postwar political settlement 39
social policy
  and business 6–12
  business benefits 51
  and business in developing economies 73–8
  and competitiveness 18–19
  East Asia 44
  economic factors 71–2, 74
  instrumental use 8–9
  legitimizing aspects 48
  needs of business 63
  role of business in 70
  South Africa 286–9
  status of 6
social pressures 48
social protection benefits, business attitudes to 71
social regulation 112
social risk mitigation 48–9
social security provisions, India 101–2
social welfare 10
socialism 39, 92
socially inclusive development 53
soft authoritarianism 43
soft regulation 114
Soskice, David 9, 68, 73
South Africa
  automotive industry 17 *see also* Motor Industry Development Programme (MIDP)
  changing role of corporate sector 272–5
  economic growth 274
  Employment and Redistribution (GEAR) 272–5
  expectations of corporate sector 273–4
  government–labour–industry partnership 272
  'interventionist-developmental' state model 271
  liberalization 273
  Motor Industry Development Council (MIDC) 276–7
  Motor Industry Development Programme (MIDP) *see* separate heading
  National Economic Development and Labour Advisory Council (NEDLAC) 273
  OEM investment and employment **279**
  post-apartheid development strategies 271
  Productive Asset Allowance (PAA) 286
  Reconstruction and Development Programme (RDP) 272–4

social policy 286–9
socio-economic aspirations 271, 272
South Africa Foundation (SAF) 271–2
Spar, D. 292
special interest groups 161
Specialty Coffee Association of America (SCAA) 301–2
Sridharan, E. 97–8
stakeholder theory 37
standards 294–5, 306
Starbucks *see also* Starbucks and Conservation International (CI) alliance
NGO activism 297–8
Preferred Supplier Program (PSP) 300
Starbucks and Conservation International (CI) alliance 17–18, 297–305
evaluation 305–7
financial assistance 303–4
stakeholder feedback 300–1
standards 299–302
support infrastructure 302–5
technical assistance 303
state–business–society relations 2–3, 5–6, 19, 65, 115, 208, 210–11, 219, 229
state capture 16, 21, 208
aims of 186
dynamics of 193
extent of influence 186
extreme mode 194–201
impact of 204–5
moderate mode 201–4
modes 186–7
and neoliberalism 185–6, 187–90
political variables 186
private sector influence on political appointments 191–4
tensions and conflict 186
uncertainty of 192
state capture studies 184–6
state, form of 67
Statement on Corporate Governance 37
Statement on Corporate Responsibility 36–7
states
attracting investors 77–82
characterization of developmental 44
control of investment 74, 77
expanding business–state relations 21
importance of international context 73–4
increasing capacity 24
Steinmo, S. 67
Stephens, John 7, 41
Stigler, George J. 34
Stiglitz, J. 66, 222
Streeck, Wolfgang 35, 38, 39, 40
structural influences 85–6
structural power 10, 13, 15, 20, 22, 47–8, 52, 64–5, 77, 85, 138, 142, 145, 150, 190–1
structural pressures 74
structural theory 64–5
structured agency 139
Subramanian, A. 4, 90, 92
SustainAbility 160, 171, 174, 176
sustainability
coffee production 298–302, 304–5
developing 306
Swank, Duane 41
Swann, Christopher 37
Swenson, Peter 9

Taft-Hartley Act 36
Taiwan 42–3, 45–6
taking a position 249
Taliercio, Robert 199
Távara, José 193
Tchernina, Natalia 211
Teague, Elizabeth 208, 216
technocracy 20
technocratic governance 12
technocrats 1, 15, 17, 192, 274–5
technological frontier 42
technological innovation, and economic development 42
Tedlow, R. S. 32
Teichman, Judith A. 139
Tendulkar, S. D. 101
Terreblanche, Sample 274
Thailand 81–2
Thelen, Kathleen 33, 38, 67
theoretical approaches
developmental state approach (DSA) 8–9, 10–12
insights and limitations 10–12

theoretical approaches – *continued*
power resources approach (PRA) 7, 10–11, 12
varieties of capitalism (VoC) 9–10, 11–12
theories of business power 64–5
Thomas, John W. 188
Thompson, G. 66
Thorp, Rosemary 189
TNC–NGO partnerships 17–18
evaluation 305–7
standards 294–6
support infrastructure 302–5
Togliatti Dialogue 218
Toledo, Alejandro 193
trade agreements 14, 19, 110–17, 119–23, 125, 127–9, 134–5, 152, 176, 178, 204, 286, 292–3, 296
trade and investment flows 66
trade negotiations 110, 113–14, 134, 137, 151
trade-offs 135
trade preferential levels (TPLs) 146
Trade-Related Aspects of Intellectual Property Rights (TRIPS) 151, 176–7
transnational capital, Central America 141
transnational corporations (TNCs)
attraction to economies 74
corporate social responsibility (CSR) policies 160
criticisms of 83–4
national bases 66
partnerships with NGOs *see* TNC–NGO partnerships
in Peru 190–1
purchase of regional and national businesses 141
response to corporate social responsibility 4
transparency, in lobbying 174
Traversari, Fernando 141, 146
tripartite bargaining institutions 40
TRIPS-plus 176–7
two-level game 14, 110, 134
two-level interface, international negotiations and domestic politics 136–7
Uganda, attracting investors 78, 79
Ugarteche, Oscar 197
UN Norms on the Responsibilities of Transnational Corporations and Other Business Enterprises with Regard to Human Rights 162–3
UNCTAD 141, 277
UNDP 218
UNICEF 84
unions/unionism, labour 5, 7–8, 10–11, 21, 22, 33, 38–40, 45–49
United Nations (UN) 3–4, 66
United States
corporate political activities 35
industrialization 31–3
labour market dualism 37
lobby regulation 170–1
lobbying 35
negotiations with Chile 121–4
pensions 37
pluralism 34–6
political economy 31
post-welfare capitalism 36–8
public interest movement (PIM) 36, 49
structural power 47, 150
welfare 33–4
Welfare Capitalism 48–9
universalism 74
US Presidential Commission on Industrial Competitiveness 285
US Senate Office of Public Records 164
Utting, Peter 2, 4–6, 25–6, 41, 138, 142, 153, 158, 160, 161, 293

Valverde, Orlando 149, 150
Van Klaveren, Alberto 124
Vander Stichele, Myriam 163, 169
varieties of capitalism (VoC) 7, 9–10, 11–12, 23, 25, 40
Varshney, A. 91, 104
Vartiainen, Juhana 46
Venkata Ratnam, C. S. 99, 101, 104
Venkatesan, V. 98
Venter, Irma 287
Ventura-Dias, V. 135, 137, 138
Vianna, Maria Lucia 249
Visser, Wessel 271
Vogel, David 32, 36, 47, 112–13, 292

Volkswagen 174–5
voluntarism 5
Voluntary Retirement Scheme (VRS) (India) 101

Wade, Robert Hunter 43, 44, 45, 50, 72, 136
Wagner Act 1935 36
Wallerstein, M. 64
Walter, Andrew 138–9
Washington consensus 4, 18, 139, 293, 294–5
water, privatization 84
Watts, P. 160
Webb, T. 162
Weigel, Marcia 213
Weisenthal, H. 65
welfare 39, 68
Welfare Capitalism, United States 33–4, 48–9
welfare growth, economic development models of 69
welfare production regimes 9
welfare provision, and economic development 70
welfare state 3, 7, 9–12, 31, 33–4, 38–9, 41, 43, 45, 52, 54–5, 63–4, 69–70
welfare state, social risk mitigation 48–9
Wetherly, P. 69
Weyzig, Francis 15, 176
Whitley, Richard 32, 38
Wilensky, W. 69
Wilson, Graham K. 35, 39
Woll, Cornelia 114, 139
Woo-Cumings, Meredith 8, 42, 45
Woodman, Arturo 196
Woolcock, Stephen 112, 128
World Bank 6, 8, 41, 45, 66, 71–3, 211, 215
World Development Reports 71–2
World Health Organization (WHO) 167
World Trade Organization (WTO) 66, 112, 161
worlds of welfare 68
WWF 160, 171, 174, 176

Yeates, N. 66
Yeltsin, Boris 211–12
Yurchak, Alexei 212

Zammit, Ann 4
Zettelmeyer, W. 298, 299